Construction and Infrastructure Disputes

A Global Handbook

Consulting Editor **Roberto Hernández-García**

Consulting editor
Roberto Hernández-García

Publisher
Sian O'Neill

Editor
Carolyn Boyle

Production
Russell Anderson

Publishing directors
Guy Davis, Tony Harriss, Mark Lamb

Construction and Infrastructure Disputes: A Global Handbook
is published by
Globe Law and Business
Globe Business Publishing Ltd
New Hibernia House
Winchester Walk
London SE1 9AG
United Kingdom
Tel +44 20 7234 0606
Fax +44 20 7234 0808
Web www.globelawandbusiness.com

Printed and bound by CPI Group (UK) Ltd, Croydon, CR0 4YY

ISBN 9781909416000

Table of contents

Preface

Cyril Chern
Dispute Board Federation

Construction is now a global business. Its international scope has become even more evident as construction companies establish a presence in different parts of the world and look for new opportunities in diverse jurisdictions.

One of several relevant aspects that any construction company will identify as a risk in new projects is the country-specific dispute resolution method, as well as those which are established by contract. This is critical to any project, as many construction and infrastructure projects involve disputes between the parties, resulting from factors including the complexity of the project, design aspects, claims, execution aspects, third-party occurrences, hardship and *force majeure*.

While most of the dispute resolution methods currently in use have proven benefits, as can be seen in some of the world's largest infrastructure projects, problems do arise. These problems have to do with the governing law of the country where the project is executed, local judicial decisions, cultural matters and other issues which generate different levels of efficiency for these dispute resolution methods in different jurisdictions. These factors sometimes are not fully known by those outside the particular jurisdiction.

That is the main objective of this book, which has been edited by Roberto Hernández. Through this important text, contractors, suppliers, subcontractors, lawyers, engineers and all those involved in the international construction industry can obtain a general overview of the construction sectors of different countries, which dispute resolution methods are allowed in each country, which dispute resolution methods are not accepted by statute, and practical matters from relevant practitioners in the construction and dispute resolution fields. Of course, owners will benefit too, since this will be a very good source of learning and using new methods that can benefit construction projects.

Having acted as arbitrator, dispute board adjudicator, mediator and conciliator, and as a barrister and party representative in many cases around the world, I am sure that this book will not only allow readers to become familiar with the various dispute resolution methods available, but will also foster the promotion of a better dispute resolution culture in the construction and infrastructure industry for the benefit of construction projects worldwide.

Cyril Chern, the secretary of the Dispute Board Federation (DBF), is also a barrister at Crown Office Chambers, London, and a chartered architect, chartered arbitrator, accredited mediator and adjudicator. He holds the degrees of BArch in architecture and engineering and

JD (Law). He is a fellow of both the Chartered Institute of Arbitrators and the Dispute Board Federation, is on both the International Federation of Consulting Engineers (FIDIC) President's List of Adjudicators and its Assessment Panel, and is a dispute board trainer for FIDIC, the DBF, and the International Chamber of Commerce.

Dr Chern is the author of Chern on Dispute Boards *(1st and 2nd editions; Wiley-Blackwell),* International Commercial Mediation *and* The Law of Construction Disputes *(Informa). He is also the co-author of* Emden's Construction Law *and its "ADR and Dispute Boards" section (LexisNexis). His newest books,* The Commercial Mediator's Handbook *and* Construction Delay and Damage, *are being published in early 2014.*

Introduction

Roberto Hernández-García
COMAD, SC

1. Disputes: a general rule or an exceptional condition?

Although people often see disputes in a negative light, they are merely the natural consequence of exercising key human rights such as democracy, freedom and fair payment for work, among many others.

For example, through democracy, people can choose the government. Some people vote for one party, while others choose a different party. The difference in the votes may become a national dispute to be resolved by a third party (eg, an electoral tribunal); if this is not done effectively, it can lead to extreme actions such as revolution.

In the case of freedom, actions that disrupt or deny freedom may cause disputes that, depending on the way in which they are resolved, can have either a positive or a negative impact – for example, the division of a society or the evolution of a nation.

Unfair payment for work is another situation that often leads to disputes, and the lack of an effective solution may cause both parties to lose out: the party which is paid unfairly will not complete the work, while the party which commissioned the work will not receive it.

Disputes are part of human nature and, although they cannot always be predicted or avoided, it is vital that we understand them and are able to resolve them effectively, efficiently and fairly, since often the resolution of a dispute offers the opportunity to evolve.

The construction and infrastructure sectors are no exception to this human process. In fact, construction and infrastructure activities often lead to disputes, since there are always matters to claim from one party to another.

2. The future of construction and construction disputes

Global construction is expected to grow by 67% from $7.2 trillion today to $12 trillion in 2020. Growth in China, India and the United States should generate 54% of the $4.8 trillion increase in global construction output. A total of $97.7 trillion will be spent on construction globally over the next decade and by 2020 construction will account for 13.2% of world gross domestic product.[1]

This forecast highlights two key issues. First, construction will become such an important activity, using so many economic and human resources, that players in

1 See "Global Construction 2020", Global Construction Perspectives and Oxford Economics.

the international construction industry will have to focus on the most efficient ways to meet this challenge from technical, financial and legal perspectives in order to carry out projects successfully. This evolution, unfortunately but inevitably, will lead to disputes.

Secondly, as a consequence of the foregoing, as the construction sector grows, the number of disputes will increase due to different variables such as the nature of works (ie, public works, private projects or public-private partnerships), failure to correct situations that have historically led to disputes, regional differences around the world and the parties involved in the projects (ie, governments, private parties or both). Ironically, many of these disputes will stem from long-standing problems in the construction sector which have not yet been definitively resolved.

Examples of these variables and their common causes have been examined in international reports. For example, one investigation shows that although the causes of disputes may vary depending on the region in which a project is performed, the general conclusion as to their roots is similar and surprisingly predictable.[2] The information gathered by the investigation is summarised in the following table:

Region	Top five causes of disputes (2011)
Middle East	• Failure to administer a contract properly. • Incomplete design information or employer requirements. • Change imposed by employer. • Failure to make interim awards on extensions of time and provide associated compensation. • Unrealistic transfer of risk from employer to contractor.
Asia	• Failure to make interim awards on extensions of time and provide associated compensation. • Unrealistic transfer of risk from employer to contractor. • Conflicting party interests. • Unrealistic contract completion date set at tender stage. • Incomplete design information or employer requirements.
United Kingdom	• Failure to administer a contract properly. • Conflicting party interests. • Unrealistic transfer of risk from employer to contractor. • Change imposed by employer. • Ambiguities in the contract.

continued on next page

2 See "Global Construction Disputes: Moving in the Right Direction", EC Harris, 2012, available at: www.echarris.com/pdf/ECH_Global_Construction_Disputes_Report_2012.pdf.

Region	Top five causes of disputes (2011)
Mainland Europe	• Failure to administer a contract properly. • Incomplete design information or employer requirements. • Ambiguities in the contract. • Failure to make interim awards on extensions of time and give associated compensation. • Change imposed by employer.
North America	• Ambiguities in the contract. • Incomplete design information or employer requirements. • Conflicting party interests. • Failure to make interim awards on extensions of time and give associated compensation. • Failure to administer a contract properly.
Overall	• Failure to administer a contract properly. • Ambiguities in the contract. • Failure to make interim awards on extensions of time and give associated compensation. • Incomplete design information or employer requirements. • Conflicting party interests.

One of the report's conclusions stated that "whilst the market may be evolving, many of the same old problems continue to create tension and ultimately prevent projects from moving forward".[3]

Although the report does not deal explicitly with Latin American countries, the author's experience confirms that some of the most common causes of construction disputes are:

- poor drafting of construction contracts;
- poor contract administration;
- poor design;
- a lack of timely recognition of extra work and extra costs; and
- in public works and public infrastructure contracts, the government's ability to skew the balance in contracts.

This means that unless there is a dramatic change in the global market, the same or similar problems and disputes will continue to recur – and will need to be avoided or handled intelligently when they arise.

Other important information that can be obtained from international reports relates to the status and perception of some of the resolution methods currently used in the construction sector.

3 "Global Construction Disputes: Moving in the Right Direction", EC Harris, 2012, page 9.

Although criticisms have been levelled in recent times at the increased judicialisation, cost and slowness of arbitration, one key report nonetheless demonstrates that international arbitration is the preferred dispute resolution method in construction cross-border disputes.[4] The report states that with regard to such disputes, "[n]eutrality and expertise of decision-maker[s] are both considered to be strong benefits of arbitration – costs and speed less so".

These two reports raise a major question: are positive steps being taken to make dispute resolution in the construction sector better, simpler and more cost effective? If the answer to this is affirmative, two further questions arise: is enough importance placed on assessing dispute resolution in the construction sector in order to make it more cost and time effective, or are the players in the construction industry using the same techniques and falling into the same traps as in the past, and thus seeing the same results?

A clear example of a method that is proving to be effective and results oriented – although not yet generally accepted – is the use of dispute boards. Although the benefits are evident in some mega-projects, such as the Panama Channel, as well as minor projects such as the Honduran Millennium Challenge Account projects, a lack of understanding and education about this model still prevents owners and contractors from implementing it.

The benefits of this model are clearly understood in Honduras, where the implementation of dispute adjudication boards has allowed for the timely and successful delivery of highway and bridge projects. According to the Honduran government, the cost of resolving disputes in this way represents an investment of approximately 0.2% of the cost of the claims, while the general understanding is that the cost can be up to 2% of the cost of the contract. This means that governments and contractors can enjoy substantial benefits from this model, as well as the successful execution of the project. But in other Latin American countries, and notwithstanding the success of dispute boards in Honduras, the model is still in the process of being digested and implemented.

3. Keeping up with developments: the purpose of this book

Although disputes in the construction sector are often negative and damaging – and are always perceived as such – in these economically challenging times construction players should not shy away from discussions about existing construction dispute methods and – more than that – from understanding what can be done, what cannot be done, which things are risky and which are positive.

In this regard, some of the matters that must currently be considered are as follows:

- Which dispute resolution methods exist in some of the world's key markets for construction, infrastructure and public-private partnerships?
- Which dispute resolution methods used in the construction industry are facing a crisis, and which others are not used or are even forbidden in some markets?

4 See "Corporate Choices in International Arbitration", PwC, 2013, available at www.pwc.com/arbitrationstudy.

- Which dispute resolution methods should be included, modified, eliminated or strengthened in order to ensure a healthier future for the construction industry in various countries?

The answers to these questions and other relevant issues form the subject matter of this book, which aims to help the reader to discover and understand the available (and unavailable) options for dispute resolution in the construction sector in different countries.

Each country chapter has been written by professional practitioners with international experience – leaders in this field in their respective jurisdictions who have kindly shared their knowledge and expertise in this relevant and unique work, and to whom we extend our most grateful thanks.

This publication is timely since its content will allow those active in the international construction arena, at a time when international construction is expected to flourish, to find relevant information to help them to make good decisions by choosing the most suitable country or dispute resolution method, or by avoiding specific problems discussed herein. For example, if a contractor wishes to carry out an arbitration in Panama, it can find information regarding the benefits of that method of dispute resolution compared with the other methods available there. If a lawyer requires information about dispute resolution in Ireland, he may use this book to research the issue before discussing it with his peers. If an engineer is scouting in India, he can read up on the issues most likely to arise. And if a party wishes to find out about the availability of arbitration in contracts with the Mexican government, this is the publication to turn to – and it can be used in more than 20 countries.

Of course, in general terms, this book provides an overview of the dispute resolution methods that work (and do not work) in different countries, offering the option to compare and contrast those methods. It is therefore a very useful tool, since it is based not on theory but on the practice of practitioners in the field.

Finally, on a personal note I can say that this work has been one of the most enjoyable in my professional and editorial life. As a construction lawyer who has worked on relevant projects both within my country and beyond it, and who has had the honour of participating in important construction law groups – such as the International Construction Projects Committee of the International Bar Association (former co-chair), the Construction Disputes Committee of the International Chamber of Commerce, Mexico (president), Division 8 of the Construction Forum of the American Bar Association Construction Forum (steering committee member) and the Dispute Board Federation (Latin American representative), I believe that this book is a unique work and an outstanding resource for contractors, owners, financiers, experts and all those involved in the sector, both in their daily lives and for special decisions, since in this fast-moving, interconnected world, good decisions must not only be taken fast, but also be made efficiently in order to achieve success in construction projects for the benefit of both the parties involved and society in general.

Ghana

Ferdinand Adadzi
David Ofosu-Dorte
AB & David

1. Introduction

The construction industry in Ghana has witnessed in recent years, and continues to witness, tremendous growth, and construction has been identified as one of the top drivers of Ghana's economy.[1] A number of factors account for this growth:

- The rapid growth in Ghana's economy in general: the country recorded an increase in GDP of 14% in 2011 and has had an average of 8% GDP growth for close to a decade.
- The fact that three successive governments have emphasised the need for accelerated delivery of infrastructure in order to support economic growth. Infrastructure development by its very nature is synonymous with construction.
- There is a huge gap in the delivery of residential accommodation and it is estimated that more than a million household units are needed to bridge the gap.
- The delivery of some strategic cross-border projects in West Africa, particularly the 400-kilometre West Africa gas pipeline (which cuts across Ghana, Nigeria, Togo and Benin).

These factors among others have fuelled growth in the sector. However, it is still estimated that about US$1.5 billion is required on a yearly basis over the next 10 years in order to meet the infrastructure gap. In other words, growth is expected to continue well into the foreseeable future. In view of the apparent gap in infrastructure delivery, both the previous and current governments have adopted public-private partnerships (PPPs) as a vehicle for infrastructural development. This is likely to boost further growth in the sector.

The increased growth in the construction industry has given rise to a corresponding increase in construction-related disputes as well as available dispute settlement methods.[2] This chapter provides highlights of the construction industry, including issues that have given rise to disputes, disputes settlement methods in use and other related matters. The chapter also indicates trends that have been observed and gives an indication of the preferred dispute settlement method favoured under Ghana's newly proposed PPP Law.

---

1 Report of Ghana National Commission for UNESCO.
2 Even though there are no hard statistics on the extent of the increase, observation by the Procurement, PPP, PFI and Infrastructure Practice Group of AB & David points to this direction.

2. Industry highlights

This section highlights legal and related issues that affect the construction industry. As noted in the introduction, the construction and infrastructure sector is one of the main contributors to Ghana's economic development. The theme of the 2012 National Budget of Ghana, "Infrastructure Development for Accelerated Growth and Job Creation", evidenced the role of the industry and its recognition in economic development. In an address by the government at the First National Building and Civil Contractors Excellence Award in 2012, it was stated that the construction industry was the second-highest contributor to the country's GDP in 2011.

Notwithstanding the adoption of PPP, the government still remains the largest investor in the construction industry in Ghana. Government investment is also undertaken through the various sector ministries. Examples of sectors where major infrastructure projects have occurred and are likely to occur include:

- road infrastructure implemented through the Ministry of Roads and Highways with the support of other agencies;
- the Ministry of Transport, which handles transport and related infrastructure (other than road construction) including the construction of railways, sea and landing ports, and airports;
- housing, water and sanitation infrastructure implemented through the Ministry of Water Resources, Works and Housing;
- oil, gas and power infrastructure implemented through the Ministry of Energy;
- health infrastructure implemented through the Ministry of Health; and
- agriculture infrastructure implemented through the Ministry of Food and Agriculture.

Since most of the projects undertaken in these sectors are government sponsored (even if the funding is secured from facilities/grants by development/donor partners), the related works, goods and services are procured under the national procurement rules.[3]

Notwithstanding the growth in the sector, it is estimated that to close the infrastructure gap in Ghana there must be consistent investment in the sector of approximately US$1.5 billion a year over the next 10 years.[4] It is also recognised that the government alone cannot undertake this investment. In that respect, it has recognised the need to involve the private sector. Thus the government adopted the National Policy for Public Private Partnership in Ghana on June 3 2011 to promote the use of private resources in infrastructure development. There is currently an ongoing consultation to prepare a PPP Law to provide a robust legal framework to facilitate private investment.

Major support has been provided by international development partners and agencies, including the World Bank, International Development Association, the

3 The Public Procurement Act 2003 (Act 663) is the law that applies where goods, works and services are funded through public funds. The act allows the use of international procurement rules of a particular donor/development agency where the funding is provided by the donor/development agency.

4 Estimate of the International Finance Corporation Report of 2012.

Millennium Challenge Corporation of the USA, the European Union, the African Development Bank and other bilateral arrangements. In 2012, the government secured $3 billion from the China Development Bank for infrastructure development in Ghana.

2.1 Key private sector players

The private players in the construction sector may be categorised as follows:

- Contractors – this category consist of both major and minor construction companies/firms. The significant feature is that large projects (projects often in excess of $10 million) are often awarded to foreign contractors. This is because there are only about 10 Ghanaian construction firms who meet the required criteria under the public procurement regime (in terms of execution of projects of similar nature, equipment and human capacity) for the execution of such projects.[5]

  There is a large group of small- to medium-scale contractors that has the capacity to execute projects up to $20 million. For many years, contractors in Ghana have been subjected to a classification system where they are graded in categories from 1 to 4 and A to B. For example, a category-A1B1 contractor is qualified to execute roads and bridges of any capacity including the major contracts that often go to foreign contractors. Foreign contractors are, however, not classified but are generally limited to projects awarded as part of an international competitive bid process for which only, in the case of roads as an example, a domestic contractor classified as A1B1 is qualified to perform. However, in order to cut costs, many foreign contractors subcontract to local firms (which thereby over time build capacity and expertise and move up in the grading system). Other similar grading systems exist for contractors who develop structure or carry out electro-mechanical works.
- Financial institutions – both local and foreign financial institutions play a key role in the sector in terms of pre-financing projects that are carried out under public procurement (that is, before the certificates mature). Another major role they play is in providing various forms of project finance in PPP-type projects. All forms of transaction structuring arrangements have thus resulted. The passage of the National Pensions Law,[6] which allows pension funds to be used to finance infrastructure projects (albeit under strict rules), is likely to increase the forms of finance available and the role of financial institutions.
- Insurance companies – Ghanaian law requires that insurance on fixed assets be obtained from Ghana except where specific exemption is granted by the Commissioner of Insurance. Accordingly, the role of the financial institutions is very much complemented by insurance companies that issue

---

5 According to report by the Ghana National Commission for UNESCO, the international contractors invariably win most of the major projects since they have the required capacity and resources. The local contractors are unable to compete with foreign contractors since the former lack capacity and the required qualifications, are ill-equipped and lack the finances required for major projects.

6 National Pension Act 2008 (Act 766).

various bonds and guarantees as well as other forms of insurance instrument.

- Technical service providers – there are various forms of technical service providers that play a key role in the local construction sector; these include architects, engineers and lawyers. Such service providers are also regulated by various statutes that affect their profession.

2.2 Related legal issues affecting the sector

These include the following:

- Standards and permits – construction works are generally regulated under the National Building Regulations 1960 (LI 1630). These regulations, however, generally apply only to the permitting systems for standards and structures, and not to civil works. There are a number of exemptions granted under the regulations. Currently (July 2013) a Land Use and Planning Bill is being considered that is aimed at widening the scope for the application of permitting standards in order to include all forms of works.
- There is no standard code that binds design standards. Therefore design standards are often prescribed by a specific sub-sector of the industry. In terms of structures, recourse to the British standard (BFC code) is allowed under the regulation regime.
- Over the years, Ghana appears to have adopted various standard forms. The UK Institution of Civil Engineers standard form was quite popular for civil works. In terms of structures, the state-owned engineering consulting company (AESL) developed and for many years used what became known as 'the pink form'.
- The influence of the Fédération Internationale Des Ingénieurs-Conseils (FIDIC) – since the mid-1980s when Ghana adopted the International Monetary Fund/World Bank structural reform programmes, both the World Bank and Ghanaian government funded projects have invariably adopted FIDIC standard contract forms. Until recently, the FIDIC Red Book was the form almost exclusively employed for public sector projects.
- The harmonised versions of FIDIC (fourth edition) are currently being used for major projects in Ghana, especially for design and build, and EPC/turnkey projects. The international agencies who funded projects in Ghana (led by the World Bank) have introduced the Multilateral Development Bank version of FIDIC.
- Dearth of legal knowledge about construction – there is little or no in-depth legal knowledge of infrastructure or construction law in Ghana: very few firms profess to have any expertise in this area. Also, disputes that have been heard in Ghanaian courts have shown that there may be a similar lack of in-depth knowledge even at the level of the judiciary. There are very few reported cases even though some major disputes have been heard in Ghanaian courts.[7] This may account for the continued reliance on London-

7 *Ballast Nedam v Horizon Marine Construction* (Supreme Court) – Suit No. 14/18/2010; *Ballast Nedam v Horizon Marine Construction* (High Court & Court of Appeal) – Suit No. AC 193/2007.

based arbitration as well as the recourse to English law in some major construction projects involving major international players in Ghana.

- Contract law – Ghana has a statute that regulates contracts[8] and this includes construction contracts. There is no specific construction contract law. Ghanaian contract law is based on common law (which is almost 100% based on English contract (common) law).

3. Issues that give rise to construction disputes

The disputes that have arisen[9] in the Ghanaian construction industry range from issues relating to project structuring or planning to issues on contract administration and post-completion issues. In particular, issues include the following:

- matters emanating from transaction structuring;
- selection of the wrong standard contract form for a particular project;
- design or technical specification, especially failure in design to fit purpose;
- implementation issues, which include:
  - delays – failure to complete within the completion date;
  - improper administration of the time extension;
  - variation;
  - cost escalation;
  - building to fit purpose; and
  - payment milestones and certification; and
- post-completion issues, including:
  - rectifying defects within the defect liability period;
  - final payment certificates; and
  - payment of a retention sum and return of a performance guarantee.

An explanation of some of these issues is provided below.

3.1 Project structure

A number of disputes in the construction industry in Ghana can be traced back to a lack of adequate planning in terms of project structuring at the start. Issues that should have been taken into account at the project structuring stage are not addressed, resulting in disputes at the implementation stage. These issues include improper allocation of risks, improper budgeting, improper identification of the relevant roles (eg, project manager, architect, engineer, employer, contractor, representatives). This is particularly prevalent in projects funded and implemented by public sector agencies. Some factors that may account for these are political or a failure to engage professionals at the planning stage.

3.2 Standard contract form

A number of disputes also result from using wrong standard contract forms. The public sector agencies favour the use of FIDIC standard contract forms, mainly the

---

8 Contract Act 1960 (Act 25) essentially modifies a number of common law principles on contract.
9 Procurement, PPP, PFI and Infrastructure Practice Group of AB & David.

Yellow and Red Books (the harmonised versions). However, the decision as to which contract form and/or edition to adopt is made by professionals (mainly engineers and not lawyers) who have no in-depth knowledge or experience in construction law. In addition, the preparation of the conditions of a particular application or special conditions sometimes fails to take into account project-specific issues, leading to disputes during implementation. Examples include cases where the Red Book was used for electromechanical work and another instance where the Red Book was used for a project to be delivered on a lump-sum basis (without proper special conditions).

3.3 Design to fit purpose: technical specification

Even though the Red Book and the Yellow Book are employed for employer-designed works, the contractor nevertheless retains some design obligation under sub-clause 5.1. In practice, the public sector employer will commission a separate entity to undertake the design and the contractor is engaged to undertake the works based on the design. The design engineer or architect may be engaged by the employer as the supervising engineer on the project. In a number of instances, disputes have arisen due to defects in the design. In such cases, even though the contractor has worked in accordance with the design, the works are not fit for purpose. In most instances, the contract between the employer and the design engineer or architect does not cover such liabilities and the special condition is not modified to require the contractor to vet the design and draw the employer's attention to such defects.

3.4 Implementation issues

Disputes arising at the time of implementation are mainly in respect of variations, delays, requests for time extensions, and cost escalation. Even though the provisions of the general conditions clearly deal with these matters, the issue has been one of compliance with the mechanism provided under the terms of the general conditions. In most public sector projects, instructions relating to the above matters (except with an increase in cost) are done at site meetings or during site inspections, without appropriate records and contrary to the contract terms. In other instances, variations and time extensions are granted by supervising engineers even though this right has clearly been reserved for the employer. Failure to comply with the terms usually gives rise to future disputes.

Cost escalation is another major source of dispute in government-sponsored projects, even though this is very limited in donor-funded projects. Most government-funded projects are rarely undertaken within the proposed accepted contract amount. Since the increased cost has not been budgeted for and further delays arise due to the complexity of the financial administration system for government budgeting and spending, completion of the construction is delayed (sometimes suspended), giving rise to a further increase in cost.

3.5 Payment delays

Government-funded projects are prone to delayed payments in terms of contractor certificates. There are instances when delays can be as much as 18 months. This leads to high interest on money borrowed by contractors and huge cost overruns.

Recently, the government has come up with a policy to reverse this unfortunate trend. For example, a ring-fenced fund has been set up by virtue of Act 536[10] which is dedicated to financing road works, resulting in a significant reduction in payment delays and cost overruns even though the problem still persists.

3.6 Fitness for purpose

A number of disputes have arisen on the ground that the completed works are not fit for purpose. A number of factors may account for this issue, but the most prevalent one is absence or lack of clarity about what the employer requires. There have been some instances where the employer's requirement has been prepared by the contractor for the employer. Sometimes, as a result of a public sector agency's lack of capacity there are few or no detailed technical studies to define the project requirements. Likewise, private party employers, in an attempt to save costs, do not engage the required professionals at the initial stages. Invariably construction according to an approved design may not fit the purpose for which the works were commissioned. This consequently leads to disputes between the parties.

3.7 Post-completion issues

A number of disputes have also arisen post-completion. These disputes may relate to: failure to remedy defects after takeover by the employer; failure by the employer to release a retention sum; settlement of accounts; and other post-completion issues.

4. Dispute settlement methods

FIDIC stipulates a three-stage dispute settlement method:

- an expert determination or engineer's determination;
- a dispute adjudication board process; and
- arbitration.

This method has been adopted in Ghana (with slight modifications).

4.1 Expert determination

The FIDIC Yellow and Red Books make provision for a number of determinations, at first instance, by the engineer appointed by the employer. FIDIC contract conditions for construction provide, under sub-clause 3.5, that whenever the contract provides for determination by the engineer, the "Engineer shall consult each Party in an endeavour to reach an agreement. If Agreement is not achieved, the Engineer shall make a fair determination in accordance with the Contract, taking due regard of all relevant circumstances." The sub-clause further provides that the "Engineer shall give notice to both Parties of each agreement or determination, with supporting particulars. Each Party shall give effect to each agreement or determination unless and until revised under Clause 20 [Claims, Disputes and Arbitration]."

This procedure is used as a pre-dispute settlement method in Ghana. The main disadvantage with this method is that since the engineer is appointed by the

---

10 Road Fund Act 1997.

employer, he is not seen as an independent person and the likelihood of bias in determination (which is reinforced when the determination is not favourable to the contractor) lessens the decision's acceptance. The contractor in most instances then proceeds to the next level of dispute settlement method permitted under the contract, namely either the dispute adjudication board (DAB) or arbitration.

Expert determination has been adopted successfully in resolving a number of contentious issues relating to construction projects in Ghana.

4.2 Dispute adjudication boards

Sub-clause 20.2 of the FIDIC General Conditions of Contract provides for dispute adjudication by a DAB appointed by the parties. There has been reluctance to use this dispute settlement method in Ghana, primarily due to the issue of cost in maintaining a DAB for the duration of the contract. In the few instances where this method has been adopted the appointment is made by the parties after the dispute starts. The scope of disputes that can be referred to the DAB includes any dispute between the parties "in connection with, or arising out of, the Contract or the execution of the Works, including any dispute as to any certificate, determination, instruction, opinion or valuation of the Engineer". This, in essence, provides a broad ambit for the parties to submit all disputes relating to the contract or the execution of the works. Even though there is currently reluctance on the part of parties to adopt this method due to associated costs, it is the authors' view that the method will be accepted over time – a view based on the fact that parties to most construction contracts that the authors have worked on recently have agreed to use a DAB. However, the special conditions are amended to provide for the appointment of a DAB when a dispute arises (rather than at the start of the contract and maintaining the DAB throughout the contract period).

4.3 Arbitration

Arbitration remains the most used dispute settlement method in construction disputes in Ghana. The reason for this may be due to the use of standard contract forms that contain standard provisions on arbitration, the perception of delays in the court processes, and the fact that major players in the sector favour the use of international arbitration (in comparison with litigation in Ghana) since they are familiar with the method.

Sub-clause 20.6 of the FIDIC General Conditions of Contract provides for the use of arbitration where the parties are unable to resolve the dispute amicably or any dispute in respect of a DAB's decision that has not become final and binding on parties. The general issue that arises in respect of this sub-clause in Ghana is the determination of the applicable arbitration rules and forum for the dispute. While most foreign contractors prefer arbitration proceedings to be conducted in accordance with the Rules of Arbitration of the International Chamber of Commerce (ICC) or the London International Arbitration Centre (LIAC) Rules, a public sector employer usually prefers the use of national arbitration rules.[11] The preference of the

11 Alternative Dispute Resolution Act 2010 (Act 798).

contractors is based on the need for neutrality in the proceedings (which is perceived as lacking in domestic proceedings under the Alternative Dispute Resolution (ADR) Act of Ghana). Public sector entities' preference for local arbitration as against international arbitration is primarily due to the high cost associated with the latter. Another emerging forum is the Singapore International Arbitration Centre, due to the increasing number of Chinese contractors in Ghana. Unlike their US and European counterparts, they appear to prefer Singapore to London as the forum for arbitration. The increasing number of Chinese contractors is due to the increase in Chinese funding sources for infrastructure projects in Ghana.

The compromise that is adopted when deciding to use international arbitration rules as opposed to national rules on some projects is using international arbitration rules (ICC or LIAC) but holding the arbitration proceedings in Ghana. However, the prevalent method, especially for major construction projects in Ghana, is the use of the ICC or LIAC (and now the Singapore International Arbitration Centre) Rules in Paris or London (or Singapore) as the case may be. In any event, the government is increasingly insisting on Ghana as the forum of arbitration even though the party autonomy principle is still observed and parties may choose foreign law.

4.4 Enforcement of an international arbitration award

One reason for the preference for international arbitration to settle construction disputes in Ghana is the enforcement method in place in Ghana. Ghana is a signatory to the Convention on the Recognition and Enforcement of Foreign Arbitral Awards (the New York Convention). The convention requires courts of contracting states/countries to recognise and enforce arbitration awards made in other countries. In addition, the ADR Act of Ghana has given further effect to the Convention. Under the act, a foreign arbitral award may be enforced by the High Court of Ghana if it is satisfied that:

- the award was made by a competent authority under the laws of the country in which it was made;
- a reciprocal arrangement exist between Ghana and the country in which the award was made or the award was made under an international convention which has been ratified;
- the party seeking to enforce the award must produced the original award or an authenticated copy; and
- there is no appeal pending against the award in any court.

The ADR Act therefore makes it easy to enforce a foreign arbitral award in Ghana through the High Court.

4.5 Emerging trends

There are a number of emerging trends in the settlement of construction disputes in Ghana. The first is using a DAB to settle a dispute and this has stopped disputes at early stages. Ideally a DAB should be appointed from the start of the works to ensure that it is familiar with the project and understands the potential issues that could cause disputes. In that respect, the DAB may function as a dispute prevention mechanism. The DAB makes a determination and where a party is not satisfied there is recourse to a more formal arbitration process. This emerging practice is due to the desire to save cost: the DAB is appointed only when there is a dispute rather than paying a DAB throughout the contract's duration.

Secondly, the proposed PPP Law in Ghana has adopted arbitration as the default dispute settlement method. This proposed law provides that "any dispute between Contracting Entity and the Private Party after they entered into the agreement shall be settled through the dispute settlement mechanism agreed by the parties in the PPP Agreement or, failing such agreement, in accordance with the Alternative Dispute Resolution Act, 2010 (Act 798)". From experience, most private parties prefer an international arbitration rule to the ADR Act for standard contract forms, so international arbitration rules (rather than arbitration under the act) will become the norm.

4.6 Other dispute settlement methods

(a) Mediation and conciliation

Even though rarely used in construction dispute settlements in Ghana, the ADR Act permits the use of conciliation and mediation as a dispute settlement method. Even though there is no statutory distinction between conciliation and mediation under Ghanaian law,[12] the choice of method is generally linked to the involvement of the appointed person (either as a conciliator or mediator). In conciliation, the involvement of the conciliator in assisting the parties to resolve the issue is less than in mediation. The authors have successfully resolved a dispute between an international organisation and a local contractor through the use of mediation.

(b) Litigation

Litigation is the second most-used method (after arbitration) for resolving construction disputes. The process is set in motion by the issue of a writ of summons accompanied by a statement of claim by the plaintiff. The writ must indicate the plaintiff's claims and reliefs. Once the writ is served on the defendant, the defendant is required to appear and file a defence (and, if applicable, counterclaim). The issues are then set down for trial. The plaintiff at the trial adduces evidence to prove its claim and the defendant also calls evidence in defence of the claims made by the plaintiff or to prove its counterclaim (if any). A determination is then made by the judge based on the facts and the applicable law.

This seemingly straightforward procedure is, however, based on the Rules of Court; and sometimes complex litigation strategies are adopted by the parties that in most instances result in undue delay in the proceedings. As there is a lack of in-depth appreciation of the issues giving rise to construction disputes, this has negatively affected judgments handed down by judges in some construction disputes.[13]

Recently, there have been a number of judicial reforms to ensure speedy

---

12 The ADR Act makes provision for the process of mediation but not conciliation.
13 This is also one of the reasons for preferring arbitration over litigation to resolve construction disputes.

resolution of comercial-related disputes. Chief among the measures is the establishment of a dedicated Commercial High Court to settle commercial disputes (including construction disputes). A striking feature of the proceedings at the Commercial High Court is the pre-trial process, where a judge is appointed to assist the parties to attempt to settle the matter without going through the trial process. The pre-trial settlement process has achieved mixed results. On the one hand, it has been suggested that it is a time-wasting process which has not achieved much success in terms dispute settlement. On the other hand, it has been stated that even though it has not achieved much success, it has assisted parties to narrow the issues that are to be determined at the trial. Whatever the position, the pre-trial process remains one mechanism provided under the rules of the Commercial High Court to resolve disputes without going through a full trial.

5. Conclusion

There has been growth in the construction sector in Ghana and the sector is one of the main contributors to Ghana's economy, but there still remains a big infrastructure gap in Ghana. Continual investment in the sector to meet infrastructure demands will sustain its growth.

Disputes arising in the sector are many and varied. Some could have been avoided by engaging professionals (including lawyers) with in-depth knowledge and experience of the sector (particularly the local issues that must be taken into account). The dispute settlement methods adopted are generally determined by the standard contract used. There appears to be a preference for using expert determination and arbitration as ADR methods. The DAB process is emerging as a pre-arbitration process but has not been tested so far. In many instances, the parties have resorted to the courts to settle disputes. Other permissible ADR methods in Ghana include conciliation and mediation. The laws of Ghana do not prohibit any particular method and the choice is determined by the contract between the parties, provided their choice does not amount to excluding the jurisdiction of the courts.

There also appears to be a preference for international arbitration even though there have been instances when Ghana is the forum.

Nicaragua

Haward Álvarez
Sergio Corrales
Terencio García
García & Bódan

As a developing country, Nicaragua is no stranger to the phenomenon of urbanisation. The domestic construction sector has enjoyed steady growth, fluctuating between 15% and 20% over the past three years. According to reports from the Nicaraguan Chamber of Construction, in September 2012 this type of activity increased by 20.5% year on year, while private investment in the construction sector had reached 48.5%.

The dynamism of this sector has translated into job creation and the registration of some 46,000 members in the Nicaraguan Social Security Institute. Construction activity also accounts for approximately 5% of Nicaraguan gross domestic product.

However, these trends present new legal issues which have thus far gone unaddressed – in particular with regard to the legal instruments through which construction activity is governed.

In terms of the public administration, construction and other service contracts are governed by the Administrative Law on Public Sector Procurement[1] and its regulations. However, there are no provisions governing construction contracts in the private sector. Private sector construction contracts are thus instruments issued by the will of the contracting parties, which govern the essential provisions for execution of the relevant construction works.

These legal instruments serve as guidelines for the resolution of unforeseen problems in the execution of the works. Private construction contracts increasingly provide for alternative dispute resolution (ADR) through non-judicial instruments, whether local or foreign. While Nicaraguan legislation lacks provisions regulating the construction industry, it does include provisions on arbitration and mediation.

This chapter outlines the ADR methods in use in the domestic construction sector, which as yet are still in their infancy. While the Nicaraguan legal framework is generally pro-ADR, such methods have not yet become common practice – probably due to misconceptions about the costs of arbitration and a legal culture that favours traditional methods (ie, litigation).

1. Legal framework and development of ADR

Every business will inevitably experience disputes in relation to performance and compliance parameters. In Nicaragua, as elsewhere, such disputes have traditionally been resolved through litigation, causing severe congestion in the courts. Given the

1 Law 737, published in the *Official Gazette* 213 and 214 on November 8 and 9 2010.

protracted nature of judicial proceedings, and judges' typically limited expertise in the specific field of the dispute, the state introduced a series of legal instruments aimed at promoting the use of ADR, which offers agile mechanisms for the swift resolution of disputes outside the congested court system.

In 2002 Nicaragua acceded to the Convention on the Recognition and Enforcement of Foreign Arbitral Awards 1958, better known as the New York Convention.[2] This strengthened legal certainty and access to justice, which in turn has assisted in attracting foreign investment and promoting economic development.

In 2003 Nicaragua ratified the Inter-American Convention on Commercial Arbitration 1975, better known as the Panama Convention.[3] It also began developing a legal framework for ADR. Among other things, this introduced to the judicial structure the Directorate for Management of Alternative Dispute Resolution, a specialised unit of the Supreme Court of Justice which provides the necessary framework, as well as institutional and technical support, to facilitate the resolution of conflicts in different areas of law – either before or during trial – through alternative processes such as mediation or arbitration.

The Nicaraguan legal system also includes additional legal provisions relating to the implementation of such methods. Thus, Article 94 of the Judicial Power Law (260/1998) provides that "in all cases that give rise to demands of family, civil, commercial, land and labour in the respective courts, before any action or proceeding the judge shall convene after the sixth day a process of mediation between the parties ... in criminal cases, mediation will be prompted by the trial's judge in any state of Judgment Instruction".

Similarly, Article 56 of the Code of Criminal Procedure (406/2001), which came into force in December 2002, provides that mediation is a viable alternative to prosecution in cases of misdemeanours, reckless or negligent offences, property offences between individuals without violence or intimidation, and less serious punishable crimes. Mediation may be requested either before a trial starts or during the proceedings, according to Articles 57 and 58.

Provision for arbitration is also made in the following laws:

- Article 76 of the Special Law on Exploration and Exploitation of Hydrocarbons (286/1998) provides for domestic or international arbitration to resolve disputes "arising in the execution, implementation and generally in all matters concerning contracts relating to this law".
- Article 8 of the Law on Foreign Investment Promotion (344/2000) provides that: "Any dispute, controversy or claim arising out of or relating to foreign investments covered by this Act may be referred to international arbitration in accordance with the prescribed provisions, without prejudice to the application of existing national laws and conventions to which the Republic of Nicaragua is party."
- Article 60 of the Law on the Electricity Industry (272/1998) provides that "disputes arising within the Operating Council and that can be resolved,

---

2 Decree 26/2002, published in the *Official Gazette* 56 on March 21 2002.
3 Decree 3362, published in *Official Gazette* 38 on February 24 2003.

shall be settled by arbitration under the terms established in the Operating Rules".

- Article 50 of the Reformed Property Law on Urban and Agrarian Land (278/1997) provides for mediation (or conciliation), and Article 59 for arbitration, to resolve disputes relating to property that arise in the circumstances set out in Article 1 of the same law.

There are also various references to these processes in the Civil Code, the Labour Code and the Code for Children and Adolescents, among others.

On June 24 2005 the Mediation and Arbitration Law (540/2005) was published in Nicaragua's *Official Gazette*. This establishes the parameters for the use of mediation and arbitration, and thus provides Nicaragua with the necessary mechanisms to facilitate international trade. The law was modelled on the United Nations Commission for International Trade Law Model Law, which is used in more than 60 countries worldwide.

2. Methods of ADR

2.1 Mediation

Article 4 of the Mediation and Arbitration Law defines 'mediation' as "any process designated as such, or any other equivalent term, in which the parties request a third person or persons, to assist them in their attempt to reach an amicable settlement of a dispute arising from a contractual or other legal relationship or that is linked to them. The mediator shall have no authority to impose a solution to the parties on the dispute."

Mediation represents a real opportunity to promote investment and legal security, and thus to enhance the business climate in Nicaragua. One of the primary advantages of this method is the parties' ability to attempt to achieve an amicable and conventional resolution of their dispute.

One key institution in charge of commercial mediation is the Antonio Leiva Perez Arbitration and Mediation Centre at the Nicaraguan Chamber of Commerce. The advantages of accessing this ADR hub include the following:

- The centre has the technical and operational capacity to handle commercial disputes, with its own code of ethics and procedural manuals for mediation and arbitration, in addition to well-equipped facilities.
- Staff have been trained in the management of arbitration and mediation proceedings through internships and the exchange of good practices with their counterparts in Mexico, Colombia, Panama and Chile.
- Corporate disputes are a specialism of the centre, which can communicate the realities of ADR to different industries and identify current and potential markets for ADR, the segments that can benefit from its expertise, and the services and options available for the resolution of disputes. The centre has also studied in detail the strengths, benefits and barriers to ADR, in order to promote its use.

2.2 Arbitration

Arbitration is a legal instrument for the non-judicial resolution of disputes by an arbitrator or arbitral tribunal, which will issue a mandatory award that is equivalent to a court judgment. Arbitration takes place by the will of the contracting parties and grants those involved the right to due process and the right to a defence, as constitutionally recognised.

Arbitration may be pursued even if the parties have not agreed on its use in advance of the dispute arising, as it may be agreed either through an arbitration clause in the contract or through a subsequent arbitration agreement.

Under Article 1 of the Mediation and Arbitration Law, any person or entity – including the state, in its contractual relations – has the right to avail itself of mediation, arbitration and other methods of ADR such as dispute boards, subject to certain exceptions set out in the law.

The Mediation and Arbitration Law provides that the following matters are excluded from arbitration:

- matters on which a final court judgment has been issued, except for matters arising from its implementation;
- matters that are inseparably linked to others in which the parties are not freely available, that are expressly prohibited by law or that require a special procedure in certain cases;
- matters relating to alimony;
- matters relating to divorce, legal separation or marriage annulment;
- matters relating to the civil status of persons or age statements;
- matters involving natural or legal persons who cannot represent themselves;
- matters which should be prosecuted;
- matters involving legal representation; and
- working arbitrations.

In Nicaragua, as elsewhere, mediation is facilitated by centres established by law for this process, or by industry or trade organisations that aim to facilitate more effective conflict management in terms of cost, time, compliance and quality of decisions.

In addition to the Antonio Leiva Perez Arbitration and Mediation Centre, there are other arbitration and mediation centres accredited in Nicaragua, such as:[4]

- the Mediation Centre of the Central American University;
- the Mediation and Arbitration Centre of the Polytechnic University of Nicaragua;
- the Mediation Centre for Fostering a Culture of Peace, established in the Department of Carazo;
- the Mediation Centre of the Democratic Lawyers Association of Jinotega, established in the Department of Jinotega; and
- the Mediation Centre of Bluefields Indian and Caribbean University.

---

4 www.poderjudicial.gob.ni/dirac1/centros.asp.

Depending on the wishes of the parties in relation to the selection of arbitrators, the proceedings may be classified as either arbitration in law or arbitration in equity. The latter is characterised by an arbitral tribunal composed of arbitrators who are professionals or technical specialists in the subject matter of the dispute, in accordance with Article 24 of the Arbitration and Mediation Law, who decide *ex aequo et bono* (ie, according to what is right and good).

Arbitration in equity is not completely detached from the law: the arbitrators must consider both basic procedural rules established by the Arbitration and Mediation Law and the principles of the Unification of Private Law Institute. However, it is possible to depart from the application of strict legal rules where the facts of the case so require, in order to ensure that the resolution is fair or just.

In arbitration in equity, each process has its own particularities and combines several scientific disciplines. Even the deadlines which the process must follow are left to the discretion of the parties, depending on the particular circumstances of the works, the terms of the contract and the parties' profiles.

The main advantages of arbitration are the speed of the process and the arbitrators' expertise in the relevant legal, technical or scientific field. Moreover, the flexibility of arbitration allows the parties to determine the procedure to be followed at their convenience. The costs of resolving a dispute through arbitration are also lower than the costs of litigation.

The arbitration process basically involves the following steps:

- request for arbitration;
- constitution of the arbitral tribunal;
- preliminary or preparatory hearing;
- presentation of the complaint;
- response to the complaint;
- hearing of test;
- presentation of the arbitral award; and
- resources.

(a) *Use of arbitration in Nicaragua*

According to statistics of the Antonio Leiva Perez Arbitration and Mediation Centre, an average of five cases were initiated each year between 2006 and 2011. Of these, 15 resulted in arbitral proceedings, while the remainder were resolved through mediation. However, these figures relate to institutional arbitration only. In accordance with Article 33 of the Arbitration and Mediation Law, the Managua courts – which handle *ad hoc* arbitration – heard a total of 34 cases from 2007 to 2012.[5]

(b) *Construction contracts and arbitration clauses*

Some of the main issues addressed in a construction contract include execution of the works, the construction plans and technical specifications, the administrative

---

5 Marenco Corea, Elsy, *"Práctica del Arbitraje Comercial en Nicaragua", Serie de Estudios Especiales* 13, April 2012.

basis, the methods and sources of funding, and the resolution of disputes.

One major shortcoming when preparing construction contracts is the lack of any regulation in national law.[6] Execution and completion of the contract, by force of Article 2480[7] of the Civil Code, fills this legislative gap and governs all aspects of the project – provided, of course, that the contract does not contravene an express rule of law.

However, disagreements between the contracting parties commonly arise, especially in case of changes to the initial terms of execution of the works, delays or cost increases, among other things, which cause conflicts to arise between different parts of the contract.

Arbitration in equity is commonly used to resolve such disputes, since the arbitrators selected may be individuals with the necessary skills to act as arbitrators and decide technical disputes submitted to them.

It is therefore imperative that the arbitration clause specify the essential aspects for submission of a dispute to arbitration and thus establish the approach to be taken to disputes, as well as the technical and scientific basis for claims.

3. Civil procedure reform

The draft of the new Code of Civil Procedure[8] makes further provision for the application of ADR in Nicaragua, including an entire chapter on the regulation[9] of ADR mechanisms as applied to civil conflicts, which complements Article 94 of the Judicial Power Law.

The draft code makes mediation a mandatory prerequisite before submission of a dispute to either arbitration or litigation, and further allows for the implementation of other forms of ADR. The establishment of new mediation centres across the country is expected as a result.

Another novel aspect of the draft code is its provisions on homologation, which recognise arbitration awards as final, binding and enforceable. Homologation may be denied only for the reasons set out in Article 63 of the Arbitration and Mediation Law. However, if a request for annulment of an arbitration award is denied by the Supreme Court, the homologation judge may review only those reasons that were not subject to the motion to vacate.

The new provisions on homologation could effectively hinder the purpose of arbitration and are arguably unnecessary. The draft would further limit the powers of arbitrators to impose precautionary measures.

4. Recommendations

The methods of ADR available under Nicaraguan law allow for the swift resolution of disputes in a cost-effective manner that reflects the will of the parties. Use of these

---

6 Except for those construction contracts regulated by the Administrative Law of Public Sector Procurement.

7 Article 2480 provides that contracts are binding according to their terms and obligations arising from equity, use or law, as appropriate.

8 Approved by Agreement 229 of the Supreme Court of Justice on November 16 and 17 2011.

9 Articles 405 to 409 of the Draft Code of Civil Procedure.

methods as the default dispute resolution mechanism is thus a win–win policy.

However, given the exigencies of construction contracts, and the fact that their terms and conditions require immediate fulfilment in order to ensure the timely completion of the works, arbitration does not present itself as the instrument that best reflects the needs of the parties to a project – and indeed, may even hinder its progress.

A more appropriate method may be resolution through a dispute board – a permanent body, composed of one or three members who are specialists in the relevant field, which is established at the beginning of the contract to assist the parties in resolving any disputes that arise during the course of the project.

According to the International Chamber of Commerce Regulation on Dispute Boards, there are several types of dispute board:

- dispute review boards, which can issue recommendations only;
- dispute adjudication boards, which can issue decisions; and
- combined dispute boards, which can issue both recommendations and decisions at the request of a party, if the other party does not object.

One of the main features of this mechanism, which makes it well suited to construction disputes, is its provision for informal assistance. At the request of either party, and if the other party does not object upon receiving prior notice, the dispute board can assist in the resolution of any conflicts that arise during execution of the works. The board may thus conduct informal visits to the construction site or meetings with the parties to determine whether they are willing to try to reach agreement.

Informal assistance is an extremely flexible process, which allows the board to meet or talk with one or both parties, and to provide opinions either orally or in note format. This ensures that the project is not delayed and there are no major setbacks, as the board is always on hand to facilitate the swift and effective resolution of any differences in opinion that arise.

The use of dispute boards and the introduction of legislation governing construction projects in the private sector would go a long way towards minimising disputes in the sector.

Another step which would assist in this regard is increased promotion of ADR throughout the country. At present, ADR is alien to the Nicaraguan legal culture – not only due to mistrust in non-judicial processes, but also due to reluctance by opposing parties to participate. Information on ADR methods and their success rates should thus be more widely disseminated among institutions such as the Nicaraguan Chamber of Construction, the Chamber of Commerce, the Nicaraguan Institute for the Promotion of Foreign Investment in Nicaragua, and the Superior Council of Private Enterprise (SCPE), which could help to encourage take-up.

The new provisions on ADR set out in the draft of the new Code of Civil Procedure are unlikely to result in greater use of ADR, as they will drive up the costs of enforcing arbitration awards and may potentially cause confusion in this regard.

There are thus three key recommendations to encourage wider use of ADR in the Nicaraguan construction sector:

- Promote and facilitate the use of dispute boards, which – due to their simplicity and costs – represent a faster, cheaper way of resolving disputes while allowing the works to continue.
- Promote conflict resolution through ADR, through the dissemination of information, training, seminars and the like.
- Ensure that future legislation does not mix up non-judicial measures such as ADR with judicial matters, as has happened with the Code of Civil Procedure reform.

Panama

Katherine González Arrocha
Adrián Martínez Benoit
ICC Dispute Resolution Services

1. Introduction

Over the past decade, construction in Panama has retained a distinguished position as one of the country's main economic activities. It has experienced steady growth since 2009, with a predicted gross domestic product (GDP) of $2 billion in 2013. In 2012, this represented 16.3% of the country's GDP. Panama's construction industry growth rate is the highest in the region, followed by Nicaragua and Honduras.

Traditionally, the majority of this activity has been divided evenly between private housing and commercial projects. A nationwide effort by the government to modernise the country's infrastructure has led to a change in this balance. Public construction work has significantly aided the industry's success since 2011. Major public works include highways, an underground metropolitan transport system and the Panama Canal expansion. These last two are both long-term construction projects that have employed the majority of the qualified workforce available in the country. They have also required foreign professionals to operate the complex machinery involved.

The industry's steady growth during the past five years has changed the country's landscape dramatically, especially in urban areas. Panama City now hosts skyscrapers, hotels and shopping centres on virtually every available corner. The majority of construction-related arbitration in Panama deals with disputes that arise from private housing and office projects.[1] These were executed mainly through works contracts for the construction of buildings, and buy–sell agreements for the sale of individual spaces within them.

Both these types of contract, if they are made between private parties, are regulated by the Panamanian Civil Code. Work contracts made with the state or state entities are governed by Law 22/2006 that regulates public procurement. Popular forms for these contracts are lump sum and turnkey, among others.[2]

The following sections describe the dispute settlement methods available in Panama.

2. Litigation

As in many countries, litigation is the default dispute-settlement method available in Panama. Construction-related disputes, which are mostly contractual, are resolved

1 See E. Britton, *"Principales Diferencias sometidas al Proceso Arbitral de Construcción"* (unpublished) for a study of works contracts and the principal disputes that arise from them.

2 See E. Rodríguez Jr, *Modalidades del Contrato de Obra* (Cámara Panameña de la Construcción 2010) for a complete study of the works contract and its most popular forms in Panama.

by the application of Book II of the Panamanian Procedural Code, which covers both provisional measures and ordinary proceedings.

Municipal courts deal with claims under US$5,000. Claims exceeding that amount fall within the scope of circuit courts: these also act as appeals tribunals for claims dealt with by municipal courts. The First Superior Tribunal deals with appeals from decisions made by the circuit courts. The Supreme Court of Panama examines annulment actions, but only for claims over $5,000.

In construction-related disputes, it is common for the claimant to request provisional measures. The Procedural Code allows them to be requested *ex parte* (Article 521(2)), with a security deposit. The requesting party must initiate ordinary proceedings no later than five days after the provisional measure is issued.

The law allows a variety of measures. The most common are the seizure of assets (Articles 523 to 553) and the stoppage of activities (Articles 554 to 557). Other non-specific measures are also allowed (Article 554), but they have a higher threshold. Owing to abusive use, a recent legislative initiative seeks to eliminate this last provision and it is currently (July 2013) under review in Parliament.

Although relatively inexpensive (aside from counsel fees), litigation is regarded as long, tedious and counterproductive: the time value in money that the parties spend litigating a dispute ends up being higher than the amount in dispute. Also, litigation counsels have found ways to delay proceedings using the norms of the Procedural Code. This, coupled with the 'normal' delay caused by busy case dockets, has driven users to other dispute settlement methods.

3. Mediation and conciliation

Alternative dispute resolution (ADR) methods have become increasingly popular in business circles in Panama over the past 15 years. Decree Law No 5 of 1999 (hereinafter Decree-Law 5) regulates arbitration, conciliation and mediation. Arbitration remains by far the most popular of them.

According to Article 58 of Decree-Law 5, a professional or an institution dully authorised by the Ministry of Government and Justice directs mediation. Article 53 bases this dispute settlement method in equity, neutrality, confidentiality and efficiency. Violation of the confidentiality of a mediation procedure means that a mediator is prohibited from acting as such in the future.

The outcome of the mediation will be recorded in a document that is fully enforceable, in the same way as an arbitral award or a court judgment (Article 56).

Most arbitration centres in Panama also provide mediation services, as does the government. In some proceedings, especially in family law, it is a mandatory stage of the proceedings. Most of the time is an option available to parties at any stage of the proceedings and it has been used successfully on several occasions. Notwithstanding this, mediation is not very popular in Panama. Like many countries in the region, there is a predominant 'litigation culture' and people are not naturally prone to sit at the negotiating table.

Conciliation holds the same status as mediation and sometimes it is provided for in buy–sell agreements and in state public work contracts. Between 10 and 20 conciliation procedures are administered each year by major arbitration centres in Panama.

4. Arbitration

The earliest accounts of arbitration regulation in Panama relate to public works contracts signed by the state. Law 6/1988 allowed a dispute arising out of such a contract to be submitted to arbitration, either by an arbitration clause inserted in the contract or by means of an arbitration agreement entered into after the dispute arose. Whichever method was used, it required the approval of the Panamanian Cabinet before any arbitrators were designated. This scheme remained untouched during the first half of the 1990s, and was reinstated via Law 56/1995.[3]

Institutional arbitration is highly popular in Panama. The most frequently used rules are those of the Panamanian Chamber of Commerce, Industry and Agriculture Arbitration Centre (the CeCAP Rules) and the Panamanian Chamber of Construction Arbitration Centre (the CESCON Rules). The majority of disputes administered by these institutions are domestic, although there was an increase in international disputes administered in 2012. According to the information provided by these institutions, about 50% to 60% of the total cases handled by them deal with construction-related issues.

Apart from those covered in Decree-Law 5, currently there is no other formal regulation of other ADR methods. However, the use of other methods such as dispute boards have received some attention recently as the Panama Canal expansion project provides for this method to deal with disputes arising from that project.

Below we will examine some of the salient features of Decree-Law 5.

4.1 International arbitration

Decree-Law 5 establishes a set of characteristics that can make an arbitration based in Panama an international arbitration. Article 5 states that an arbitration is international when it contains certain foreign elements that qualifies it as such. The 'international' character may also be determined by a conflict-of-law rule.

Further developing this definition, Article 5 details five grounds that make arbitration international. The first establishes that if parties to an arbitration agreement had their domiciles in different states when it was signed, the arbitration resulting from the agreement will be deemed international. The second focuses on the place (or seat) of the arbitration: if it is different from the parties' domicile, the arbitration will be deemed international. Performance and fulfilment of the contract is the focus of the third ground: if it is to be sited in a country different from that of the parties' domicile, then the arbitration is deemed international. The fourth ground is a simple conflict-of-law rule that makes arbitration international if the dispute is closely connected to a country different from that of the parties' domicile. Finally, ground five establishes that an arbitration that deals with matters relating to international commerce or with activities with transnational or extraterritorial effects is also deemed international, regardless of the parties' domiciles.

However, this 'internationality' of arbitration under Decree-Law 5 does not detach it from Panamanian law. Article 6 states that the application of Decree-Law 5

---

3 See G. Martinez, *"El Arbitraje en los Contratos de Obra Pública del Estado"* (unpublished, 2013) for a detailed account of these and other past arbitration regulations in Panama.

and Article 5 does not mean that a breach of Panamanian public policy is authorised. Furthermore, Decree-Law 5 applies to international arbitrations without prejudice to international treaties subscribed to by Panama.

4.2 The arbitration agreement

Before discussing how the arbitration agreement is regulated under Panamanian law, we need to look at Article 3 of Decree-Law 5. This provision describes the types of arbitration that can be seated in Panama according to law or according to what is right and just (*ex aequo et bono*). If the parties do not specify in the arbitration agreement which type of arbitration they require, the arbitration will be *ex aequo et bono*.

The Republic of Panama is one of the very few countries of Latin America that provides this ruling. Although it may be argued that this provision could be hazardous for some cases, the practice developed during the past decade in Panama has been positive in general terms. The Panamanian Supreme Court of Justice has affirmed on several occasions that awards decided *ex aequo et bono* "are rendered in accordance with good judgement, stripped from legal formalities, inspired by justice, which entails 'give to each its own', so that it does not have to imperatively decide applying the rules of law, without these entailing that not awarding a cause implies the violation of parties' rights".[4] The court has also stated that the purpose of arbitration *ex aequo et bono* is that "arbitrators, by their experience and utilising the rules of logic, render a measured award, based on natural justice without the rigorous limitations established by the law".[5]

Further judgments have developed the relationship between equity and the law. In a 2010 decision, the court held that when deciding *ex aequo et bono* the arbitrators "apply natural justice, which entails the application of the law, but not in stringent observance of the rigid prescriptions of substantive law".[6] That same year, in a December decision, the Court stressed the fact that in arbitrations *ex aequo et bono* the arbitrators decide "without the stringency of [formal] justice and what is embodied in the law, but rather in accordance with their education and appreciation of the dispute at hand, which allows them to broaden their decision-making capacity, in other words, they are not conditioned to make an award in accordance with [the Panamanian] legal system".[7] In this same decision, the Court stated that "in some circumstances the concept of equity must not be separated from the law, given that under some circumstances the law must be applied to guarantee justice".[8]

Based on this jurisprudence, there is thus a general trend towards allowing arbitrators a large spectrum of action when deciding based on equity. This does not

---

4 Judgment of April 22 2002, Supreme Court of Panama. Translated from the original in Spanish by the authors.

5 Judgment of September 7 2001, Supreme Court of Panama. Translated from the original by the authors.

6 Judgment of June 22 2010, Supreme Court of Panama. Translated from the original in Spanish by the authors.

7 Judgment of December 29 2010, Supreme Court of Panama. Translated from the original in Spanish by the authors.

8 *Ibid.*

mean that arbitrators can depart from the general rules of logic, justice, natural justice or even substantive law, if it directs them to a decision based on equity.

Regarding the arbitration agreement, Article 8 indicates that this can take the form of either an arbitration clause inserted in a contract before the dispute arises or a separate agreement concluded between the parties after the dispute has arisen. A third type of arbitration agreement is foreseen: a unilateral declaration followed by the later addition of the other party or parties involved in the dispute. In fact, according to Article 7, when there is no prior agreement to arbitrate and a dispute arises, any party may send a written notice to the other indicating its willingness to submit to arbitration. Acceptance of such an offer must be made within seven days of its receipt.

Article 7 also expressly recognises the capacity of the state and its subdivisions to submit their present or future disputes to arbitration. This capacity is also expressly provided for in the text of the Panamanian Constitution. The constitution, as well as Article 7, underline that the arbitration agreement does not require cabinet approval or a favourable opinion from the Attorney General. Only in cases where there is no arbitration agreement in the contracts entered into by the state and its subdivisions is cabinet approval and a favourable opinion from the Attorney General required in order to submit the dispute to arbitration.

The arbitration agreement must be in written form. Article 9 is flexible in this respect, and includes any exchange of documents between the parties via fax, email or any other way that acknowledges the parties' will to arbitrate. This agreement, however, must at least designate the method of appointment of arbitrators and the rules of procedure. Reference to a valid and existing set of procedural rules (such as those from a specific domestic or international arbitration institution) is allowed.

Local practitioners have criticised the wording of this provision.[9] It steers away from the widespread criteria championed by the New York Convention and the United Nations Commission on International Trade Law (UNCITRAL) Model Law. Both legal instruments solely require the agreement to be in writing. Some have affirmed that the absence of the requirements in Article 9 in an arbitration clause may deem it invalid. There is no decision yet on the interpretation of this provision, nor has any arbitration agreement been declared invalid because of the absence of these requirements.

Decree-Law 5 establishes which matters arbitration agreements can cover. Article 2 excludes matters that are related to non-freely disposable rights, especially those that deal with the exercise of public powers and the protection and guardianship of minors. Matters that are already judged, regardless of the nature of their decision (by an award or by a judgment), are also outside the scope of arbitration agreements.

Article 11 describes the effects of the arbitration agreement. Firstly, it states that the parties must respect the arbitration agreement. Secondly, they must formalise the constitution of the arbitral tribunal and collaborate fully in the performance and

9 See K González Arrocha and L. Sánchez Ortega, *"Arbitraje Comercial Internacional en Panamá: Marco Legal y Jurisprudencial"* in A Hierro and C Conejero (eds), *El Arbitraje Comercial Internacional en Iberoamérica: Marco legal y jurisprudencial* (second edition, La Ley, 2012) pp583, 587–588.

finalisation of the arbitration procedure. All these obligations on the parties are developments of the more general principle that agreements must be kept.

The negative effect of *kompetenz-kompetenz* is also guaranteed in Article 11: domestic courts are obliged to immediately transfer the file to the arbitral tribunal or to an arbitral institution when faced with an arbitration agreement; government authorities are also required to abstain from making determinations between two parties that have subscribed to an arbitration agreement. Still, Article 11 allows the request for provisional measures to be made to domestic courts, although this should not be considered a waiver of the arbitration agreement.

This provision also establishes the autonomy of the arbitration agreement from the contract that contains it. The last paragraph of Article 11 clearly establishes the principle of separability of the arbitration clause: the nullity of the main contract will not necessarily entail the nullity of the arbitration clause.

4.3 The arbitral tribunal

Article 13 of Decree-Law 5 indicates that, unless otherwise agreed by the parties, foreign nationals may be nominated as arbitrators. The only restriction made by the Decree Law is that when the arbitration is based on law,[10] the foreign arbitrator should be a lawyer (not necessarily registered in Panama; he could be a lawyer from a different country). The same rule applies to nationals.

Tribunals are composed of one or three members, according to Article 12. In the absence of any determination by the parties, the number of arbitrators will be three. An exception to this rule is made in the last paragraph of this provision: in multiparty arbitrations, parties may agree on a different number of arbitrators to make up the tribunal.

With regard to the method of constitution of the arbitral tribunal, Article 14 establishes that parties may agree this amongst themselves or in accordance with the procedure established by the appointing authority of their choice. When neither of these ways is possible, there is a fallback procedure established in Article 15. In the case of tribunals composed of three arbitrators, each party nominates one arbitrator. These arbitrators will then designate a third one, who will be the president of the tribunal. In multiparty arbitrations, parties may jointly designate members of the tribunal when no conflict of interest prohibits it. Parties have 20 days to make their designations, starting after one party has notified the other party of the need to arbitrate.

Ad hoc tribunals have special rules. If a party fails to make its designation within the 20 days, the arbitration procedure moves forward with the appointed arbitrator. This arbitrator will act solely.

In tribunals composed of only one arbitrator, parties will have a deadline of 20 days after one of them has notified the other of the need to agree on an arbitrator. If parties fail to agree on a nomination, the appointing authority will make the decision.

Unlike arbitral laws in other countries and the UNCITRAL Model Law, Decree-

10 See comments in this respect in section 3 above.

Law 5 does not mandate recourse to the domestic courts for aid in the constitution of the arbitral tribunal. In a unique way, the Panamanian law only makes reference to a third person or an appointing authority, which is commonly understood as a duly authorised arbitral institution. The Panamanian legislator went even further: Article 10 establishes that when various appointing authorities are competent, the first one to receive an arbitration request from one of the parties is deemed competent to administer the proceedings and make the designations mandated by law. Thus, it has become standard practice in Panama that arbitration agreements that do not provide for an arbitration institution are assigned by the unilateral will of the claimant to the institution of its choice. It could be argued that the simple language of 'a third person' (Article 10) may be interpreted in a broader and more inclusive way: domestic tribunals may well be considered 'a third person'. However, this possibility is only foreseen based on an agreement between the parties and not as the default position if the parties fail to agree.

As commonly found in other domestic regulations, arbitrators are required to be impartial and independent from the parties when appointed and throughout the arbitration. Article 16 covers all matters related to this topic. First, arbitrators should abstain from accepting appointments if they know of any fact or circumstance that may jeopardise their independence and impartiality. Secondly, parties may challenge arbitrators when they are aware of such facts or circumstances. No arbitrator may be challenged by a fact or circumstance pre-existent to his appointment, unless he is a party-appointed arbitrator.

If an arbitrator does not accept a challenge made by a party, the challenging party may present its challenge before the arbitral tribunal within three days of the arbitrator's decision to not accept the challenge. The tribunal will establish a procedure for the challenge, and its decision on the matter will be final. Substitution of an arbitrator will be made under the rules agreed by the parties; when no rules have been agreed, it will be made by the appointing authority.

Article 17 establishes the positive effect of the principle of *kompetenz-kompetenz*. In tune with all modern arbitral regulations, tribunals seated in Panama may decide the scope of jurisdiction, including the invalidity, inexistence or inefficacy of the arbitration agreement, and therefore its lack of competence.

The positive effect of *kompentz-kompetenz* was not always a given in Panama. In 2001, Article 17 was declared to be unconstitutional. The Supreme Court declared that the state could not waive its power to administer justice. It was also deemed that Article 17 violated the human right of access to justice, as it prevented recourse to domestic tribunals. To sum up, the court stated that domestic tribunals should resolve any challenge to an arbitral tribunal jurisdiction. Happily, this situation did not stay as such for long: a 2004 constitutional amendment guaranteed the arbitral jurisdiction in the constitution's text, including the principle of *kompetenz-kompetenz*, and reinstated Article 17 of Decree-Law 5.

Panamanian law grants arbitral tribunals the power to issue provisional measures. The law indicates that in order to enforce these measures, the arbitral tribunal may seek the assistance of a circuit judge and the judge must enforce the measures within a period of 10 working days. Some arbitration practitioners in

Panama have interpreted this rule as allowing the arbitral tribunals to enforce interim measures based on the fact that the rules indicate that the arbitral tribunal may seek the assistance of a circuit judge. Furthermore, they consider that in view of the modifications made to the Panamanian Constitution in 2004, the arbitral tribunal is empowered to execute interim measures. Article 202 of the Panamanian Constitution indicates that "the administration of justice may also be exerted by the arbitral jurisdiction in accordance with the law".

4.4 The arbitration procedure

Article 18 lays down the general principle for the conduct of the arbitral procedure by the tribunal. Arbitrators will apply the rules accorded by the parties; if no such rules exist, the applicable rules of the arbitration institution that administers the procedure will govern the proceedings. If there are no arbitration institution rules applicable, the tribunal will determine the procedural rules. The president of the arbitral tribunal has the final word on the interpretation of any applicable procedural rule.

Panamanian law also includes some general principles basic to any adversarial dispute settlement method. Article 19 guarantees equality between the parties and the right to be heard. It also establishes that if a party does not appear to the proceedings, or if the validity of the arbitration agreement or the authority of the arbitral tribunal to decide the dispute is challenged before domestic courts, it will not stop the proceedings.

Tribunals seated in Panama are not limited to carrying out the arbitral proceedings within the country's borders. Article 20 allows parties to designate the place where the various acts related to the arbitration (hearings, witness examination, etc) will be held. The applicable institutional rules will apply if no such designation is made. The tribunal may also decide the place where some concrete acts will be held, letting the parties know about this decision in advance. Although no mention is made in this provision, it is clear that decisions of this kind by the arbitral tribunal do not contravene the parties' agreements or the applicable arbitration rules.

As to the language of the arbitration, Article 20 ensures that party autonomy and institutional rules are respected by indicating that the language agreed by the parties or the one designated by the applicable arbitration rules will govern the proceedings. However, the same provision introduces a more restrictive approach when both parties are Panamanian. In such a case, the language will always be Spanish.

This language limitation may pose difficulties for international arbitrations seated in Panama. It limits the participation of foreign counsel in these arbitrations by confining the pool of available legal professionals. This is one of the provisions that disappears in the draft arbitration law, which is scheduled to be approved in the second half of 2013 by the Panamanian legislature.[11]

No other significant determinations regarding the arbitration procedure are made. Article 21 indicates that the procedure will start with the notice of arbitration from one party to the other in *ad hoc* arbitration, or the filing of the arbitration

11 See section 4.9 below.

request by one party before the competent arbitral institution. Article 22 provides minimal guidelines for the filing of the arbitration request and the answer to the request; time limits are established by the parties' agreement or by the applicable arbitration rules. Article 23 gives the arbitral tribunal the power to decide the dispute by relying solely on documents, if the parties so agree.

4.5 The law applicable to the dispute

Regarding applicable law, Article 26 of Decree-Law 5 establishes two different standards. Firstly, in domestic arbitrations the tribunal will apply the rules of law. The use of this wording gives the tribunal enough room to cherry-pick the most suitable provisions on which to base its decision, including international norms and principles. This is laid out in Article 27, which indicates that the arbitral tribunal will bear in mind the provisions of the contract, commercial customs and the UNIDROIT Principles on International Commercial Contracts.

Secondly, when the arbitration is deemed international in accordance with the criteria established in Article 5, the applicable law will be procured as stated in Article 43(3): the tribunal will decide the dispute in accordance with the law designated by the parties or by the applicable arbitration rules. Failing an agreement, the arbitral tribunal will choose the law, by the application or otherwise of a conflict-of-law rule. In this process, the tribunal will consider the uses of commerce, the content of the contract and the rules of international private contracts.

Article 43 allows the tribunal to find the applicable law via a conflict-of-law rule, but it also allows it to select an applicable law without resort to any conflict-of-law rules. The inclusion of a resort to a conflict-of-law rule is only a guideline for the tribunal to take into account in its determination of the law applicable to the dispute. In this respect, Article 43 is very similar to Article 1511 of the French Code of Civil Procedure, which allows the arbitral tribunal to apply the rules of law it considers appropriate.

4.6 The award

A time limit of six months is established for the award to be made by the arbitral tribunal, starting from the tribunal's last member's acceptance. This time period may be different if parties agree otherwise or if a different time limit is established in the applicable arbitration rules. Article 25 allows this period of time to be extended.

Awards will be made in writing and will be signed by all members of the arbitral tribunal. In case there is no agreement of the tribunal or a majority position cannot be distinguished, the award will be rendered by the tribunal's president.

The minimum requirements the award must have are contained in Article 29: the parties and the dispute must be identified; the arbitral tribunal must explain the basis and scope of its jurisdiction; the seat of the arbitration and other related facts must be also present; and the evidence must be systematically examined, including the parties' arguments and the decision of the tribunal. The tribunal's reasoning must be included when it decides according to law. Article 30 allows parties' settlements that finalise a dispute to be recorded in the form of an award if the parties request the arbitral tribunal to do so.

The award will be notified to the parties in the manner they have agreed on or that established in the applicable arbitration rules. If it cannot be done this way, the secretary of the arbitral tribunal will make the notification; in the absence of the secretary, the president of the tribunal will do so.

Parties have five days from the notification of the award to request that the arbitral tribunal corrects any clerical errors in the award or make an interpretation of the award.

Article 33 places the end of the arbitral tribunal's mandate at the date the award is duly notified to the parties, or when a requested interpretation of the award is issued. The award has the effect of a matter already judged.

4.7 Means of recourse

An award issued by tribunals seated in Panama can only be subject to an application to set it aside on the grounds laid out in Article 34. These are divided into two different groups.

The first group is further subdivided on the following grounds: the invalidity of the arbitration agreement; the improper constitution of the arbitral tribunal; the failure of due notification to one of the parties of the request for arbitration or any other act within the procedure; decisions beyond that which is sought (*ultra petita*); or awards rendered under violence, malfeasance or bribery. The party who commenced the set-aside proceeding must prove these. The second group deals with awards that decide disputes that are not subject to arbitration in accordance with Panamanian law, or where the decision by the arbitral tribunal is contrary to Panamanian public policy. Article 34 states this ground can be proven by the tribunal that entertains the set-aside application.

Article 35 establishes a time limit of 15 days after the award is notified or after an interpretation request is fulfilled for any set-aside application to be filed.

4.8 Recognition and enforcement of foreign awards

The Panamanian law establishes a procedure that is applicable to both foreign awards *per se* and international awards (as defined through Article 5) that have been rendered by arbitral tribunals seated in Panama.

Applications for recognition and enforcement will be addressed to the Fourth Chamber of the Supreme Court of Panama. Panama has ratified the New York Convention of 1958, and so the requirements that Article 43 establishes for such applications to be filed are identical to the ones contained in Article IV of the Convention. Likewise, the grounds for denying recognition and enforcement in Article 41 of the Panamanian law mirror those of Article V of the Convention.

A few judgments by the Supreme Court have addressed issues pertaining to the recognition and enforcement of foreign awards. In March 2001, the court rejected a request made by a Panamanian corporation to refuse recognition and enforcement of an International Chamber of Commerce award made in Mexico, based on an alleged violation of Panamanian public policy. The court reasoned that public policy "is nothing more than to achieve that a foreign judgment does not violate the competence of the national forum, abiding by the Magna Carta and other legal provisions in force, congruently with the obedience foreign judgments must display towards authorities".[12] More importantly, the court added that the understanding of public policy "must be studied on a case by case basis" and "its violation cannot be invoked generically".[13]

In February 2005, the court rejected a party's request to deny the recognition and enforcement of a domestic award deemed international in accordance with Article 5. The appellant, a Panamanian oil and gas processing company, argued that it was deprived of exercising its right of defence because the arbitral tribunal did not admit an expert opinion, which it considered essential to the outcome of the case. The court rejected this argument and affirmed that the award did not violated public policy and was enforceable. It reasoned that the arbitral tribunal was fully capable of admitting or rejecting all evidence presented before it. Furthermore, the court held that it was not an appeal court for arbitral tribunals, and added that "it cannot elucidate whether the arbitral tribunal appreciated in due form the adduced evidence". It also affirmed the binding character of arbitral awards, both to the parties involved and the state courts, stating that "arbitrators are judges in their own right, and their decisions have coercive force towards the rest of the judiciary and administrative community, thus giving parties greater security that their claims, recognised through arbitral awards, shall be respected".[14]

4.9 Changes ahead: the 2013 proposal for a new arbitration law

A draft text for new legislation on national and international arbitration is under review at the Panamanian National Assembly, the country's highest legislative body, at July 2013. Its aim is to keep the legal framework that regulates domestic and international arbitration in Panama up to date. While Decree-Law 5 regulates arbitration, mediation and conciliation, the new draft text focuses only on arbitration.

The draft new law incorporates provisions aimed at addressing modern trends of international arbitration. It maintains the favourable aspects of Decree-Law 5 but also incorporates new aspects based mainly on the modifications made to the UNCITRAL Model Law in 2006. Like Decree-Law No. 5, the bill regulates domestic and international arbitration in a single legal instrument.

Now arbitrators can hold any nationality, unless otherwise agreed by the parties. In international arbitrations they may or may not be lawyers; in arbitrations to be decided according to law they must be practising lawyers. Regarding multiparty arbitrations, a provision has been included that deals with the composition of the arbitral tribunal. Decree-Law 5 is silent in this respect, and this provision is sure to bring clarity to the composition of the arbitral tribunal when there are multiple claimants and/or multiple respondents.

The provision indicating that the arbitral tribunal decided *ex aequo et bono*, if not

12 Judgment of March 23 2001, Supreme Court of Panama. Translated from the original in Spanish by the authors.

13 *Ibid.* Translated from the original in Spanish by the authors.

14 Judgment of February 14 2005, Supreme Court of Panama (Judge Winston Spadafora Franco). Translated from the original in Spanish by the authors.

otherwise expressly provided in the arbitration agreement, is replaced by a provision indicating that the arbitral tribunal shall decide *ex aequo et bono* only if the parties have granted the tribunal such power.

Provisional measures, a subject not considered in detail in Decree-Law 5, enjoys detailed regulation in the draft law based on the UNCITRAL Model Law. Chapter V of the new draft law focuses on this topic, and gives the arbitral tribunal powers to issue such measures, detailing the requirements that must be met before it does so. It also regulates how provisional measures requested before the constitution of the arbitral tribunal will be dealt with. A provision on recognition and enforcement of provisional measures issued by arbitral tribunals seated outside Panama is also included.

Smaller but equally important additions are made. For example, an article on rules of interpretation is included. It states that at all times the law shall be interpreted taking into account its international origin, the necessity to promote uniformity in its application, and good faith. This provision assures any interpretation of the law to be anchored in international arbitration theory as developed by legal instruments such as the New York Convention and the UNCITRAL Model Law.

5. Other dispute settlement methods

5.1 Dispute boards

Dispute boards are not used in Panama's private construction industry and this method is unknown in local business circles. Still, two of the current government's major public infrastructure works provide for dispute boards: the Panama Canal expansion project and the building of an underground transport system in Panama City.

The impact of these dispute boards in the local construction environment is still unknown. Aside from this, dispute board proceedings are confidential. Hence, for the time being, little practical experience can be extracted from them.

5.2 Expert determination

Currently, this method is not used but experts' reports are often used in litigation and arbitration, either at the request of the parties or at the request of the judge or arbitral tribunal.

6. Conclusion

From the dispute resolution methods reviewed, we can conclude that arbitration is the most popular method for construction businesses in Panama. During the past 15 years it has become so popular that an arbitration clause is now present in virtually all buy–sell agreements for new properties, insurance, guarantee bonds and other contracts relating to construction operations. Furthermore, it seems that arbitration will acquire more strength and will continue to grow as the preferred method in this field should the new draft arbitration law be approved soon.

Mediation and conciliation remain unpopular dispute settlement methods in

Panama. This is in part due to cultural traits common to many countries of the region that share a civil law system. An effort is being made to promote these methods, especially through the state's judiciary, by making it a mandatory stage of the proceedings or an option available to parties at all stages of the procedure. This practice has enjoyed limited success in business circles.

Dispute boards are still a relatively unknown phenomenon in Panama, even though they are currently instituted in two major government-led infrastructure projects. This method is sure to reach the private domestic construction sector, given its increased worldwide popularity; however, at the time of writing (March 2013), there are few (if any) private projects that warrant their use.

The views expressed in this article are those of the author and not necessarily those of the ICC International Court of Arbitration or its Secretariat.

Canada

Bruce Reynolds
Sharon Vogel
Borden Ladner Gervais LLP

1. Introduction

Canada's construction industry is well established and continues to grow, pumping billions of dollars into the economy each year. For instance, the 2012 Canada Year Book for the construction industry, published by Statistics Canada, notes that "construction accounted for 6.0% of Canada's GDP in 2011, contributing $76.5 billion".[1] The yearbook also provides the total value of building permits issued in 2011: C$74.0 billion, which was up 2.1% from the value of permits issued in 2010. Of this, C$44.5 billion was issued in respect of residential buildings and C$29.5 billion was for non-residential building permits, most of which related to commercial building projects (C$16.3 billion).[2]

The Canadian Construction Association compiled construction industry highlights of the 2013 Federal Budget which demonstrate the continued importance of growth in the construction industry. These include:

- More than C$53 billion in investments, including over C$47 billion in new funding in support of local and economic infrastructure projects over 10 years under a new Building Canada Plan starting in 2014–15, including:
  - C$32.2 billion over 10 years under a Community Improvement Fund to build roads, public transit, recreational facilities and other community infrastructure across Canada;
  - C$1.25 billion for the renewal of the PPP Canada Fund to continue supporting innovative ways to build infrastructure projects through public-private partnerships (PPPs); and
  - C$6 billion to provinces, territories and municipalities under current infrastructure programmes in 2014–15 and beyond; and
- significant investments in First Nations infrastructure such as roads, bridges and energy systems, as well as other First Nations infrastructure priorities, including:
  - C$155 million over 10 years from the new Building Canada Fund, in addition to allocations from the Gas Tax Fund; and
  - approximately C$7 billion over the next 10 years under existing programming to build, operate and maintain infrastructure on reserves.[3]

---

1 Statistics Canada, "Construction Year Book" (2012), Government of Canada, www.statcan.gc.ca/pub/11-402-x/2012000/chap/construction/construction-eng.htm.
2 *Ibid.*
3 Canadian Construction Association, Federal Budget 2013, www.cca-acc.com/pdfs/en/budget/2013Budget.pdf.

Canada is a leader in the development of PPP projects. Statutory and regulatory frameworks have been established at both the federal and provincial levels. For example, in 2002 the federal government introduced the Canada Strategic Infrastructure Fund Act.[4] The legislation promotes PPP projects "by creating a programme pursuant to which eligible recipients are provided with contributions for the carrying out of large-scale strategic infrastructure projects that contribute to economic growth or quality of life in Canada or that advance Canada's objectives with respect to infrastructure".[5] In 2009 PPP Canada Inc, a crown corporation, was created to manage and invest the PPP Fund, worth C$1.25 billion. PPP Canada is tasked with advising the federal government on PPP projects and determining the PPP eligibility of major projects seeking federal funding by weighing their PPP options.[6] PPP Canada explains the PPP Canada Fund as follows:

> *The PPP Canada Fund is a merit based program, designed to incent the use of PPP procurement in delivering public infrastructure projects. Eligible projects can receive up to 25% of the direct cost of construction supported through non-payable contributions, repayable contributions, loans or loan guarantees. The $1.2 billion is committed over a 5 year period starting 2009/10 and is allocated to PPP Canada on an annual basis, subject to approval by Parliament. The Government of Canada recently announced in Budget 2013 its commitment to renew the PPP Canada Fund by an additional $1.25 billion beginning in 2014.*[7]

There have been five rounds of submissions of proposals to PPP Canada, the first of which launched in October 2009. PPP Canada announced the launch of Round Five on April 15 2013 by way of a press release.[8] The focus of Round Five was on "public infrastructure projects that promote jobs and stimulate economic growth".[9] PPP Canada indicated that it would be giving priority to proposals in the following areas:

- transportation;
- water/wastewater;
- solid waste disposal; and
- brownfield redevelopment of contaminated sites.[10]

PPP Canada also advised in its Round Five release that "[t]o date, the Government of Canada has announced PPP Canada Fund commitments toward 15 PPP projects across Canada, totaling over $715 million to projects with more than $3.2 billion in capital costs".[11] PPP Canada anticipates further announcements in the months following this April 15 2013 press release.

---

4 SC 2002, c 9, s 47.
5 Bruce Reynolds, Sharon Vogel and Yvan Houle, "Canada" in Robert S Pecker, ed, *Construction 2012 in 35 Jurisdictions Worldwide* (London: Law Business Research Ltd, 2011) 43 at p45.
6 *Ibid.*
7 PPP Canada, "PPP Canada Launches Round Five of the PPP Canada Fund" (April 15 2013), www.PPPcanada.ca/_files/file/FINAL%20ROUND%20FIVE%20LAUNCH%20DOCUMENTS/RELEASE_PPP%20CANADA%20LAUNCHES%20ROUND%20FIVE%20OF%20THE%20PPP%20CANADA%20FUND%20.pdf.
8 *Ibid.*
9 *Ibid.*
10 *Ibid.*
11 *Ibid.*

2. Dispute resolution regime

Canada has adopted various alternative dispute resolution mechanisms which may be utilised in the context of a construction dispute, including negotiations, mediation, arbitration, dispute resolution boards (DRBs), referees and project neutrals. Some construction disputes continue to be resolved through the traditional litigation process as well.

Canada is a federal state comprising 10 provinces and three territories, all but one of which have a common law legal system. The exception is the province of Quebec, which is a civil law jurisdiction. The Canadian Constitution allocates powers between the federal and provincial levels of government. Provinces are allocated a number of important powers, the most significant of which is the power to make laws in relation to "property and civil rights in the Province". In general terms, this head of power gives the provinces the right to legislate over construction matters.[12] There is a federal court with trial and appellate divisions, but its jurisdiction is limited to certain strictly federal matters (eg, intellectual property, income tax and admiralty). Each province has a court system composed of a superior court with broad jurisdiction, specialised provincial courts with jurisdiction over family matters, minor criminal charges and small claims, and a court of appeal. Judges of the superior court and the court of appeal are appointed by the federal government, but the courts are administered by the provincial government.

2.1 Litigation processes designed to encourage early resolution of disputes

Negotiation is usually the first resolution method attempted by parties and their representatives in a construction dispute.[13] If initial negotiations are unsuccessful, provincial and territorial rules of court prescribe the steps to be taken within the context of the civil litigation process to encourage settlement. For example, under Ontario's Construction Lien Act,[14] an order may be obtained requiring the parties to attend a settlement meeting. Such meetings are held in a courtroom, but a judge is present only at the outset and conclusion of the settlement meeting, such that most of the meeting takes place in the presence of the parties to the dispute and their counsel only. The person in charge of conducting the meeting is selected by a majority of those present at the meeting. If the parties are unable to select a person to be in charge, the Construction Lien Act mandates that the person who "took out the appointment" for the meeting will conduct it. If the parties can resolve any issues at the meeting, they are to be set out in a statement of settlement, which is then filed with the court.[15] Ontario's Rules of Civil Procedure[16] also provide for mandatory mediation for civil actions commenced in the cities of Toronto or Ottawa, or the County of Essex, on or after January 1 2010.[17] If such efforts at early resolution fail, the parties can continue through the traditional litigation processes of discovery of

---

12 See RB Reynolds, "A Canadian Approach to the Minimization of Construction Insolvencies", in *Contemporary Issues in Construction Law* (London: Construction Law Press, 1996).

13 Reynolds, Vogel and Houle, note 5 above, at p47.

14 RSO 1990, Chapter C30.

15 *Ibid*, s61.

16 Courts of Justice Act, RRO 1990, Reg 194.

17 *Ibid*, Rule 24.1.04(1).

documents, oral examinations for discovery, interlocutory motions, pre-trial conferences and ultimately trial.

2.2 Alternative dispute resolution mechanisms

Mandatory civil procedure aside, it is important in settling construction disputes that parties consider which method of alternative dispute resolution is most likely to achieve the following goals in the context of the specific matter at hand:

- Efficient and expeditious resolution of disputes – matters should be disposed of in a timely manner at the least possible expense so that they are not allowed to fester or evolve (devolve) into larger disputes.
- Procedural fairness – the process should not favour one party over the other, and should allow for disputes to be addressed without negatively affecting the ongoing work or the relationship between the parties. Ideally, the mechanism should identify and discourage frivolous claims, and should not penalise a party for raising legitimate claims.
- Certainty and finality of result – an effective dispute resolution mechanism will achieve a certain and final result, whenever possible.

Below is a discussion of the various alternative dispute resolution methods available in Canada which may be used to achieve these goals.

(a) *Stepped negotiations*

Most Canadian construction contracts include a procedure involving structured or stepped negotiations for resolving disputes. Such clauses identify representatives from each organisation who are responsible for meeting at first instance and attempting to resolve a dispute when it arises, failing which the dispute is elevated to a higher level of management for further negotiation, prior to being turned over to other methods of resolution involving a third party. Such procedures generally include requirements for full disclosure and prompt exchange of information.[18]

One disadvantage of this process is that if the information exchanged between the parties is insufficient, the likelihood of resolution is significantly diminished.[19] Another disadvantage is that stepped negotiations can be slow, particularly if they are not carried out at the same time as an adjudicated process. If stepped negotiations are unsuccessful and the parties must engage in subsequent processes, resolution of disputes can be delayed significantly.[20]

On the other hand, stepped negotiations can provide an advantageous avenue of resolution for parties that do not wish to involve third parties in their dispute:

- Negotiations can result in a swift resolution of a dispute if the parties "communicate well and engage in principled negotiation";[21] and

---

18 P Bruner and P O'Connor, *Bruner and O'Connor on Construction Law* (West Group Publishing, 2002).
19 *Ibid.*
20 W Earle, *Drafting ADR and Arbitration Clauses for Commercial Contracts* (Toronto: Carswell, 2010), at pp1–6.
21 P Bruner, *"'Rapid Resolution' ADR – The Future is Now"*, American Bar Association Forum on the Construction Industry 2011 Mid-Winter Meeting, New York, at p8.

- The negotiation may involve several levels of authority within the organisations, with the result that "the dispute will be examined by people with different concerns, viewpoint and agenda, and perhaps with a healthy distance and detachment from the dispute".[22] However, this advantage of a stepped negotiation process applies only if the individuals attempting to resolve the claim have the requisite distance and detachment from the dispute.

(b) *Mediation*

Mediation is increasingly being recognised in Canada as an effective means of resolving legal disputes. The number of mediators available to participate in the resolution of construction disputes is also increasing. Many mediators are familiar with construction law issues and include former judges and counsel who specialise in construction law.[23]

Mediation is a process by which the parties select a neutral third party without decision-making power, the mediator, to assist them in resolving issues in dispute. Typically, the mediator meets with the parties separately and communicates with each party on behalf of the other, providing views on the dispute at the same time. In meeting with the parties, the mediator attempts to get a sense of each party's perspectives and to identify the barriers to settlement. The mediator then tries to break down barriers to settlement using a variety of tactics and strategies, including "highlighting the parties' common interests"[24] and identifying a settlement zone, within which both parties would consider an agreement or settlement to be fair.

Mediation can be an extremely useful tool for resolving disputes. It is relatively low in cost and usually short in length, ensuring both cost and time efficiency. Mediation also has the potential to preserve the business relationship between the parties after the dispute between them is settled. Further, mediation is confidential, maintaining the parties' privacy in respect of the dispute. Mediation also presents the possibility of negotiating unique solutions that may not arise in a rights-based process.[25]

As previously noted, the Ontario legislature has recognised the advantages of mediation and has made it mandatory in civil actions "in order to reduce cost and delay in litigation and facilitate the early and fair resolution of disputes".[26]

While mediation has certain advantages for resolving construction disputes, it may not always succeed. Mediation will be unsuccessful or inappropriate when:

- it is merely being used as a tactic to delay resolution;
- there is a power imbalance that a mediator is unable to manage;
- legal questions or matters of policy or principle are involved that make it difficult to reach a negotiated resolution, particularly where the mediator is not an evaluative mediator;

---

22 *Drafting ADR*, note 20 above, at pp1–6.
23 Reynolds, Vogel and Houle, note 5 above, at p48.
24 George W Adams, *Mediating Justice: Legal Dispute Negotiations*, 2nd edn (CCH Canada Limited, 2011), at p245.
25 *Drafting ADR, supra* note 19 at pp1-12.
26 Rules of Civil Procedure, *supra* note 15, Rule 24.1.01.

- the fact-finding process is not sufficiently advanced such that the parties are not adequately prepared;[27]
- the case involves fundamental wrongdoing such as fraud, corruption or intentional torts; or
- there is a history of animosity and conflict between the parties, such that resolution discussions and problem solving would be inhibited by bad faith and hostility.[28]

(c) Arbitration

In arbitration, the parties set out their positions in respect of the dispute and an impartial third party, the arbitrator, decides the case. As opposed to mediation, arbitration is an adversarial process, focusing on the parties' rights rather than their interests. Instead of reaching a collaborative agreement, the parties either win or lose certain aspects of the dispute, depending on the arbitrator's final determinations.[29]

The construction industry was one of the first industries in North America to accept arbitrations as a contractually agreed-upon method of dispute resolution. In Canada, binding arbitration is well known and well developed in the construction industry and has governing legislation in the form of provincial statutes such as Ontario's Arbitration Act, 1991.[30] The key to an effective contractual arbitration provision is that the process be mandatory, rather than voluntary or subject to a veto.

There are many advantages to conducting a private arbitration as opposed to litigating. For instance, arbitrations may better maintain business relationships, and they can preserve confidentiality.[31] George W Adams in *Mediating Justice: Legal Dispute Negotiations* has identified further advantages of the arbitral process:

- a civilised method of 'fighting it out';
- procedural fairness and party satisfaction;
- better fact finding;
- protection of rights; and
- the intrinsic good of enhancing a client's autonomy and individuality.[32]

Arbitration should resolve disputes in a timely and cost-effective manner. It is recognised, however, that arbitration by its nature, and given the procedural steps involved, can sometimes be a lengthy process (although no more lengthy than a trial). An effective arbitration process will include the following elements:

- a well-drafted agreement that requires mandatory, binding arbitration and clear rules for the conduct of the arbitration;
- a selection process for arbitrators with the requisite construction law, construction industry and case management knowledge and experience;[33]

---

27 *Rapid Resolution*, note 21 above, at p13.
28 *Mediating Justice*, note 24 above, at p282.
29 *Ibid* at p378.
30 SO 1991, Chapter 17.
31 Reynolds, Vogel and Houle, note 5 above, at p47.
32 *Mediating Justice*, note 24 above, at p378.

- a requirement for early disclosure of positions;
- limits on oral discoveries and document disclosure;
- effective arbitrator control of pre-hearing motions and the hearing; and
- a reasoned decision.[34]

Even an arbitration that incorporates the above elements can become a time-consuming and expensive process, which has led various jurisdictions to explore alternatives such as mediation, adjudication, dispute resolution boards, expert determination and referees.

(d) *Mediation-arbitration*

Mediation-arbitration ('med-arb') combines mediation and arbitration into one dispute resolution process. In a med-arb setting, the third neutral party acts as both a mediator and an arbitrator. The process typically begins with mediation, followed by arbitration if the parties are unable to resolve their dispute during mediation. At the arbitration stage, the mediator-arbitrator can reach a decision, ensuring finality of dispute resolution. Also, the parties may settle some aspects of their dispute at the mediation stage and proceed to allow the arbitrator to decide the remaining issues at arbitration.[35]

The advantages of med-arb process include the following:

- The power of the neutral third party ultimately to impose a decision on the parties provides an incentive for the parties to act reasonably and to carefully consider any of the third party's comments regarding the positions of the parties or suggestions for resolution.
- The mediation component of med-arb allows the parties to maintain control at the outset of the resolution process, allowing for interest-based resolution before proceeding to a rights-based binding decision;
- If the mediation segment of the process does not result in resolution, the arbitration component ensures finality and "provides a clear end point within a reasonably acceptable timeframe, giving the parties an incentive to agree".[36]
- In the event that arbitration is required, the parties do not incur further costs in finding a new third party to act as decision maker.
- At arbitration, the mediator-arbitrator is more likely to be informed of the nuances of the parties' positions and have a better understanding of the details of the case than a fresh arbitrator.[37]

One perceived disadvantage of med-arb is that the mediator-arbitrator receives information from each party privately before arriving at a final decision. This is in contrast to traditional arbitrations, where the arbitrators hear evidence and positions

---

33 *Rapid Resolution*, note 21 above, at p15.
34 *Ibid.*
35 *Mediating Justice*, note 24 above, at p386.
36 *Ibid* at pp386–7.
37 *Ibid* at p387.

in the presence of all parties in an open hearing. The med-arb process makes the arbitrator privy to information that the opposing party may be unaware of, causing a lack of transparency which is not inherent in standard arbitrations. As noted by George W Adams, "there is little chance of removing information from the mind of an arbitrator acquired during the mediation phase or of a party successfully reverting to an earlier position unless, in the latter event, the party can establish that it was prejudiced by its greater candour or the failure of conditions upon which its offer was premised". As such, the mediation portion of med-arb can shape the ultimate outcome of a subsequent arbitration.[38]

Other potential negative effects of the med-arb model include the following:

- The parties may be less candid during mediation because the mediator-arbitrator is involved in both processes.
- The parties may feel coerced into a mediated settlement if the mediator-arbitrator threatens to use his arbitral powers.
- The mediator-arbitrator's neutrality may be called into question if the parties suspect that information conveyed during mediation has shaped the arbitral award.[39]

To mitigate these problems with the med-arb model, parties may decide to make the arbitral award non-binding. If the process becomes advisory only, parties will be able to obtain a better sense of how their dispute might be resolved under a binding decision-making process and continue negotiations to resolve issues on their own.[40]

(e) *Dispute resolution boards*

Another alternative dispute resolution mechanism accepted, though not widely used, in Canada involves dispute resolution boards (DRBs). A DRB is composed of anywhere between one and three construction experts retained prior to the commencement of a construction project. DRBs usually consist of three members: one nominated by the contractor, one nominated by the owner and one nominated by the other two members, who then becomes the chair of the DRB. This selection process is intended to create an impartial board.

Once selected, the board familiarises itself with the project, attends at the project site on a regular basis (monthly or quarterly), obtains reports from the project managers of the owner and the contractor, follows the development of the project and provides advisory opinions with respect to any disputes that may arise. These opinions can be provided during regularly scheduled meetings or following an *ad hoc* hearing. The objective of DRBs is to resolve disputes as they arise, rather than waiting until the completion of the project when disputes can become more expensive and difficult to resolve.

The advantages of DRBs include the following:

- They allow for 'real time' dispute resolution.[41]

---

38 *Ibid* at p388.
39 *Ibid* at p388.
40 *Ibid* at p390.
41 G McEniry, "It's Time for More DRBs in Canada", *The Revay Report*, vol 29, No 2, June 2010.

- They are considered to be relatively inexpensive.
- They allow for better relationships between the parties because problems are not allowed to "fester and contaminate other problems that may arise later".[42]

Disadvantages of DRBs include the following:
- Concerns may arise over the impartiality of the DRB.
- DRBs may make recommendations that do not fall within the ambit of the contract.
- DRBs may not be effectively utilised by project participants if the contract is not drafted in such a way as to permit expeditious and efficient review by the DRB.[43]
- The advisory opinion of a DRB is not usually binding, such that an intransigent party can ignore it.

(f) *Referees and project neutrals*

Some construction contracts provide for a referee, who is usually a technical expert and who presides over a full hearing in the form of an informal arbitration. The referee will review the evidence presented and will make a written, non-binding decision or recommendation.

In addition, construction contracts may include reference to a 'standing project neutral'. If this is the case, one or more individuals will be identified in the contract or appointed later and are on call to assist the parties in agreeing on dispute resolution procedures, facilitating negotiations, mediating disputes and/or recommending proposals for settlement. The key element of this individual's role is the "early neutral evaluation of the facts and law in the dispute".[44]

(g) *Expert determination*

A variation on the notion of a referee or a project neutral (see (f) above) is to provide in a construction contract for expert determination involving the referral of a dispute to be resolved on an expedited basis by an expert with the necessary experience and qualifications to resolve it.

The expert may be agreed to by the parties and jointly appointed, or may be appointed by the court if the parties cannot agree. The expert must have no interest, financial or otherwise, in the conduct of the project or any business affairs of any entity involved in the project. Such experts may be appointed on a dispute-by-dispute basis, with each expert having the qualifications and experience relevant to the issues in respect of the particular dispute in relation to which the expert is appointed. The expert may be given the jurisdiction to determine the appropriate process for timely and cost-effective resolution of the dispute, including:

---

42 K Lawrence, "Effectively Employing the Independent Decision Maker, Project Neutral and Dispute Resolution Board ADR Options", ABA Forum on the Construction Industry 2011 Mid-Winter Meeting, New York.

43 G McEniry, note 41 above.

44 *Rapid Resolution*, note 21 above, at p11.

- soliciting submissions and documents from both parties;
- requiring some or all of the evidence to be provided by affidavit;
- directing that parties provide such documents, test results or other things as the expert may require;
- requiring examinations and inspections of the project, and convening meetings of the parties; and
- taking such measurements, tests and audits of such processes and procedures as are necessary in order to allow the expert to make a determination of the dispute.

Such determination by an expert is usually subject to a right to require that the dispute be arbitrated or litigated, failing which the expert's determination is final and binding.

3. Proposals for the future of alternative dispute resolution in Canadian construction

'Adjudication' is a term that first began to be used in the construction industry in the United Kingdom during the late 1970s.[45] Adjudication is not a process that is widely used in Canada currently. The essential difference between adjudication and arbitration is that adjudication is an interim binding procedure subject to revision by either arbitration or litigation, unless the parties agree that the decision of the adjudicator is to be binding.[46] Like arbitration, contractual adjudication involves a process whereby the parties to a contract submit a dispute to an independent third party, whose decision is binding. Unlike arbitration, however, an adjudicator's decision usually binds the parties only until it is revised in subsequent arbitration or litigation.[47] Significantly, while adjudication is structured as an interim procedure, surveys from the United Kingdom have shown that it vastly reduces, if not eliminates, appeals and further arbitration. In other words, the UK experience shows that the parties by and large end up accepting the interim decision of the adjudicator.[48]

Although adjudication in the United Kingdom is statutory, it can also be provided for through contractual provisions. In his paper "The Adjudication Option: The Case for Uniform Payment & Performance Legislation in Canada",[49] Duncan Glaholt makes a persuasive argument for the adoption of adjudication as a proven mechanism for the resolution of construction disputes in Canada, based on an analysis of the experience from the United Kingdom and other jurisdictions.

As noted, the UK adjudication process is statutory, having been enacted under the Housing Grants, Construction and Regeneration Act, 1996, which provided the following basic scheme to address the resolution of disputes in construction contracts:

---

45 Hudson's *Building and Engineering Contracts,* 12th edn, Chapter 11, at p1373.
46 *Ibid* at p1376.
47 *Ibid.*
48 Duncan Glaholt, "The Adjudication Option: The Case for Uniform Payment & Performance Legislation in Canada" (2006), 53 *CLR* (3d) 8.
49 *Ibid.*

- minimum procedural requirements enabling parties to provide for reference of disputes to an adjudicator for summary determination according to a set timetable and within a very short period of time (28 days), while work on the project continues;
- a statutory default scheme if minimum procedural requirements are not met by the parties in their contracts;
- the right of any party to a written construction contract to seek adjudication by serving notice on both the other party and the adjudicator;
- nomination of the adjudicator by a nominating body if agreement is not possible. The adjudicator is selected within a week and the dispute is determined within four weeks. The adjudicator hears one dispute at a time; the adjudicator has 28 days from referral to make a determination which is binding and enforceable for the life of the project;
- the assistance of the courts in the implementation of any adjudicator's determination;[50] and
- selection of adjudicators from a roster, and requirement that they conduct proceedings in accordance with the rules of natural justice, act impartially and inform the parties if they are taking into account information obtained from their own knowledge and experience, or from other sources, and of the conclusions they might reach taking those other sources into account.[51]

The key benefits of adjudication, according to the UK experience, are as follows:

- It provides for an expedited process that results in an interim binding decision by a third party.
- It is relatively inexpensive.
- It has demonstrated an ability to keep money flowing on a project, pending completion and the determination as to whether certain funds are due and owing, while preserving the parties' rights to have the interim decision revised or reversed at the conclusion of the project.
- There is a high frequency of the ultimate acceptance of the decision of the adjudicator.
- There is a proven and significant reduction in litigation.

The disadvantages of adjudication include the following:

- The tight timeframes of many adjudication systems means that there may be insufficient time to properly prepare the case; and
- Procedural safeguards such as oral and documentary discovery are unavailable.[52]

The adoption of contractual adjudication for the purpose of resolving construction disputes in Canada could lead to faster, more cost-efficient dispute resolution, decreasing litigation in the construction industry. Moreover, adjudication

---

50 *Ibid* at pp16–17.
51 *Ibid* at p22.
52 *The Adjudication Option*, note 48 above.

allows the parties to reconsider their positions after the adjudicator makes a decision, and to determine whether pursuing further arbitration or litigation is appropriate according to their interests and rights. However, the adoption of statutory adjudication in Canada would be difficult to reconcile with existing lien legislation in the common law provinces and territories, as well as with the right of legal hypothec in the province of Quebec.

4. Conclusion

The foregoing represents an overview of the various methods of dispute resolution utilised in the construction industry in Canada. Obviously, parties are free to choose the alternative dispute resolution mechanism that best suits the project at issue, but the above is an attempt to describe the most common mechanisms. From the above summary, it is clear that alternative dispute resolution is growing in popularity in Canada, as parties look to alternative mechanisms to reduce the time and cost often associated with traditional litigation.

Mexico

Roberto Hernández-García
COMAD, SC

1. Introduction

According to the last census, carried out in 2010, Mexico has a population of 112.3 million, distributed across 31 autonomous states and the Mexican capital (the Federal District, also known as Mexico City).

Construction is a key activity in the Mexican economy. According to a 2012 report of the Mexican Chamber of the Construction Industry (CMIC),[1] the industry generated 5.6 million jobs in 2011, with five indirect jobs generated for every 10 direct jobs. Construction is currently the sixth main economic activity in Mexico, contributing approximately 6.7% to gross domestic product.

Notwithstanding the 2008 global financial crisis, the Mexican construction sector enjoyed positive results in both 2011 and 2012, as did the economy in general – this coming in the wake of 21 consecutive months of negative figures for 2009 to 2010. Since mid-2010, results have picked up and are still improving, although solid figures on the prospects for 2013 are not yet available.

Nevertheless, some of the most significant and relevant projects under way are public projects, which often involve infrastructure development. The government entities most active in the construction sector, investing in public works and privately funded public projects, are:[2]

- Pemex – the state-owned oil company;
- the Ministry of Communications and Transport;
- the Ministry of Environment and Natural Resources;
- CFE3, the state-owned electricity utility;
- the Ministry of Public Security;
- the Ministry of Public Education;
- the Mexican Social Security Institute;
- the Ministry of Health; and
- the Ministry of Energy.

According to another CMIC report[3] on competition in infrastructure, during 2011 and 2012 Mexico ranked fourth in terms of competitiveness in infrastructure

1 *"Presentación ejecutiva del Entorno Actual y Futura (sic) de la Industria de la Construcción en México", Gerencia de Economía y Financiamiento, Cámara Nacional de la Industria de la Construcción* (CMIC) November 2012.
2 *Ibid.*
3 *"Competitividad en Infraestructura 2012–2013", Gerencia de Economía y Financiamiento, Cámara Nacional de la Industria de la Construcción* (CMIC), September 2012. The report refers to the World Economic Forum report of Global Competitiveness in 144 countries.

in Latin America, after Panama, Chile and Uruguay, and ahead of Brazil, El Salvador and Costa Rica.

In December 2012 Mexico elected Enrique Peña Nieto as its new president for the 2012 to 2018 term, making the PRI (which had previously governed for 75 years until 2000) the country's new ruling party. His agenda for the construction of public infrastructure will be reflected in the National Infrastructure Plan (not available at the time of writing), and will include the first important projects in several schemes, including under the 2012 Public-Private Partnership (PPP) Law and its regulations.

Speaking of his plans, the Mexican president stated:

> *I trust entirely that the strategic alliance between governments and the private sector strengthens and opens the ability to carry out major infrastructure projects in order to upgrade our competitiveness, to attract more investments, but most of all to generate more employment, which is one of the major goals that my government has and that Mexico as whole has.*[4]

It seems likely, therefore, that Mexico will see a lot of major construction projects in both the public and private sectors in the near future. As a consequence it is important to be aware of the relevant available resolution methods, in order to improve such projects' chances of success.

For the purposes of this chapter, the Mexican construction sector is divided as follows:

- pure public construction projects, governed by the Public Works and Related Services Law and its regulations;
- Pemex Law construction and infrastructure projects;
- PPPs; and
- private construction projects.

2. Pure public construction projects

'Public' refers to construction projects where the owner or client is:

- the federal government through its branches or powers (executive, legislative and judicial), ministries, entities or any bodies under federal government control;
- any of the 31 states or the Federal District government (executive, legislative and judicial branches), ministries, entities or any bodies under their control;
- Pemex; or
- autonomous entities under the Mexican Constitution, such as the Central Bank and the National Commission on Human Rights.

The main statutes governing public construction contracts in Mexico at the federal level are:

- Article 134 of the Mexican Constitution;
- the Public Works and Related Services Law;
- regulations fleshing out the details of that law, as issued by the executive branch;

4 www.eluniversal.com.mx/notas/895771.html.

- the Pemex Law, which regulates the organisation, powers and activities of Pemex, including the administrative contracting provisions made thereunder; and
- specific public works regulations for the contracting of public works contracts by Congress, the judiciary, autonomous entities and so on.

The main statutes governing public construction contracts in Mexico at the state level are:

- the articles of each state constitution that regulate public contracts;
- the corresponding state law on public works and related services (each state's law has a different name);
- regulations fleshing out the details of those law, as issued by the executive branch; and
- specific public works regulations for the contracting of public works contracts by the state congress or judiciary.

This chapter focuses solely on the federal level, since the most relevant projects are those sponsored by the Mexican federal government or by the states using federal funds, which are regulated by federal rules.

2.1 Article 134 of the Mexican Constitution

Article 134 of the Mexican Constitution provides the constitutional basis for public procurement. It establishes that government contracts, including those for public works, are to be awarded through public bids, in order to guarantee the best conditions for the Mexican state (except for restricted bidding and direct awards under certain and specific conditions established in the laws). No guidance is specified by Article 134, which is an empowering provision only; specific guidance is provided by the Public Works and Related Services Law, its regulations and other norms.

The importance of this provision is that any violation of the rules governing public contracts can be understood, directly or indirectly, as a violation of this constitutional provision, with serious consequences.

2.2 Public Works and Related Services Law and its regulations

This law regulates:

- the procedures for awarding public works contracts (eg, by public bid, invitation to three parties or direct award);
- the types of public works contract and their content (ie, the rights and obligations of the parties);
- the inspection and auditing of public works contracts;
- the procedures for challenging awards;
- sanctions on bidders and contractors; and
- dispute resolution methods.

As most federal public construction/infrastructure projects are governed by this law, several specific matters are highlighted below.

(a) ***Project delivery methods***

The Public Works and Related Services Law recognises the following kinds of public works contract:

- Lump-sum or fixed-price public works contracts – construction projects which are to be paid for at a fixed, non-variable price. This kind of contract is not subject to variation or adjustment, except for some conditions established in the law;
- Unit price public works contracts – construction projects which are to be paid for in work units, with each unit having a fixed price and being paid on completion. This kind of contract is subject to variation and adjustment, with certain methods established in the law;
- Mixed public works contracts – construction projects to be paid partly on a lump-sum basis and partly on a unit price basis; and
- Services related to public works contracts – services related to public works projects other than construction services (eg, technical studies, investigations, supervision).

This law and its regulations establish the specific details and regulations for each type of contract, as well as its possibilities and limitations.

(b) ***Dispute resolution methods envisaged in the Public Works and Related Services Law***

Conciliation:[5] This dispute resolution method empowers the Ministry of Public Function[6] to act as conciliator. It is a widely used procedure whereby both the government (as client) and the contractor can request the ministry to assist them in the resolution of disputes arising from public works contracts or related services. The procedure starts with a request for conciliation from either party, to which the other party responds. Live hearings follow, in which ministry officials act as conciliators to promote the reaching of agreement. If the parties reach an agreement, this will be binding on the parties; if it is not complied with, it can be enforced by the competent courts. If the parties fail to reach agreement, they file a claim in another forum, such as a federal tribunal, or proceed to arbitration. In any case, and at any stage, either party can pull out of the procedure; where this happens, the process is automatically closed, leaving the parties to restart the claim via another applicable route.

Conciliation has played an important part in the evolution of federal public works contracts in Mexico. One clear benefit of the system is that it allows parties to present their claims and disputes face to face and, with the help of the Ministry of Public Function, to filter out minor problems and prioritise major issues. Sometimes the parties present their cases in a very formal, 'judicial' way – this unfortunately

6 Articles 95 to 97 of the Law on Public Works and Related Services.

7 As at July 2013 the Ministry of Public Function is still operating, but the Organic Law of the Federal Public Administration has been modified in order to dissolve the Ministry. References made to this ministry are made advisedly, therefore, as its role and function may have changed by the time this is published.

misses the point of the process, which is intended to be more informal, enabling the parties to resolve their dispute amicably. Counsel with experience and sensitivity to this method of dispute resolution are thus invaluable. A major challenge for any party involved in conciliation is to ensure compliance with administrative public order laws, and the ministry's input can be helpful in achieving this goal. The barometer for evaluating the success or otherwise of this procedure will be the intention and will of the parties, as expressed in the document and as evidenced in the hearings. The parties will normally adopt very strong positions at the beginning of the process, but a good conciliator will help the parties to reach agreement on more and more issues as they go through the process, until as many points as possible – if not all points of dispute – have been resolved. If, however, no clear, specific results appear to have been achieved, one of the parties will usually express its will to terminate the process and proceed to arbitration or litigation.

Arbitration:[7] The Commercial Code has a specific chapter on arbitration (Title 4), which is based on the United Nations Commission on International Trade Law Model Law. The law allows government entities and ministries to agree on arbitration proceedings only in case of disputes relating to the interpretation of contractual clauses or the execution of a contract. Arbitration is excluded for two specific cases (called 'exorbitant state clauses') that are included in all public works contracts without exception:

- administrative rescission (ie, unilateral termination by the state for breach by the contractor without the intervention of a judge or an arbitrator); and
- early termination for the convenience of the government (also called 'advance termination').

Where public officials include an arbitration clause or agree to arbitration, according to the internal guidelines of the agency or entity, it will be clearly established which administrative unit and/or (director-level) public official is responsible for deciding whether to include an arbitration clause or sign an arbitration agreement.

Arbitration is not the general rule for dispute resolution in public works contracts in Mexico. Its use is rather limited to public works contracts which have been subject to International Chamber of Commerce (ICC) arbitration clauses. These kinds of contract include:

- financed public works contracts concluded by the Federal Commission of Electricity;[8] and
- major public works contracts signed by Pemex.

Under Article 1457(II) of the Commercial Code, an arbitration award can be declared null and void by a competent judge if the judge determines that, according

7 Articles 98 to 101 of the Law of Public Works and Related Services.

8 Financed public contracts are agreements governed by the Public Works and Related Services Law, which oblige the contractors to finance the works with private funds and deliver the works ready for operation. Some people consider this kind of contract as the first type of PPP agreement in Mexico.

to Mexican legislation, the subject of the dispute is not arbitrable or the award is contrary to public policy. Obviously, since public works contracts are public contracts subject to laws of public order, this loophole exposes many cases to judicial revision. In this context, Mexico has seen cases in which Pemex and CFE have requested the annulment of arbitration awards based on breach of public policy rules. Needless to say, such annulment efforts have not been well received by the private sector.

Against this backdrop, an in-depth evaluation of the present and future status of arbitration in government contracts is therefore required. As at July 2013, several proposals had been presented to Congress and the authorities, but the issue remains open, since Mexico needs to define clearly its position on this matter.

Tribunals:[9] The most frequently used dispute resolution channel in federal public works contracts are the federal tribunals. Two kinds of federal tribunal have competence over public works contracts, depending on when the case arose:

- the federal Judiciary; and
- the Federal Tax and Administrative Tribunal.[10]

The federal tribunals which have shown expertise in public works contracts are respected in Mexico and exhibit high levels of professionalism. As they are independent in their decision making, they sometimes adopt differing criteria on some issues; but the Mexican judicial system allows clear routes for challenging wrong, illegal or abusive decisions and has a body of precedent to help determine the issues, and the public has free access to all jurisprudence. There are no specialised construction courts to hear public works matters, but the tribunals hear more public works cases by the day and have built up a considerable body of expertise. There is some question over the role of the courts when annulling arbitration awards arising from public works contracts on the grounds of public order; further clarity here would be welcome in future to increase legal certainty for the parties.

Other dispute resolution methods:[11] The law establishes in general that "other resolution methods can be agreed among the parties in order to solve disputes that arise about interpretation and performance of public works contracts".

Since government officials have a duty to do only what the law allows them to do, and are permanently audited, there have been very few cases in which other methods have been used. For example, CFE has included the role of independent expert for technical, administrative and financial matters in its privately financed projects, which has had some positive results; but it has also led to many problems, since the decisions of such independent experts can be challenged on the grounds of manifest error. Another dispute resolution method which has not yet been accepted in Mexico is the dispute board model, which some organisations are working hard to promote. A relevant contract in the water and sewage sector included an ICC clause

---

9 Article 103 of the Public Works and Related Services Law.

10 After the Organic Law of the Federal Tax and Administrative Tribunal was modified in 2007, this tribunal became competent on this matter.

11 Article 102 of the Law on Public Works and Related Services.

that never became operational.

Overall, no other methods of dispute resolution have been effectively implemented in or are being used in public works in Mexico.

2.3 Pemex Law[12]

Pemex, the state-owned oil company, is a major government client at the national level. In 2008, after a public, multi-sector consultation, a special law regulating its operation and powers was introduced: the Pemex Law.

One of the most important achievements of the law was to create a special new public procurement regime for Pemex, which then became subject to two systems:

- one regime for procurement and contracts relating to substantive oil-producing operations, which are Pemex's core business activities; and
- a second regime for the purchase of goods, services and public works unrelated to Pemex's core business.

Today, therefore, Pemex can invite bids for public works contracts under either the Pemex Law or the Public Works and Related Services Law, although in recent times it has tended to use the Pemex Law to avoid the limitations of the Public Works and Related Services Law, since the latter is less flexible. The essential difference between the Pemex Law and the Public Works and Related Services Law is that Article 60 of the Pemex Law allows Pemex to conclude, with individuals and companies, such works and services contracts as best achieve its ends without imposing any kind of predetermined delivery methods. Thus, the law gives Pemex the freedom and flexibility to choose an appropriate contracting scheme, with only certain (essential) limited restrictions – mainly relating to principles established in the Mexican Constitution and the Oil Law. This has enabled Pemex to begin a new chapter and create new model contracts that are not tied to the formalistic and limited principles imposed by the Public Works and Related Services Law.

All this means that many different options may be explored when considering dispute resolution in relation to Pemex works contracts, including those set out next.

(a) Tribunals and arbitration

According to Article 72 of the Pemex Law, Pemex and its subsidiary organs are governed by applicable federal laws and all disputes in which they are involved, except for those which must be arbitrated, are to be resolved by the federal tribunals, with no obligation for Pemex to provide any security or guarantee in case of an unfavourable decision, even in judicial proceedings. The general directors have the power to agree to arbitration under Article 5 of the law.

(b) Foreign tribunals

Article 72 also allows Pemex, in international transactions, to agree to be governed

12 According to the Pemex Law, its actions are considered "commercial acts" and construction is a "commercial matter". Therefore, Pemex could be theoretically considered as a commercial enterprise. However, Pemex is a decentralised organ of the federal state, ruled by specific legislation under the control of the government, and therefore it is not really a commercial enterprise.

by foreign law and be subject to the jurisdiction of foreign courts, as well as to agree to arbitration, where appropriate.

(c) *Conciliation*

Disputes arising from contracts that are concluded under the Pemex Law can be subject to the conciliation procedure established in the Public Works and Related Services Law and its regulations, notwithstanding that the governing law of the contract is not the latter.

(d) *Internal procedures established in Pemex contracts*

For many years, Pemex has required the use of an internal dispute resolution procedure before allowing contractors to present claims in conciliation or arbitration, or before the courts. Although this theoretically represents an opportunity to resolve disputes between the parties, in many cases this effectively delays the resolution of disputes, since the procedure is quite complicated and is usually deployed as a means for Pemex to buy time.

(e) *Outlook*

Pemex plays a significant role in Mexico's national economy. It is still the keeper of the country's most valuable natural resource, from both a practical and political point of view. It has been struggling for years to evolve from a state-oriented to a commercially oriented company. The laws that govern the entity and the regulations that audit and sanction its public officials have not helped it achieve full growth and independence, with implications for dispute resolution. As a state-owned company (technically, a decentralised organ of the federal public administration), Pemex is still too limited by laws which tend to hinder the full achievement of its objectives and purposes. Legal action against Pemex can be (informally) interpreted as an act against the nation, public order and/or the interests of the people. Pemex's structure and future should arguably be re-evaluated in order to define its position in the coming years, and to determine whether it will become a relevant and powerful industry player or continue to be bound by limitations as a state entity.

3. Public-private partnerships

Although PPPs are not strictly construction projects, they are a contractual framework through which to develop infrastructure projects with the concurrent participation of the public and private sector.

In 2012 the federal PPP Law was enacted. According to Article 2, a 'PPP' is "any project that is carried out within any scheme in order to establish a long-term contractual relationship between the public [sector] and the private sector for the rendering of services to the public sector or to the final user, and in which infrastructure is provided totally or partially by the private sector with the purpose of providing social benefits and investment in the country".

This law and its regulations provide for the dispute resolution methods for PPP projects set out below.

3.1 Good-faith negotiation

The PPP Law provides that, as a first resort, the parties should attempt to resolve technical and financial disputes through good-faith negotiations (Article 134). The parties must set a time frame for negotiation and within which a settlement must be reached. If agreement is not possible, the parties may initiate a procedure before a so-called 'expert committee', as outlined below.

3.2 Expert committee

Article 134 of the PPP Law provides that an expert committee formed by three experts – one chosen by each party and the third agreed by both experts – may be established to resolve technical and financial disputes. The law establishes a procedure for filing the claim, responding to the claim and conducting hearings. At the end of the process, the experts committee will report on its findings. If the report is unanimous, it will be binding on the parties; if not, the parties are free to bring the dispute to arbitration or before a tribunal, depending on the nature of the dispute.

3.3 Conciliation

Disputes arising from contracts that have been executed under the PPP Law can be subject to the conciliation procedure established in the Public Works and Related Services Law or the Law on Acquisitions, Leases and Services of the Public Sector, even where these laws do not directly apply to the relevant PPP project.

3.4 Arbitration

Parties can agree on an arbitration clause or an arbitration procedure in order to resolve their disputes. Arbitration must be agreed by law, and shall be performed under the terms of the Commercial Code Regulations on Arbitration (under Article 139 of the PPP Law). The law establishes clearly that the arbitration will be governed by federal Mexican law, the proceedings will be held in Spanish and the award will be obligatory and binding on both parties. Only the 'amparo' procedure (ie, the judicial procedure for constitutional protection) can be used to challenge an arbitral award. The law expressly provides that the revocation of concessions and authorisations in general, as well as acts of authority, shall not be subject to arbitration in this kind of project, and that disputes relating to the legal validity of any administrative act can be challenged only via the federal tribunals.

3.5 Tribunals

Federal tribunals are competent to resolve any dispute involving the interpretation or application of the PPP Law, as well as any agreements concluded based on the law or any provisions that arise therefrom (Article 140). The competent authorities can take any necessary measures to ensure that the development of the project or provision of the service of the contract is not interrupted (Article 141).

3.6 Outlook

As the PPP Law is new, there is no real experience of dispute resolution of PPP schemes under this law at the time of writing. However, it seems clear that because of the way it is written, conflicts are bound to arise over its interpretation. This is because although disputes can be subject to resolution through arbitration or by an expert committee and arbitration, where the case involves interpretation of the law the federal tribunals are competent to hear the dispute. Since public officers must establish the legal grounds and motives for their decisions, it is clear that in most cases there will be a direct or indirect interpretation of the law, giving rise to a conflict of competence between the arbitrators and the tribunals. It is also clear that the judicial authorities will face a steep learning curve in trying to understand the nature of projects and their schemes in order to efficiently manage dispute resolution processes.

Another important matter in relation to dispute resolution under the PPP Law is that the law requires parties which initiate any administrative or judicial action under the law to provide guarantees against any damages, losses or liquidated damages that may arise as a result, and also establishes fines for frivolous actions by contractors. These provisions could be understood as a type of 'false claim' regulation, notwithstanding that this issue is not clearly regulated under Mexican law.

4. Private construction contracts

As discussed, Mexico is a federation with 31 states and a Federal District (Mexico City). Each of these has its own civil code, which usually includes a chapter regulating several issues – such as family, property and contracts, including construction contracts – in more or less detail.

Each state civil code primarily establishes the delivery methods for construction contracts (eg, lump-sum, unit price or general terms), but not the dispute resolution methods *per se*. Therefore, this chapter does not focus on the civil codes, but rather on the dispute resolution methods that can be used in private sector contracts.

According to Article 75 of the Commercial Code, construction companies and construction contracts are commercial enterprises and instruments, and since the commercial legislation is a federal/national law (not a state law), all construction companies and construction contracts are regulated by the Commercial Code law and principles.

Private construction contracts can generally include any measure as agreed by the parties (as the will of the parties being the supreme law of the contract is a general principle under Mexican law). Therefore, there are no limitations on project delivery methods and other agreements, including dispute resolution methods. That said, it is possible for parties to private contracts to agree on any dispute resolution method, as long as they do not violate public policy matters established in the Civil and Commercial Codes. This means that private construction contracts can be very flexible as to content and also as to chosen dispute resolution methods.

The usual dispute resolution methods found in private construction contracts are as follows:

- Tribunals – in private construction contracts, parties can resort to either federal (judicial) or local (state) courts to resolve their disputes under the constitutionally enshrined principle of 'simultaneous competence'. This means that parties can opt to sue under the local (state) procedural civil code before the local courts, or under the Commercial Code before the federal courts.

- Arbitration – parties can freely agree to arbitration, except where special restrictions apply, especially in relation to public order rules (which rarely apply to private construction projects). The Commercial Code has a specific chapter on arbitration (Title 4), which is based on the United Nations Commission on International Trade Law Model Law. Therefore, arbitration in Mexico has the elements of a good arbitration regime.
- Mediation – in private contracts, parties can opt for negotiation or mediation of their disputes, without limitation.

Other dispute resolution methods such as expert determination and dispute boards, although not forbidden, are not generally used in relation to private construction contracts.

5. Efforts to promote effective dispute resolution procedures

Some important associations and players in Mexico are advocating more effective dispute resolution for the construction sector, in order to secure better conditions for owners and contractors alike.

5.1 International Chamber of Commerce Mexican Construction Disputes Committee

As the worldwide leader of dispute resolution methods, the ICC participates in the resolution of construction disputes across the globe and has a relevant presence in Mexico (ICC Mexico). About eight years ago, the Arbitration Commission of ICC Mexico formed a Dispute Boards Committee. As time went by, this committee became increasingly active, becoming the first national committee to translate the ICC Dispute Board Rules into Spanish. The committee comprises companies, construction lawyers, experts and government officials, and is active in discussions promoting the safe and legal implementation of effective dispute resolution methods for both the public and private sectors. Every year, the committee hosts a seminar on the legal and technical aspects of public and private construction contracts and issues, including dispute resolution, as well as hosting ordinary sessions to keep participants updated on legal changes, sector problems and so on. In 2012 the committee began to participate in ongoing discussions on proposed modifications to the Public Works and Related Services Law. The group has also provided a dispute resolution training programme to Pemex, and is a permanent adviser to federal authorities on construction and dispute matters. This committee has been an international promoter of dispute boards across Latin America.

5.2 Arbitration Centre of the Construction Industry

Legally established in 2011 and operational since 2012, the Arbitration Centre of the Construction Industry (CAIC) was set up to fill a vacuum which some in the industry had identified – namely, the absence of a more focused and specialised body charged with promoting arbitration and other alternative dispute resolution (ADR) instruments such as dispute boards, expert determination and mediation within the construction and ancillary (eg, engineering, design, architecture) sectors. It has drafted state-of-the-art provisions on arbitration and ADR, and its model clauses are now adopted in a variety of domestic and international construction contracts (as well as in other fields).

The CAIC stages an annual lecture on the topic, presented by an internationally renowned figure in international arbitration,[13] and also hosts a specialised seminar on arbitration[14] at which, once a month, experts from all over the globe debate a current topic in the arbitration and/or construction field.

The CAIC's overall position is that it should be possible for all disputes arising from construction contracts in Mexico and Latin America to be referred to mediation, arbitration, expertise or dispute boards, no matter how big or small.

5.3 Mexican Arbitration Centre

This national arbitration centre has also been active in promoting the effective resolution of construction disputes.

5.4 Dispute Board Federation

The Dispute Board Federation recently appointed the author as its representative in Mexico and Latin America in order to promote the use of this dispute resolution method in infrastructure projects. Agreements have been concluded with established organisations such as the CAIC, and collaboration between such organisations is expected to encourage the use of dispute boards in the Latin American region.

6. Conclusion

Mexico has experienced much important activity in the construction and infrastructure sector in recent years. Although dispute resolution methods are clearly established by the laws outlined in this chapter, their importance and the need for clarity and predictability in the industry still need to be more widely accepted and practised.

In contracts, certain issues still present grave problems, such as the prohibition against arbitrating rescissions or advance termination, or any other matter regarding public order rules. These may create burdens for private companies and individuals, preventing big players from entering into important contracts. The future of dispute resolution in public contracts depends a lot on future judicial interpretations and possible legislative reform.

Alternative dispute resolution methods such as dispute boards could give a significant boost to some major public projects which are beleaguered by disputes instigated and adjudicated after the projects are finished, causing major headaches.[15] A major initiative to promote dispute boards is under way, and by 2015 these are expected to become a regular feature in government contracts.

---

13 Via the *Conferencia Magistral* "José Luis Siqueiros".
14 Along with the *Universidad Iberoamericana* (Mexico).
15 Dispute boards have been successfully implemented in projects elsewhere in Central and South America.

Finally, an important matter that may affect the future of dispute resolution (specifically arbitration) is the new Amparo Law, which governs constitutional control suits before the federal courts. This now establishes that some private parties can be considered 'authorities' under some conditions. Some people consider that arbitrators can, at some point, be considered as 'authorities' similar to government entities. This could create severe problems for arbitration in Mexico, as it could mean that all arbitral awards may be subject to review by the federal courts as if they were decisions of government authorities or regular tribunals.

Although issues relating to dispute resolution in the construction and infrastructure sector have not been completely resolved, and many still remain to be defined, it is clear that both the problems and solutions are foremost in the minds of stakeholders in Mexico. There should thus be positive developments in the coming years, as laws are interpreted, clear regulations are introduced and players in the field can make greater use of methods such as dispute boards in major infrastructure projects without any fear.

United States

David Arola
Cadian T Baker
Jerry Brodsky
Danielle J Cole
Peckar & Abramson PC

1. Introduction

The United States is a federal republic of 50 states, a federal district and territories.[1] The federal government has three branches: executive, legislative and judicial, as do the governments of each state. Following the principle of balance of power among the three branches which guided the designers of the US Constitution, each branch of government, at the federal and state levels, has a role in the legal systems and processes which govern the resolution of all civil disputes in the United States, including disputes arising in large construction projects in the private and public sectors, and including, in particular, 'mega-projects' for infrastructure development and public-private partnerships (PPPs).

This chapter provides an overview of the legal and regulatory framework and systems which govern construction disputes, particularly those arising in large and complex construction projects and PPPs.

1.1 Executive

The executive branch of the federal and state governments where a construction project is built affects construction disputes by:

- contracting for public works, and
- enacting and enforcing regulations affecting design and construction activity, including financing.

The executive branch, through its various departments, agencies, boards, commissions and committees, regulates many aspects of the design and construction activity such as: use (eg, transportation, defence, energy, education, homeland security), use permits, licensing, environmental impact, among other things. This regulatory framework covers rulemakers, rules, enforcement personnel, hearing officers and public agency administrators.

Compliance, or lack of compliance, with executive regulations is often the source of construction disputes. In some cases the disputes are between a private actor and a public agency; in other cases the dispute is between two or more private actors, but arises from regulatory enforcement and penalties. Public agency or administrative disputes are often aired and resolved, in the first instance, within the executive

1 The territories politically associated with the United States are: Puerto Rico, Guam, the Virgin Islands of the United States, the Northern Marianas and American Samoa.

branch, through administrative legal proceedings. These disputes and proceedings can relate to a wide range of aspects of the design and construction activity, such as standards, licensing, inspections, environmental protection, compliance, labour standards and practices, and other aspects of safety and welfare for which the executive branch is responsible.

In addition to the regulatory framework, the executive branch (federal or state), through one of its departments or agencies, is usually the public contracting entity for public works, including infrastructure projects and PPPs. This means that the initial dispute resolution legal process for disputes involving regulatory compliance is typically between a private actor (concessionaire, designer, builder, contractor, developer, lender) and a public agency (part of the executive branch) involving some aspect of regulatory compliance (regarding rules enacted by the executive branch), and is heard by hearing officers (employed by the executive branch) in a process created and administered by the executive branch. Court (judicial branch) appeals from administrative agency decisions are available in certain cases.

Finally, among the powers reserved to the executive branch which affect construction disputes are the enforcement of the laws enacted by the legislative branch and the judgments and orders of the judicial branch.

1.2 Legislative branch

Like its executive counterpart, the legislative branch of the federal and state governments where a construction project is built regulates design and construction activity by providing statutes and rules within its competence governing key aspects of design and construction projects, public and private, such as:

- standards, licensing, inspections, environmental protection, compliance, labour standards and practices and other aspects of safety and welfare;
- rules of procedure and evidence for judicial proceedings involving civil disputes, including laws and rules for the enforcement of judgment and court orders; and
- statutory civil remedies and causes of action which can be asserted in judicial or other legal proceedings involving construction disputes, as well their prescription.

Rules and statutes are enacted by the legislatures, enforced by the executive, and, when disputes arise, tested for constitutionality and interpreted by the judiciary.

1.3 Judicial branch

The judicial branch of the federal and state governments means federal and state courts. For civil disputes, each state has a court system which includes a trial court, appellate courts and a state supreme court. In parallel, on the federal side, there are trial courts, appellate courts and the US Supreme Court. Trial courts are called United States district courts and courts of claims. There are 94 federal judicial districts in the United States. Of the 94 districts, 89 cover the 50 states, with the remaining five covering the US territories.

Access to federal courts is limited to cases in which there is federal subject matter as well as jurisdiction over the parties. Subject matter jurisdiction exists when the dispute involves a question of federal law, including federal statutes, admiralty and bankruptcy, and in certain cases not involving questions of federal law but nevertheless involving citizens of different states or countries.

Decisions from the district courts and court of claims can be appealed to the US circuit courts of appeals. There are 13 judicial circuits covering the 50 states and territories and federal circuit. Appellate circuit court decisions, as well as decisions of the state supreme courts, can be appealed to the US Supreme Court, which has discretionary review jurisdiction.

In addition to the interpretation of statutes and review of administrative agency decisions, the courts (federal and state), are the forum in which contractual disputes involving construction projects, public and private, are often resolved (including enforcement of private arbitration agreements and awards) and arguably have the most significant effect on the resolution of construction disputes.

Federal and state[2] courts in the United States follow a common law legal system. Through published judicial decisions interpreting statutes and rules, as well as contracts, contract documents and other types of documents generated as part of complex construction projects, courts decide legal and contractual issues in construction disputes. Those decisions, in the case of federal courts, are published and can make precedent for other courts to follow. In the case of state courts, jurisprudence generally evolves from published appellate and state supreme court decisions.

Disagreements between courts of the same level are resolved by the appellate courts. Disagreements among the appellate courts are resolved by the corresponding state supreme court or US Supreme Court. 'Tie breakers' among the states or between the state and federal courts are resolved by Article VI, Section 2, of the US Constitution (known as the 'supremacy clause'), which provides that:

> *This Constitution, and the Laws of the United States which shall be made in Pursuance thereof; and all Treaties made, or which shall be made, under the Authority of the United States, shall be the supreme Law of the Land; and the Judges in every State shall be bound thereby, any Thing in the Constitution or Laws of any State to the Contrary notwithstanding.*

Accordingly, the manner in which each of the branches of government affects the resolution of construction disputes can be illustrated as in the diagram on the next page.

In summary, the legal and regulatory framework and systems which govern construction disputes, including those arising in large and complex construction projects and PPPs, are multiple and complex.

We now look at general and specific information about the federal legal system as well as the legal systems of California, Florida, Georgia, Illinois, Maryland, New Jersey, New York and Virginia, as well as the District of Columbia, which govern such construction disputes.

---

2 Except for the State of Louisiana, which has a civil law system.

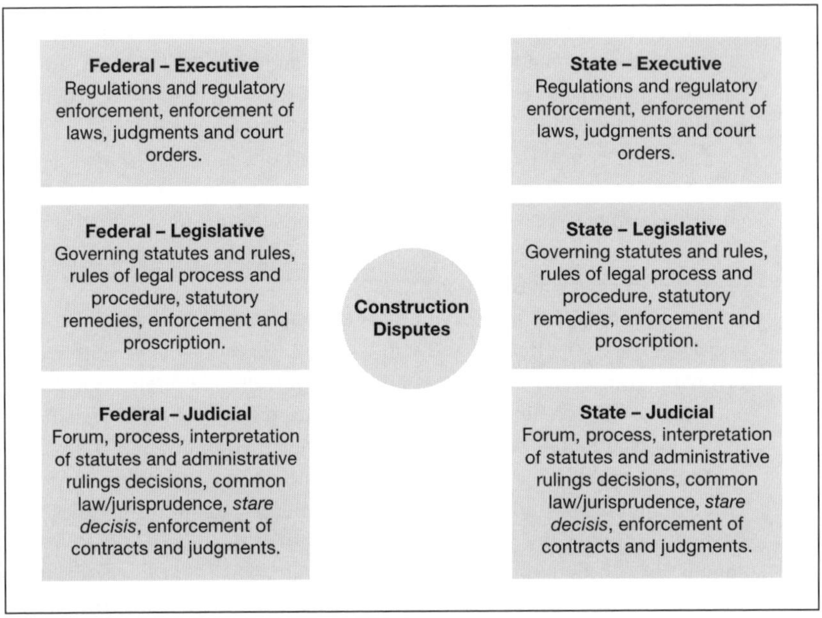

2. Resolution of disputes on construction, infrastructure and PPP projects under federal and state laws

2.1 Federal government contracts

When the federal government causes a change in a project, either by directive or constructively, the contractor has two means to obtain additional compensation and/or time: a request for equitable adjustment; or a claim. These actions are not mutually exclusive, and thus contractors frequently seek a request for equitable adjustment first and, if that fails, submit a claim. It should, however, be noted that submission of a request for equitable adjustment is not prerequisite to a claim, so a claim may be submitted without having first pursued a request for equitable adjustment.

The Contract Disputes Act 1978[3] is the statutory framework governing the submission of claims against the federal government, establishing procedures and requirements for asserting and resolving claims which are subject to the act. The act applies to all express or implied contracts to which an executive agency of the federal government is a party for the procurement of:

- property, other than real property in being;
- services;
- construction, alteration, repair, or maintenance of real property; or
- the disposal of personal property.

The Contract Disputes Act requires claims to be submitted, in writing, to the

3 41 USC, Sections 7101–7109.

contracting officer for decision within six years after accrual of the claim. The act extends the contracting officer's authority to cover all matters 'relating to the contract', including claims for breach of contract. While the act does not define the word 'claim', that term is defined in the Federal Acquisition Regulations, which state:

> *Claim, as used in this subpart, means a written demand or written assertion ... seeking, as a matter of right, the payment of money in a sum certain, the adjustment or interpretation of contract terms, or other relief arising under or relating to the contract. A claim arising under a contract ... is a claim that can be resolved under a contract clause that provides for the relief sought by the claimant. However, a written demand or written assertion by the contractor seeking the payment of money exceeding $100,000 is not a claim under the Contract Disputes Act until certified. A voucher, invoice or other routine request for payment that is not in dispute when submitted is not a claim under the Act. The submission may be converted to a claim under the Act by complying with the certification requirements of this clause, if it is disputed as to liability or amount or or is not acted upon in a reasonable time.*[4]

This provision of the Federal Acquisition Regulations identifies the mandatory elements of a claim, but does not provide instruction to the contractor on the manner in which a claim is to be written. There is no 'official' written format to be followed in presenting a claim; however, a contractor must take care to ensure that its written claim submission meets the minimum requirements set out in the Federal Acquisition Regulations as the contracting officer cannot consider a claim that fails to meet this threshold. Pursuant to the Federal Acquisition Regulations, the claim submission to the contracting officer must, at a minimum, contain:

- a written demand/statement of claim asserting specific rights and requesting specific relief;
- clear indication of the monetary sum sought, stated as a 'sum certain'; and
- a request for issuance of a final decision.

The statement of claim must contain a sufficient level of detail to inform the contracting officer of what is being claimed, and to allow for a meaningful review of the claim. It must include specific facts explaining what occurred, why the contractor is not financially responsible for the additional work or cost, and must include relevant documentation supporting those assertions such as provisions of the contract, specifications, design documents, etc. The statement of claim must be sufficiently detailed to allow negotiation: so a contractor risks dismissal of a claim if adequate data and backup support are not included in the written claim submission.[5]

All claims must be submitted to the contracting officer for decision. While this may be accomplished by delivery of the claim to the representative of the contracting officer with specific instruction that it be forwarded to the contracting officer, it should be noted that jurisdiction under the Contract Disputes Act 1978 has

---

4 48 CFR, Section 52.233-1.

5 *H L Smith v Dalton*, 49 F 3d 1563 (Fed Cir 1995) (invoices, detailed cost breakdowns, and other supporting financial documentation need not accompany a CDA claim as a jurisdictional prerequisite); see *also Transamerica Ins Corp v United States*, 973 F 2d 1572 (Fed Cir 1992); *Kanag'Iq Constr*, 51 Fed Cl 38.

been challenged by the government where a claim was not signed by the contractor, but by its counsel. While the Armed Services Board of Contract Appeals (ASBCA) concluded that the attorney could submit claims on behalf of the contractor, claims submissions should be signed by an authorised official directly employed by the contractor to avoid potential jurisdictional issues that could potentially result in the dismissal of an otherwise proper claim submission.[6]

A claim seeking monetary relief must state the exact amount of the relief sought or must otherwise contain sufficient information to permit the claim amount to be determined through a simple arithmetic calculation.[7] While most claims seek monetary relief, Section 52.233-1 of the Federal Acquisition Regulations permits claims to be asserted that seek "an adjustment or interpretation of contract terms or other relief arising under or relating to this contract".[8] Claims for money damages cannot be disguised as a request for an interpretation of the contract.

The requirement that the contracting officer issue a final decision will be met if it is reasonably clear from the contractor's submission that this is the action requested. The request to issue a final decision need not be made in any particular form as long as the basic requirements of the Contract Disputes Act are met. Despite this implied flexibility, best practices dictate that a contractor should explicitly request that the contracting officer issue a final decision on the claim unless there are specific, compelling, reasons why a request for final decision is not desirable (eg, where the contractor is negotiating with the contracting officer and would prefer not to have its submission considered as a formal claim).

The Contract Disputes Act requires contractors to certify that claims in excess of $100,000 are made in good faith, are accurate and complete, and that the claim reflects the amount the contractor believes it is entitled to recover. Under the Federal Acquisition Regulations, the value of all additive and deductive changes must be aggregated and the total sum thereafter considered against the $100,000 threshold for certification (eg, the Federal Acquisition Regulations would require certification of a claim for an additive change of $40,000 and deductive change of $70,000 as the sum of these amounts exceeds the $100,000 threshold).[9] Section 33.207(c) of the

---

6 *Ebasco Env'tl*, ASBCA No 44547, 93-3 BCA, Paragraph 26,220 (ASBCA stated that the government cited no authority for the proposition that the contractor itself must sign the claim, but further stated its holding did not address the question as to whether the contractor's lawyer could certify the claim on behalf of the contractor).

7 *Hamza v United States*, 31 Fed Cl 315 (1994); *United Tech Corp*, ASBCA Nos 46880 and following, 96-1 BCA, Paragraph 28,226.

8 48 CFR, Section 52.233-1; see, *eg*,, *Summit Contractors*, AGBCA 81-136-1, 81-1 BCA Paragraph 14,872 (Section 907 of the Federal Courts Administration Act of 1992, Pub L No 102-572, amended 28 USC. Section 1491(a)(2), specifically grants jurisdiction over non-monetary claims "concerning claims of termination of a contract, rights in tangible or intangible property, compliance with cost accounting standards, and other non-monetary disputes on which a decision of the contracting officer has been issued" to the Court of Federal Claims; distinguished by *John Hackler and Co*, AGBCA No 82-221-1, 85-2 BCA, Paragraph 17,957 ("This circumstance may be contrasted with cases previously decided by this Board where review of amended complaints did not show that claims had been made to a Contracting Officer"). In *Summit,* above, the appeal was taken for protective purposes and dismissed as premature. While not apparent from the ruling, no claim had in fact been made to the contracting officer. The letter dated June 17 1980, which the contracting officer alleged was a claim, made no demand for payment or other relief, and was part of a long dialogue between the parties regarding disagreements over the administration of a timber sale).

9 48 CFR, Section 33.207(d).

Federal Acquisition Regulations requires the certification provided by the contractor to contain the following language:

I certify that the claim is made in good faith; that the supporting data are accurate and complete to the best of my knowledge and belief; that the amount requested accurately reflects the contract adjustment for which the contractor believes the Government is liable; and that I am duly authorized to certify the claim on behalf of the contractor.[10]

The Contract Disputes Act requires that claims by and between the contractor and government relating to a contract must be submitted within six years of the claimant receiving actual knowledge of the basis for the claim,[11] but that limitation period does not apply to fraud claims asserted by the government against a contractor.[12]

Once a valid claim is submitted, the contracting officer must issue a final decision on the claim. For claims of $100,000 or less, the final decision must be issued within 60 calendar days of receipt of the claim.[13] For claims in excess of $100,000, the contracting officer must issue a final decision, or inform the contractor when a decision will be issued, within 60 days of receipt of the claim submission.[14] The contracting officer must, thereafter, issue the decision within a "reasonable time".[15] If the contracting officer fails to issue a final decision within the specified time limits, the contractor may consider the claim to have been "deemed denied" and may thereafter file an appeal with the board, or file suit in the court of federal claims.[16]

The Contract Disputes Act provides two methods by which a contractor may appeal the final decision of a contracting officer: by filing with the applicable board of contract appeals within 90 days of receipt of the final decision, or by filing an action in the court of federal claims within one year of receipt of the final decision.[17] The provisions of the Contract Disputes Act state that the contracting officer's decision is final, conclusive, and not subject to review by any forum, tribunal or government agency unless a contractor commences an appeal or suit within the stated time limits.[18] If a contractor fails to file within the prescribed time periods, the contractor will be without further recourse to pursue the claim.

2.2 California

California was among the first states to enact legislation permitting the use of PPPs. During the period from 1989 to 2009, legislation was enacted authorising state and local government agencies to contract with private entities for the construction of certain transportation and infrastructure projects, and to utilise private investment capital to finance such projects.[19]

---

10 48 CFR, Section 33.207(c).
11 41 USC, Section 7103(a)(4)(A).
12 *Ibid.*
13 41 USC, Section 7103(f)(1).
14 41 USC, Section 7103(f)(2)(A)–(B).
15 41 USC, Section 7103(f)(3).
16 41 USC, Section 7103(f)(5).
17 41 USC, Section 7104(a)(b).
18 41 USC, Section 7103(g).
19 See eg, 1989 Cal ALS 107, 1989 Cal AB 680, 1989 Cal Stat Ch 107; 1996 Cal ALS 796, 1996 Cal SB 1420, 1996 Cal Stat Ch 796; 1996 Cal ALS 1040, 1996 Cal AB 2660, 1996 Cal Stats Ch 1040; 2006 Cal ALS 32, 2006 Cal AB 1467, 2006 Cal Stats Ch 32; 2006 Cal ALS 44, 2006 Cal AB 713, 2006 Cal Stats Ch 44.

The California Government Code contains statutory provisions on infrastructure financing.[20] The provisions of this statutory scheme reflect the findings of the California legislature that in the absence of the ability to utilise private sector investment capital "some local governmental agencies will not be able to adequately, competently, or satisfactorily retrofit, reconstruct, repair, or replace existing infrastructure and will not be able to adequately, competently, or satisfactorily design and construct new infrastructure".[21] As a result, the legislature enacted the provisions of the California Government Code governing Infrastructure Financing, granting local government agencies broad authority to utilise private sector investment capital to design, construct, develop, finance, maintain, improve, repair and operate fee-producing infrastructure.[22] The Code defines 'fee-producing infrastructure' projects and facilities broadly, to include any project or facility whose operation "will be paid for by the persons or entities benefited by or utilizing the project or facility".[23] The infrastructure financing statutes expressly exclude the power to design, construct, finance or operate a state project from the grant of authority to local governments.[24]

Neither the legislation concerning PPPs nor the resulting enabling statutes enacted by the state of California have addressed the manner in which disputes between the parties to such agreements are to be resolved. In the absence of statutory or contractual provisions on this, the default method of dispute resolution in California is litigation in a state or federal court of competent jurisdiction. Litigation is the default method of resolution of all disputes in California and is thus not limited to disputes arising between parties to a PPP, but would likewise apply to disputes arising on all infrastructure and construction projects.

Provisions of both the California Government Code and California Public Contract Code are relevant to disputes involving public entities, so these Codes should be carefully reviewed prior to submission of a claim against a public entity to ensure compliance. Title 1, Division 3.6 of the California Government Code addresses public liability, Part 3 of which sets forth a series of statutory provisions governing claims against public entities.[25] The Public Contract Code "is the basis of contracts between most public entities in this state and their contractors and subcontractors".[26] The term 'public entity' includes the "state, county, city, city and county, district, public authority, public agency, municipal corporation, or any other political subdivision or public corporation in the state".[27] The Public Contract Code includes sections addressing relief of bidders,[28] claims and disputes,[29] and arbitration of public works contract claims.[30]

---

20 Cal Gov Code, Sections 5956–5956.10 (2013).
21 Cal Gov Code, Section 5956.1 (2013).
22 *Ibid.*
23 Cal Gov Code, Section 5956.3 (2013).
24 Cal Gov Code, Section 5956.10 (2013).
25 Cal Gov Code, Sections 900 and following.
26 Cal Pub Contract Code, Section 1100.7.
27 Cal Pub Contract Code, Section 1100.
28 Cal Pub Contract Code, Sections 5100 and following.
29 Cal Pub Contract Code, Sections 9201 and following.
30 Cal Pub Contract Code, Sections 22200 and following.

The state courts of several large cities/counties in California, including those in Los Angeles and San Francisco, have distinct departments created to manage the litigation of complex disputes.[31] The types of complex matters handled by such departments include those requiring "exceptional judicial management", such as "antitrust, securities claims, construction defects, toxic torts, mass torts, and class actions".[32]

The state of California and its courts encourage the use of alternative dispute resolution (ADR) in furtherance of findings by the California legislature that "peaceful resolution of disputes in a fair, timely, appropriate, and cost-effective manner is an essential function of the judicial branch of state government under Article VI of the California Constitution".[33] Mediation is the most common method of ADR utilised. Title 11.6 of the California Code of Civil Procedure sets out a series of statutes addressing civil action mediation and pilot programmes permitting court-referred 'judicial arbitration' and mediation in Los Angeles County and other counties electing to participate.[34] While all parties to civil actions are encouraged to participate in mediation, participating courts have the authority to order civil actions with an amount in controversy of no more than $50,000 to mediation.[35] Judicial arbitration involves the referral of small civil cases to non-binding arbitration as a means of seeking an efficient and equitable method of resolution that saves litigants both the time and expense of costly litigation.[36] Judicial arbitrations are governed by several provisions of California law.[37] Judicial arbitration awards are not binding unless the parties so stipulate or are deemed to have accepted an award by failing to file a timely request for trial *de novo*.[38]

California has enacted a state arbitration act, the California Arbitration Act, which provides a statutory framework for the resolution of disputes that parties have contractually agreed to arbitrate.[39] The act allows arbitral tribunals to encourage parties to settle their dispute using mediation, conciliation or other procedures during the arbitration process.[40] As is the case in all US states, the Federal Arbitration Act governs agreements to arbitrate set out in contracts involving interstate commerce.[41]

2.3 Florida

In Florida, the manner of resolving construction disputes is determined by the parties' agreement and, in certain cases, by statutes which designate litigation as the

31 See, eg, *Complex Civil Litigation Program,* Los Angeles Superior Court, www.lasuperiorcourt.org/ComplexCourt/UI/ (last visited March 2013); *Complex Civil Litigation,* California Supreme Court of San Francisco, www.sfsuperiorcourt.org/divisions/civil/litigation (last visited March 2013).

32 See Cal R of Court 3.400 (a) (2013), Cal R of Court 3.400 (c) (2013).

33 Cal Civ Proc Code, Section 1775 (2013).

34 Cal Civ Proc Code, Sections 1775 and following (2013).

35 Cal Civ Proc Code, Section 1775.3 (a), Cal Civ Proc Code, Section 1775.5 (2013).

36 See Cal Civ Proc, Code Section 1141.10 (2013).

37 Cal Civ Proc, Code Sections 1141.10 and following; see also Cal R of Court 3.810 to 3.830; see, eg, S F Unif, Rule 4.1; Orange Supreme Court, Rule 446; San Diego Supreme Court, Rule s 2.24–2.29; and Los Angeles Supreme Court, Rules 12.0–12.14.

38 Cal Civ Proc Code, Section 1141.20 (2013).

39 Cal Civ Proc Code, Sections 1280 and following.

40 Cal Civ Proc Code, Section 1297.301 (2013).

41 9 USC, Section 3.

dispute resolution process for certain construction disputes, such as those against public entities and sureties on public bonds, and lien foreclosure actions against land owners.[42] Absent a contractual provision or applicable statute, construction disputes are resolved through litigation in civil courts (state or federal). In the case of construction disputes involving decisions of public agencies, disputes are resolved through an administrative process, including hearing officers and hearings, within the agency or state administrative process.[43]

Within the state circuit court system, most complex construction disputes are assigned to the complex business litigation (CBL) courts, which have been created by administrative orders in several judicial circuits as sections of the general civil jurisdiction division or general jurisdiction division in each respective circuit.[44] Each CBL court has adopted separate procedures and forms applicable only to that court. Rulings of one CBL court are not controlling on the other CBL courts.

Though litigation is the default method of resolving construction disputes in Florida, parties may agree by contract to pursue resolution through arbitration or mediation.[45] The Florida Arbitration Code[46] governs the interpretation and enforcement of contractual arbitration clauses, except for those in contracts involving interstate commerce, which are governed by the Federal Arbitration Act.[47]

The process or selection of arbitrators, as well as other particulars of the contractual arbitration process, are generally defined as part of the arbitration agreement or, in the case of institutional arbitration forums, by the procedural rules of the selected forum. In the absence of an agreement or if the agreement fails to establish a fundamentally fair method of appointment,[48] the court, on application of a party, appoints the arbitrator(s)[49] which, to be considered, must either:

- be a member of the Florida bar (the chief arbitrator must have been a member of the Florida bar for at least 5 years); or
- serve on the arbitration panel with the written consent of all parties.[50]

The right to arbitration under an agreement may be waived by taking actions inconsistent with the arbitration provision. The court, and not the arbitrator(s), determines whether a party to an arbitration agreement has waived its contractual right to arbitration by its subsequent conduct.[51]

Mediation is also a common method of dispute resolution utilised in construction

---

42 eg, Fla Stat, Section 255.05 (2012; surety bonds on public works), Chapter 713, Florida Statutes (lien actions against private land owners or lessees, private bond actions against sureties).

43 eg, Fla Admin Code, Rule 28-106.201 (2013).

44 See, eg, 11th Judicial Circuit Administrative Order No 1-11-04, FL ST 11 J CIR 1-11-04.

45 The court may refer an action to arbitration, except where the dispute has to do with bond estreatures, *habeas corpus* or other extraordinary writs, bond validations, civil or criminal contempt, or any other matter specified by the chief judge in the circuit: Fla R Civ P 1.800 (2013).

46 Fla Stat, Sections 682.01–682.22 (2012), *legis pending* H B 693, 2013 Leg, 115th Reg Sess (Fla 2013).

47 9 USC, Section 1 and following. See *O'Keefe Architects, Inc v CED Construction Partners*, Ltd, 944 So 2d 181, 184 (Fla 2006); *Wachovia Securities, LLC v Vogel*, 918 So 2d 1004, 1007 (Fla 2d DCA 2006); see also, *Buckeye Check Cashing v Cardegna*, 824 So 2d 228 (Fla 4th DCA 2002).

48 Fla Stat, Section 682.04 (2013), *legis pending* H B 693, 2013 Leg, 115th Reg Sess (Fla 2013).

49 Fla Stat, Section 682.04 (2013), *legis pending* H B 693, 2013 Leg, 115th Reg Sess (Fla 2013); Fla R Civ P 1.810(a).

50 *Ibid.*

disputes, particularly those involving large, complex and multi-party claims. Mediation may be contractually or voluntarily agreed by the parties (before, during or even after litigation or arbitration), or may be ordered by the court.[52] If a party fails to appear at a scheduled court-ordered mediation without first having obtained the court's permission, sanctions may be imposed by motion by an opposing party or on the court's own motion.[53] Settlement agreements reached at a court-ordered mediation become, once signed by all parties, enforceable agreements.[54]

Florida is one of the few states to have embraced the use of PPPs within its statutory framework. The Florida Statutes provide Florida's legal framework for PPPs in the transportation sector. Section 334.30 of the Florida Statutes authorises the Florida Department of Transportation (FDoT) to enter into agreements with private entities for the building, operation, ownership or financing of transportation facilities.

FDoT has also adopted its own rule within the Florida Administrative Code governing proposals for public-private transportation facilities and has issued public-private transportation facilities rough-draft guidelines (revised October 12 2004) to provide proposed guidelines for the solicitation, receipt and evaluation of proposals from private entities, and the rendering of an agreement with FDoT for the construction and operation of safe, convenient and economical transportation facilities.

FDoT's PPP programme includes the use of dispute resolution boards (DRBs) for resolution of disputes between FDoT and the contracting party.[55] Projects worth $10 million and above are assigned a project DRB and the governing rules and procedures are included in the bid specifications of the project. All other projects have access to a regional disputes resolution board for hearings. FDoT maintains a listing of qualified DRB board member candidates. Under the FDoT DRB process each party selects one DRB member, who must be approved by the other party, and the two selected members choose a third member, who usually chairs the board. A DRB meets periodically, usually at the project site, and reviews pending disputes and disagreements during project execution. FDoT procedures provide for monthly meetings for the first six months, and then bimonthly until project completion.

Florida's PPP legislation, however, does not specifically address resolution of disputes arising in PPP projects. Therefore, dispute resolution in PPP projects, as well as other complex construction disputes, is still a matter of contract or, in certain specific cases, of statute.[56]

---

51 "All questions concerning the scope or waiver of the right to arbitrate under contracts should be resolved in favor of arbitration rather than against it": *GBR3 v Largo Dev Corp*, 807 So 2d 723 (Fla 3d DCA 2002), quoting *Beverly Hills Dev Corp v George Wimpey, Inc*, 661 So 2d 969, 971 (Fla 5th DCA 1995); see also *Florida Educ Assoc v Sachs*, 650 So 2d 29 (Fla 1995).

52 See Fla Stat, Section 44.102 (2012); Fla R Civ P 1.710 (2013).

53 See Fla R Civ P, 1.720(b)–(f) (2013).

54 See Fla R Civ P, 1.730(b) (2013). However, at least one court has held that a mediated settlement agreement which was not signed by counsel but was signed by the parties was not rendered unenforceable based upon such a technical deficiency where the parties conducted themselves as if they had reached a binding agreement. *Jordan v Adventist Health System/Sunbelt, Inc*, 656 So 2d 200 (Fla 5th DCA 1995).

55 *Office of Construction: DBR Operating Procedures*, www.dot.state.fl.us, www.dot.state.fl.us/construction/CONSTADM/drb/OperatingProcedure.shtm (last visited 23 March 2013).

56 *Ibid.*, at n 19.

2.4 Georgia

Georgia has enacted a statutory framework to allow the Georgia Department of Transportation (GDoT) to enter into PPP agreements to fund or finance transportation projects.[57] Section 12-5-23.3 of the Official Code of Georgia (OCGA) permits the Georgia Water Resources Department to privatise the operation and maintenance of publically owned waste water treatment facilities. The state has also enacted additional statutory provisions that embrace the use of PPPs in contexts not affecting the construction industry.[58] The Georgia statutes addressing PPPs do not address the resolution of disputes between the parties.

The manner of dispute resolution on a PPP project, or a project involving construction or infrastructure more generally, will typically be dictated by the terms of the relevant contract. To the extent that the contract at issue does not require a specific method of dispute resolution, the default method of resolution will be litigation in a state or federal court of competent jurisdiction.

As is the case in all US states, venue and jurisdiction largely determine whether a litigated dispute proceeds before a Georgia state or federal court. The residency of the parties to the dispute, the type of claims asserted, the relief requested (monetary, injunctive, declaratory) and the value of any monetary claims are relevant considerations in making this determination.

Georgia's capital and largest city, Atlanta, sits primarily within the geographic boundaries of the counties of Fulton and Dekalb. Parties to disputes involving Georgia PPP, infrastructure or construction projects that will be litigated in Fulton County should be aware of the existence of the Fulton County Superior Court's business court.[59] Rule 1004 of the Atlanta Judicial Circuit governs Fulton County Superior Court business case division.[60] The business case division was created for the express purpose of handling complex business disputes, including those brought under specific business-related statutory acts, those involving large contractual claims, business tort claims, and other complex commercial claims for which damages in excess of $1 million are sought.[61] Cases may be assigned to the business case division upon joint request of the parties, by motion of a party, or by request of the Superior Court judge assigned to that case.[62] Judges of the business case division, in consultation with the parties, have authority to "order non-binding mediation, arbitration, or other means of alternative dispute resolution as dictated by the needs of a particular business case".[63] The divisional judges themselves, with the consent of all parties, may conduct such non-binding mediation, arbitration or other means of alternative dispute resolution.[64]

---

57 OCGA, Section 32-2-80 (2012).

58 For example, OCGA, Section 31-43-12 Commission on Men's Health's development of PPPs designed to educate Georgia's men on health-related issues; OCGA, Section 50-29-12 State agencies, authorities, and boards authorized to establish pilot projects to serve as models for the application of technology; and, OCGA, Section 50-12-31 Creation of the Georgia Arts Alliance to foster support of the arts, education, economic development, and tourism.

59 Atlanta Judicial Circuit, Superior Court of Fulton County, business court, www.fultoncourt.org/business/.

60 See generally, www.fultoncourt.org/business/BusinessCourtRule sAmendedOctober2012.pdf.

61 *Ibid.* at Paragraphs 2–3.

62 *Ibid.* at Paragraph 5.

63 *Ibid.* at Paragraph 12.

64 *Ibid.*

Georgia law encourages the use of ADR to secure the early and efficient resolution of disputes. "The Georgia Constitution of 1983 mandates that the judicial branch of government provide 'speedy, efficient, and inexpensive resolution of disputes and prosecutions'."[65] A Commission on ADR was established by the Supreme Court of Georgia in furtherance of this constitutional mandate for the purpose of examining "the feasibility of using court-annexed or court-referred alternative dispute resolution processes to complement existing dispute resolution methods" and to "prepare recommendations for a statewide, comprehensive ADR system".[66] As a result of the Commission's work, the Alternative Dispute Resolution Rules applicable to Georgia courts were created and enacted by the Georgia Supreme Court,[67] later supplemented by the Georgia Model Court Mediation Rules governing the mediation process.[68]

The Georgia ADR Rules define ADR as "any method other than litigation for resolution of disputes" and further identify common methods of ADR to include mediation, arbitration, case evaluation, early neutral evaluation, 'multi-door courthouse', summary jury trial, mini-trial, and 'settlement week'.[69] The 'multi-door courthouse' is not an ADR process, but is a concept wherein a wide range of ADR processes are made available to the parties with:

> *skilled intake workers direct[ing] disputants to the most appropriate process or series of processes, considering such factors as the relationship of the parties, the amount in controversy, anticipated length of trial, number of parties, and type of relief sought. Mediation, arbitration, case evaluation or early neutral evaluation, summary jury trial, mini trial, and various combinations of these ADR processes would all be available in the multi-door courthouse.*[70]

'Settlement week' is, likewise, not an ADR process, but involves a week-long moratorium on pending litigation during which courts select cases deemed appropriate for ADR.[71] "Mediation is the ADR process most often used during settlement week".[72]

The Georgia Commission on Dispute Resolution operates under the Georgia Supreme Court and is responsible for many tasks, including the administration of Georgia's statewide comprehensive ADR programme, overseeing the development of all court-annexed or court-referred ADR programmes, as well as ensuring the quality of, and approving, all such ADR programmes developed and utilised by Georgia state courts.[73] The Uniform Rules for Dispute Resolution Programs governing all ADR programmes utilised by Georgia state courts are contained within Appendix A of the Georgia ADR Rules.[74] Statements made during court-annexed or court-referred ADR proceedings or as part of the intake process for those proceedings are not subject to

65 Ga Alternate Disp Resol Note (2013).
66 *Ibid.*
67 Ga Alternate Disp Resol I-VIII (2013).
68 Ga Mediation Rules I-XIII (2013).
69 Ga Alternate Disp Resol I (2013).
70 *Ibid.*
71 *Ibid.*
72 *Ibid.*
73 Ga Alternate Disp Resol II, IV (2013).
74 Ga Alternate Disp Resol IV (2013); see *also* Ga Alternate Disp Resol Appx A (2013).

disclosure nor may they be used in evidence in subsequent administrative or judicial proceedings.[75]

The Uniform ADR Program Rules govern mediations, non-binding arbitrations, case evaluations, early neutral evaluations, summary jury trials, mini trials, or combinations of such ADR processes utilised through court-annexed or court-referred ADR programmes.[76] By Rule 2.1 of the Uniform ADR Program, the judge presiding over a civil case may, at any time, refer such case to mediation, non-binding arbitration, case evaluation, early neutral evaluation or a multi-door programme.[77] Rule 2.5 provides that access to such ADR processes may also be granted upon the petition of a party to the dispute.[78] Parties likewise have the right under Rules 3.1 and 3.2 to petition the court to remove the case from the ADR process or to refer the case to an alternative process than that to which it has been referred.[79]

The Georgia Arbitration Code provides a statutory framework governing contractual agreements to arbitrate.[80] Except as otherwise provided by contract or by law, including within the provisions of the code itself, the arbitration code operates as the default law governing "all disputes in which the parties thereto have agreed in writing to arbitrate and shall provide the exclusive means by which agreements to arbitrate disputes can be enforced".[81] A written agreement to submit any existing controversy to arbitration is enforceable without regard to the justiciable character of the controversy and confers jurisdiction on the courts of the state of Georgia to enforce it and to enter judgment on an award.[82]

The Federal Arbitration Act governs contractual agreements to arbitrate contained within contracts involving interstate commerce and provides the means by which such agreements are enforced.[83] The phrase 'involving commerce' has been interpreted to include any transaction having an impact on interstate commerce.[84] The act "preempts any state law that conflicts with its provisions or undermines the enforcement of private arbitration agreements. To the extent that state law stands as an obstacle to the accomplishment and execution of the full purposes and objectives of Congress, it will be preempted by the [Federal Arbitration Act]".[85] To the extent that a provision of the Georgia Arbitration Code conflicts with the act, the code "must yield to the paramount federal law" and is thus preempted.[86] Construction projects typically involve interstate commerce at a base level, as materials used on

---

75 Ga Alternate Disp Resol VII (2013).
76 Ga Alternate Disp Resol Appx A (2013).
77 *Ibid.*
78 *Ibid.*
79 *Ibid.*
80 OCGA Section 9-9-1 and following.
81 OCGA Section 9-9-2 (2012).
82 OCGA Section 9-9-3 (2012).
83 9 USC. Section 1 and following.
84 *Citizens Bank v Alafabco, Inc*, 539 US 52 (2003).
85 (citations and punctuation omitted). *Langfitt v Jackson*, 284 Ga App 628, 634–635 (2007); *Results Oriented v Crawford*, 245 Ga App 432, 436 (2000); *Southland Corp v Keating*, 465 US 1, 16 (1984), *Volt Information Sciences v Bd. of Trustees*, 489 US 468, 477 (1989).
86 See *Primerica Financial Svcs v Wise*, 217 Ga App 36, 41 (1995); see *also Langfitt v Jackson*, 284 Ga App 628, 635 (Ga Ct App 2007).
87 See *Krut v Whitecap Housing Group, LLC*, 268 Ga App 436 (2004).

the job routinely pass through interstate commerce.[87] As a result, construction contracts are generally found to involve interstate commerce, thereby invoking the provisions of the Federal Arbitration Act.[88]

While substantive provisions of the Federal Arbitration Act may govern a dispute, the applicability of the act does not result in a wholesale pre-emption of the entire field of state arbitration law relevant to a dispute involving interstate commerce.[89] Parties must thus be aware that the provisions of both the Federal Arbitration Act and Georgia Arbitration Code may be found applicable to a dispute arbitrated under Georgia law.[90] Procedural mechanisms within the provisions of the code that are consistent with the act's goals and do not undermine its purposes or objectives are not pre-empted.[91] Georgia courts have found that choice-of-law provisions within a contract which state that the contract is "governed by the law of the place where the project is located" evidences the parties' intent to abide by the state rules of arbitration, further finding that enforcing the state arbitration rules "is fully consistent with the goals of the [Federal Arbitration Act]".[92] Understanding the interplay of the act and code, as well as the implications resulting from the trigger and application of both arbitration acts, is important at both the contracting and dispute resolution stages.

The state of Georgia recently enacted the Georgia International Commercial Arbitration Code, Sections 9-9-20 to 9-9-59, for the purpose of "encourag[ing] international commercial arbitration in [Georgia], enforc[ing] arbitration agreements and arbitration awards, facilitat[ing] prompt and efficient arbitration proceedings consistent with [the act], and provid[ing] a conducive environment for international business and trade".[93] The code applies to international arbitration agreements entered into on and after July 1 2012, the effective date of the act.[94] The code expressly states that its provisions apply to "international commercial arbitration, subject to any agreement in force between the United States and any other country" with certain provisions applying only when Georgia is the *situs* of the arbitration proceedings.[95] An arbitration is considered 'international' for purposes of the code if:

- the parties' places of business are located in different countries "at the time of the conclusion of such arbitration agreement";
- the location of the arbitration identified in or by the terms of the arbitration agreement is outside the country in which the parties have their places of business;
- any place where a substantial part of the obligations of the commercial relationship are to be performed is situated outside the country in which the parties have their places of business;

---

88 See *GF/Legacy Dallas, Inc v Juneau Constr Co, LLC*, 282 Ga App 14 (2006); *Krut v Whitecap Housing Group, LLC*, 268 Ga App 436 (2004); *Wise v Tidal Constr Co*, 261 Ga App 670 (2003); see *also Allied-Bruce Terminix Cos v Dobson*, 513 US 265 (1995).

89 *N Augusta Assocs P'ship v 1815 Exchange*, 220 Ga App 790, 791 (1996).

90 *Ibid*.

91 *Ibid*; see also *Simmons Co v Deutsche Fin Servs Corp*, 243 Ga App 85, 88–89 (2000).

92 *N Augusta Assocs P'ship*, 220 Ga App at 791, citing *Volt Information Sciences*, above.

93 OCGA, Section 9-9-20 (2012).

94 See OCGA, Title 9, Chapter 9, Article 1, Part 2, Note (2012).

95 OCGA, Section 9-9-21 (a)–(b) (2012).

- the place with which the subject matter of the dispute is most closely connected is situated outside the country in which the parties have their places of business; or,
- the parties have expressly agreed that the subject matter of the arbitration agreement relates to more than one country.[96]

Where the International Commercial Arbitration Code governs a disputed matter, courts have no authority to intervene except as provided within the act.[97] If the controversy between the parties is within the scope of the code, "the arbitration agreement shall be enforced by the courts of this state in accordance with this part without regard to the justiciable character of the controversy".[98] The provisions of the code address and govern a variety of procedural aspects of the international commercial arbitration process including, but not limited to, matters of interpretation, written communications, waivers, judicial intervention and enforcement, jurisdiction, interim measures of protection, appointment of arbitrators, the arbitration hearing, and procedures following the hearing to confirm or appeal the award.[99]

2.5 Illinois

The state of Illinois has enacted several PPP-enabling statutes to facilitate the use of PPP agreements for the development, financing, construction, management and operation of transportation projects. These PPP-enabling statutes include those contained within the Illinois Public Private Partnerships for Transportation Act,[100] the Public Private Agreements for the Illiana Expressway Act,[101] and an Illinois statute promoting the development of high-speed rail and magnetic levitation transportation.[102] Illinois also has a PPP-enabling statute within the Riverdale Development Authority Act, which allows for the use of PPPs on a variety of projects beyond those involving transportation.[103] The stated purpose of that act is to "facilitate and promote the redevelopment of vacant and underutilized brownfield property" within the specified geographic area "and to enhance the economic benefits generated by the former uses of the property with development that will attract new residences and businesses and create new and better housing and job opportunities within the area".[104] The Riverdale Development Authority (RDA) has responsibility for promoting development within the area by "assist[ing] in the planning, development, acquisition, construction and marketing of residential, industrial, commercial, or freight-oriented projects".[105] The 'projects' contemplated by the act are defined as "industrial, commercial, freight-oriented or residential

96 OCGA, Section 9-9-21 (c) (2012).
97 OCGA, Section 9-9-26 (2012).
98 *Ibid.*
99 See *generally* OCGA, Section 9-9-20 and following.
100 630 Ill Comp Stat 5/1 and following.
101 605 Ill Comp Stat 130/1 and following.
102 20 Ill Comp Stat 2705/2705-450 (2013).
103 70 Ill Comp Stat 516/1 and following.
104 70 Ill Comp Stat 516/5 (2013).
105 70 Ill Comp Stat 516/20 (2013).

projects or any combination thereof provided that all uses shall fall within one of those categories", including buildings, structures, improvements, machinery, equipment, whether related to "an addition to or renovation, rehabilitation, or improvement of any existing capital project", as well as:

> *site improvements and new construction involving sidewalks, sewers, landscaping and all appurtenances and facilities incidental thereto such as utilities, access roads, railroad sidings, truck docking, and similar facilities, parking facilities, railroad roadbed, track, trestle, depot, terminal, intermodal facilities, switching and signaling equipment, or related equipment and other improvements necessary or convenient thereto, solid waste and wastewater treatment and disposal sites and other pollution control facilities, resource or waste reduction, recovery, treatment, and disposal facilities, open spaces, streets, highways, and runways.*[106]

The breadth of authority granted to the RDA under the act includes the power to "enter into agreements with businesses, form PPP entities and appropriate funds to such entities as needed to achieve the purposes of the Act".[107]

Although Illinois law includes several PPP-enabling statutes, none specifies a method by which disputes between the parties to such agreements are to be resolved. Unless the relevant PPP agreement specifies an alternative means of resolving a dispute between the parties, disputes will be resolved through litigation in a court of competent jurisdiction. This would likewise be the case for parties involved in disputes on infrastructure and other construction projects unless otherwise provided by contract or other authority governing the project.

The system of state trial courts in Illinois includes the Illinois court of claims. The Illinois Court of Claims Act[108] grants the court of claims exclusive jurisdiction over a variety of claims including all "claims against the State founded upon any law of the State of Illinois or upon any regulation adopted thereunder by an executive or administrative officer or agency; ... claims against the State founded upon any contract entered into with the State of Illinois ... [and] claims against the State for damages in cases sounding in tort".[109] Since the state of Illinois and its transportation agencies are the public entities with authority to enter into PPPs under the Illinois Public Private Partnerships for Transportation Act, the Public Private Agreements for the Illiana Expressway Act and the statute addressing high-speed rail and magnetic levitation transportation development, disputes with such entities relating to a PPP agreement would fall within the exclusive jurisdiction of the court of claims.[110]

The Court of Claims Act expressly states that Illinois general assembly will not make an appropriation to pay a claim against the state unless an award has been made by the court of claims.[111] The state may consent to resolve a dispute in a forum other than the court of claims; however, valid consent may only be provided by

106 70 Ill Comp Stat 516/10 (2013).
107 70 Ill Comp Stat 516/25 (2013).
108 705 Ill Comp Stat 505/1 and following.
109 705 Ill Comp Stat 505/8 (2013).
110 See 630 Ill Comp Stat 5/1 and following; 605 Ill Comp Stat 130/1 and following; 20 Ill Comp Stat 2705/2705-450 (2013), and 705 Ill Comp Stat 505/8 (2013).
111 705 Ill Comp Stat 505/23 (2013).

action of the general assembly.[112] Officers and agencies of the state have no "authority to waive laws that are for the benefit of this State".[113] Before seeking final determination of a claim filed with the court of claims, a party must exhaust all other available administrative or judicial remedies and sources of recovery.[114]

The state of Illinois and its courts embrace ADR as a means of achieving expedited resolution of disputes. Numerous statutory acts, state court rules and local rules have been enacted to encourage the use of ADR and facilitate ADR processes, including (but not limited to) the Uniform Mediation Act,[115] Uniform Arbitration Act,[116] International Commercial Arbitration Act,[117] Illinois Supreme Court Rules governing mandatory arbitration[118] and mediation programmes,[119] and the local rules of the circuit court of Cook County.

Illinois' Uniform Mediation Act applies to:

- mediations required by statute, by court or administrative agency rule, or by referral of a court, administrative agency, or arbitrator;
- mediations which the parties and mediator have agreed will be privileged against disclosure; and
- other mediations conducted by an individual holding himself out as a mediator.[120]

Among other issues, the act addresses privilege against disclosure, confidentiality, disclosure of conflicts of interest by a mediator, and participation in the mediation.[121]

The Illinois Supreme Court Rules include provisions governing mandatory arbitration proceedings conducted by the judicial circuits.[122] Judicial circuits within the Illinois state trial court system are permitted to adopt rules by which to conduct arbitration proceedings as long as such rules are consistent with the provisions of the Illinois Supreme Court's Rules governing mandatory arbitration.[123] By way of example, "the mandatory arbitration program of the Circuit Court of Cook County, Illinois, is governed by the Supreme Court Rules for the Conduct of Mandatory

---

112 *J L Simmons Co v Capital Dev Bd*, 98 Ill App 3d 445, 447 (Ill App Ct 4th Dist 1981) citing *Crane Paper Stock Co v Chicago & Northwestern Ry Co*, 63 Ill 2d 61 (Ill 1976); *Edelen v Hogsett*, 44 Ill 2d 215 (Ill 1969).

113 *J L Simmons Co*, 98 Ill App 3d at 447 (action to enforce arbitration award against state board dismissed for lack of jurisdiction as board lacked authority to agree to arbitration of contract dispute).

114 705 ILCS, Section 505/25 (2013); See, for example, *Schuepfer Plumbing, Inc v State*, 52 Ill Ct Cl 151 (1997; subcontractor's failure to timely file its statutory notice of mechanics lien and failure to timely file its complaint to foreclose on the mechanic's lien constituted a failure to exhaust remedies prior to filing action against the state seeking payment for labour, materials, tools, and equipment provided for a project as required by 705 ILCS Section 505/25); *Herlhy Mid-Continent Co v State*, 54 Ill Ct Cl 429 (2001; motion to dismiss contract claim against Illinois Department of Transportation (IDOT) based on claimant's alleged failure to exhaust administrative remedies with IDOT by failing to file a required sub-contractor certification during the administrative review process was denied as claimant presented its claim to all three levels of review and obtained a decision at each level, resulting in full exhaustion of remedies).

115 710 Ill Comp Stat 35/1 and following.

116 710 Ill Comp Stat 5/1 and following.

117 710 Ill Comp Stat 30/1-1 and following.

118 Ill Sup Ct, Rule 86 (a) (2013).

119 Ill Sup Ct, Rule 99 (2013).

120 710 Ill Comp Stat 35/3 (2013).

121 710 Ill Comp Stat 35/1 and following.

122 Ill Sup Ct, Rule 86 (2013).

123 *Ibid.*

Arbitration Proceedings".[124] Civil actions seeking relief solely limited to a monetary award in an amount not in excess of the limit specified for the applicable circuit or county within such circuit are subject to mandatory arbitration.[125] The rules set out procedures for: the appointment, qualification and compensation of arbitrators; scheduling hearings; discovery; conducting the hearings; and the issuance of awards and judgments.[126] Within 30 days of the issuance of an arbitration award, a party may pay the requisite fee and file a written notice of rejection of such award and request that the matter proceed to trial.[127] If no party to the arbitration files a notice of rejection of the arbitrator's award and requests to proceed to trial within the specified time frame, a party "may move the court to enter judgment on the award".[128]

The Illinois Supreme Court Rules likewise include provisions governing mediation programmes conducted by the judicial circuits.[129] The Illinois Supreme Court must review and approve the rules established by a judicial circuit for the operation of mediation programmes.[130] The Rules of the circuit court of Cook County provide sets of procedures governing mediation related to both law division major-case court-annexed civil mediation[131] and chancery division court-annexed civil mediation.[132] The rules governing court-annexed civil mediation in both the law division major case and chancery division provide for cases to be referred to mediation by the court, by motion of a party, or upon the agreement of the parties.[133] Both divisions allow a party to file a motion seeking to set aside or modify the referral to mediation within 14 days of the entry of the order of referral.[134]

Illinois federal district courts have likewise demonstrated their support for the use of ADR by enacting local rules governing ADR procedures. By way of example, local rule 16.4 of the US district court for the Central District of Illinois adopts a set of rules "pursuant to the Alternative Dispute Resolution Act 1998 to make available to litigants a program of court-annexed dispute resolution processes designed to provide quick, inexpensive and satisfying alternatives to engaging in continuing litigation".[135] The Rule thereafter notes that the "court establishes mediation, summary jury trials and summary bench trials as the forms of alternative dispute resolution available to litigants in all civil actions".[136] Parties are encouraged to use the ADR processes created by the rules.[137] Cases may be referred to mediation at any time, but only by agreement of the parties.[138] Parties may also consent to the summary jury trial of a civil case, with the proceeding thereafter being "conducted by a judge other than the assigned judge".[139]

124 Ill R Cir Ct Cook Co, Rule 18.2 (2013).
125 Ill Sup Ct, Rule 86 (2013).
126 See generally Ill Sup Ct, Rule 86 and following.
127 Ill Sup Ct, Rule 93 (2013).
128 Ill Sup Ct, Rule 92 (2013).
129 Ill Sup Ct, Rule 99 (2013).
130 *Ibid.*
131 Ill R Cir Ct Cook Co, Rule 20.01 and following.
132 Ill R Cir Ct Cook. Co, Rule 21.01 and following.
133 See Ill R Cir Ct Cook Co, Rule 20.02, Ill R Cir Ct Cook Co, Rule 21.02.
134 *Ibid.*
135 CD Ill, Rule 16.4(A).
136 *Ibid.*
137 CD Ill, Rule 16.4(D).
138 CD Ill, Rule 16.4(E)(2).
139 CD Ill, Rule 16.4(F).

Aside from the availability of court-annexed ADR proceedings, the state of Illinois enacted the Illinois Uniform Arbitration Act to provide a statutory framework by which contractual agreements to arbitrate are governed.[140] The act governs binding arbitration proceedings in Illinois absent either a contractual choice of law provision to the contrary or an underlying contract affecting interstate commerce.[141] As is the case with all state arbitration acts throughout the United States, the Federal Arbitration Act applies to arbitrated disputes involving interstate commerce, thus pre-empting the Illinois Uniform Arbitration Act even where the relevant contract contains a choice-of-law provision specifying the governing law as that of the state of Illinois. Parties to contract for construction are well advised to understand the differences between the federal and the Illinois Uniform acts, as well as how those differences may impact any future arbitrated dispute. The statutory provisions of the acts differ in several respects, including as to the method of appointing arbitrators when not specified by contract,[142] as to the timeframe in which a party must move to vacate an arbitration award,[143] and as to appeals.[144]

In addition to the Illinois Uniform Arbitration Act the state of Illinois has enacted the Illinois International Commercial Arbitration Act, which sets out an extensive statutory framework by which international commercial arbitrations are to be governed.[145] That act expressly states that its provisions apply to "international commercial arbitration, subject to any agreement in force between the United States and any other country or countries" with certain provisions applying only when Illinois is the *situs* of the arbitration proceedings.[146] An arbitration is considered 'international' for purposes of the act if:

- the parties' places of business are located in different countries "at the time of the conclusion of execution of that agreement";
- the location of the arbitration identified in or by the terms of the arbitration agreement is outside the country or countries in which the parties have their places of business;
- any place where the predominant part of the obligations of the commercial relationship is to be performed or the place with which the subject matter of the dispute is most closely connected is situated outside the country in which the parties have their places of business; or
- the parties have expressly agreed that the subject matter of the arbitration agreement relates to more than one country.[147]

Where the act governs a disputed matter, courts have no authority to intervene except as provided in the act or federal law.[148] The provisions of the act address and

140 710 Ill Comp Stat 5/1 and following.
141 See generally 710 Ill Comp Stat 5/1 (2013).
142 Compare 710 Ill Comp Stat 5/3 (2013), 9 USC, Section 5 (2013).
143 Compare 710 Ill Comp Stat 5/12 (b) (2013), 9 USC, Section 12 (2013).
144 Compare 710 Ill Comp Stat 5/18 (2013), 9 USC, Section 16 (2013).
145 710 Ill Comp Stat 30/1-1 and following.
146 710 Ill Comp Stat 30/1-5 (2013).
147 *Ibid.*
148 710 Ill Comp Stat 30/1-25 (2013).

govern a variety of procedural aspects of the international commercial arbitration process, including (but not limited to) court referral of claims subject to arbitration and granting of interim measures, composition of the arbitral tribunal, jurisdiction of the tribunal, conduct of the proceedings, and the issuance of an arbitration award.[149]

2.6 Maryland

Maryland is one the few US states that has embraced the use of PPPs within its statutory framework. The Maryland Transportation Code provides broad, general powers to the Maryland Department of Transportation, under which PPP-enabling statutes have been enacted.[150] Section 4-406 of the Maryland Transportation Code identifies the types of agreement that may be considered PPPs and details the oversight and reporting requirements applicable to such partnerships. The code does not address the resolution of disputes on projects involving PPPs; as such, the manner of dispute resolution would either be dictated by the terms of any agreement between the parties to the dispute or would default to litigation.

As is the case with other US states, the manner of resolving disputes arising out of a construction project is often dictated by the agreement of the parties as set forth in the relevant contract. If a contract does not exist between the parties to the dispute, or if the relevant contract does not specify an agreed method of dispute resolution, the default is for the dispute to be resolved through litigation in state or federal court. Default resolution by litigation is not dependent on the nature of the project to which the dispute relates, but instead applies generally to all disputes in the United States, including disputes arising within projects involving infrastructure, PPPs, or construction generally.

The litigation of complex construction cases typically involves testimony by experts. In Maryland:

> *[t]he admissibility of expert testimony generally is subject to evaluation according to three requirements:*
>
> - *the witness qualifies as an expert on the topic about which he or she intends to testify;*
> - *the subject is appropriate for expert testimony; and*
> - *there is an adequate factual basis supporting the testimony.*[151]

Though litigation is the default method of resolving disputes, parties may agree by contract to pursue resolution through arbitration or mediation. The provisions of the Federal Arbitration Act govern the arbitration of disputes where the contract at issue involves interstate commerce.[152] While disputes arising from construction projects typically involve interstate commerce, thus triggering application of the act, Maryland has enacted other state statutes that provide for arbitration of certain disputes, including the statutory framework set forth in the Maryland Uniform

149 See 710 Ill Comp Stat 30/1-1 and following.
150 Md Transportation Code Ann, Section 4-205 (2012).
151 *Exxon Mobil Corp v Ford*, 2013 Md LEXIS 79 (Md App 2013); Md R. 5-702.
152 *Handyman & Remodeling Servs, LLC et al v Judith Schedule et al*, 183 Md App 44, 49 (2008).

Arbitration Act.[153] Section 3-202 of that act states that "[a]n agreement providing for arbitration under the law of the State confers jurisdiction on a court to enforce the agreement and enter judgment on an arbitration award."[154]

Where there is no contractual agreement between the parties to submit a dispute to an alternative dispute resolution proceeding, Title 17, Chapter 100 of the Maryland Rules of Procedure gives courts the authority to refer all or a portion of a civil case to alternative dispute resolution.[155] As defined by the rules, 'alternative dispute resolution' means "the process of resolving matters in pending litigation through arbitration, mediation, neutral case evaluation, neutral fact-finding, settlement conference, or a combination of those processes".[156] A court may not require the parties to participate in an ADR proceeding if a timely objection to the referral is filed.[157] Arbitrations conducted under Title 17, Chapter 100 of the rules of procedure are non-binding, though the parties may elect to use binding arbitration.

While the litigation of disputes between non-governmental entities in Maryland proceed before state and federal courts based on a variety of factors including the state of residency of each party and the type and value of the claims asserted, disputes involving public contracts proceed before the Maryland State Board of Contract Appeals. The Maryland State Finance and Procurement Code gives that state board exclusive jurisdiction over the claim of a contractor involving the award, breach, performance, modification or termination of a public contract.[158] The dispute resolution procedures set forth in the State Finance and Procurement Code contain specific notice and claim requirements, particularly with respect to timing and explanation of the claim.[159] All claims are required to be reviewed first by the head of the unit involved in the procurement at issue.[160]

Although there are no statutory provisions providing different standards or procedures for the admission of evidence, including expert testimony, before the Maryland State Board of Contract Appeals, it is noted that, in practice, the board does not adhere as strictly to the rules of evidence as would be typical in a matter litigated in Maryland circuit courts.[161] Though either party may appeal a decision by the board, a contractor must exhaust its administrative remedies before filing suit in circuit court.[162]

With respect to the use of dispute review boards (DRBs), it is noted that there are no provisions under Maryland public contracting law that specifically address or require the use of the DRBs; however, the database maintained by the Dispute Review Board Foundation indicates that DRBs have been utilised on disputes involving the Washington Metropolitan Area Transit Authority and the Baltimore Metro.[163]

---

153 Md Courts and Judicial Proceedings Code Ann, Sections 3-201 and following.

154 Md Courts and Judicial Proceedings Code Ann, Section 3-202 (2012).

155 Md, Rule 17-201 (2013).

156 Md, Rule 17-102 (2013).

157 Md, Rule 17-202 (2013).

158 Md State Finance and Procurement Code Ann, Sections 15-201 and following.

159 Md Courts and Judicial Proceedings Code Ann, Section 15-219 (2012).

160 Md Courts and Judicial Proceedings Code Ann, Section 15-218 (2012).

161 Md Courts and Judicial Proceedings Code Ann, Section 15-216 (2012); Md State Government Code Ann, Section 10-213 (2012).

162 *McLean Contracting Co v Maryland Transp Auth*, 70 Md App 514 (1987); Md State Government Code Ann, Section 10-222 (2012).

163 www.drb.org/manual/Database_2005-State.xls.

2.7 New Jersey

Statutory authority permitting the use of PPPs in New Jersey is presently limited to that contained within the State College Contracts Law. The law allows public colleges or institutions of higher education to enter into PPP agreements permitting private entities to assume full financial and administrative responsibility for on-campus construction projects, operations and facilities management, "provided that the project is financed in whole by the private entity and that the State or institution of higher education, as applicable, retains full ownership of the land upon which the project is completed".[164] In the wake of recent events devastating the state of New Jersey, legislation has been proposed, and remains pending at July 2013, before the New Jersey Senate which would expand the authorised use of PPPs, permitting counties and municipalities to partner with non-profit entities for projects relating to water management, storm shelter construction and flood/hurricane resistance.[165]

Neither the State College Contracts Law nor the recently proposed legislation addresses the method by which disputes are to be resolved between the parties to a PPP agreement. Any method of dispute resolution is thus likely to be dictated, if at all, by the terms set forth within each PPP agreement. In the absence of contract terms to the contrary, the default method of dispute resolution would be litigation in a court of appropriate jurisdiction. In the state courts of New Jersey, all cases involving more than $15,000 are heard in the law division of the Superior Court. Cases in which money damages are not sought (eg, labour matters, injunctions) are heard before the chancery or general equity divisions of the superior court.

New Jersey state and federal courts encourage parties to explore expedited resolution of disputes through alternatives to full-blown litigation. Although not mandatory, many processes exist within the judicial system to assist parties achieving this end, including various statutes, and court rules provide alternative mechanisms by which parties may seek to resolve disputes.

The New Jersey Court Rules specifically include a programme addressing dispute resolution. In this regard, the rules detail the Complementary Dispute Resolution (CDR) programmes available to parties engaged in litigation in New Jersey superior and municipal courts.[166] The rules state that the CDR programmes "constitute an integral part of the judicial process, intended to enhance its quality and efficacy" and notes that "[a]ttorneys have a responsibility to become familiar with available CDR programs and inform their clients of them".[167] The CDR programmes embrace ADR beyond mediation of disputes, providing various means by which the parties may seek early resolution of a dispute pending in litigation under judicial supervision, including:

- through adjudicative processes (non-binding arbitration; settlement proceedings before a panel of neutrals; summary jury trials resulting in issuance of non-binding advisory opinions as to liability, damages, or both);
- evaluative processes (early neutral evaluation, a pre-discovery presentation of facts and legal contentions to a neutral evaluator, who provides assessment

164 NJ Stat, Section 18A:64-85 (2013).
165 S 2632, 215th Leg, Reg Sess (NJ 2012).
166 NJ Court Rules, Rule 1:40 and following.
167 NJ Court Rules, Rule 1:40-1 (2013).

of the strengths/weaknesses of positions and assists in narrowing the dispute and proposing discovery guidelines;

- neutral fact-finding by a neutral, agreed upon by the parties, who investigates and analyses a dispute involving complex or technical issues, and then makes non-binding findings and recommendations);
- facilitative processes (mediation), hybrid processes (mediation-arbitration, where, following mediation, unresolved issues are arbitrated);
- a 'mini-trial process', where parties present facts and legal contentions to a neutral, panel of party-selected representatives or both, to define disputed issues, assist settlement negotiations, or issue non-binding/binding advisory opinions as agreed by the parties); and
- "any other method or technique of complementary dispute resolution permitted by guideline or directive of the Supreme Court".[168]

The rules governing the CDR have been structured in a manner that allows for flexibility and modification by the courts, with respect to programmes offered to assist parties in achieving resolution, requirements for participation, and assignment to non-court administered programmes.[169]

The CDR regime also specifically provides that the complementary dispute resolution programmes to be offered shall include "arbitration of civil actions in accordance with Rule 4:21A".[170] New Jersey Court Rule 4:21A provides for mandatory, non-binding arbitration of certain actions screened and identified as appropriate for arbitration, including actions involving contracts, commercial claims, negligence claims, and actions on a book account or instrument of obligation.[171] Prior to the scheduling of such arbitration or within 15 days thereafter, the parties may opt out of arbitration by submission of a certification stating that the case involves novel legal issues or unusually complex factual issues, or is otherwise ineligible for arbitration.[172] Removal of a case from arbitration must be pursued by motion to the presiding judge if more than 15 days have elapsed since the scheduling of arbitration.[173]

Within 30 days of an award by the arbitrator, a party may file a notice of rejection of the arbitration award and demand a trial *de novo*.[174] When demand for a trial *de novo* and payment of the requisite amount of $200 towards the arbitrator's fee has been timely made by a party, the action is returned to the trial calendar for the trial *de novo* scheduled to occur within 90 days thereafter.[175] New Jersey Court Rule 4:21A-6 further provides that a party demanding a trial *de novo* "may be liable to pay the reasonable costs, including attorney's fees, incurred after rejection of the award", thereafter detailing circumstances that will limit any further award of reasonable

168 NJ Court Rules, Rule 1:40-2 (2013).
169 NJ Court Rules, Rule 1:40-2, 1:40-10, 1:40-11.
170 NJ Court Rules, Rule 1:40-9 (2013).
171 NJ Court Rules, Rule 4:21A-1 (2013).
172 *Ibid.*
173 *Ibid.*
174 NJ Court Rules, Rule 4:21A-6 (2013).
175 *Ibid.*

costs upon motion.[176] Procedures for dismissing the action upon settlement and for confirming an arbitrator's award are likewise set out in Rule 4:21A-6.[177]

The New Jersey Alternative Procedure for Dispute Resolution Act is applicable to contractual agreements which specifically reference the act and thereby invoke its provisions.[178] Under the act, party- or court-appointed umpires are given authority to resolve all claims, issues and disputes arising from the agreement.[179] The rules of evidence do not apply to hearings conducted before one or more umpires under the act, resulting in proceedings that are less formal than those encountered in traditional judicial processes.[180] Awards issued by an umpire must be made in accordance with the principles of substantive law, and must be accompanied by written findings of fact and conclusions of law.[181] The act provides a mechanism by which an umpire's award may be vacated, modified or corrected, including specific provisions detailing the time frame in which a party may apply to the superior court for such an order, the standard of review, and the parameters under which such relief will be granted.[182]

Though the State of New Jersey has taken steps to enact the aforementioned Alternative Procedure for Dispute Resolution Act, in the context of disputes arising out of larger construction projects it is likely that contractual provisions addressing alternative dispute resolution will involve mediation and/or arbitration. Contractual agreements to arbitrate will be governed by either the New Jersey Arbitration Act[183] or the Federal Arbitration Act. Even though the NJAA operates as the default arbitration act governing contractual agreements to arbitrate in New Jersey, the importance and application of the FAA cannot be ignored as most, if not all, construction cases involve interstate commerce, thereby resulting in pre-emption by the FAA.[184] Parties should, nonetheless, be aware of the provisions of the NJAA and of its potential application to disputes subject to a contractual agreement to arbitrate. The NJAA is a version of the Uniform Arbitration Act which has been modified in certain respects, including by provisions that:

- allow the parties to expand the scope of judicial review;[185]
- require equivalent levels of interest disclosures by all arbitrators, whether party-appointed or neutrals;[186]
- prohibit party-appointed arbitrators from serving if interests are not properly disclosed;[187] and
- require vacation of an arbitration award for evident partiality of both party-appointed and neutral arbitrators.[188]

176 *Ibid.*
177 *Ibid.*
178 NJ Stat, Sections 2A:23A-1 and following.
179 NJ Stat, Section 2A:23A-5 (2013).
180 NJ Stat, Section 2A:23A-11 (2013).
181 NJ Stat, Section 2A:23A-12 (2013).
182 NJ Stat, Section 2A:23A-13 (2013).
183 NJ Stat, Sections 2A:23B-1 and following.
184 See *eg, Estate of Ruszala v Brooklyn Living Communities*, 1 A 3d 272 (App Div 2010).
185 NJ Stat, Section 2A:23B-23 (2013).
186 NJ Stat, Section 2A:23B-12 (2013).
187 *Ibid.*
188 *Ibid.*

The US district court for the District of New Jersey utilises both mediation and arbitration to assist in early resolution of litigated disputes. USDC District of New Jersey Local Civil Rule 301.1 governs mediation and grants each district court judge and magistrate judge the authority to refer most civil actions to mediation with or without the consent of the parties.[189] Actions which are not subject to mediation under Rule 301.1 are described in Rule 72.1(a)(3)(C).[190] Court-ordered arbitration of disputes pending before the US district court for the district of New Jersey is governed by Local Civil Rule 201.1 which provides for the compulsory arbitration of civil actions "pending before the Court where the relief sought consists only of money damages not in excess of $150,000 exclusive of interest and costs and any claim for punitive damages".[191] A matter may be exempted from arbitration as provided in Local Civil Rule 201.1(d). If a matter proceeds through the arbitration process, an award shall be issued by the arbitrator as provided in Local Civil Rule 201.1(g). A party may file a demand for a trial *de novo* with the district court within 30 days of the filing of the arbitration award, or within 60 days when the US government or any employee or agency thereof is a party, with service of such demand to be accomplished within the same time frame.[192] When demand for a trial *de novo* has been timely filed and served by a party, the action is placed on the trial calendar and treated as if the arbitration did not take place.[193] If no trial *de novo* is demanded, the arbitration award filed by the arbitrator will be "unsealed and entered as the judgment of the court after the time period for demanding a trial de novo, pursuant to [Local Civil Rule] 201.1(h), has expired ... [t]he judgment so entered shall be subject to the same provisions of law, and shall have the same force and effect as a judgment of the Court in a civil action, except that it shall not be the subject of appeal".[194]

2.8 New York

While New York has not yet enacted a statutory framework expressly addressing PPPs, the Innovative Infrastructure Development Act[195] provides various New York state transportation agencies, such as the NY Department of Transportation, Bridge Authority, Thruway Authority, with the requisite authority and flexibility to enter into PPP agreements as a means of financing and delivering transportation infrastructure projects. The act neither addresses nor mandates the use of a particular form of dispute resolution; thus in the absence of a contractual agreement between the parties to the contrary, the default method of dispute resolution is litigation.

The manner of resolving disputes arising out of a construction project is typically dictated by the agreement of the parties as set forth in the relevant contract. If a

---

189 USDC DNJ L Civ R 301.1 (2012).
190 *Ibid.*
191 USDC DNJ L Civ R 201.1(d)(1) (2012).
192 USDC DNJ L Civ R 201.1(h)(1) (2012).
193 USDC DNJ L Civ R 201.1(h)(2) (2012).
194 USDC DNJ L Civ R 201.1(g) (2012).
195 The Innovative Infrastructure Development Act, Section 5445, 234th Leg, Reg Sess (NY 2011), was introduced to the New York Senate in May 2011, during the 234th Legislative Session, and as at July 2013 has yet to be enacted.

contract does not exist between the parties to the dispute, or if the relevant contract does not specify an agreed method of dispute resolution, the default is for the dispute to be resolved through litigation in state or federal court. Default resolution by litigation is not dependent on the nature of the project to which the dispute relates, but instead applies generally to all disputes, including those related to construction projects.

In New York, disputes between private parties are litigated in the state trial courts. Certain jurisdictions within the state have commercial components to the state trial courts that hear commercial disputes. Courts of this nature can be found in the counties of New York, Kings, Queens, Nassau, Suffolk, Westchester, Onondaga and Albany, as well as in the districts around Rochester and Buffalo.

If a state agency is a party to the litigation, the dispute will be heard in the state court of claims – for example, cases involving the New York Department of Transportation. Cases involving the New York Bridge Authority and the New York Thruway Authority are typically heard in a state trial court in the county where the project was located, or where the authority in question has its main office. Though not mandated by statute or otherwise, dispute review boards have been used by several New York transportation authorities and agencies.

Even though litigation is the default method of resolving disputes, parties may agree by contract to pursue resolution through arbitration or mediation. New York State and the various municipalities rarely participate in arbitration.

New York did not adopt the Uniform Arbitration Act, but it has enacted laws governing the arbitration of certain disputes as set out in Section 75 of its Civil Procedure Law and Rules. Although not identical, Section 75 of the Civil Procedure Law and Rules is similar to the Uniform Arbitration Act.

Absent a contractual agreement to the contrary, Section 75 of the Civil Procedure Law and Rules operates as the default law governing arbitrations in New York. Close attention must be paid, however, to the interplay between Section 75 and the Federal Arbitration Act. In *Diamond Waterproofing Systems,* the Court of Appeals of New York held that the FAA governs all written agreements to arbitrate in contracts affecting interstate commerce.[196] The US Supreme Court has interpreted the Federal Arbitration Act's reach broadly, such that most if not all New York-based construction projects are covered by the act.[197]

Section 75 of the Civil Procedure Law and Rules governs the arbitration proceedings when the application of the Federal Arbitration Act is not triggered by law or contract. There are significant differences between the provisions of New York law and those of the act. For example, under New York law, arbitrators do not have the power to award punitive damages even if the parties agree that they do.[198] Parties should also be aware that Section 7502-03 of the Civil Procedure Law and Rules allows a party to avoid arbitration of disputes over statute of limitations issues, and

196 See *Diamond Waterproofing Systems, Inc v 55 Liberty Owners Corp*, 4 NY 3d 247, 793 NY S 2d 831, 826 NE 2d 802 (2005).

197 See *Citizens Bank v Alafabco*, 539 US 52 (2003); *Wein & Malkin, LLP v Helmsley-Spear, Inc*, 540 US 801 (2003).

198 See *Garrity v Lyle Stuart, Inc*, 40 NY 2d 354, 386 NYS 2d 831 (1976).

Section 7513 prohibits the award of attorneys' fees in arbitration proceedings absent agreement of the parties.

2.9 Virginia

Virginia was an early leader among US states in embracing PPPs and enacting a statutory framework governing the use of such agreements. Virginia codified these regulations in the Public-Private Transportation Act 1995[199] and the Public-Private Education Facilities and Infrastructure Act 2002.[200] Neither of those acts requires the use of a particular method of dispute resolution, nor do they otherwise address the resolution of disputes arising between parties to a PPP agreement. As a result, absent a contractual agreement to the contrary the default method of resolving a dispute arising out of a PPP agreement would be litigation.

As is the case with other US states, in Virginia the manner of resolving disputes arising out of a construction project is often dictated by the agreement of the parties as set out in the relevant contract. If a contract does not exist between the parties to the dispute, or if the relevant contract does not specify an agreed method of dispute resolution, the default is for the dispute to be resolved through litigation in the state or federal courts of Virginia. Default resolution by litigation is not dependent on the nature of the project to which the dispute relates, but instead applies generally to the resolution of all disputes, including those arising on projects in Virginia involving infrastructure, PPPs or other types of construction.

Although disputes between private parties are litigated in both state and federal courts in Virginia, claims against a governmental entity must be made in compliance with the Virginia Public Procurement Act.[201] The act contains specific requirements addressing claims and notice of claims, particularly with respect to timing. The claim procedures set forth in the act include the submission of the claim to the public body for consideration and decision. Strict compliance with the claims procedures of the act is required, as is receipt of a decision by the public body on the claim (absent its failure to render a decision within the times set forth by contract or statute), before a contractor may initiate legal proceedings related to the claim.[202] A contractor may also opt to seek compensation for a denied claim through an administrative appeal or through direct legal action in the manner and within the time period provided by the act.[203] The provisions of the act do not expressly exclude the application of the act or its requirements from projects involving PPPs. Likewise, there is no provision in the Virginia Public Procurement Act that requires disputes between private parties on a project involving state or municipal funding to adhere to the dispute procedures set out in the act; however, it is noted that the contracts on such projects often contain the same notice requirements to protect the prime contractor. Section 2.2-4366 of the act expressly authorises governmental entities to submit disputes to arbitration and to "utilize mediation and other alternative dispute resolution

---

199 Va Code Ann, Sections 56-556 – 56-575.
200 Va Code Ann, Sections 56-575.1 – 56-575.17
201 Va Code Ann, Sections 2.2-4300 and following.
202 Va Code Ann, Sections 2.2-4363–2.2-4365.
203 *Ibid.*

procedures". However, any such procedures are non-binding and are subject to the provisions of Section 2.2-514 of the Virginia Code regarding the settlement and compromise of disputes involving state interests.[204]

Beyond the context of litigated disputes subject to the Virginia Public Procurement Act, the state of Virginia and its courts encourage the use of alternative dispute resolution to facilitate early resolution. Courts in Virginia are granted explicit authority under Section 8.01-576.5 of the Virginia Code to refer the parties to a contested dispute to a free 'orientation session' during which dispute resolution options are discussed with a neutral who "screen[s] for factors that would make the case inappropriate for a dispute resolution proceeding, and assist[s] the parties in determining whether their case is suitable for a dispute resolution process such as mediation".[205] The parties are able to opt out of participation in the orientation session as provided in Section 8.01-576.6.

In addition to those statutory provisions authorising court-referred dispute resolution proceedings, the Virginia code provides a framework by which the parties to a civil proceeding may "elect to have a summary jury trial on the issues of the case" to facilitate resolution.[206] Under the summary jury trial procedures, the judge having jurisdiction over the case likewise presides over the summary trial during which summaries of the issues and evidence are presented on behalf of each party.[207] The submission of witness testimony and documentary evidence is not permitted unless stipulated or agreed to by the parties.[208] Except by written agreement of the parties submitted to the court before the start of the proceedings, any verdict issued by the jury is neither binding nor admissible in any subsequent trial of the case.[209] The provisions of Virginia law addressing court-referred dispute resolution proceedings and summary jury trial proceedings apply generally to litigated matters and would thus be available to parties involved in any construction dispute as an option to facilitate early resolution.

The state of Virginia does not require the use of dispute review boards (DRBs) to facilitate the disputes arising in connection with public construction projects, including those involving PPPs or infrastructure. Nonetheless, as is the case in the nearby jurisdictions of Washington DC and Maryland, the DRB Foundation's database reflects the Virginia Department of Transportation's use of DRBs on certain projects.[210]

Parties may agree by contract to resolve disputes through arbitration rather than litigation. As is the case in other US states, Virginia has enacted a state arbitration act modeled after the Uniform Arbitration Act. The Virginia Uniform Arbitration Act[211] provides the statutory framework for the resolution of disputes where the parties have contractually agreed to go to arbitration. The act governs binding arbitration

204 Va Code Ann, Sections 2.2-4366, Section 2.2-514.
205 Va Code Ann, Section 8.01-576.5 (2013).
206 Va Code Ann, Sections 8.01-576.1–576.3.
207 Va Code Ann, Section 8.01-576.3 (2013).
208 *Ibid.*
209 *Ibid.*
210 www.drb.org/manual/Database_2005-State.xls.
211 Va Code Ann, Sections 8.01-581.01 and following.

proceedings in Virginia absent either a contractual choice-of-law provision to the contrary or an underlying contract affecting interstate commerce. The Federal Arbitration Act applies to disputes involving contracts that affect interstate commerce.[212]

2.10 Washington DC

The District of Columbia (DC) has yet to enact a statutory scheme authorising the general use of PPPs. However, some laws and regulations, such as the New Town at Capital City Market Revitalization Development and Public/Private Partnership Act of 2006, have been enacted allowing for the use of PPPs in specific circumstances.[213] The most common method of enabling the use of PPPs in DC has involved the promulgation of a regulation allowing the mayor to enter into a specific PPP agreement. As the laws and regulations authorising the use of PPP agreements in DC have, to date, been project specific, the method of resolving disputes arising from such PPPs is not addressed in broad statutory language but is instead dictated by the contract terms set out within each agreement. In the absence of contract terms to the contrary, the default method of dispute resolution would be the same as is generally seen throughout the US – litigation in a court of appropriate jurisdiction.

While litigation before a court is the default method of resolving disputes between private parties, under DC law access to a traditional judicial process is limited in disputes involving governmental entities or government funding since a contractor may not file a lawsuit until all required administrative remedies have been exhausted.[214] Claims falling within the jurisdiction of the District of Columbia Contract Appeals Board (DCCAB) must be initiated and determined through the administrative processes of the board before subject matter jurisdiction will vest with a court. The DCCAB maintains exclusive jurisdiction over disputes in which a governmental entity of the district is a party, as well as those disputes arising from construction projects involving state or municipal funding.[215] The DCCAB thus has exclusive jurisdiction over protests or claims arising from the administration or award of contracts by the District of Columbia, as well as over appeals from a final decision issued by the contracting officer on a claim arising under or relating to such a contract.[216] A decision issued by the DCCAB may be appealed to the District of Columbia Court of Appeals within 120 days of receipt of a copy of such a decision.[217]

Although participation in alternative dispute resolution is not mandatory, the DCCAB provides for, and encourages the use of, ADR as a means of achieving early resolution of claims.[218] The Code of DC Municipal Regulations, Section 27-217, does not mandate a particular method of ADR but instead provides that the code "will consider the use of any technique proposed by the parties which is deemed to be fair,

---

212 *MC Constr Corp v Gray & Co*, 17 F Supp 22 541 (WD Va 1998).
213 DC Code, Section 6-1062.02(1).
214 *Davis & Assoc v Williams*, 892 A 2d 1144 (DC App 2006).
215 DC Code, Section 2-360.03.
216 DC Code, Sections 2-360.03–2-360.04; see also, *Francis v Recycling Solutions, Inc*, 695 A 2d 63 (DC App 1997).
217 DC Code, Section 2-360.05 (2012).
218 Code of DC Municipal Regulations, Section 27-217.

reasonable, and in the best interest of the parties, the Board, and the resolution of disputes".[219] Section 27-217 of the code identifies examples of available ADR techniques, including:

- mediation;
- non-binding neutral case evaluation involving either informal or formal proffers of evidence to include mini-trials;
- binding, non-appealable decision by a board judge; and
- use of a modified version of any of the above techniques or other ADR techniques not requiring the direct involvement of the board.[220]

DC's public contracting laws do not specifically address the use of dispute review boards (DRBs) on projects involving PPPs, infrastructure or other construction. Nonetheless, the database maintained by the Dispute Review Board Foundation evidences the use of DRBs on disputes involving the Washington Metropolitan Area Transit Authority. [221]

The DC state courts likewise encourage, but do not mandate, the use of ADR to facilitate early resolution of disputes pending before the courts. Though no provision of the DC Code or other regulation codifies the use of mini-trials, the procedure has been used by some courts to facilitate settlement.[222] Subject to a few exceptions unlikely to be incurred in the context of a dispute involving a construction project, all matters litigated before the civil division of the District of Columbia Superior Court are eligible for referral to non-binding arbitration through the Superior Court civil arbitration programme.[223] Though Rule 1 specifies any such arbitration is non-binding, it provides procedures by which the parties may agree to binding arbitration.[224] A party to a non-binding arbitration that wishes to, in effect, appeal an arbitration award must file a demand for a trial *de novo* within 15 days after the filing of the award, which demand returns the case to the court's trial calendar.[225] The trial *de novo* is then conducted as though no arbitration proceeding occurred.[226]

Arbitration of construction disputes is most commonly encountered in situations where the parties have agreed, by contract, to arbitrate any disputes that may later arise. DC has enacted a framework to govern such arbitrations as codified in the District of Columbia Revised Uniform Arbitration Act.[227] The act governs all agreements to go to arbitration, whenever made.[228] Nonetheless, the Federal Arbitration Act[229] applies in any case where the contract at issue affects interstate commerce.[230]

---

219 *Ibid.*
220 *Ibid.*
221 www.drb.org/manual/Database_2005-State.xls.
222 See *Bahura v SEW Investors*, 754 A 2d 928, 932 (DC App 2000).
223 DC Supreme Court, Civ Arbit Rule I.
224 *Ibid.*
225 DC Supreme Court, Civ Arbit Rule XI.
226 *Ibid.*
227 DC Code Sections 16-4401 and following.
228 See *Giron v Dodds*, 35 A 3d 433 (DC App 2012).
229 9 USC, Sections 1 and following.
230 *Hercules & Co Ltd v Beltway Carpet Service, Inc*, 592 A 2d 1069 (DC App 1991).

3. Conclusion

Anyone considering participation in a construction project in the United States should know that the number of government agencies – state and federal – with jurisdiction over any particular project will vary and depend to a large extent on the location of the project, and also on the extent to which public funds are, directly or indirectly, used for the project.

Many or all of the government agencies with jurisdiction over a project require that the owner of the project (whether public or private) obtain a permit to perform the portion or aspect of the project regulated by each particular government agency. In addition, many of these government agencies require inspection and final approval of the portions of the work or aspects of the project which are subject to the various agency jurisdictions. These permitting, inspection and approval requirements are often transferred contractually to the entity that contracts with the public owner for the design and construction of the project, and compliance with all of the foregoing regulation is invariably included among the requirements for project delivery and payment.

Brazil

Fabio P Alem
Victor Madeira Filho
Madeira, Valentim & Alem Advogados

1. Introduction

Brazil has faced long periods without consistent investment in infrastructure and construction, which has left it lagging behind other global players. As a result, infrastructure limitations – particularly in the logistics and energy sectors – have hindered its economic development.

Over the past two decades Brazil has tried to enhance the quality of its infrastructure, in order to support sustained economic growth and to provide Brazilians with a better quality of life. The Brazilian economy was reorganised by drastically reducing inflation, and other measures were taken to increase productivity and services quality as well as to improve security for investors. Faster and more specific methods to resolve conflicts using arbitration and other alternative dispute resolution (ADR) methods, without depending exclusively on the traditional Brazilian judicial system (considered by many as slow and bureaucratic), were devised.

There is still a lot to do before Brazil becomes a world market leader, and the construction/infrastructure sectors will benefit further from the 2014 World Cup and the 2016 Olympic and Paralympic Games in Rio de Janeiro.

The private and public sectors are interested in developing and executing projects that will enable Brazil – the fifth-biggest economy in the world – to be on a par with the other BRIC countries of Russia, India and China. Such achievements, however, depend on the public and private sectors, as well as domestic and international investors. The Brazilian government has created specific construction/infrastructure investment plans: direct investment is facilitated through the Growth Acceleration Programme and indirect investment is promoted through tax benefits or other federal incentives. Other social and education plans are also being implemented by the Brazilian government, with the support and participation of the private sector.

Regardless of the measures that have been taken by the Brazilian government, only a few private companies are taking the opportunity to participate, despite the potential in a broad range of fields, notably construction/infrastructure, technology and education.

Access to the Brazilian market is hampered by lack of knowledge and insecurity about Brazil's legal and dispute resolution systems. Thus, Brazil needs to take measures to drastically reduce corruption levels and bureaucracy. It also needs to enhance the security of business transactions by having clear laws and rules, and a faster, more solid dispute resolution system – particularly in connection with strategic construction/infrastructure projects that are necessary to Brazil's development in many areas.

2. Construction and infrastructure sectors

The public and private sectors are supporting a broad range of construction/infrastructure projects that are strategic and relevant to the country's development. Such projects have a high demand for labour, equipment, raw materials, steel, cement and other construction materials, as well as related services such as design, management, civil works, erection, assembly and supervision. In 2011, it was estimated that the construction/infrastructure industry represented 16.4% of Brazil's gross domestic product (GDP), which in that year was worth the equivalent of US$2.3 trillion. Between 2012 and 2020 Brazil expects to receive approximately $809.4 billion of investment for construction/infrastructure projects.

Despite the efforts of the public and private sectors, large-scale projects face several difficult challenges, including inadequate contract models, construction management difficulties, bureaucracy relating to licences and permits, lack of skilled manpower, strong environmental control, social disturbances (from indigenous and labour unions or associations, and Brazil's Landless Rural Workers' Movement, among others), legal restrictions and other common issues relating to large-scale construction projects, whether private or public funded. For example, according to ANEEL (the Brazilian electricity regulator), of the 28 hydroelectric power plant projects under way, 20 are currently delayed. Such delays are mainly due to difficulties in obtaining licences and environmental permits, judicial embargoes, lack of execution efficiency and productivity, as well as strikes and social disturbances.

Among the challenging hydroelectric power plant projects that have been started, three are destined to be in the largest top 15 in the world. One of these projects is Belo Monte Dam, a large project in the northern region next to the Amazon area. It is costing R18 billion (approximately $8 billion) and is expected to be the world's third-largest hydroelectric power plant. Belo Monte has faced, and is still facing, serious construction problems due to environmental issues, indigenous and workers' social movements, and strikes. Other examples are the Jirau and Santo Antonio Dams (the latter has now started commercial operation), also in Brazil's northern region, which have also faced similar difficulties.

Regardless of the challenges, the construction/infrastructure market is still growing and new business opportunities are being created. Moreover, upcoming major sport events in 2014 and 2016 have made the Brazilian market even more interesting to major companies and investors. There are also many public projects that could be great opportunities for domestic or international companies.

The soccer stadium projects relating to the 2014 World Cup are still in the execution stage; only two have been concluded and most are over budget and behind schedule. These delays prompted serious discussions between FIFA and the Brazilian government, which have been temporarily resolved. Everybody involved is aware that the 2014 World Cup local organisation committee will need to get the work done before the competition starts, even though this will be costly, in order to maintain credibility.

The overall government investment planned to host the 2014 World Cup is over $12 billion. Private investments are also being made, mostly with government support, to provide better accommodation facilities, transport, catering, telecommunications and other services related to major sporting events. According to the government, the total investment in this event is about R33 billion (around US$14.6 billion). However, expected income from tourism during just the month that the 2014 World Cup takes place is R9.4 billion.

Unfortunately, a lot less than what was initially expected was effectively implemented. Many urgent contracts – with their related high costs – will be necessary to fulfil what is expected of a country hosting such a major event. Consequently, the amount spent by the government is greater than expected and the infrastructure may not be the best.

The 2016 Olympic and Paralympic Games will hopefully have a significant impact on the infrastructure and economies of Rio de Janeiro and other areas. Rio de Janeiro is currently experiencing an increase in the cost of living, services and real estate prices, as well as greater exposure and interest from international companies. Roughly $15 billion is expected to be invested in Rio de Janeiro exclusively on infrastructure investments.

One of the most recent examples is the large investment made by a company owned by Donald Trump, which will develop five business towers in the city centre, next to the port of Rio de Janeiro, an area that the city government intends to transform in the next few years into a new business and commercial centre. According to the developers, work will probably start in the second half of 2013 and sales are expected to reach R3 billion.

Many other construction/infrastructure projects are being developed throughout Brazil, such as the renovation of airports and ports, the construction of new rail links and roads to improve logistics and increase productivity and exports, as well as the construction of millions of new low-cost houses. The Brazilian government is stepping up the sale of infrastructure concessions, having already issued public concessions for airports in São Paulo, Campinas and Brasília, which are being expanded to cope with the major sporting events in 2014 and 2016. It is also preparing to offload R133 billion of road, rail and port concessions. Together with each project comes a number of social investments that will increase Brazil's economic capacity in the future. Many relevant education programmes are being created by all levels of the Brazilian government (federal, state and municipal), which will also boost the Brazilian economy.

All of these initiatives have increased the number of public concessions and public-private partnerships (PPPs), with the possibility that international companies will be able to participate in public bids. The need for more specific and detailed contracts has created more specialised practice areas for lawyers. Specialised contracts include DBBs (design-bid-build), EPCM (engineering, procurement and construction management), EPC (engineering, procurement and construction), alliance/partnering, DBOOT (design, build, own, operate, transfer) and bespoke versions of international standard forms.

The most common models for public construction contracts are still the traditional public schemes (ie, concessions, permissions and public works bids). However, due to the recent need for private investment in critical construction/infrastructure projects relating to major sporting events in 2014 and 2016, the PPP model has been used more consistently with relative success. One PPP example relating to the 2014 World Cup is the Mineirão soccer stadium construction in Belo Horizonte, in the state of Minas Gerais, which was completed on time and is considered an example of good practice to be followed. Other PPP models are being executed in Brazil, but the majority of the public contracts still use the traditional public concession model. Perhaps one of the legacies that the above-mentioned major sporting events will give to Brazil is the development and use of more effective scheme models, such as the PPP model.

In Brazil, large-scale construction projects typically require direct financing by the investor without the contractor having to provide the land or even pre-finance construction. Such projects are normally financed by a project finance structure, led by a senior bank – in many cases by publicly owned banks and by the Brazilian Development Bank (BNDES), the main financing agent for development in Brazil. Regardless of whether investors are public or private, they normally require insurance (performance) bonds and bank guarantees, as well as contractual rights, such as step-in rights, parent company guarantees and warranties.

During times like these, disputes often arise and many ultimately must be resolved by the legal system. Disputes over delays, inefficiencies, changes to the contracted scope of work, change orders/out-of-scope issues, differing site conditions, economic imbalances in the contract and defective scope, as well as enforcement of bonds (performance and/or advance payment bonds) and insurance policies, are the most frequent disputes in Brazilian construction projects and usually involve significant amounts of money.

In view of the risks involved in such disputes, owners, contractors, designers, suppliers, managers, insurance companies and sponsors require more specialised, technical, speedy and reliable methods of dispute resolution methods. The Brazilian dispute resolution system needs to provide domestic and international companies/investors with the security that any controversy will be resolved rapidly, be definitive, have substance and be settled by a specialised judge or arbitrator.

3. Frequently used dispute resolution methods for construction/ infrastructure projects

In parallel with the economic and financial aspects mentioned above, Brazil can be considered a real player in the world market only if it can demonstrate internationally that its legal system is solid and that dispute resolution will be undertaken by qualified and expert judges (or arbitrators) within a reasonable period of time.

The Brazilian legal system is a complex system based on codified statutes that have been modified over the years to accommodate the inevitable influence of common law. Regardless of the recent investments in technology and training, an increase in personnel, and new rules to provide more security and speed to judicial proceedings, the conclusion of a lawsuit still takes a long time (around six to eight years at first and second instances) in comparison with other methods such as arbitration, which takes roughly 12 months to reach a final award.

In spite of the modifications that are being made to the Brazilian judicial system, notably in the largest economic centres (the southeast, southern and central-west areas), the Brazilian judicial system is still slow and less effective compared with other methods of dispute resolution, such as arbitration, mediation, dispute resolution boards (DRBs) and dispute adjudication boards (DABs).

The wide range of appeals that may stay the proceedings, the low productivity of the judicial system and the existing difficulties linked to the enforcement of final judicial decisions are some of the problems faced by conflicting parties that appear before the Brazilian courts.

In Brazil, arbitration has grown considerably during the past 10 years, since the Federal Supreme Court decided that the Brazilian Arbitration Law was fully in accordance with the Federal Constitution. Such growth stemmed from the need to obtain a faster and more specialised method of resolving controversies, as well as from the relevant support provided by the judiciary that gave strength to the arbitral awards and avoided attempts by losing parties to obtain annulments. Currently 10% of arbitration cases under way before the International Chamber of Commerce involve Brazilian companies. The number of proceedings managed by the Centre of Arbitration and Mediation of the Brazil–Canada Chamber of Commerce grew from 63 in 2011 to 319 in 2012, which shows the effectiveness of changes to the arbitration market in Brazil.

Arbitration is a natural choice for Brazilian companies and lawyers, due to Brazil's civil law background. Both private and public companies are willing to use arbitration as an alternative method to resolve disputes. Brazilians are also learning that using other methods to resolve controversies more amicably is usually better for business. Thus, large and mid-size companies are increasingly more concerned about saving time and money and finishing a project on time, than being the winner or loser in an arbitration proceeding.

Once arbitration was established in Brazil, the construction sector started using it as the main method to resolve disputes. International arbitration institutions are commonly used by Brazilian companies to administrate large-scale arbitrations, mainly because of their past experience of complex cases. Brazilian institutions, however, are developing their expertise and increasing their participation, contributing to a sharp increase in the number of arbitrations.

Other methods to resolve controversies are also used in the construction sector. DRBs have been used:

- on the São Paulo Metro Line 4, a PPP construction project that started in 2004 and is due to end in 2013;
- for the Belo Monte and Jirau hydroelectric power plants currently under way; and
- for the Jurong Aracruz shipyard in Espírito Santo State.

Ad hoc methods such as the creation of specialised groups (technical, procurement and legal) that work to manage and resolve potential claims during project execution are also used. In Brazil, such methods are still being developed but are seen as an interesting option, mainly for complex and large-scale projects in which the stakes involved are high.

Infrastructure construction projects are technically complex, time consuming and of significant value, and involve a spectrum of participants with different interests. Claims and disputes arising out of construction projects are almost inevitable and most end up becoming disputes. Construction project disputes often involve very technical subject matter that needs to be dealt with by a specialised arbitrator, hand-picked by the parties, rather than by a national court judge with little or no prior knowledge or experience in the field. An arbitrator's specialised competence normally increases the quality of the decision, but also the efficiency of the proceedings, with more detailed and specialised production of evidence and cross-examination hearings.

Other areas related to infrastructure – oil and gas, technology, transportation, mining, equipment and product supply – are also now widely using arbitration as the main method for resolving conflicts in Brazil. Financial and corporate matters are also commonly subject to arbitration; again, these are complex issues that require arbitrators to have very specific knowledge.

The parties involved in construction and infrastructure project negotiations must be made aware of the importance of drafting a clear and executable arbitration clause that can then be used to resolve any controversies. Drafting an arbitration clause can sometimes be forgotten during contract negotiations, but this omission could jeopardise future conflict resolution.

There are several methods used for drafting an arbitration clause. One of the most commonly used in complex cases is multi-tier clauses. This method provides the parties with the opportunity to search for previous, less-litigious ways to resolve the conflict. Normally, multi-tier clauses establish the following methods of ADR: negotiation; conciliation or mediation; and adjudication or, in some instances, expert determination.

Ad hoc arbitration has decreased over the years, while institutional arbitration has risen, mainly in connection with complex infrastructure projects. The predictability of procedures and how the arbitration will be managed have given more security to the parties involved. Initially, most arbitration proceedings were managed by international arbitrators but now domestic institutions are more commonly used because of their growing knowledge and expertise. In short, Brazilians are getting more used to seeing arbitration as a solid and reliable alternative method of dispute resolution than traditionally complex and protracted litigation.

Institutions have different areas of specialisation – for example, energy, capital markets, construction/engineering, labour. There are others, however, that are multi-service arbitration institutions and these are also improving their services. The majority of construction and infrastructure projects have chosen well-known domestic or international institutions to manage their dispute resolution proceedings. International institutions most used by Brazilian companies are the Centre of Arbitration of the International Chamber of Commerce, the American Arbitration Association, the International Centre for Disputes Resolution and the London Court of International Arbitration. Domestic institutions most commonly used by Brazilian companies are the Centre of Arbitration and Mediation of the Brazil–Canada Chamber of Commerce (CAM-CCBC), the Centre of Arbitration and Mediation of the São Paulo's Federation of Commerce (CAM-FIESP) and the Centre of Arbitration and Mediation of Fundação Getúlio Vargas (FGV).

There are also specific aspects to be considered in construction and infrastructure cases, notably with regard to expert examination. In such cases, there is considerable potential in the market for specialists who can act as experts in complex cases. The support of international consultants in all types of infrastructure project is most welcome and should be viewed as an opportunity in this very specialised market.

Foreign companies intending to enter Brazil's specific and complex market need to take into consideration its legal security and dispute resolution aspects, as well as making a strategic analysis of the market and economy.

4. Least-used or forbidden dispute resolution methods

Brazilians are accustomed to having a third party or a neutral party decide their controversies, so even when there are provisions to resolve disputes by using experts to support the parties, most controversies end up in court or use arbitration. So less aggressive dispute resolution methods are rarely used effectively in Brazil. The forbidden methods are those that are contrary to the Federal Constitution or federal law, which are seen as contrary to public order – for example, non-compliance with the due process of law or the international treaties signed by Brazil, or, among other things, the Federal Constitution principles.

A well-known method of resolving conflicts relating to international investment is ADR under the International Centre for the Settlement of Investment Disputes (ICSID) Convention rules. However, in Brazil this method cannot be used, as Brazil still has not signed the ICSID Convention (Washington Convention) and the dispute resolution procedure relating to the Convention on the Settlement of Investment Disputes between States and Nationals of Other States is not applicable to Brazil. As a result, some of the Mercosur regulations are also not applicable to Brazil. Investors in infrastructure construction projects must also be aware that any dispute resolution involving Brazil will not consider the state of Brazil as party to the dispute, but only the private or public company that is directly related to the case.

Finally, the International Federation of Consulting Engineers contract models are not commonly used by Brazilian companies (which have their own contract models, as previously mentioned).

5. Dispute resolution in Brazil

Significant reforms to the Brazilian judicial system include training at all levels, an increase in the number of court judges and second-instance judges, as well as the creation of more specialised courts. While the effects will only be felt in the long term, in the meantime Brazilians are learning how to use more effectively ADR methods such as negotiation, mediation, adjudication and arbitration. Brazilians understand that, at the outset, good project management of a large-scale infrastructure construction project is more important to all parties involved than having to resort to arbitration later to resolve conflicts.

Brazil has recently approved the application of the United Nations Convention on Contracts for the International Sale of Goods (CSID) through Decree-Law 538/2012. This positions Brazil as one of the global players in the international sale-of-goods market, mainly as a strong exporter. The approval of CISD shows the Brazilian government's commitment to creating a safer platform for other countries to do business with Brazilian companies based on global rules. This is a strong signal to foreign entities that Brazil is seeking to become a worldwide player in many fields.

Many attempts to modify the current Arbitration Law (Law 9307/96) have occurred over the past decade, but most stalled because arbitration in Brazil was in its consolidation phase. After 10 years of discussion, Brazil is facing a fresh attempt to modify or create a new Arbitration Law through a bill (Law 2.937/11) which aims to increase the number of cases in which the judiciary can review the merits of an arbitral award. If such a modification progresses (which is unlikely) all of the innovation and benefits to the litigation and commercial market brought by the current Arbitration Law will be wasted.

In principle, the current Arbitration Law should remain unchanged and the security it gives investors and international companies will be maintained and even expanded in the future.

6. Conclusion

It is clear that Brazil is going through a period of change and consolidation, with financial and economic improvement, and it has the potential to become a major international player in many areas.

Brazil's recent signing of the CISD, which will provide more security for international sale-of-goods transactions, is one measure among others taken by the Brazilian government to convince the international community that doing business with Brazil is safe, or at least low risk.

While Brazil maintains its traditional position of not signing up to the ICSID Convention, this should not deter international investors, as the Brazilian system is being improved to provide more security to investors in the public and private sectors. In order to achieve its intended goals and to continue its sustainable growth, investment will have to be made in many fields associated with the legal and dispute resolution system – again, to provide the necessary security to investors and companies that are active in the Brazilian market.

Currently, arbitration is the ADR method most commonly used to resolve conflicts relating to construction/infrastructure cases. Other ADR methods such as DRBs, adjudication or expert determination, are used to a lesser extent. This provides companies with a faster and more structured way to obtain a more specific resolution to complex or strategic conflicts.

Chile

Oscar Aitken
Carey y Cía

---

1. Introduction

The Chilean engineering and construction industry has evolved in line with a general consistent and solid growth pattern in the Chilean economy over the past last three decades or so. As a result of the development of the mining industry, with major international companies assuming important positions within the Chilean market, engineering and construction contract standards have become more and more sophisticated, including their dispute resolution mechanisms.

At present, Chile has a well-developed engineering and construction industry, with large international and global contractors and major regional and local contractors co-existing with many of the mid- and small-sized contractors and construction companies.

From a legal perspective, the Chilean legal system has belonged to the civil law tradition, favouring a 'civil law' type of construction agreement. However, in the past two decades or so, a 'common law' type of contract has been more and more customary for larger projects, particularly in the mining and energy industry and for projects where international project financing arrangements have been used. Such contracts are usually 'Chileanised' to work under Chile's legal system. At present no standard forms of agreement are used in the country, and foreign or international forms such as FIDIC or NEC are rarely used.

Each construction industry has its own distinctive features. For example, the practices and standards found in mining or energy can be quite different from those found in the housing, office or general industrial sectors. However, and with few exceptions, arbitration is overall the preferred dispute resolution method when direct negotiation fails to resolve a dispute.

At the time of writing the construction sector is very active, resulting in a 'contractor's market' (seeing increased costs, scarcity of labour, reluctance of contractors to take unreasonable risks, etc).

2. General overview

Most of the traditional dispute mechanisms are available in Chile, with some more frequently used than others. They are outlined next.

2.1 Arbitration

Arbitration is statistically the preferred route for dispute resolution. Most contracts for medium-sized and upwards projects will contemplate a prior step of direct negotiations at various levels, whether or not as a precondition to triggering arbitration.

Contracts for smaller projects may not expressly contemplate any prior negotiation process, but it is certainly common practice to exhaust all reasonable negotiating efforts before engaging in arbitration or mediation. As the number of key players in the Chilean construction sector is fairly small, contractors will be motivated to avoid initiating arbitration as far as possible, as any such action could potentially damage their reputation. Owners appreciate that, for certain kinds of work, having issues with one contractor shortens the list of contractual partners for future projects, potentially leaving them tied to a contractor whose work they might not be completely happy with. This has resulted in the creation of hubs and long-term alliances between owners and contractors, which help minimise the number of disputes (at least unresolved ones), with both parties being incentivised to be reasonable.

At present, mid-sized and large contracts will mostly employ institutional arbitration rules: namely those of the Santiago Chamber of Commerce Arbitration and Mediation Center (CAM Santiago). CAM Santiago offers specific rules for international or domestic arbitration and for both arbitration of law and *ex aequo et bono*. UNCITRAL and *ad hoc* arbitration are also used. ICC rules are used for a fair number of projects, usually where international contractors or project financing is involved.

Typically, arbitration in mid-sized and large projects or with some international component will be arbitration at law, meaning that the arbitration tribunal will rule on the dispute applying the substantive law chosen by the parties. Small local projects frequently favour arbitration *ex aequo et bono*, particularly if the contract draft is prepared by the contractors; it is common for certain contractors also to push for this system since it presents them with more flexibility under owner-prepared contracts.

2.2 Mediation

The uptake of mediation is quite low, but increasing. Institutional mediation services are available locally from CAM Santiago. As mediation is usually not binding, parties see this method as time-consuming/expensive and not very different from direct negotiation. The existence of 'ITOs', as we see further below in section 3.2, has also affected the use of mediation, which is more commonly found in contracts with international parties.

In summary, despite its internationally recognised effectiveness and the fact that the Center of Arbitration and Mediation of the Santiago Chamber of Commerce (CAM Santiago) offers institutionally assisted mediation, this form of dispute resolution is not widely used in Chile.

2.3 Expert determinations

Expert determinations are not frequently used and, when used, are normally restricted to certain technical aspects that could lead to disputes. In most cases, the expert determination tends to be non-binding. In a minority of cases, such determination would be binding (unless and until challenged through arbitration).

2.4 Dispute resolution boards

Dispute resolution boards are very rarely used. There is no legislation dealing with dispute adjudication boards and there appears to be some reluctance to use them. The writer is, however, aware of a couple of projects where dispute resolution boards have been employed.

A rather unique dispute resolution mechanism that has been quite successful in Chile is the 'expert panel', as set out in the concessions (PPP) legislation (see section 5 below).

2.5 Litigation

Last but not least, litigation is always present as a dispute resolution mechanism. Litigation most typically happens in construction contracts where contract parties involve the State of Chile, state-owned companies, governmental agencies, the armed forces or similar type of 'owners'. Decennial liability (applicable to certain work) is also typically handled through litigation, particularly when the claimant is not the party who commissioned the construction work but acquired the property later on.

3. Most commonly used dispute resolution mechanisms

3.1 Direct negotiation

Whether or not formally agreed upon in the contract as a dispute resolution mechanism, direct negotiation is almost always the first mechanism of choice for the parties to try to find a resolution to their dispute.

Sophisticated contracts and/or contracts for larger projects will typically include a 'stepped' negotiation procedure. The process will begin with the site-level project teams, then move to project directors and, ultimately, to upper-level executives (general managers, CEOs, etc). Some contracts may involve 'project control' groups or teams as a second tier.

In recent years, some contractors have been trying to convince owners to include a new direct negotiation mechanism which consists of forming, as from the execution of the contract, a 'claim/steering committee' of senior representatives of the contractor and owner (and agents or administrators, when applicable). Although contractors claim that this system tends to have the effect of reducing claims, such a system can present problems to owners, as it is the contractor who is in control of the site, relevant information, workers, etc. When the system is incorporated, it will usually be 'non-binding' – designed as just a step within the contract dispute mechanism.

3.2 ITO determinations

ITO (*Inspección Técnica de la Obra*) corresponds to specialised entities that: oversee the construction from a technical perspective; approve or pre-approve payment statements or progress payment requests etc; and are often contractually empowered to issue determinations, clarifications, instructions and similar directions to the contractor on technical matters. The scope of their authority varies from contract to contract. They have been in use in Chile for decades.

These entities are hired and paid by owners but, although they represent owners' interests, many of them, because of their size and reputation, are not necessarily seen by contractors as merely an owner's *alter ego.*

ITO determinations (taking this word broadly) are often binding unless challenged by arbitration.

In the normal course of a construction project, many technical disputes are solved at the ITO level, usually with participation of the owner and other owner parties (such as architects).

ITOs are more powerful and dominant in certain industries (such as housing, commercial, office and general industrial buildings) and less common or totally absent in others (eg, mining and to some extent energy industries). In an effort to make an international comparison, they resemble an 'owner's engineer' (but they do not design anything and often have no engineering title) and have some 'expert' authority.

3.3 Arbitration

Arbitration is recognised by statute in Chile and has been widely used since at least the late 19th century. Certain disputes arbitration can even be mandatory (ie, the dispute cannot be resolved in the ordinary courts). Arbitration is by far the most widely used mechanism for dispute resolution in the construction industry. The exact form it takes will vary depending on the size of the project, nationality of the parties, the industry, etc.

Arbitrators (and arbitration in general) are deemed by statute to be part of the judiciary and are regulated by the Organic Code of Courts and the Code of Civil Procedure. The most significant consequence of this is that arbitrators are subject to the disciplinary powers of the Supreme Court – which can review arbitration awards in cases of abuse or serious fault (fraud, corruption or serious abuses when issuing the award) under a remedy known as *'Recurso de Queja'* – which cannot be waived under public policy rules since it pertains to the disciplinary powers of the Supreme Court. Under this remedy, the Court will not address incorrect interpretations of the law, or facts, nor review the merits of the award in general: it is not an appeal but a very last and ultimate resort for extreme situations, and thus can be filed only where no other remedy is available to the parties.

Until fairly recently, Chilean law did not distinguish between local or international arbitration. However, in 2004, Chile enacted Law 19.971 on International Commercial Arbitration, following the UNCITRAL Model Law (1985 version). Chile is also party to numerous treaties on international arbitration, most importantly, the New York Convention.

Chilean courts enforce local and foreign arbitration awards on a regular basis and also provide support in terms of installation or establishment of the arbitration tribunal, injunctions, forced summon of witnesses and other types of aid the arbitrators may need but which they cannot procure for themselves. The local courts will generally not interfere with arbitration awards except as highlighted below.

(a) Local arbitration

Local arbitration can deal with the remedies of appeal or others that the parties may have agreed upon either directly or as a consequence of the type or arbitration entered into. For example, under a full domestic arbitration of law with no waiver of remedies, all remedies will generally be available against the award, allowing the competent Court of Appeals to review it by means of an appeal and/or annulment remedy on procedural grounds as well as the Supreme Court, by means of annulment remedies based both on procedural grounds or substantive violation of the law.

In addition, certain very limited and restricted remedies are available in respect of local arbitration, and generally cannot be waived, including:

- *Recurso de Queja* sometimes translated as 'remedy of complaint' or 'disciplinary remedy' for cases of gross abuse, fraud, etc; and
- *Recurso de Casación en la forma*, based on *ultra petita* or lack of jurisdiction; and in respect of international arbitration, to the remedy of annulment.

Some legal commentators also argue – on constitutional grounds – that despite clear language to the contrary in the International Arbitration Act, the remedy of complaint is always available against the judgment passed by the Court of Appeals on an annulment remedy filed against international arbitration awards issued in Chile (and not directly against the arbitral award, as in that kind of case other remedies would be available to the parties).

(b) ***International arbitration***

Law 19.971 makes specific provisions determining that local courts may be involved for:

- injunctions;
- appointment of arbitrators, provided that there is no agreement on the identity of the arbitrator by the parties (where the agreement establishes that the dispute must be solved by one arbitrator) or the co-arbitrators (where the agreement provides that the dispute must be solved by three arbitrators);
- challenging of an arbitrator (provided that the arbitrator has previously dismissed the challenge filed by one of the parties);
- replacement or substitution of an arbitrator;
- lack of jurisdiction (provided that the arbitrator has previously dismissed a defence based on that lack of jurisdiction); and
- annulment remedies.

(c) ***Types of arbitration***

A first approach would require a distinction between local arbitration and international arbitration. Local arbitration is governed by the Civil Procedural Code and the Judiciary Code and international commercial arbitration is governed by Law 19.971 (as well as general principles set out in Chilean procedural regulations, which relate only to due process).

Arbitration may also be divided into: arbitration of law; 'mixed' arbitration; and arbitration *ex aequo et bono*. Strictly speaking, both the arbitration of law and mixed arbitration involve the dispute being decided according to applicable law. The difference is that the arbitration of law is also subject to the statutory procedural rules under the Code of Civil Procedure (whereas in mixed arbitration, the procedural rules are as set out by the parties or the arbitration institution or, ultimately, by the arbitrator himself, subject only to certain minimum due-process rules established in the Code of Civil Procedure).

Under the arbitration *ex aequo et bono*, arbitrators make a decision by applying the rules of prudence and equity and the procedural rules set out by the parties, the arbitration institution or the arbitrator himself, subject to minimum rules of due process set out in the Code of Civil Procedure.

Arbitration can also be institutional or *ad hoc*. Most arbitration in the past was *ad hoc*, whereby the parties would appoint the arbitrators and set out the procedural rules. Where the parties fail in such *ad hoc* arbitration proceedings to appoint individuals to serve as arbitrators, any of them may resort to the local courts to designate an arbitrator.

Local institutional arbitration has been expanding exponentially, with the Center of Arbitration of the Santiago Chamber of Commerce currently the preferred institution, both for domestic as well as international cases. The centre's case law is online at www.camsantiago.com, although the website does not yet include the lists of arbitrators (appointed by specialised committee) available for local and international arbitrations.

The ICC is probably the second choice of arbitration institution, used in construction industry disputes in Chile for larger, more complex international construction projects, especially following the 2012 amendments to the ICC Regulations. There is also a small, less-used local institutional arbitration service called Centro Nacional de Arbitrajes (CNA; see www.cna.cl).

In terms of user preferences, the following general situations apply:

- Local contractors, particularly those that are small or medium-sized, tend to prefer arbitration *ex aequo et bono* as a way to try to overcome harsh, one-sided owner's written agreements.
- Owners and larger, more sophisticated contractors tend to choose mixed institutional arbitration.
- Lenders will almost never accept arbitration *ex aequo et bono* in financed projects.
- International owners dealing with international contractors sometimes choose foreign arbitration in the United States, Canada or Europe. They are typically institutional, ICC or triple-A.

(d) Enforceability of arbitration awards

Local arbitration final awards are enforced just like any regular court awards. Courts will assist the arbitration tribunal on this where necessary – for example, to foreclose and auction assets, or to issue preventive injunctions. Awards issued during the arbitration procedure, such as injunctions, summons to witnesses, etc, can also be enforced with the aid of the courts, if the parties do not voluntarily comply with them.

In relation to international arbitration, the general principle is that foreign arbitration awards are fully enforceable except where they may be contrary to

Chilean public policy. In order to enforce, an authorisation procedure known as 'exequatur' must be followed before the Supreme Court. The Court will first look for any international treaty applicable in Chile, and then confirm that any requirements for enforcement under such a treaty are met. Any arbitration awards coming from any of the countries that are signatories of any of the following international treaties to which Chile is a party will be subject to the terms and conditions for enforcement set out in those treaties:

- New York Convention (1958);
- Panama Convention (1975);
- Washington Convention (1965); and
- International Private Law Code (also known as the 'Bustamante Code' of 1928).

If no international treaties apply, the Supreme Court will look into the International Arbitration Act 19.971. Following the Model Law, that act provides requirements for recognition identical to those set out in Section V of the New York Convention. Thus foreign arbitration awards issued in another country can be denied enforcement when:

- the party against whom enforcement is being sought demonstrates that:
  - the party to the arbitration agreement was under some incapacity;
  - the arbitration agreement is not valid under the laws to which the parties have subjected it, or under the law of the country where the award was issued;
  - the party against whom the award is invoked was not given proper notice of the appointment of an arbitrator or of the arbitral proceedings or was otherwise unable to present his case;
  - the award deals with a dispute not contemplated by, or not falling within the terms of the submission to arbitration, or contains decisions on matters beyond the scope of the submission to arbitration, provided that, if the decisions on matters submitted to arbitration can be separated from those not so submitted, that part of the award which contains decisions on matters submitted to arbitration may be recognised and enforced;
  - the composition of the arbitral tribunal or the arbitral procedure was not in accordance with the agreement of the parties or, absent such an agreement, was not in accordance with the law of the country where the arbitration took place; or
  - the award has not yet become binding on the parties or has been set aside or suspended by a court of the country in which, or under the law of which, that award was made; or
- the court finds that:
  - the subject matter of the dispute is not capable of settlement by arbitration under Chilean law; or
  - the recognition or enforcement of the award would be contrary to public policy.

Injunctions issued by foreign arbitration entities over assets located in Chile may be difficult or impossible to enforce if not voluntarily complied with, given that injunctions under Chilean law are provisional (thus not fulfilling the requirement that they be a final judgment). Likewise, arbitration awards directly referring to or affecting assets located in Chile may be difficult to enforce on grounds of public policy given that Article 16 of the Chilean Civil Code provides that assets located in Chile are governed by Chilean law. Monetary awards are generally not a problem to enforce in Chile.

(e) *Discovery*

As Chile is a civil law jurisdiction, discovery procedures under local institutional arbitrations (as well as under local courts) tend to be much more limited than under most common law jurisdictions. Parties agreeing to common law arbitration rules and/or appointing arbitrators from a common law background may provoke typical problems of excessive and time-consuming discovery (discrediting the key feature of arbitration, namely that it is supposed to be simpler and faster than litigation).

Parties may request an arbitrator to order the production of certain documents which relate directly to the matter at issue, provided the documents are not confidential (Article 349, Civil Procedural Code). Such a request may be granted either against the opposing party or against a third party (which may request that the document be presented at its home or offices, and in which case the request must be executed through an ordinary court, given that the third party has not subscribed to the arbitration agreement). The expenses related to this document production must be paid by the petitioner.

Prior to instituting proceedings, parties may file a pre-trial interim measure before the ordinary courts. Such a request involves a petitioner (in most cases a potential plaintiff) asking the court to order the potential opposing party to:

- provide sworn depositions related to its ability to stand trial; representation; and name or domicile of representatives;
- exhibit an object at issue in trial;
- exhibit certain documents; and/or
- acknowledge a signature in a private document (which can also be requested by the future defendant).

Arbitrators can enforce their decision through ordinary courts. If the court orders one of the parties to exhibit certain documents and that party refuses to do so, it will be banned from using the documents in the proceedings and the judge may impose a fine, order the arrest of the party in contempt (for a maximum of two months) and/or issue a search warrant. If a third party refuses to comply with the court's order without cause, the judge may impose a fine and/or order the arrest of that person.

Additionally, as a pre-trial interim measure in cases where there is imminent danger of damage to or loss of evidence, the potential plaintiff can request the judge to order an expert (appointed by the court) to draft a report, to personally inspect certain facts, or to issue a certificate attesting to any relevant circumstances.

The future litigant may also request that the court orders the deposition of the opposing party or a witness if there is any reason to believe this might not be forthcoming later.

Having said all that, Chilean law allows any request for an interim measure (even if the request is not expressly provided for by law), as long as it fulfils certain requirements established by the Civil Procedural Code.

(f) *Injunctions*

Once an arbitration tribunal has been established, it will have jurisdiction to issue injunctions. However, if the injunctions are not voluntarily observed, it will need the assistance of the local courts, which will normally enforce the injunctions.

Prior to establishment of an arbitration tribunal, the parties may resort to the local courts to seek injunctions without waiving their arbitration agreement by doing so. Once the arbitration tribunal is established, it will have to either confirm or release any injunction issued by the local courts. The local courts will set a timeframe within which the injunction applicant must file suit (not longer than 30 days) and will also require solid proof of the merits warranting the measure as well as provision of a security.

Injunctions issued by foreign arbitration entities over assets located in Chile may be difficult or impossible to enforce if not voluntarily complied with.

3.4 Disputes involving contracts with the State of Chile

In 1978 the Chilean Government passed Decree-Law 2349, which explicitly recognised contractual stipulations submitting disputes to international tribunals as 'common practice', for both private and state-owned entities, thereby unambiguously declaring as valid those stipulations that submit controversies to the jurisdiction of foreign tribunals, including arbitration, contained in agreements signed between the State of Chile – including its organs, institutions or companies – and entities that have their main business centre abroad. Decree-Law 2349 also openly permits the State of Chile to waive immunity of the enforcement of such contracts.

However, Decree-Law 2349 does not apply: to contracts concluded in conformity with Decree-Law 600 of 1974, which is commonly applicable to foreign companies in Chile; to concession contracts over state-owned property; and to contracts which specifically exclude foreign tribunals or mandate national tribunals.

Regarding concession contracts, it is important to bear in mind that disputes that arise in contracts signed in accordance with the Concessions Act of the Ministry of Public Works, can be resolved through ordinary litigation before the Court of Appeals or through a special Arbitration Commission where it is not international (see further section 5 below).

An important group of contracts which are excluded from the terms of Decree-Law 2349, and subject to special legal provisions, relate to public works' contracts concluded by the State of Chile. Disputes relating to such contracts must be resolved through general administrative proceedings, for which appeals must be submitted to the ordinary courts (with arbitration excluded as a possibility).

In sum, the general rule is that disputes relating to contracts with the State of

Chile must be submitted to international arbitration; excluding the following:

- contracts concluded in conformity with Decree-Law 600;
- public works contracts; and
- concession contracts, which may be submitted only to a national arbitration commission, in accordance with the Concessions Act.

4. Litigation

4.1 Overview

Litigation is still used as a dispute resolution mechanism, particularly for certain types of disputes.

The procedures set out in the Code of Civil Procedure are not intrinsically time-consuming, but the caseload of the courts tends to result in litigation being drawn out in excess of five – or as much as 10 – years.

Problems of corruption generally do not arise in the Chilean courts, but the system is prone to problems in complex construction disputes (as compared with arbitration) in terms of: delay or the length of the process; rigidity of rules of evidence; and, in some cases, low levels of available expertise.

As at July 2013, major reforms to the civil procedure system are under discussion, significantly raising the possibility of the current written procedures being replaced by proposed new oral procedures – so this may all change in the near future.

4.2 Litigation cases, subject matter and users

Litigation is still preferred by some public entities and publicly owned companies, mostly as a matter of policy rather than because of legal considerations. Recurrent litigants include the municipalities, the armed forces and related entities, the Ministry of Public Works and the Housing Ministry.

Decennial liability (in its broad sense) is also typically handled by the courts, particularly if the claimant was not the party who entered into the construction contract. Under the General Construction and Urbanism Act and its Ordinance: the owner/first seller (real estate developer) is liable for damages resulting from defects in design, materials and workmanship; the designer, for defects in design if they caused damages; and the contractor or builder, for defects in materials, supplies and workmanship. Each of them may in turn sue each other and their subcontractors back in the chain, if the defect was ultimately caused by any of them.

Liabilities regarding defects in the supporting structure do not expire before a 10-year period, counting from the date of certification of the work; five years from certification in the case of non-structural installations and other building works; and, in relation to finishing works, three years counting from the date of the first sale/purchase agreement. (This regime was originally intended to protect homeowners, albeit that the act now applies to all defects cases.)

Under the system of decennial liability, the owner of a building may sue the contractor under the act even where there is no privity. Such suits tend to proliferate after earthquakes, instigated either by owners or by insurers exercising subrogation rights.

The above-mentioned act provides that these claims shall be heard under 'summary proceedings', which in Chile involves a shorter procedure in which basically a claim is served, and a hearing for response summoned after five days from service of process. Evidence is rendered in a time frame of eight working days. Such time frames can be extremely hard on constructors/developers.

Under Article 19 of the act, class actions under the Consumer Protection Act are specifically allowed, although with some differences from normal consumer class actions. This provision was amended as a consequence of political pressure after the 2010 earthquake.

5. Expert panels and arbitration commission under the Concessions Act

The Public Concessions Act DFL MOP 164 of 1991, as amended, establishes a technical panel (Article 36). This is a permanent panel which operates for all concessions subject to the Concessions Act and is vested with the authority to decide monetary and technical disputes arising between the parties. The technical panel resembles a dispute review board.

The Concessions Act also states that disputes arising from the interpretation, application or execution of a concession contract may not only be resolved through litigation (through the Court of Appeals) but also by an Arbitration Commission, which is governed by a series of rules and provisions that differ somewhat from those of general arbitration tribunals.

The Concessions Act also expressly states that the technical panel shall not exercise jurisdiction and shall issue non-binding recommendations. The parties are free to bring the dispute to arbitration or litigation, where the recommendation issued by the technical panel can be considered by an Arbitration Commission or the Court of Appeals. Nevertheless, prior to resorting to those procedures in connection with monetary or technical matters, the parties must have allowed the dispute to be reviewed by the technical panel.

The technical panel is made up of professionals as follows: two lawyers, two engineers and one economist appointed by the High Public Administration Council. The professionals remain in post for six years and cannot be re-elected. The panel is partially replaced every three years. The authority finances the administrative costs of the panel, and half of the members' fees; the other half is financed by the concessionaires subject to the Concessions Act.

The Arbitration Commission must be established at the beginning of the concession and its members will generally remain in office for the duration of the concession contract. The commission is made up of three professionals, two at least of whom must be lawyers. The members are chosen by the parties of the concession contract from a list of 20 lawyers short-listed by the Supreme Court; and from a list of 10 professionals presented by the Antitrust Court. Both lists will partially renew themselves every five years and the commission members will be paid, in equal parts, by the bidder and the Ministry of Public Works. Ordinarily, parties to the concession contract must file their complaints to the commission within two years of the launch date of the project if the complaint originated during the construction period, or within two years from the disputed event (or news of it) if it happened during the execution phase. The Arbitration Commission must decide the dispute in accordance with applicable law, but is not tied by procedural and evidential rules. Final judgments of the Arbitration Commission cannot be appealed. More on the technical panel can be seen at their website at www.panelconcesiones.cl.

6. Investment arbitration

Although less utilised, investment arbitration may also lend itself to resolving construction-related disputes under investment protection treaties. Chile has 53 of such treaties in place.

Chile is signatory of the Washington Convention setting out the International Center for Settlement of Investment Disputes ICSID (or CIADI in Spanish), as well as of several investment protection treaties.

In 2004 the CIADI awarded a Malaya company US$6.8 million in connection with a case involving a construction of a commercial and residential complex that was frustrated by permitting/zoning matters.

Chile has only had three cases in the ICSID, and only one related to construction. More on the case can be found in https://icsid.worldbank.org/ICSID/FrontServlet.

7. Conclusion

Albeit with advantages and disadvantages, all of the dispute resolution methods described here work in Chile, although arbitration is generally regarded as the most effective.

There is considerable room for expansion of other less-used procedures, such as dispute boards and expert determinations. Specific legislation may need to be passed to accelerate their use and acceptance, particularly in the case of dispute adjudication boards.

The new civil procedure law reform currently (July 2013) under discussion may also boost litigation and should be closely monitored. The reform is aimed, among other things, at expediting procedures and reducing the time needed to resolve disputes – currently the greatest problem presented by litigation.

New legislation or clarity within the case law would also be very welcome in relation to choice of foreign law.

Colombia

Maria Alejandra Arboleda González
Carolina Posada Isaacs
Posse Herrera Ruiz

1. Introduction

This chapter considers:

- common disputes arising from construction and infrastructure contracts;
- dispute resolution rules applicable to construction, infrastructure and public-private partnership (PPP) contracts in Colombia; and
- relevant jurisprudence regarding construction, infrastructure and PPP contracts in Colombia.

The major judgments of Colombian courts are also examined. These are relevant to anyone interested in executing construction agreements, especially with state parties (including the state, state entities, state enterprises, enterprises in which the state and private individuals have an interest and the public stake is 50% or more, and private individuals that perform public functions).

2. Common disputes arising from construction and infrastructure contracts

Construction and infrastructure projects in Colombia are subject to neither a particular standard contract nor any specific regulation, so International Federation of Consulting Engineers (FIDIC) models, adapted to the needs of Colombian law, are commonly used.

The Red, Yellow and Silver Books are the most common FIDIC forms for standard agreements among Colombian public and private owners. There are frequent disputes arising from construction contracts relating to the quality of the work, late completion, longer stays on site and cost overruns.

By default, any dispute is resolved by the Colombian courts, but parties should agree to use alternative dispute resolution (ADR) methods, since:

- judicial procedures are very slow;
- ADR experts tend to be better informed than the judiciary;
- ADR procedures are speedier than court proceedings; and
- more court decisions are challenged as compared with decisions reached using ADR methods, such as arbitration.

Both the judicial procedures and the principal ADR methods are analysed in the following sections.

3. Dispute resolution rules applicable to construction, infrastructure and PPP contracts

In a construction contract where no state parties are involved and no ADR methods have been selected by the parties, disputes must be brought before the civil courts.

Disputes equivalent to US$29,475 and above must be brought before the civil circuit court. The civil district court has jurisdiction over any appeal and any motion to revise the judgment rendered by the civil circuit court. Disputes involving sums less than this amount must be filed before the municipal civil court.

The highest court in the civil jurisdiction is the Supreme Court, which hears the extraordinary motion of annulment of a judgment and the revision motion, over which the civil district court does not have jurisdiction. Regarding arbitration, the Supreme Court has jurisdiction over revision motions against domestic awards,[1] annulment motions against international awards rendered in Colombia, and *exequatur* requests.[2]

For disputes arising from construction contracts involving state parties, the procedure must be filed before the courts of the administrative jurisdiction.

According to the Administrative Procedural Code, the courts have jurisdiction over administrative acts and omissions, and private and public contracts where the state has exceptional powers to unilaterally terminate, modify or interpret the contract, or impose what is called *caducidad* – which means that if the contractor severally breaches a contract with the state party which could serve to halt performance of the contract, the state party may issue an administrative act terminating the contract. The effect of such a decision is that the contractor will be unable to execute any contract with any state party during the next five years.

The State Council is the highest tribunal in the administrative jurisdiction. It is competent to hear annulment motions against arbitral awards where one of the parties to the arbitration is a public entity or someone who performs public functions.[3] In addition, there are administrative courts and administrative district courts.

According to Article 141 of the code, any party to a state contract may file a lawsuit requesting a declaration of the contract's validity or nullification, and may also request revision, breach, damages and liquidation of the contract.

Parties to construction contracts may – and most of the time do – agree on ADR methods to resolve their disputes. Colombian law and jurisprudence have acknowledged ADR and have regulated some methods, such as conciliation, arbitration, *amiable compositeur* and technical arbitration (similar to expert determination).

The fact that some forms of ADR, such as dispute review boards and expert determination, are not regulated does not mean that they are forbidden. In fact, in Colombia there is no special provision which expressly forbids the use of any specific ADR method. However, some restrictions apply – for example, some specific matters are not arbitrable according to jurisprudence.[4]

According to the principle of free will, any person has the power to dispose of,

1 Law 1563/2012, Article 46.
2 Law 1563/2012, Article 68.
3 Law 1563/2012, Article 46.

with binding effect, their interests and rights and thus create rights and obligations, provided that the public order and custom are respected.[5] And "from these freedoms arises the freedom to contract as a manifestation of the principle to which reference has been made, and in accordance with which individuals can execute binding agreements that they wish".[6] Hence, parties to a contract may agree on any ADR method, as long as it is not forbidden by law or the specific matter is not prohibited.

In contrast to private persons, the state can do only what the law expressly allows it to. So the state's ability to agree upon ADR methods in its contracts is limited to the methods expressly recognised by law.

Fortunately, Law 80 – the General Contractual Statute for Public Administration – contains a strong pro-ADR statement, as Article 68 indicates that:

> *The entities referred to in Article 2[7] of this statute and contractors will seek to solve in an agile, fast and direct way the differences and discrepancies arising from the contractual activity.*
>
> *To this end, when the differences arise they will* make use of mechanisms for contractual dispute resolution under this Act and conciliation, amicable composition and settlement *[emphasis added].*

---

4 In arbitrations with state-owned entities, the arbitration tribunals may not resolve upon the legality of:
- administrative acts (they may only decide on the economic effects of these acts); or
- the application of 'exceptional powers' of the administration, which are unilateral interpretation, unilateral modification, unilateral termination and caduciad. However, the economic consequences of the above can be submitted to arbitration.

Other matters that are not arbitrable are those involving:
- fundamental rights;
- civil status;
- public policy;
- labour issues;
- administrative proceeding under law for antitrust; and
- consumer disputes – according to Law 1480/11, it is considered abusive to compel a consumer to agree on an arbitration clause.

5 Constitutional Court, Judgment of December 3 2008. Justice Dr Rodrigo Escobar Gil, Ref D-7379.

6 *Ibid.*

7 Unofficial translation: Article 2, Law 80: definition of entities, public servants and services.
For the purposes of this Law:
1°. State entities are:
a) The Nation, regions, states, provinces, the capital district and special districts, metropolitan areas, municipal associations, indigenous territories and municipalities, public institutions, industrial and commercial state companies and the enterprises where the State and private individual hold an interest and the public funds are 50% or superior and indirect decentralised entities and other legal persons where there is majority of public participation, regardless of the name they adopted, in all areas and levels.
b) The Senate, the House of Representatives, the Supreme Judicial Council, the General Prosecutor's Office, the General Comptroller, the departmental district and municipal comptrollers, the General Attorney's Office, the National Registry of Civil Status, ministries, administrative departments, superintendencies, special administrative units and, in general, agencies or departments of the State to which the law grants the capacity to execute contracts.
2°. Public servants are:
a) Individuals who provide dependent services to entities referred to in this article, except for associations and foundations of mixed participation in which only their legal representatives and managers, executives or consultants or their equivalent on whom the execution of contracts is delegated.
b) Members of the public corporations that have the capacity to enter into contracts on their behalf.
3°. Public services are:
Those destined to meet collective needs in a general, permanent and continuous way, under the State's direction, regulation and control, as well as those by which the State seeks to preserve order and ensure the fulfilment of its purposes.
[Paragraph repealed by Act 1150 of 2007, Article 32: For the sole purpose of this law, cooperatives and associations formed by local authorities are also state entities, which shall be subject to the provisions of this statute, especially when they enter into inter-administrative agreements on behalf of such entities.]

Contractual administrative acts may be revoked at any time provided that they have not been subject to a final judgment.[8]

Article 69 of Law 80 reinforces the above-mentioned principle by pointing out that authorities may not prohibit the use of direct mechanisms for dispute resolution arising from state contracts, and makes specific reference to arbitration in the following terms: "Entities will not prohibit the provision of the arbitration clause or the execution of commitments to resolve disputes arising from state contracts."[9] Hence, state parties to a contract may agree upon conciliation, arbitration and *amiable compositeur.*

Regarding PPPs, on January 10 2012 a new statute for their regulation (Law 1508/2012) entered into force in Colombia. According to Article 3, the statute:

applies to all contracts in which State agencies contract a private investor for the design and construction of infrastructure and related services, or for the construction, repair, improvement or equipping of said infrastructure, all these activities necessarily involving the operation and maintenance of the infrastructure. The contracts can also relate to infrastructure for the delivery of public services.[10]

Law 1508/2012 does not provide any specific dispute resolution regulation, so the rules of Law 80 apply to such contracts, since state parties are involved.

3.1 Arbitration

In recent years, Colombia was urged to implement fresh legislation, since the provisions regarding arbitration were piecemeal and there was limited regulation of international arbitration cases. The previous rules[11] exclusively established the criteria for determining whether arbitration was international, the law applicable to international arbitration and the concept of a foreign award.

Colombia is not known as an attractive seat for international arbitration, despite its strategic location in Latin America and the significant increase in Latin American arbitration cases over the past decades. Moreover, Colombia has experienced dramatic economic and commercial development in recent years, thanks to wholesale changes in national security. This has led to the execution of several bilateral investment treaties, as follows as at July 2013:

- with China (2012), India (2012), Peru (2010), Switzerland (2009) and Spain (2007) – in force;
- with the United Kingdom (2010) and Japan (2011) – signed but still pending approval by one of the parties; and
- with Russia, Azerbaijan, Kuwait and Singapore – at the negotiation stage.

In addition, free trade agreements with an investment chapter have been concluded as follows as at July 2013:

- with Mexico, Chile, the North Central America Triangle (Guatemala, El Salvador and Honduras), Canada and the United States – in force;

---

8 Unofficial translation of Article 68, Law 80.
9 Unofficial translation of Article 69, Law 80.
10 Unofficial translation.
11 Law 315/96 regulated international arbitration in Colombia before Law 1563/2012.

- with the Pacific Alliance (Peru, Mexico and Chile), Costa Rica, Israel and South Korea – signed but still pending approval by one of the parties; and
- with Panama, Turkey and Japan – at the negotiation stage.

Over recent years, foreign investment has been progressively increasing year on year; imports and exports doubled in 2012.[12]

With the increased investment and rapid growth of commerce, Colombia has had to make numerous and significant investments in infrastructure. As is customary in large construction contracts, an arbitration clause is included (sometimes along with another ADR method, such as previous negotiation, expert determination, mediation); and if a foreign party is involved – which is generally the case – the arbitration agreed on is international. Therefore, new arbitration legislation, especially for international arbitration, was urgently needed, since foreign parties to large infrastructure contracts always sought international arbitration, but were uncertain of the rules that applied when a dispute arose.

Due to the lack of regulation and uncertainty about the rules, it was usual to agree on international arbitration based outside Colombia. Having international arbitration based outside Colombia for contracts performed in Colombia is more costly in terms of legal fees, displacement of the hearings, possible displacement of the arbitral tribunal to the project site to collect evidence, and possible *exequatur* if the award is to be executed in Colombia.

Thus on October 12 2012 Law 1563 – the new Arbitration Statute – entered into force to remedy such deficiencies. It has three main chapters, on national arbitration, *amiable compositeur* and international arbitration.

For national arbitration, two types of arbitration were introduced: institutional and *ad hoc*. This is relevant to large infrastructure projects with national arbitration clauses, since the arbitration is always administered by an institution when there is a state party to the arbitration agreement. However, if there is a state party, the applicable rules of procedure will be those in Law 1563, and not the institutional rules.

Article 8 prohibits an arbitrator and secretary from exercising their functions in more than five tribunals at a time where state parties are involved.

The arbitration term was rigorously limited to six months, extensible only for a further six. This limitation probably sought to make arbitration more effective, but a one-year maximum term for complex arbitrations such as those arising from large infrastructure projects may be insufficient. Experience indicates that one of the most time-consuming stages during an arbitral proceeding is expert determination, due to the complexity of construction projects, differences between expert reports when each party has a different expert, and difficulties in finding experts that the parties will accept – all of which take time.

Regarding international arbitration, Law 1563/2012 adopted, with some modifications, the United Nations Commission on International Trade Law

12 In only the first 10 months of 2012, direct foreign investment reached $14 billion: www.portafolio.co/economia/inversion-extranjera-colombia-crecio-14-octubre.

(UNCITRAL) Model Law on International Arbitration. The benefits of an arbitration system based on the UNCITRAL Model Law are well known and clearly reflect Colombia's pro-arbitration position.

The Arbitration Statute made a significant modification to the first article of the model law, which sets out the criteria for determining whether arbitration is international. It did not include the criteria established in Articles 1(b)1 and 1(c) of the model law, which indicate that arbitration is international when "the place of the arbitration is situated outside the State in which the parties have their places of business" and "the parties have expressly agreed that the subject matter of the arbitration agreement relates to more than one country".

Thus, the Arbitration Statute acknowledges three criteria for determining whether arbitration is considered international in Colombia:

- The parties to an arbitration agreement have, at the time of concluding that agreement, their domiciles in different states; or
- The place where a substantial part of the obligations of the commercial relationship is to be performed, or the place with which the subject matter of the dispute is most closely connected, is situated outside the state in which the parties have their domiciles; or
- The dispute submitted to arbitration affects the interests of international trade (this criterion is not in the model law).

This last criterion increases the scope of international arbitration, since it has been widely interpreted by French jurisprudence as including any dispute arising from a cross-border transaction of goods, services or payments.[13] Under this interpretation, almost any transaction with an international element may be subject to possible international arbitration.

Additionally, Article 64 of the arbitration statute reinforces the pro-international arbitration principle in Law 1563/2012, as it stipulates that "in the interpretation of international arbitration the international character and the necessity to promote uniformity and the *pacta sunt servanda* must be observed".[14]

Finally, according to Colombian law, the only motion that may be filed against an international arbitration award granted in Colombia is an annulment motion, on the same grounds stated in Article V of the New York Convention on the Recognition of Enforcement of Foreign Arbitral Awards (the New York Convention), to deny the recognition of foreign arbitral awards.

Law 1563/2012 modified the last paragraph of Article V(2)(b) of the New York Convention as a ground for annulment, specifying that the award must be contrary

---

13 "For the arbitration to be international, it is sufficient that the economic transaction under consideration involves the cross border movement of goods or services or a cross border payment. ...The payment for the work was to be made partially in Tunisian dinars and partially in French francs. ... Hence the operation presupposed the cross border transfer of material, a cross border transfer of technology as well as cross border payments. It thus has an international character and the arbitration is an international arbitration." France No. 25, *Ministry of Public Works v. Société Bec Frères*, Cour d'Appel [Court of Appeal], Paris, Not Indicated, February 24 1994 in Albert Jan van den Berg (ed), *Yearbook of Commercial Arbitration 1997 – Volume XXII, Volume XXII* (Kluwer Law International 1997) pp682–690.

14 Unofficial translation of Article 64 of Law 1563/2012.

to the international public policy of Colombia, rather than just the national public policy. It thus upgraded this ground for annulment and made it more difficult for an award to be annulled, since international public policy is a narrower concept.

The Colombian Supreme Court has clarified that the international public policy "is limited to the basic principles or fundamental institutions, which serve as illustration: the prohibition to abuse of rights, good faith, the arbitral tribunal impartiality and the right to due process", and that "the breach of a peremptory rule of the 'forum' of the judge of the *exequatur*, *per se*, does not imply the breach of said institution".[15]

However, even when the Supreme Court has given a general notion of what is required, the public policy standards are not very clear and there is no certainty as to what a judge might consider as a violation of international public policy.

This is a global problem, as Professor Gary B Born has pointed out: "the public policy exception is unpredictable and expansive. As first-year conflicts teachers around the world invariably recite, public policy is an unruly horse that carries its rider to unpredictable destinations."[16]

When recognising foreign arbitral awards,[17] the Arbitration Statute has adopted, as an exact transcription, the same grounds that can be used to deny the recognition of a foreign award in Article V of the New York Convention.

3.2 *Amiable compositeur*

Article 59 states that "*amiable compositeur* is an alternative dispute resolution method, by which two or more individuals, an individual and one or more public entities, or several public entities or whoever performs public functions, delegate on a third party, called *amiable compositeur*, the power to solve – its decision is enforceable for the parties – disposable contractual disputes".[18]

There is no extensive regulation of *amiable compositeur* – just three articles in Law 1563/2012 that state the concept mentioned above, the effects of the decision, the appointment of the *amiable compositeur* and the applicable rules of procedure.

Regarding the effects, the decision of the *amiable compositeur* has the same effect as the settlement agreements. Article 60 of Law 1563/2012 adds that the decision will be in equity (by default), unless the parties agree otherwise or the *amiable compositeur* decides to apply any rules of law.

Finally, Law 1563/2012 states that the rules of procedure for *amiable compositeur* are those established by the parties; where there is lack of agreement, the rules will be those of the arbitration institution where the respondent party is based. Parties may decide upon the number of *amiables compositeurs* and their method of appointment. If there is no agreement, one *amiable compositeur* is appointed by the arbitration institution where the respondent is based.

---

15 Unofficial translation. Supreme Court of Justice, Civil Chamber, Justice Dr Ruth Marina Díaz Rueda, Judgment of July 27 2011.

16 Gary B Born, (2001) *International Commercial Arbitration – Commentary and materials*, Kluwer Law International, second edition, p816.

17 An award by an arbitral tribunal based outside Colombia.

18 Unofficial translation of Article 59 of Law 1563/2012.

3.3 Conciliation

In Colombia, conciliation is a mandatory step in some legal proceedings, so it is one of the most commonly used ADR methods – not because the parties agree on it, but because they have to use it.

The most important characteristic is that the conciliation agreement is a matter already judged and is enforceable.[19]

Regarding state parties, Article 56 of Decree 1818/1998[20] establishes that disputes that fall under the competence of the administrative jurisdiction may be settled though conciliation. This includes contractual disputes (Article 161 of the code).[21]

3.4 Technical arbitration – expert determination

In Colombia, there is no specific regulation for expert determination. The most similar ADR method is technical arbitration, which is not defined by law (Law 1563/2012 only makes reference by saying that the arbitral award may be in law, equity or technical); but jurisprudence has established that "technical arbitration is a form of arbitration by which arbitrators solve a particular dispute based on certain specific knowledge of a particular science, art, or occupation. However, being a type of arbitration, it consists of the general elements of arbitration".[22] Hence, it is not really an expert determination, but rather an arbitration, with all its legal requirements, resolved by an expert. It is possible for both private and state parties to agree on technical arbitration for technical matters.

3.5 Other ADR methods – dispute boards

Other ADR methods (eg, dispute boards and expert determination) that are not regulated by Colombian law may be agreed on by private parties, but unlike those subject to regulation (eg, arbitration and conciliation) they lack judicial value. Thus, they produce only the same effects as contracts and there is still the chance that the losing party will file a judicial claim against the decision.

If the parties agree that some disputes can be resolved by a dispute board or expert determination and undertake to comply with the decision, which shall be final and binding, but one subsequently refuses to comply with the dispute board's or expert's decision, this ultimately constitutes a breach of contract that would have to be resolved by an ADR method that is subject to regulation (eg, arbitration), or the national courts.

4. Relevant jurisprudence regarding construction, infrastructure and PPP contracts

4.1 *Consorcio Miel v ISAGEN*

The State Council recently rendered an annulment judgment filed against an

19 Decree 1818/1998, Article 3.

20 Statute of alternative dispute resolution methods.

21 As stated above, according to Article 87 of the APC, any party to a state contract may file a lawsuit requesting the declaration of the contract's existence or its nullity, and may also request conviction, damages, revision or breach, among others.

22 Unofficial translation. Constitutional Court, Judgment C-035/2008 of January 23 2008, Justice Dr Manuel José Cepeda, Ref: D-6898.

International Chamber of Commerce (ICC) award with Colombia as the seat of the arbitration, in *Consorcio Miel v ISAGEN SA ESP*, by which the award was partially annulled.

ISAGEN is a company controlled by the Colombian Ministry of Mines and Energy, with a public shareholding below 90%. The consortium was integrated by Constructora Norberto Odebrecht S/S, Alstom Power Brasil Ltda (today Alstom Hydro Energía Brasil Ltda), Kvaerner Energy SAS and Alstom Power Italia SpA.

ISAGEN filed an annulment motion alleging six legal grounds[23] established in Article 163 of Decree 1818/1998, which regulated arbitration in Colombia at the time. However, only the ground on the award being rendered *ex aequo et bono* (ie, according to what is fair and just) succeeded and the award was partially annulled.

The State Council decided that a decision is *ex aequo et bono* not only when the judge leaves aside the law applicable to the dispute, but also when, even though the judge makes reference to the applicable law, he does not explain the analysis of the evidence that gives rise to the decision. That is, that the judge's decision is based on his beliefs.[24]

This ground for annulment is the most relevant, as it has been the most successful in annulling arbitration awards where state parties are involved.

In *Consorcio Miel v ISAGEN* the arbitral tribunal, based on the applicable law, developed the concept of generalised loss of production, which it defined as "the conduct of the owner or his representative contrary to the good faith which, by an abuse of its contractual and legal prerogatives, affects the performance and utility produced by the work to the constructor".[25] The State Council observed that the award did not mention the specific evidence that proved the bad-faith conduct of ISAGEN, which led to the conclusion (in the award) that ISAGEN had indulged in generalised loss of production conduct.

In general, the State Council censured the lack of evidence-based arguments for the arbitral tribunal to condemn certain audit actions during the performance of the contract as contrary to the good-faith principle, when bad faith must be proven under Colombian law – for example:

---

23 The alleged grounds for annulment by ISAGEN:
1. Absolute nullity of the arbitration agreement for illegal object or cause. Absolute or relative nullity of the arbitration agreement on grounds that were alleged in the arbitration proceedings that have not been cleared or validated in the course of it (Article 163 [1] Decree 1818 of 1998).
2. The arbitral tribunal was not legally constituted, circumstance that was alleged on due time by my client (Article 163 [2] of Decree 1818 of 1998).
3. Failed to enact, without legal justification, evidence requested on due time and have not taken the necessary steps to practice the evidence, as such omissions are relevant for the decision and have been claimed in due time and form (Article 163 [4] Decree 1818 of 1998).
4. The award was rendered after the expiration of the time fixed for the arbitration or the extension (Article 163 [5] of Decree 1818 of 1998).
5. The award was rendered ex aequo et bono *when it should be in law, a fact that appears evident in the award (Article 163 [6] of Decree 1818 of 1998).*
6. The award decided on matters that were beyond the arbitrator's competence and more was awarded than requested (Article 163 [8] of Decree 1818 of 1998).

24 State Council, Third Chamber, Justice Dr Hernan Andrade Rincón, annulment Judgment of November 29 2012, ref: 39332.

25 Unofficial translation. Paragraph from the arbitral award dated July 2 2010 in the case *Consorcio Miel v ISAGEN*, cited by the State Council, Third Chamber, Justice Dr Hernan Andrade Rincón, annulment judgment of November 29 2012, ref: 39332.

> *[t]he statement made by the Tribunal indicated that before the proactive and diligent attitude of the Consortium 'the auditing reacted by imposing a series of penalties, and then refusing to return them. The obligation to repay the penalties regarding Milestones 9, 10, 11 and 7 offers little legal doubt – and yet, the Owner and Auditor,* in a breach which looks to be deliberate, refused to return them'. *It is to note that in this regard the award was issued with adherence to the most intimate convictions of the arbitrators, since, as stated, even when bad faith is not presumed but must be proven, it was assumed based on the 'breach which* looks *to be deliberate', without, at least, any reference to any evidence establishing that the defendant's actions had been contrary to good faith*[26] *(original emphasis).*

Finally, the State Council decided that "it is reasonable to conclude that the arbitrators, according to their personal and intimate conviction over what they considered just and equitable and for reasons that are not expressly reflected in the award, estimated that the auditor had acted in bad faith, leading to the conclusion that in this respect the award was rendered not by law as it should, but *ex aequo et bono* and, therefore, concerning this issue the award shall be annulled".[27]

This recent annulment decision may be criticised as intrusive, since the State Council basically censured the award for not specifying which piece(s) of evidence led to the conclusion that the auditor and/or ISAGEN was acting in bad faith when imposing the penalties, or the auditor's performance was not up to the expected standards, among other things. But the same judgment recognised that the arbitral tribunal arrived at its conclusions based on "an overall review of the auditing performance" and an analysis of the "very extensive evidence presented during the proceedings, heard during eight sessions of witnesses and experts, [and] studied the thousands of pages of allegations made". So, the arbitral tribunal affirmed that its decision was a consequence of the evidence studied, but the State Council considered that because there was no express indication of the piece of evidence which led to the conclusion, the award was rendered *ex aequo et bono.*

The implication of this reasoning is that the arbitral tribunal exceeded its jurisdiction and violated the arbitral agreement, as it gave the arbitrators power to decide based on Colombian law, but they did not apply the parties' choice of law and rather decided *ex aequo et bono*. This is a serious allegation. Moreover, the ICC Rules of Arbitration, selected by the parties, clearly state that "[t]he arbitral tribunal shall assume the powers of an amiable compositeur [emphasis added] or decide *ex aequo et bono* only if the parties have agreed to give it such powers"[28].

Even with the criticisms, the judgment shows a more positive State Council view towards international arbitration, compared with past decisions.[29] In this decision, the State Council dismissed all of the arguments attacking the validity of the arbitral agreement, and there was no hesitation regarding the possibility of state entities, or

26 Unofficial translation. State Council, Third Chamber, Justice Dr Hernán Andrade Rincón, annulment Judgment of November 29 2012, ref: 39332.

27 Unofficial translation. State Council, Third Chamber, Justice Dr Hernán Andrade Rincón, annulment Judgment of November 29 2012, ref: 39332.

28 ICC Rules of Arbitration, Article 21(3).

29 For example the *Termorio* case.

enterprises such as ISAGEN, agreeing upon international arbitration. For example, the judgment stated: "[T]he Ml-100 contract from 1995 and the arbitral clause and its modifications were executed by a State entity and several foreign companies, which complies with the first criterion of Law 315 of 1996,[30] which is to be domiciled in different States."

Conclusively, even when the award was partially annulled, in Colombia it is absolutely clear that it is possible to agree on international arbitration in contracts with state parties. Any shadow of a doubt on this matter has been dissolved as a result of the *Termorio* case.

4.2 Judgment SU-174

Another case worth mentioning is the *sui generis* Judgment SU-174 rendered by the Colombian Constitutional Court on March 14 2007, in which the court made significant statements regarding arbitrability and choice of law in construction disputes with state entities.

This case related to a concession contract for the construction, maintenance and operation of a public road, executed by Concesiones de Infraestructuras SA (CISA) and Valle del Cauca State. The disputes regarding termination of the contracts were resolved by an arbitral tribunal through domestic arbitration in Cali, Colombia. On March 11 2004, the State Council upheld the award against the annulment motion filed by Valle del Cauca. The same losing party then filed an *acción de tutela*, which is a constitutional claim for the protection of its fundamental right of due process. On May 11 2005 the Constitutional Court overturned both the State Council's judgment and the arbitral award, so unilateral termination Resolution 095 was maintained.

However – and this is the interesting part – on March 14 2007 the plenary of the Constitutional Court rendered a new judgment overturning its own decision as it considered that the subject matter decided by the arbitral tribunal was arbitrable, so Valle del Cauca's constitutional right to due process was violated neither by the award nor by the annulment decision of the State Council.

For the purposes of construction and infrastructure contracts with state entities, the Constitutional Court distinguished between the validity and legality of administrative acts and the economic aspects of acts rendered in connection with a state contract, and concluded:

> *It is entirely possible that for the resolution of these exclusively economic disputes, arbitral tribunals do not examine the legality or question at all the validity of administrative acts; if the dispute is economic, the core aspects of its decision have to do with issues such as the existence, content, scope and conditions of the financial obligation in dispute; in other words, whether there is a contractual debt, and how it is to be quantified. There is no need to make pronouncements on the validity of contractual administrative acts for taking a decision on these issues.*[31]

The Constitutional Court stated: "the importance given by the Constitution to

---

30 Law 315 of 1996 was the international arbitration act in force at the time of the arbitration.

31 Unofficial translation. Constitutional Court, Justice Manuel José Cepeda, Judgment SU-174/07 of March 14 2007.

the autonomy of the parties as the basis of each arbitration proceeding, and that the parties' will enabling principle of arbitration justice has been one of the cardinal axes of constitutional doctrine on the subject, under Article 116 of the Constitution."[32]

4.3 Further commentary

The judgments described in sections 4.1 and 4.2 highlight some important features of arbitration in Colombia:

- Arbitration has a jurisdictional nature, so the arbitral awards are final decisions and are subject only to an annulment motion;
- In state contracts, public entities may agree upon arbitration clauses and commitments; and
- The constitutional action for the protection of fundamental rights (*acción de tutela*) is not admissible against arbitral proceeding decisions and annulment judgments.

4.4 *Exequatur* decisions

Another important aspect to consider regarding international arbitration, which is the most popular mechanism of resolving disputes arising from large infrastructure contracts, is the position of the Supreme Court concerning the *exequatur* of international or foreign awards.

Fortunately, the Supreme Court adopts a favourable position towards granting *exequatur*, as revealed in the two latest *exequatur* decisions rendered in 2011. In those judgments, the court strictly applied the international standards of the New York Convention.

In the judgment of December 19 2011, the Supreme Court studied the *exequatur* request of an ICC arbitral award rendered in Paris, which resolved disputes between the national railway company Ferrovías and Ferrocarriles Nacionales de Colombia SA (Fenoco). The court's decision was clearly in favour of arbitration, as it indicated that its analysis was going to be conducted exclusively according to the New York Convention criteria:

> *The foreign nature of the decisions for which recognition is pursued, [arbitral awards]...,* imposes on the Court to review the case under the rules set forth in the "Convention on the Recognition and Enforcement of Foreign Arbitral Awards", *adopted by the United Nations Conference on 'commercial arbitration', June 10, 1958, Colombia approved by Law 39 of 1990, which was also signed and ratified by France.*
>
> *The aforementioned convention adds* the only causes that may lead to denial of recognition of the award, *placing them into two groups depending on the actions taken by the party affected by the judgment, to demonstrate the lack of agreement or arbitration clause or procedural defects in the integration of the arbitration tribunal, or arising out of the decision in this regard from the competent authority of the country where recognition is sought*[33] (emphasis added).

---

32 Unofficial translation. Constitutional Court, Justice Manuel José Cepeda, Judgment SU-174/07 of March 14 2007.

33 Unofficial translation. Supreme Court of Justice, Civil Chamber, Justice Dr Fernando Giraldo Gutiérrez, Judgment of December 19 2011.

Through the judgment of November 20 1992, the Supreme Court had insisted that the only requirements that the interested party must comply with when requesting the *exequatur* of a foreign award are those required by the New York Convention:

> *the special requirements to be met by the interested party to obtain the recognition, is that,* along with the lawsuit, the arbitral award and the agreement under which the parties agreed to submit to arbitration in writing are attached, *either original or duly authenticated copy and official translation if they were not in the official language of the country where the award is invoked*[34] *(emphasis added).*

Such position was reaffirmed in the judgment of July 27 2011, where the Supreme Court stated that when the stipulated requirements are met, the court has the power to grant the *exequatur* of the foreign award:

> *Given that the contract where the arbitration clause was contained, as well as the "arbitral award", were each presented in a certified copy, it emerges as a corollary that the conditions which enable the Court to grant the claimed recognition are satisfied, since the differences of the parties from the "Joint Operating Agreement-JOA" may be resolved by arbitration, and the recognition or enforcement of the award is not contrary to domestic public order (a) and b), numeral 2 Article V of the Convention).*[35]

Even when the Supreme Court's position regarding which criteria (those of the New York Convention or those of the Civil Procedural Code) should be used to assess *exequatur* requests was unclear, and when it was likewise unclear whether it was possible to request the *exequatur* of partial arbitral awards, the judgments confirm, beyond doubt, that the only criteria applicable are those of the New York Convention.

This is very important for large infrastructure projects, since a contractor needs to know how it can execute an international arbitration award in Colombia relating to a contract with a Colombian party, what the requirements are and the Supreme Court's position towards the *exequatur* proceeding.

5. Conclusion

ADR methods should be used in construction and infrastructure contracts performed in Colombia. The most commonly used and safest option until now has been domestic or international arbitration, since the Arbitration Statute and the decisions of the three different courts illustrate the arbitration-friendly approach that is applied to ADR mechanisms in Colombia.

The essential aspects that a foreign contractor needs to be aware of when entering into a large infrastructure agreement in Colombia, most probably with state entities, include:

- domestic and international arbitration regulation;
- arbitrability;
- the courts' interpretation of objective and subjective arbitrability;

34 Unofficial translation. Supreme Court of Justice, Civil Chamber, Justice Dr Héctor Marín Naranjo, Judgment of November 20 1992.

35 Unofficial translation. Supreme Court of Justice, Civil Chamber, Justice Dr Ruth Marina Díaz Rueda, Judgment of July 27 2011.

- the motions that can be filed against a domestic or international award; and
- the grounds of revision for the recognition and enforcement of an international award in Colombia.

With the new Arbitration Statute and the courts' arbitration-friendly decisions, Colombia should now be viewed as a desirable international arbitration base for large infrastructure contracts. However, there is much that needs improvement in relation to ADR methods concerning construction and infrastructure projects. Colombia urgently needs regulations on dispute boards, which have proved to be an excellent tool to expedite the resolution of constant disputes that may arise during the performance of construction contracts.

In addition, expert determination must be recognised as an ADR method for state contracts, and decisions thereunder should be given final and enforceable status.

Peru

Jonnathan Bravo
Jaime Gray
Navarro Sologuren, Paredes, Gray Attorneys

1. Introduction

Peru has experienced significant micro and macroeconomic growth in recent years despite the global economic crisis that has affected other countries so adversely. In 2008, Peru achieved a gross domestic product (GDP) growth rate of 9.8%, and in 2010 and 2011 GDP increased by 6% and 6.5% respectively.

At the end of 2011, with GDP at an equivalent of US$17.6 billion, the Peruvian economy had recorded 10 years of consecutive growth at rates above the Latin American average. The following graph shows Peruvian GDP for the period 2000 to 2011.

Gross Domestic Product 2000–11 (US$ millions)[1]

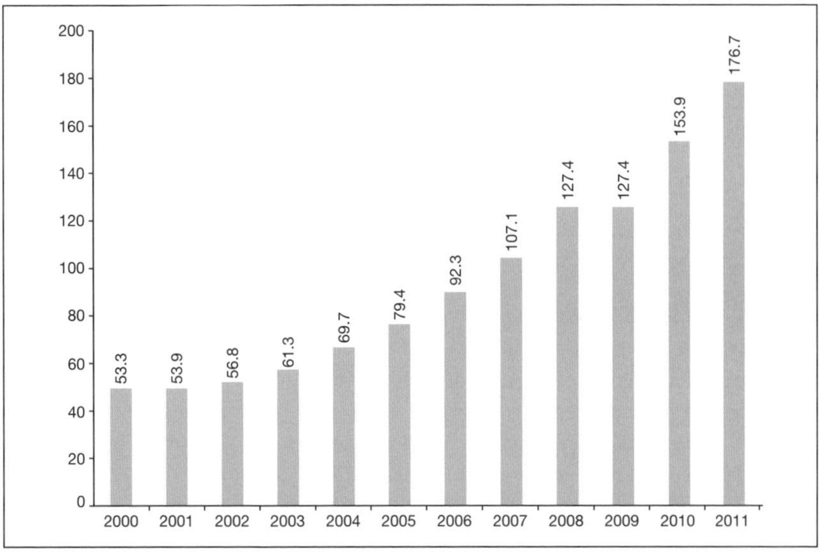

Source: BCRP. Prepared by: PROINVERSION

In 2012 the growth trend continued. The International Monetary Fund, in its Public Information Notice dated February 14 2013,[2] said about Peru:

1 See: www.proinversion.gob.pe/0/0/modulos/JER/PlantillaStandardsinHijos.aspx?ARE=0&PFL=0&JER=62.
2 See: www.imf.org/external/np/sec/pn/2013/pn1318.htm.

Strong economic performance and sound macroeconomic management continued in 2012. Economic growth is estimated at 6 percent of gross domestic product (GDP) in 2012, and the economy is near its potential... Economic activity was driven by domestic demand, in particular investment, as the weak external environment is taking a toll on exports and widened the external current account deficit. Inflation declined to 2¾ percent (y-o-y) in December 2012, falling within the inflation target band (1–3 percent) as the adverse supply shocks unwound after being above the upper limit of the target band during the first ten months of 2012.

Moreover, the same source predicts growth in Peru will continue in 2013:

Directors considered near term fiscal policy to be broadly adequate and took note that the 2013 budget targets a surplus. While the current fiscal framework has served Peru well in reducing debt and building public sector savings, Directors saw merit in strengthening the framework by establishing an appropriate anchor which aims at ensuring prudent management of non-renewable resources and intergenerational equity, and enhancing the predictability of public spending.

Impressive though recent GDP growth has been, figures relating to construction activity have been even more positive. In a report prepared by the Banco Central de Reserva del Peru in December 2012[3], sustainable growth in construction activity was recorded as follows:

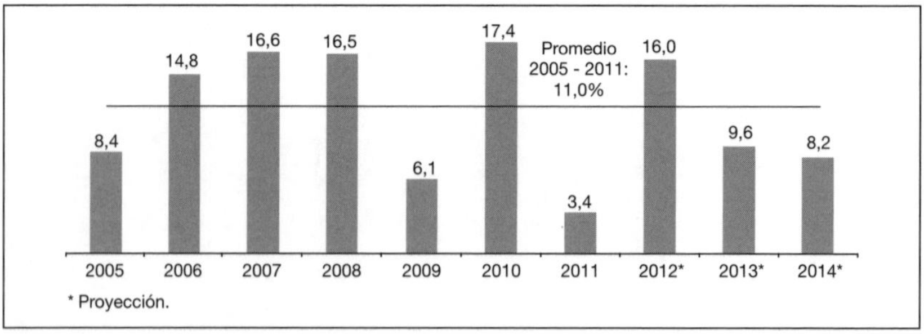

With this growth in construction activity, concern among professionals to have projects completed on time and in line with the contractual scope has led them to a greater awareness of the need for both better contracts and improved mechanisms to protect their interests.

One of the mechanisms considered particularly important in a contract is the dispute resolution method. Parties are not always at liberty to choose the method for resolving controversies. It will depend on the funding source for projects in Peru. In this context, the following section offers an overview of the dispute resolution methods that are used in the construction industry.

2. Public projects

In contrast with some other countries, in Peru there does not exist a liberal regime

3 See: www.bcrp.gob.pe/docs/Publicaciones/Reporte-Inflacion/2012/diciembre/reporte-de-inflacion-diciembre-2012.pdf.

of dispute resolution methods. That is, parties are not allowed to choose the dispute resolution method they consider most appropriate; it depends on whether or not the project is public or private. And if the project is public, it depends on whether or not the Public Procurement Law and its regulations are applicable. Consequently, there are specific laws that make mandatory the use of certain dispute resolution mechanisms when there is some sort of public financing involved.

In Peru there is no law that regulates all the ways in which the state may contract with a private investor. By contrast, there are different rules – depending on the kind of contract and investment – to be applied to each case. Thus, the Public Procurement Law, for example, regulates all those contracts where the state acquires goods, requires services or needs infrastructure work to be carried out. In other words, the state does not act as a seller. When the state decides to sell goods, other specific rules are applied.

On the other hand, the Concession Law for Public Infrastructure Works regulates all those contracts where the state has previously granted a concession to a private entity for the construction, exploiting and/or operation of an infrastructure work or a public service. In these contracts there is a much larger investment than in those procurements and contracts entered into under Public Procurement Law, basically because of the magnitude of the works.

Meanwhile, the Framework Law on Public-Private Partnership (PPP) regulates contracts where both the state and a private investor are jointly involved in the construction, exploiting and/or operation of an infrastructure project. The private investor obtains a concession awarded by the state too, but in these cases the participation of the state is greater – where experience, technology and efficiency mechanisms combine to benefit both parties.

In all the regulations mentioned above, then, there is a non-liberal regime of dispute resolution methods. The only mechanisms that may be used by parties in public projects are described below.

2.1 Conciliation

Conciliation is considered as an alternative dispute resolution method where parties appoint a recognised, independent and impartial third person who is responsible for carrying out the conciliation process. The conciliator proposes different solutions to assist the parties in resolving the dispute, but does not impose a solution; it is for the parties to decide on the best solution to their controversy. In Peru, conciliation is regulated by the Conciliation Act, which establishes the procedures, general rules and legal institutions of the conciliation process.

Conciliation is a dispute resolution mechanism that can be used by parties in those contracts that are regulated by the Public Procurement Law. Article 52 of this law states in part:

> *Any dispute between the parties about the implementation, interpretation, resolution, absence, ineffectiveness, or invalidity of the contract will be resolved by conciliation or arbitration under the agreement of the parties, having requested the initiation of these proceedings at any time prior to the date of completion of the contract.*

As can be seen, the Public Procurement Law expressly provides for the possibility of resolving disputes during the execution of a contract through conciliation or arbitration. Because arbitration will be dealt with in the next section, here we confine ourselves to describing conciliation.

In Peru, conciliation is a mechanism that can be used by itself. For example, in contracts where the Public Procurement Law applies, parties may agree to conciliation as the only dispute resolution method, thus excluding arbitration. However, it is unusual for parties to decide on conciliation as the only dispute resolution method. By contrast, conciliation is often chosen by parties as a pre-arbitration mechanism.

Thus, there can be a kind of multi-tiered clause where conciliation is the first method to be used when there is a controversy. If parties do not agree and, therefore, no conciliation is made, they may resort to arbitration as a final mechanism to settle disputes. In consequence, the conciliation mechanism becomes dysfunctional because parties are forced to go into it (as this has previously been agreed) knowing that the controversy will inevitably end in arbitration. That is, parties often have no intention of reconciling, making conciliation an unnecessary step prior to arriving at arbitration.

As stated by Paredes and Gray, "However, reality has delegitimized [conciliation's] function and nature being considered just as a prerequisite to the exercise of judicial action, precisely because of the absence of a culture of conciliation".[4]

When conciliation is used well by parties, disputes can be resolved without the resulting higher costs in terms of time and money. However, this usually happens in few cases because contractors prefer to extend the lifetime of the contract to charge owners the costs, penalties and interests incurred up to the issuance of an arbitration award. Furthermore, there are public officials who prefer not to make decisions regarding disputes in contracts because of a possible audit that could put them in serious trouble.

2.2 Arbitration

Largely as a result of the inevitable inefficiency and slowness of the judicial process, arbitration in recent years has become the dispute resolution method most frequently used by professionals in public works contracts, construction and infrastructure works. Arbitration has been seen as a more effective mechanism to resolve disputes. The dynamic of these contracts does not allow agents (contractors and owners) to run out of time and money as would be the case in a judicial process.

As a result of the nature of construction and infrastructure works contracts, there is a need for a more dynamic and specialised dispute resolution mechanism.[5] Indeed, arbitration was considered such a useful alternative to the judicial process that the

4 Paredes, Gustavo and Gray, Jaime, *"Mecanismos alternativos de resolución de disputas en construcción", Revista de Derecho Administrativo, Círculo de Derecho Administrativo*, Lima, Peru: Year III, No 4, January 2008.

5 We recognise, of course, that arbitration is not a new method. Professionals have been focusing their attention on it in recent years in the search for a better dispute resolution method to be applied in construction contracts. In this regard, we agree with José de Vicente y Caravantes when he says that "It is enough to stop and observe the events taking place in society, the way individuals tend to treat each other, and the way they end simple controversies that separate them, to understand that arbitration should have been one of the primary needs and one of the first practices of mankind." In: Vicente y Caravantes, José de. *Tratado histórico, crítico filosófico de los procedimientos judiciales en materia civil, según la nueva ley de enjuiciamiento*. Madrid: Gaspar y Roig. 1856. Page 11.

Public Procurement Law – as seen in the previous section – established the requirement for its use in cases where conciliation is not the preferred dispute resolution method. This mechanism has become so widely used in contractual practice and, specifically, in public projects, that people might believe it is the only dispute resolution mechanism permitted by law. However, as previously noted, the Public Procurement Law provides for the possibility to use both arbitration and conciliation as methods to resolve controversies. Neither arbitration nor conciliation is excluded and, consequently, it is feasible to agree on either one individually.

Regarding the supposed belief that arbitration is the only dispute resolution mechanism that can be used under the Public Procurement Law, it is appropriate to consider what the State Procurement Tribunal (*Tribunal de Contrataciones del Estado*)[6] of the state Procurement Supervisory Body (*Organismo Supervisor de las Contrataciones del Estado – OSCE*)[7] said about it: "public procurement regulations establish the obligation to arbitrate any disputes that may arise during performance of the contract and regulate certain general provisions regarding the dispute settlement procedure".[8]

Again, while this seems to imply that that arbitration is the only mandatory method to resolve disputes in public projects under the Public Procurement Law, this is not in fact the case. If arbitration is considered as obligatory, it is not because the law so determines but because it has become the custom (contractual practice).

For other projects executed under the Concession Law for Public Infrastructure Works,[9] there is provision for the possible use of arbitration as a dispute resolution mechanism. Article 17 of the Concession Law for Public Infrastructure Works states in part:

> *The State may submit patrimonial disputes regarding the concessions referred to in this law to international or local arbitration, in accordance with the provisions of article 63 of the Peruvian Political Constitution.*

Consequently, this law does not establish the obligation to use arbitration as a dispute resolution method. The wording determines that this mechanism is permissible but not mandatory. It would therefore be possible to agree on the use of conciliation or resort to judicial processes.

However, the wording of Article 17 is not entirely clear. Some professionals think that arbitration is mandatory. For them, the wording "The State may..." means the state may or may not decide to submit controversies to a resolution method. But if the state does decide to submit them, then that mechanism must be arbitration.

In practice, all concession contracts in Peru use arbitration as the dispute resolution method since it provides greater security for the investor. We can therefore say that its use is more a matter of accepted national custom than an obligation enacted in a law.

On the other hand in PPP projects the Framework Law on Public-Private Partnership provides for the mandatory use of arbitration as the only dispute

---

6 Settlement body for disputes between entities and bidders during the selection process. Applicable sanctions of suspension or debarment to suppliers and contractors violating the law.

7 Specialised technical agency responsible for promoting compliance with public procurement regulation.

8 Pronouncement N° 094-2012/DSU, February 20 2012.

9 Supreme Decree N° 059-96-PCM and Supreme Decree N° 060-96-PCM.

resolution method. Article 9.6 states:

> *Public-Private Partnerships contracts must include arbitration as the dispute settlement mechanism and must include provisions governing the procedure and grounds for renegotiation.*

The parties, therefore, cannot use any other mechanism as there is the express statutory obligation to go to arbitration to settle disputes.

2.3 Dispute boards

There are cases where, despite the fact that an infrastructure project is conducted by the state as a contractual party, the Public Procurement Law is not applied. That is because this particular law assumes that contracts are entered into with public investment involved, and contracts with private investment are excluded from the application of the Public Procurement Law. Contracts executed under specific procedures of international organisms, cooperation agreements and others with the same characteristic are also excluded.

In recent years, there have been contracts signed through certain public entities with some international agencies to grant the necessary financing for major construction projects (especially in the water and sewage disposal sector). These international organisms themselves set rules and mechanisms applicable to contracts signed by the state with a constructor for infrastructure works and large projects.

Similarly, for infrastructure, construction, supervision and consulting projects, the World Bank and the JICA (formerly JBIC; see below), for example, establish specific dispute resolution methods or oblige states to use contract models, such as FIDIC contracts, in which the resolution method applied is either multi-tiered or involves dispute boards (DBs).

Although DBs are becoming better known to professionals in the Peruvian construction industry, there remains much to be done before the method becomes universally used as an efficient tool to resolve controversies in contracts. Peruvian economic growth has encouraged both national and foreign investors to participate in private and public infrastructure projects. Consequently, the construction industry here has become more globalised; more technical construction information has been shared, contracts have been improved by mechanisms developed abroad and more expertise has been acquired.

However, the DB – as an alternative resolution method in construction – has not yet come to be as fully understood and appreciated as it should be. In consequence, although DBs are being used in Peru, there is considerable room for improvement in their usage. There are good arbitrators that have not as yet performed well as DB members; nevertheless, since they already have the knowledge required to resolve disputes, they surely have the capability to acquire sufficient expertise to operate effectively in the DB context.

Many infrastructure projects in Peru have involved financing institutions and international organisations. One which has been more involved in recent years has been the Japan International Cooperation Agency, JICA, mentioned above. This agency has funded many projects in Peru and required the employment of certain contractual mechanisms so that money may be invested more efficiently.

Sewage treatment plant (Huachipa, Peru)[10]

Source: SEDAPAL

One of the JICA requirements for those receiving funding for the execution of infrastructure projects is the use of FIDIC[11] contracts. As is well known, contracts developed by FIDIC include a DB as a dispute settlement mechanism. Thus, Peru has executed projects under contracts where the DB should have worked to prevent disputes arising.

However, during the negotiation of contracts, through ignorance or the lack of a thorough understanding of the nature of a DB, its true function is misrepresented sometimes. The result is a system which, while theoretically aimed at resolving disputes, in fact does not. That is, parties modify (eg, as the result of an incorrect translation) the DB clause included in the FIDIC model contracts, turning the DB into a different mechanism that functions negatively rather than positively in the dispute resolution process.

Despite the above, it is true to say that DBs are now being used more frequently in Peru. However, as suggested, a thorough understanding of the function, structure and nature of a DB is a prerequisite to achieving success. To broaden the appeal and interest in this mechanism it is vital that we determine fully and objectively the incentives and disincentives for using the DB as an alternative method of dispute resolution in the field of construction, and communicate effectively the conclusions to all interested parties. In this way, everyone concerned can form their own opinion.

10 For more information about this and other works, see: www.sedapal.com.pe/c/document_library/get_file?uuid=83aaef9b-40f1-4806-98aa-d38bcca57262&g

11 International Federation of Consulting Engineers (FIDIC) is an international organism designed to promote and implement strategic goals and to disseminate information and resources of interest to its members. FIDIC has published standard forms of contracts for works and for clients, consultants, sub-consultants, joint ventures and representatives.

Finally we should point out that the legal impediment to the use of DBs or any other dispute resolution method is not applicable in public projects in which the Public Procurement Law and its regulations are not applicable either.

3. Private projects

For all projects in which the state does not participate or where no public funds are involved, there is a liberal regime of dispute resolution methods. In other words, there is no rule establishing any mandatory mechanism. Parties are free to determine the method that best suits their interests and needs in the context of the project concerned. Usually, parties agree on arbitration as the method to resolve disputes. In some other cases, parties establish a multi-tier dispute resolution method. In these instances, parties define stages and separate procedures for the settlement of disputes. Typically, there is a clause that lets parties negotiate controversies as a first tier. Conciliation is used as a second tier, and arbitration as a third and final tier of dispute resolution.

Provision for judicial process can be found in some contracts, but the tendency is not to resort to it, especially in large projects. DBs are not typically used as a resolution method, although nowadays they are being employed in some projects by professionals and construction activity agents.

3.1 Negotiation

Negotiation, like conciliation or arbitration, is an alternative dispute resolution method that can be used not only in the construction sector but in any area where disputes arise. It is a mechanism whereby parties interested in resolving their disputes may reach agreement to end any conflict.

Negotiation is a process through which each party presents its interests and ideas to reach a fair and efficient solution for both, if possible. However, unlike conciliation, mediation or arbitration, there is no involvement of a third party in the solution process; the parties themselves (or their representatives) must reach an agreement. This, however, does not exclude the possibility of a third party, a friendly facilitator, from assisting in the solution process. The role of this person, then, will be solely to direct the negotiation to make parties focus on reaching a fair solution.

It is common practice to use this method in construction and infrastructure project contracts. It is inevitable that, during the contract execution, disputes arise that oblige parties to negotiate an appropriate solution. Sometimes transaction, or compromise, is used as a legal device (regulated in the Peruvian Civil Code) for both parties to reach an agreement conceding benefits, accepting some conditions and proposing others. On many occasions, controversies end in such negotiation, generating more savings in cost and time than conciliation, mediation or arbitration.

It is not necessary to specify in a contract the use of negotiation to resolve controversies. This method can always be used if parties agree to it when a dispute arises. Sometimes, parties do not realise they are using it because negotiation has become common practice in the Peruvian construction industry. As individual interests and private investment are involved, parties know the best way to resolve a dispute is by discussing possible solutions. They realise – or should realise – that it is costly to get involved in a process where a third person will decide a controversy and receive payment in exchange (in addition to the costs of legal fees, investigation, time, technical support, etc).

3.2 Mediation and conciliation

Both mediation and conciliation are dispute resolution methods in which there is the participation of a third person. The role of this person is what makes the difference between mediation and conciliation. Whereas in mediation the third person – without proposing any kind of solution – leads parties to resolve any disputes, in conciliation the third person may propose solutions that parties may accept or not. Consequently, in conciliation the participation of the third person is more active than in mediation.

As may be appreciated, the solution to a controversy depends, always, on the parties. They will decide if the dispute is to be resolved by implementing any solution as it applies to them. In Peru, there has been a great effort to promote the correct use of conciliation, with the passing of the Conciliation Act specifying conciliation as a mechanism to resolve controversies prior to entering into any judicial process. Conciliation has thus been perceived as a means to lightening the judicial caseload.

Nevertheless, as observed by professionals in Peru, conciliation has been misunderstood and, despite its regulation, has merely become a preliminary mechanism generating unnecessary costs in terms of time and money, prior to embarking on a judicial process. If parties wish to take controversies to a conciliation process, they must simply agree to it. Peru has several institutions that provide infrastructure and conciliators for the resolution of disputes. In the field of construction, conciliation is rarely considered as a controversy resolution mechanism. Owners and constructors usually establish a multi-tier clause in which negotiation is the first tier and arbitration the second.

However, Peru does not have a mediation law. Mediation is a method by which parties could choose to resolve their controversies and, as mentioned above, there are institutions that provide it as a service. But despite that, mediation is not a dispute resolution mechanism commonly adopted by parties in contracts for construction and infrastructure projects.

3.3 Arbitration

Arbitration is the most widely used dispute resolution mechanism for public construction and infrastructure projects in Peru. In private projects, contract parties almost always agree an arbitration clause whereby parties submit disputes to an *ad hoc* or institutional arbitration.

Ad hoc arbitrations are characterised mainly by the fact that the arbitrators organise and conduct the arbitration process themselves. Institutional arbitrations, on the other hand, imply the existence of arbitral institutions responsible for organising the process while arbitrators conduct it. Moreover, arbitral institutions provide not only the organisation and management of arbitrations, but they also offer the infrastructure necessary for a good and efficient process. Each institution has a list of recommended arbitrators, and parties may appoint one of them if they so wish.

Peru does not have specific arbitration rules for the construction industry. However, professionals these days are dealing with so many conflicts related to construction and infrastructure works contracts that they are coming to realise the need for specialisation. This explains why there is currently a growing interest in creating an Arbitration Court for Construction in one of the more prominent arbitration centres in Peru.

Peru has a specific law that regulates arbitration proceedings and supplements those regulations prepared and incorporated by each arbitral institution. The Arbitration Act, last modified in 2008, received good reviews from those involved in these processes on a day-to-day basis. Although the Arbitration Act is not perfect, it has remained fully in force and is generally applied in all arbitration proceedings where required.

Parties are allowed to opt for either international or domestic arbitration. Major project contracts, however, usually have a domestic arbitration clause included. In spite of the large amount of investment involved in these projects, taking conflicts to international arbitration is still costly. Most conflicts taken to arbitration are regulated under the ICSID rules and this happens only when the state and a private investor are contract parties.

3.4 Litigation

Bearing in mind that private projects imply a liberal regime for dispute resolution methods, the legal jurisdiction remains as a mechanism to resolve controversies if parties so decide. It may be that parties have expressly established in the contract the submission of disputes to legal jurisdiction, in which case parties will be forced to resolve issues that way (unless parties agree later to submit controversies to another mechanism, usually arbitration). However, it can also happen that parties have not established any mechanism to resolve controversies, in which case disputes will be resolved under the general rules of judicial proceedings (again, unless parties agree to resort to another method). In any case, the mechanism selected by parties must be established in writing.

Parties hardly ever agree to go into litigation to resolve controversies related to construction and infrastructure projects. They know that it is better to resolve them by any means other than litigation. This explains why legislators decided to oblige parties to employ conciliation or arbitration for disputes arising in public projects. Even in cases where parties have not established any particular method to resolve controversies, when a dispute arises they tend to decide on conciliation or arbitration to settle them.

There are no state courts specialising in construction, infrastructure or PPP disputes. Whenever a case is submitted to a judicial process, it is usually dealt with by the Commercial Court and parties are required to explain as fully and accurately as possible the conflicts in question, the circumstances, business objectives, evidence and any other data relevant to the contract concerned. In other words, they need to adequately inform judges so that the latter thoroughly understand the nature of the conflict they are dealing with. Only then can parties feel assured that they will receive at least an informed decision.

4. Conclusion

We should bear in mind that is important for the owner and the constructor to have a dispute resolution method that works efficiently, irrespective of what that method is called. It is important to consider the nature of construction and infrastructure works contracts. These contracts are essentially dynamic, not only because of the number of controversies that may arise during the execution of works but because the owner (in private projects) or the state (in public projects) needs to have the works completed.

In public projects there are additional factors to consider in relation to disputes arising. The state is usually reluctant to extend the execution time due to promises made to its citizens. We have also stressed that price and time are extremely important in construction activities because of the implications they generate for parties.

Consequently, it is necessary to stop and think about the functions of the resolution methods in use in Peru. It is time to undertake a review of how arbitration – as the main method employed – has helped in dispute resolution, to review the reasons for still using the present mechanisms and to re-examine other methods that could be more frequently used, such as mediation or conciliation, considering that they are aimed at finding a 'win–win' solution for the parties. It is also time to be honest with ourselves and ask if the methods most often used in Peru really work as originally intended; it is time to reflect on the words the Fox used when speaking to the Little Prince: "what is essential is invisible to the eyes".[12]

Once we have fully evaluated the status of the Peruvian dispute resolution system, there should be more studies made, for example, of DBs. Academic debates about the use of DBs and other effective mechanisms should be organised to discuss their implementation in public procurement regulation.

When a contractor or an employer is asked what kind of dispute resolution method is preferable for the resolution of controversies arising during the execution of a construction project, he will usually answer:

> *I do not care what the resolution method is. All I need is a way for me and my counterpart to promptly resolve any issues and if we cannot agree on how to resolve them, then the method should allow the decision-maker (judge, arbitrator or whoever is designated to make the decision) to decide in favor of the party which has proven their case and has supported the facts with evidence.*

A similar answer to that question would be given by an American, Chinese, German or Peruvian. In other words, the need for a resolution method with the above characteristics is universal. However, of all the resolution methods employed in construction and infrastructure projects in general, it is the DB – in our opinion – that is the dispute resolution method that best meets the requirements for dealing with construction activity controversies, particularly in Peru.

---

12 De Saint-Exupery, Antoine, *The Little Prince*, Reynal & Hitchcock Editorial: USA, 1943, chapter 21.

Uruguay

José Luis Echevarría Petit
Echevarría Leunda & Echevarría Petit

1. Introduction

The Uruguayan economy has been growing strongly over the past seven years, after a major crisis in 2002 due to currency devaluations in Argentina and Brazil (neighbouring countries and important buyers of the country's products).

During this economic growth, Uruguay received foreign direct investment in many sectors, construction being one of the most important. These circumstances improved employment in the sector, and this increase was accompanied by a growth in salary of more than 70% – factors that allowed more people into the housing market. The government also passed a law for social housing construction that meant an increase in the construction of low-cost houses over the 2010–12 period.

For all the above reasons, construction, both industrial and housing, grew strongly and with it the need for flexible and agile dispute resolution methods to solve differences between developers, contractors and subcontractors. To a lesser extent, dispute resolution methods have been used for labour disputes. Even though labour disputes can be submitted to arbitration, and have been in some cases in the past, its application is very rare and it is unusual to see arbitration clauses in labour contracts or collective agreements between unions and employers.

As explained below, no alternative dispute resolution (ADR) methods are banned in Uruguay, so they are all applicable to a very wide range of matters and in fact, many of these methods were used in construction contracts in the past, and continue to be used today.

Arbitration is the binding method for dispute resolution under the Public-Private Partnerships Law passed in 2011, and regulations approved in 2012, which will start to show results as soon as the first PPP projects are awarded.

The Uruguayan General Procedure Code has a specific chapter regarding arbitration, which states the freedom to choose arbitration for all matters – apart from some criminal and family law matters – that are not forbidden by law.

Arbitral awards can only be challenged for nullity on four specific grounds, as described in section 2.2(i), giving arbitration stability and certainty as a method.

International or domestic arbitration is allowed, either institutional or *ad hoc*, and based in law or in fairness.

2. Arbitration

Arbitration is not a new phenomenon in Uruguay as it was the chosen dispute resolution method for matters related to corporations in the Commercial Code, which dates from 1866. For more than 100 years, all aspects referring to commercial corporations had to be solved by arbitration, so it became a widely used ADR method in Uruguay.

Article 6 of the Constitution states: "In the international treaties that the Republic signs, it will propose that all difference that may arise between the parties shall be decided by arbitration or other pacific means." Uruguay has also ratified a list of important treaties and conventions regarding arbitration and, as will be explained, this tendency was fortified by the growth of direct foreign investment.

Furthermore, the Industrial Promotion Law passed by Parliament in 1998 states that any dispute arising from the application or interpretation of the law between an investor and the Uruguayan state can be submitted to arbitration based in law. This shows a clear and wide acceptance of arbitration, but also a clear decision by the Uruguayan state to be part of arbitration in certain disputes with individuals, giving national and foreign individuals more certainty of fair and equal treatment, which is very important in public infrastructure projects. In fact, many public construction contracts contain arbitration clauses, with all the advantages that this method has as opposed to the traditional jurisdictional suits against the administration.

The Uruguayan Chamber of Commerce has organised a court of arbitration and has a wide list of arbitrators, some of which were appointed by the chambers of different industries, thus giving the parties the chance to appoint specialised arbitrators suggested by the different chambers.

Under the rules of the chamber, each party appoints an arbitrator (these can be from the list or not), and both arbitrators appointed by the parties appoint the president of the tribunal from the list of court arbitrators.

2.1 Main reasons for the adoption of arbitration

The use of arbitration is growing worldwide as a result of several factors, and Uruguay has been part of this trend.

One of the main reasons that arbitration is the preferred dispute resolution method stems from the lack of a specialised jurisdiction for certain sectors. This is the case in construction which, despite being a civil law matter, has its own special features that should be considered when discussing and deciding disputes. Many technical aspects arising in construction disputes are unfamiliar to civil judges.

Another important reason to use ADR is its agility. As well as being provided with a final and non-appealable decision, the parties can choose a short procedure, taking less time to arrive at the final arbitral award. An important advantage of arbitration is that parties are able to decide by mutual agreement the term within which the award shall be issued. This gives parties the key to short and agile procedures.

Confidentiality is another feature of arbitration that is appreciated by the parties to a contract, and the Chamber of Commerce's arbitration court has very strict confidentiality clauses in its arbitration rules. Section VI of the rules contain Articles 46 to 49 that ensure a specific arbitration is kept confidential, as is the information disclosed during arbitration and the award. The arbitrators and the Chamber itself are committed to confidentiality.

2.2 Arbitration regulation

Legal regulation of arbitration is contained in the General Procedure Code.

(a) *Matters that can be resolved by arbitration*

Under Article 472 of the General Procedure Code, any particular or collective dispute can be subject to arbitration.

Only matters expressly excluded from arbitration by law (and there are no such laws at present) and matters that cannot be settled or disposed of freely by the parties fall outside the application of arbitration. The matters that are excluded from arbitration are criminal law matters and some aspects of family law that cannot be settled under Uruguayan law.

(b) *Recognition of arbitral awards*

The code states that the law recognises *de jure* all arbitral awards either issued by *ad hoc* or institutional tribunals. This means that the state gives validity to all arbitral awards and therefore, once the arbitral award is issued, there is no need for agreement or approval by the judicial power.

General *de jure* recognition shows the low level of state intervention in arbitration, which is critical when deciding the applicable law and site of arbitration. Uruguay has a very liberal approach to arbitration, shown by this low level of state intervention.

(c) *Arbitration clause*

When parties to a certain contract wish to submit all their disputes to arbitration, an arbitration clause is included in writing in the contract. If no written clause is included in the contract, there is no way of making the parties subject to arbitration.

The inclusion of the written clause entitles a party to make a resisting party go to arbitration. The General Procedure Code has a provision stating that a judge can sign an arbitration commitment on behalf of a resisting party. Once the commitment is signed by the judge and the other party, arbitration can begin and any further absence or resistance of the party has a detrimental effect on its case.

Even in cases in which there is no arbitration clause in a contract, parties can agree to submit to arbitration voluntarily. In other words, the inclusion of a written clause is essential to force a resisting party, but absence of the clause is not an obstacle for parties willing to submit their differences to arbitration, despite not having agreed on that at contract execution.

(d) *Arbitral commitment*

Once one party decides to submit a dispute to arbitration, it has to notify the arbitral institution (or the appointed arbitrator) and the other party of its intention to submit to arbitration. Once notice is given, both parties must sign an arbitral commitment. This commitment is the key arbitration document and it must be executed before a notary public or a judge in a hearing.

The arbitral commitment contains the appointment of the arbitrators, all the issues that the arbitrators have to decide, the procedure to be followed, the decision about whether the arbitration will be founded in law or in fairness, and the term in which to issue the award.

(e) ***Freedom to choose the tribunal***

Parties can choose to submit their differences either to an institutional arbitration or to an *ad hoc* tribunal; both kinds are used in contracts.

Notwithstanding the freedom to choose, there is a strong tendency to adopt the Chamber of Commerce institutional arbitration terms in most contracts stating arbitration as the dispute resolution method.

(f) ***Kompetenz-kompetenz***

The principle under which the arbitral tribunal has the competence to decide whether or not it is competent, in each particular case, is practically unanimous in international arbitral regulations and Uruguay is no exception. It is known as *kompetenz-kompetenz.*

This principle is set forth in Article 26 of the Chamber of Commerce's arbitration rules and is paramount when the validity of the contract or of the particular arbitration clause is challenged for nullity by one party.

(g) ***Freedom of arbitral procedure***

Article 477 of the General Procedure Code states that the parties shall determine, in the arbitral commitment, the procedure to be followed in the arbitration, which means that the parties have freedom to decide which is the most suitable procedure for them, provided the procedure fulfils the requirements of fair and due process.

Default procedure: The General Procedure Code sets a default procedure where parties are silent. In such cases, the ordinary procedure stated in the same code must be followed by the tribunal. This ordinary process has basically three phases:

- A written phase, in which the plaintiff files its claim including all documents that it intends to use as evidence, the name of all witnesses, the information that it is going to ask from public or private third parties, and any other evidences that it wishes to bring to the arbitration. Once filed and notified to the defendant, it has 30 calendar days to file its defence, including, as in the claim, all the evidence.
- The oral phase, composed of a preliminary hearing in which the tribunal tries to help parties to settle their disputes; but if settlement is not reached, the parties ratify their positions, and the tribunal details the issues to be resolved and the evidence to be produced. If all evidence cannot be examined in the preliminary hearing, a second hearing is held. After all evidence is produced, each party makes its final remarks.
- An award issuance phase, in which the tribunal studies all the evidence and issues the award.

Chamber of Commerce court procedure: This procedure is very similar to the default position described above, but it contains a confidentiality clause, which is not included in the General Procedure Code. This Chamber of Commerce rule allows the parties to introduce particular variations to suit their needs.

Tailored procedure: Under Uruguayan law, there is freedom to choose the arbitral procedure, so parties can agree a certain procedure different from the ones described above, or a customised version of one of them, as long as those procedures respect the principles of due process.

(h) Award

One very important aspect contained in the General Procedure Code refers to the term for the tribunal to issue the award. That term is set by the parties in the arbitral commitment, and can be set in business or calendar days. The arbitral tribunal must issue the award within the term. This is paramount, because the consequence of exceeding the term is nullity.

(i) Challenges to the arbitral award

The General Procedure Code sets a very restricted path to challenge arbitration awards, which provides a great deal of certainty and stability.

The award can only be challenged on the grounds of nullity, and this can only arise in four possible cases:

- The award is issued after the expiry of the term set by the parties in the commitment.
- The award is on matters not included in the arbitration commitment.
- The award does not decide matters included in the arbitration commitment.
- The refusal of the tribunal to receive certain evidence that was essential for ruling the case.

This is a definitive list, so no other cause of nullity is admitted. Only the first and the last cause of nullity affect the whole award, while the other two just partially affect the award, especially the part of it relating to the undecided issues.

Nullity challenges are decided by a civil appeal court, composed of three judges.

Jurisprudence on challenges to arbitral awards filed by losing parties is very reassuring as judges have ruled against most of those challenges, charging the losing party (the plaintiff of the challenge) with all expenses. This discourages such challenges when they are not founded on one of the four cases of nullity.

(j) Award enforcement

Under the General Procedure Code, arbitral awards, when not instigated by the parties spontaneously, can be enforced before the tribunal that would have been competent to decide the case if an arbitration clause had not been included by the parties.

The procedure for enforcing domestic awards is the same as that for enforcing a decision of a state judge or tribunal, and is set forth in Articles 372 to 376 of the General Procedure Code.

Enforcement starts with a presentation of the award before the state judge that would have been competent if the case was submitted to state jurisdiction. The judge orders the defeated party to pay the award. If the party does not comply, the judge issues a seizure injunction and enforces the award, with all costs bound by the resisting party.

2.3 Investment protection arbitration

Besides the international conventions ratified by Uruguay regarding international arbitration, the country has signed several international agreements for foreign investment protection, setting arbitration as the dispute resolution method.

The countries with which Uruguay has investment protection treaties are the following:

Albania	Armenia
Australia	Austria
Barbados	Belorussia
Belgium	Bolivia
Bulgaria	Canada
Chile	China
Costa Rica	Croatia
Cuba	Czech Republic
Ecuador	Egypt
El Salvador	European Union
Finland	France
Germany	Greece
Holland	Hungary
India	Indonesia
Israel	Italy
Latvia	Lebanon
Lithuania	Luxembourg
Malaysia	Mauritius
Mexico	Morocco
Nicaragua	Panama
Paraguay	Peru
Poland	Portugal
Qatar	Romania
San Marino	Saudi Arabia
Slovenia	South Africa
South Korea	Spain
Sweden	Switzerland
Thailand	Turkey
United Kingdom	United States of America
Venezuela	Vietnam

These treaties allow nationals of these countries to file a claim against Uruguay in an international court of arbitration if the investor is treated unfairly or with discrimination, breaching the obligation of the state under the protection treaty.

2.4 Enforcement of international arbitral awards

Domestic arbitral awards are enforced by the tribunals of the state as explained above.

Enforcement of foreign arbitral awards, according to the General Procedure Code, is done according to the treaties signed by Uruguay applicable to the case, or according to the procedure set by law for the enforcement of foreign judicial decisions.

To enforce foreign awards under the General Procedure Code (in other words, when no other procedure is set by the treaties signed by Uruguay and the country of origin of the award), a petition must be filed before the Supreme Court of Justice, which will notify the party against which it will be enforced, giving it 20 days to file its defence. The resolution is final and is not appealable. If the decision of the Supreme Court is to enforce the award, the interested party must follow the same procedure explained for domestic awards.

Uruguay has ratified many international conventions on arbitration, for example:

- the New York Convention on the Recognition and Enforcement of Foreign Arbitral Awards;
- the Inter-American Convention on International Commercial Arbitration (Panama 1975);
- the Inter-American Convention on the Extraterritorial Validity of Foreign Judgments and Arbitral Awards, (Montevideo, 1979); and
- the Protocol on Cooperation and Jurisdictional Assistance in Civil, Commercial, Labour and Administrative Matters (Mercosur, Las Leñas, Argentina).

Having ratified international conventions that ensure the validity and enforcement of foreign judgments and arbitral awards, Uruguay allows parties to agree upon a foreign institutional or *ad hoc* arbitration to decide differences between parties. This helps create a very positive and secure environment for foreign construction companies to develop projects in Uruguay.

3. Other ADR methods

3.1 Conciliation

There is no rule forbidding ADR methods in Uruguay, so mediation, conciliation, dispute review boards, expert determination and other procedures are accepted in Uruguay.

Conciliation is a type of mediation in which a specialised judge helps the parties to settle their differences, without having the competence to decide the case if an agreement is not reached. Conciliation is the most common way of dispute resolution besides the jurisdictional suit.

Conciliation is obligatory as a preliminary procedure, and any prospective plaintiff must follow it before filing any lawsuit. Conciliation is conducted, as explained above, by special judges that do not have the competence to decide on the case. The judges help the parties settle their differences, even proposing settlement alternatives.

If there is no settlement, a minute stating that the conciliation was unsuccessful is issued, and that document must be attached to any claim filed before the judge appointed to rule on the case.

An important feature of conciliation is that all arguments stated during the hearing are not included in the minute, and therefore parties' views on the particular case cannot be used against them in the suit if the conciliation is unsuccessful.

3.2 Mediation

Another ADR method used in Uruguay is mediation. This differs from conciliation in that the individual helping the parties, who is not a judge but a mediator, does not usually propose ways to settle the dispute but simply helps the parties to discover their own interests and a way to negotiate with each other to reach a solution to their dispute.

The Uruguayan Chamber of Commerce has a list of mediators and, to be included on that list, each individual has to follow a certain curriculum and participate in mediations in countries in which mediation is obligatory – for example, Argentina.

Mediation is sometimes included as a preliminary phase of dispute resolution. It is usual to find clauses that state that the parties should try to settle their differences amicably within a certain term, and if this negotiation does not succeed, then they should file for mediation. Only when this method proves to be unsuccessful does arbitration take place.

3.3 Dispute review boards

Although dispute review boards (DRBs) are admitted under Uruguayan law on disposable matters (the same as arbitration, conciliation and mediation), this is not a method usually used in Uruguay.

There is no regulation or provision in Uruguayan law regarding this method, which has nevertheless proved very useful in many parts of the world.

3.4 Expert determination

This ADR method (which the author includes in most construction contracts), is rarely used in Uruguay. It has proved to be the best way to resolve relatively minor differences that tend to sour the relationship between parties, and it can be used to avoid conflict escalation. Many technical aspects of a contract can be solved by expert determination in a clear and agile fashion.

Some of the technical aspects that can be solved by expert determination are common disputes – for example, quality of material, craftsmanship quality, certification of work, preliminary acceptance and final acceptance of works.

This swift way of solving everyday differences also works as an incentive to show good faith during contract execution, particularly when the cost is borne by the defeated party. Another advantage of this method is its agility, which avoids unfair situations persisting over time that detrimentally affect both parties.

The difficulty of finding an expert who meets the approval of both parties is well worth the effort in the long run, often avoiding having to proceed to arbitration.

4. The construction sector

Construction has always been a strong industry in Uruguay, and has been growing apace during the past eight years. During 2012, 12,000 direct and 11,000 indirect jobs were created in the construction sector. The overall growth of the sector's gross domestic product during 2012 was 12%. Moreover, according to social security administration information, direct employment in construction grew from 43,193 employees in February 2008, to 70,142 in August 2012, more than 74% growth in four years. Considering direct and indirect jobs, the total number is 115,000, representing 6.7% of the country's active population.

One of the factors that fostered such growth in this sector is a new law for social housing (Law No 18.795, Access to Social Interest Housing) that creates important tax benefits for developers of social housing projects. These developers receive substantial rebates in net income tax, net worth tax, value added tax and importing tax. This new law provides a great incentive for companies that were mainly involved in high-value housing to engage in new low-cost projects but with more advantageous tax incentives.

Infrastructure and housing are the most developed subsectors of the construction industry in Uruguay. Construction of industrial plants has also gained in importance over the past years. For example, cattle slaughter plants and cellulose pulp plants contributed to the industry's growth owing to substantial investments in these industries.

The public sector was less active than the private sector and was unable to capture private sector funds for public sector infrastructure, despite the unanimous approval of a public-private partnership law in 2011.

This situation is about to change, as the government has already issued requests for proposals for a prison, highways and an oil and gas port within Montevideo Bay (the last opened on February 22 2013).

Many public sector projects are being studied – for example convention centres, railways and deep water ports, among others. This means that the future of construction in Uruguay looks bright and will definitely demand specialised arbitration skills.

5. Arbitration in public construction

Some decades ago, there was no possibility of including arbitration in public contracts. Today, there is no problem with the government including arbitration clauses in its contracts to help solve disputes.

5.1 Arbitration in PPP contracts

The Uruguayan pro-arbitration position is ratified by the inclusion of obligatory arbitration in the new Public Private Partnerships Law (Law 18.786), passed by Parliament in 2011. Article 54 of the law states:

> *Controversy solution: Conflicts arising from the application, interpretation, execution, accomplishment and extinction of contracts signed under this law shall be solved by parties by arbitration. Arbitrators shall be appointed by the parties by mutual agreement, or otherwise, according to article 480 the General Procedure Code, and shall decide based in law. The arbitral award will be unappealable.*

As PPPs are agreements between public and private sector entities, this legal rule means that the Uruguayan state has decided to be judged by arbitration when a dispute arises between one of its bodies and a private sector company.

This PPP law was approved by unanimous vote of the deputies and senators, which sends a strong signal to foreign companies considering participating in Uruguayan PPP projects.

Regulation of this law, approved by the Executive Power in 2012, sets the principle of the arbitral clause's autonomy and the competence of the arbitral tribunal to decide on the existence and validity of the clause. It also states the independence of the arbitral clause from the contract, assuring the validity of the arbitral clause even in the case of the contract becoming null.

5.2 Arbitration in other public contracts

Besides providing for arbitration in PPP contracts, arbitration is usually stated as the dispute resolution method in many other public contracts, especially in construction.

The following paragraphs refer to specific cases where public contracts contained the arbitral clause and it was effectively put into practice by the parties. To show a consisten adoption of arbitration in public contracts, these sampled cases range from 1989 to the present:

- In 1989 a Uruguayan local authority signed a construction contract with a private company to build some of its sewage system components. During construction, the administration modified some units, resulting in more material and work for the contractor. The contract had a provision allowing the administration to modify the obligations under the contract within certain limits. The administration made use of such a clause, but the dispute arose from the price to be paid for that modification, due to a lack of unitary prices to be applied to the modification. It was solved by the arbitral tribunal in three months.
- In 1993, the state water and sewage company entered into arbitration with a contractor regarding the application of higher costs and compensations for early completion. The dispute was solved by the arbitral tribunal in three and a half months.
- In 1994, the state power company entered into a contract with a foreign company and its Uruguayan subsidiary that included an arbitration clause, which was set in the terms of reference. In 1998 a dispute arose that led to an arbitral commitment, which was signed in September 1998. The dispute referred to the existence of a right of compensation for early completion in favour of the contractor. Several hearings were postponed by mutual agreement of the parties. The arbitral tribunal proposed a settlement that the parties did not accept at the beginning but finally did. The whole procedure, including conciliation, took six months.
- In 1997, the University of the Republic in Uruguay entered into a construction contract containing an arbitration clause with a local contractor. A dispute arose regarding the term of the contract and the

interpretation of a clause on labour costs. The arbitral commitment was signed in March 1997, and the arbitral award resolving it was issued on June 1997.

- In 2005, the contractor of a transmission line construction contract signed in 1998 with the state energy company, started an arbitration procedure. The contractor claimed that decisions taken by the state company had generated progressive delays in the execution of the works, slowing cash flow and causing damage to the contractor's business. The arbitration was solved within eight months from the arbitral commitment.

6. Conclusion

Uruguay has had long experience in the arbitration field as this ADR method has been adopted for civil and commercial disputes for more than 100 years.

Arbitration is also part of the country's international strategy, as set forth in the constitution. It has also become a guarantee for foreign investors who perceive that the Uruguayan state is ready to be judged by arbitrators (local and international) on questions relating to foreign investment, public construction contracts and PPPs.

Inclusion of arbitration in the constitution and in laws approved by a unanimous vote of all of the political parties shows a consistent support of and confidence in arbitration. This is also shown by the inclusion of arbitration in many public construction contracts.

International treaties and conventions approved by Uruguay show an international commitment in favour of arbitration as a preferred ADR method.

The low level of state intervention in arbitration, and the very restrictive grounds for challenging the arbitral award, make Uruguay one of the preferred sites for arbitration in South America.

Very low corruption numbers – Uruguay is ranked 20, one notch below the United States, according to Transparency International, 2012 – assures transparency of the whole process.

Construction, both public and private, is steadily growing and is predicted to do so in future, resulting in more intensive use of arbitration. Arbitration will continue to be an agile, specialised, confidential and fair way to solve the disputes of an ever-growing construction sector in Uruguay.

Australia

Jonathon DeBoos
Andrew Stephenson
Clayton Utz

1. Introduction

Australia exported A$54 billion of resource commodities in 2004–05. The Bureau of Resources and Energy Economics (BREE) forecasts that in 2012–13 Australia's resources and energy commodity export earnings will be A$184 billion.

This increase in demand for resources has seen Australia become home to some of the largest construction projects in the world. According to BREE, there are a total of 364 projects in the construction pipeline, ranging from A$651 billion to $693 billion in total. Of these, 87 projects with a combined value of A$268 billion either have started or are about to start.[1]

While many of these projects relate to resources such as coal, iron ore, copper, gold and uranium, by far the largest projects are those in the liquefied natural gas (LNG) sector. These include Chevron, ExxonMobil and Shell's A$43 billion Gorgon LNG project, Total SA and Inpex Corp's A$34 billion Ichthys LNG project, Chevron's A$29 billion Wheatstone LNG project and Woodside's A$14.9 billion Pluto LNG project. Analysts expect that these and other projects will result in Australia overtaking Qatar as the world's largest exporter of LNG by 2020.[2] Australia also has many other infrastructure projects. Billions of dollars' worth of construction is under way in the road, rail, water and electricity sectors.[3]

It is thus inevitable that Australian projects will be the subject of some of the biggest construction disputes in the world, making efficient dispute resolution of critical importance to Australia's economic future.

1.1 Brief overview of Australia's legal system

The Commonwealth of Australia is a federation of six states – New South Wales (NSW), Queensland, South Australia, Tasmania, Victoria and Western Australia – and two major mainland territories – the Australian Capital Territory and the Northern Territory. Under the Australian Constitution, the Commonwealth is granted legislative power in specific areas, with the states retaining all residual powers.[4] The

1 John Barber, Tom Shael, Nina Hitchins and Adam Bialowas, *Resources and Energy Major Projects October 2012*, http://www.bree.gov.au/documents/publications/mimp/REMP_Oct2012.pdf.

2 AFP, "Australian gas rush set to overhaul Qatar's lead", July 22 2012, accessed at www.news.com.au/business/markets/australian-gas-rush-set-to-overhaul-qatars-lead/story-e6frfm30-1226432124541 on February 6 2013.

3 Australian Government Department of Infrastructure and Transport, *Investment in Australian Infrastructure*, September 2012.

4 Section 51 of the Australian Constitution.

matters governed by Commonwealth legislation that are relevant to construction projects include those relating to interstate and international trade and commerce, corporations, taxation, intellectual property, immigration and workplace relations. The Australian Capital Territory and the Northern Territory function as states in most respects, with the major exception being that the Commonwealth Parliament can override any legislation of their parliaments.

The Commonwealth, the states and the territories each have their own legislature and court system. Accordingly, construction projects in Australia will be governed by both Commonwealth and state/territory legislation. The Australian court system is discussed below.

Being a former British colony, Australia has inherited the common law tradition.

2. Construction project dispute resolution

The complexity of international construction projects makes it inevitable that issues will arise during the course of a project. Where possible, these issues must be resolved at an early stage to prevent the relationship between the parties souring and escalating into dispute. There are a number of approaches used on construction projects in Australia aimed at doing just that.

2.1 Contract administrator

The most common method of project-level dispute resolution is the appointment of a contract administrator, who is referred to variously as the architect, engineer or superintendent. The contract administrator is the first port of call once an issue has been identified. His decision is usually binding, but subject to review by arbitration, court and possibly expert determination. Historically, the contract administrator was an employee or consultant of the owner, which meant that he was required to act as the owner's agent and obliged to promote the owner's interests. Nonetheless, when performing a dispute resolution role, the contract administrator was required to act fairly, justly and with skill towards all parties.[5]

The principal drawback to the traditional model is the contract administrator's perceived lack of neutrality, which can seriously hamper effectiveness in resolving issues.

One approach to solving the perceived lack of neutrality is to split the contract administrator's role into two positions. A neutral party who is formally engaged by both parties to the contract can perform the independent certification functions. As in the case of a traditional contract administrator, the independent certifier's decision will usually be binding but not final. The fundamental difference from the traditional administrator's role is that the independent certifier is not solely employed by the owner. The perceived loss of influence and additional expense may make this approach less attractive to the principal, but it is likely to reduce dispute costs and may even attract lower tender prices.

A second approach is to institute an 'appeal' process whereby the decision of the contract administrator can be referred to an independent adjudicator or a dispute review board (DRB). DRBs are discussed next.

2.2 Dispute review boards

The purpose of a DRB is to deal with the everyday commercial tensions that arise during a project before they become disputes and to provide a mechanism for effectively dealing with problems that do become disputes.

The concept originated in the United States in the 1980s and was principally used in major civil engineering works. The use of DRBs in Australia has increased significantly since 2003, with at least 24 major projects in Australia having used them since.[6] The use of DRBs in Australia will continue, with the NSW Transport Infrastructure Development Corporation (TDIC) having announced that it will use DRBs on all projects valued in excess of A$50 million and the Queensland Department of Main Roads having included DRBs as an option in its major design-and-construct standard form.

A DRB usually consists of a panel of three respected, impartial and experienced industry or technical experts. More members may be appointed for larger projects. The board is most effective when it is established at the start of a project, ideally as part of the construction contract. This enables it to keep up with the project's progress through regular site inspections, progress reports, project documents and regular contact with key project personnel. When issues arise, the board then has sufficient background to enable it to resolve them as quickly as possible. Having a board from the start of a project also regulates the parties' behaviour:[7] parties are less likely to send unfriendly correspondence when it could attract the board's disapproval.

One of the key issues is whether a DRB's decision should be binding. Broadly, there are three options:

- The decision is entirely non-binding and merely advisory.
- The decision is binding subject to review by an arbitral tribunal or court.
- The decision is entirely final and binding (where such DRBs are also known as dispute adjudication boards).

In Australia, the second option is the most common; that is, the board's decision is binding, but subject to review by (typically) arbitration or court proceedings (on a *de novo* basis). This means that the board's decision will be binding on the parties in the interim while allowing commercial relations to continue.

Experience to date suggests that a board decision will rarely be reviewed. Presumably, this is owing to the respect the parties have for the board members' opinions. Further, boards are usually used in projects when it is important to maintain commercial relations, so it is often in the parties' best interests to accept the decision as binding and move on with the project.

A DRB is based purely on a contract. Therefore the parties must agree upon all of the rules and the procedure to be followed in order for them to work properly. This is in contrast to arbitration (see section 5 below), in which the parties' agreement is supported and regulated by legislation.

---

5 See, for example, *Perini Corporation v Commonwealth* [1969] 2 NSWR 530.

6 R Finlay, "Dispute Board Concepts Internationally – Divergence or Convergence – Australian Perspective", paper delivered at the 12th Annual DRBF International Conference, May 2012.

7 P Gerber, "Construction Dispute Review Boards" (1999) 10(1) *ADRJ* 9 at 15.

The parties' agreement is typically set out in a combination of the construction contract and a tripartite agreement between the parties and the board members. The construction contract will tend to deal with issues such as whether the board's decisions will be binding and the procedure for replacing a board member. The tripartite agreement will tend to deal with more administrative matters such as the fees, confidentiality and limitation of board members' liability.

3. Administrative dispute resolution

As in the United Kingdom, Australia has introduced a statutory payment and adjudication regime for the construction industry. The purpose of this regime is to provide reasonable assurance that cash will flow in the manner anticipated by the contract.

The first problem that the legislation attempts to address arises when a party higher up the contractual chain refuses to make a due payment. Before the introduction of the legislation, only a court or arbitrator could force it to pay. The cost and time of obtaining a judgment or award means that a party higher up the contractual chain can put commercial pressure on the claimant by withholding payment.

The second problem is that a party higher up the contractual chain may become insolvent. A subcontractor, for example, cannot recover a debt owed by the contractor from the owner because, generally, the subcontractor has no direct relationship with the owner. This usually means that when an insolvent head contractor is wound up, the subcontractor will not get paid, other than as an unsecured creditor.

From 1999 to 2009, each Australian state and territory enacted its own security-of-payment legislation to protect contractors and subcontractors against these risks.[8] This legislation gives any person that carries out construction work or supplies related goods and services under a construction contract a statutory right to receive progress payments. It also entitles contractors, subcontractors and suppliers to pursue disputed progress payments by referring them to a rapid adjudication process.

The NSW act was the first of these acts, and the others are generally consistent with it. However, the acts vary in how efficient they are as a means of obtaining payment. Accordingly, the security-of-payment regime is used more in some states and territories than others. For example, the regime is used more in NSW than in Victoria, due in part to the unique aspects of the Victorian regime that make it less attractive to claimants. The main distinguishing feature is that claimants cannot take into account certain 'excluded amounts' when calculating the amount due for payment. In short, these 'excluded amounts' include variations that have not been

---

8 Building and Construction Industry Security of Payment Act 1999 (NSW); Building and Construction Industry Security of Payment Act 2002 (Vic); Building and Construction Industry Payments Act 2004 (Qld); Construction Contracts Act 2004 (WA); Construction Contracts (Security of Payment) Act 2004 (NT); Building and Construction Industry (Security of Payment Act) 2009 (ACT); Building and Construction Industry Security of Payment Act 2009 (SA); Building and Construction Industry Security of Payment Act 2009 (Tas).

agreed between the parties, claims for compensation for latent conditions (ie, unforeseen ground conditions) or time-related costs, or any other claims for damages arising under, or in connection with, the contract. This and other distinctive features of the various regimes are discussed further below.

3.1 Overview of the process

Under the security-of-payment acts, if a construction contract makes provision for progress payments, the legislation effectively turns the contractor's contractual entitlement into a statutory one. Where the contract does not provide for progress payments, then certain default provisions entitling the contractor to monthly progress payments take effect.

Following service of a progress claim, the owner must respond with a payment schedule setting out the amount that the respondent believes to be due and giving reasons for any difference from the payment claim. Generally, the respondent is required to issue its payment schedule within the earlier of the time required by the contract or 10 business days from when the progress claim was served.[9]

If the amount shown in the schedule is less than the amount claimed (or if the respondent fails to pay), the claimant may apply for adjudication.[10] This triggers the appointment of an adjudicator. The respondent is entitled to make a written response to the claimant's adjudication application,[11] but apart from that, the acts do not prescribe the procedure to be followed. In New South Wales, Queensland, Australian Capital Territory, South Australia and Tasmania, the respondent cannot include in its adjudication response any reasons for withholding payment that were not included in its payment schedule. This requirement makes it vital that respondents in those jurisdictions provide thoroughly reasoned payment schedules.

The adjudicator generally must make his determination within 10 business days of being appointed, unless the parties agree otherwise.[12] In Victoria, the respondent can seek a review of the determination by another adjudicator where the adjudicated amount exceeds A$100,000 and the respondent considers that the determination contains an excluded amount.[13] This entitlement is not available in the other Australian jurisdictions.

If the respondent does not pay the amount due under the adjudicator's determination, the claimant may give notice of its intention to suspend work and

---

9 Section 14(4) of the NSW act; Section 15(4) of the Victorian act; Section18(4) of the Queensland act; Section 16(4) of the ACT act. Cf Section 14(4) of the SA act (15 business days); Sections 19(2) and (3) of the Tasmanian act (20 business days in the case of a 'residential structure' where the respondent is the owner and not a building practitioner, or 10 business days in other cases).

10 Section 17 of the NSW act; Section 18 of the Victorian act; Section 21 of the Queensland act; Section 26 of the Western Australian act; Section 8 of the Northern Territory act; Section 17 of the South Australian act; Section 21 of the Tasmanian act.

11 Section 20 of the NSW act; Section 21(2) of the Victorian act; Section 27 of the Western Australian act; Section 29 of the Northern Territory act; Section 22 of the ACT act; Section 20(1) of the South Australian act; Section 23 of the Tasmanian act.

12 Section 21(3) of the NSW act; Section 22(4) of the Victorian act; Section 25(3) of the Queensland act; Section 33(3) of the NT act; Section 1(3) of the South Australian act; Section 24(1) of the Tasmanian act; cf Section 31(1) of the Western Australian act (the applicable time limit is 14 days or by agreement between the parties).

13 Division 2A of the Victorian act.

may also obtain an adjudication certificate, which can be filed in court as a judgment for a debt.[14]

The Australian Capital Territory is the only jurisdiction in which the security-of-payment legislation contains an express right to appeal an adjudicator's determination on a question of law.[15] However, while the other jurisdictions do not contain an express right to challenge an adjudicator's decision, courts may intervene if:

- the adjudicator failed to comply with the 'basic and essential' requirements of the relevant act;
- the adjudicator has denied natural justice to a party (having regard to the relatively limited scheme put forward by the acts for the provision of natural justice); or
- the adjudication decision was procured by fraud in which the adjudicator was complicit.[16]

The security-of-payment acts do not affect any other rights that parties may have under contract, and do not affect any civil proceedings that may start under the contract.[17] Accordingly, it is often said that an adjudicator's determination is binding, but not final. Therefore, any payment made pursuant to the security-of-payment acts is only on an interim basis and will be subject to any final reckoning of the parties' respective entitlements under the dispute resolution procedure applicable to the contract.

4. Court system

Australia has state and federal court systems, both of which are adversarial in nature. The effect of having an adversarial system is that the parties themselves initiate the proceedings and determine which legal and factual issues the court is to decide. The federal courts' jurisdiction is broad and encompasses almost all civil matters arising under Australian federal law.[18] However, the Federal Court deals with only a limited range of issues likely to arise in the context of construction disputes. Other than questions about arbitration procedure in international arbitrations, most disputes that arise on construction projects are dealt with by state courts.

In the state jurisdictions, the court hierarchy is made up of a number of different courts. Small matters are generally dealt with by the lower courts:

- the magistrates court (or local court),[19] which deals with less serious civil cases; and
- the district court (or county court),[20] which sits above the magistrates/local court in the state court hierarchy and deals with more serious claims.

---

14 Section 25 of the NSW act; Section 27 of the ACT act; Section 33 of the Victorian act; Section 27 of the Tasmanian act; Section 25 of the South Australian act; Section 45 of the NT act; Section 31 of the Queensland act; Section 43 of the Western Australian act.

15 Section 43(2).

16 *Brodyn Pty Ltd t/as Time Cost and Quality v Davenport* [2004] 61 NSWLR 421.

17 Section 32(1) of the NSW Act; Section 47 of the Victorian act; Section 45 of the Western Australian act; Section 100 of the Queensland act; Section 47 of the NT act; Section 10 of the Tasmanian act; Section 32 of the South Australian act; Section 38 of the ACT act.

18 See www.dfat.gov.au/facts/legal_system.html.

19 The equivalent of the magistrates court in New South Wales and Western Australia is the local court.

20 The equivalent of the district court in Victoria is the county court.

The most relevant court for construction disputes will generally be the local supreme court, which is the superior court in each state. In some states, such as Victoria and New South Wales, specialist lists facilitate the conduct of construction disputes. In Victoria, for example, the Technology, Engineering and Construction List (TEC List) is a specialist list which draws together three groups of related disputes under one management regime.[21] Matters to be admitted to the TEC List include cases that relate to:

- the supervision or inspection of the construction, design or execution of TEC works, or their design or execution;
- the supervision, construction, design or execution of TEC works;
- the manufacture or provision of TEC works;
- the performance or the products of TEC works; or
- the sale or supply of such products.[22]

In New South Wales, the supreme court manages a similar list (now called the Technology and Construction List) which, much like the Victorian TEC List, hears cases involving complex technological issues and building or engineering contract disputes.[23]

These specialist lists ensure that there are appropriate mechanisms to manage the unique features of construction litigation, such as the length of time taken to hear cases and the volume of documents involved in typical construction disputes. The stated objective of the TEC List in the Supreme Court of Victoria is to:

> *provide for the just and efficient determination of TEC cases, by the early identification of the substantial questions in controversy and the flexible adoption of appropriate and timely procedures for the future conduct of the proceeding which are best suited to the particular case.*[24]

In some Australian jurisdictions the intermediate courts (in the case of Victoria, the county court) have unlimited jurisdiction in respect of construction disputes. This makes the intermediate courts a potentially cheaper option for construction project disputes.

However, as discussed further in section 5 below, in circumstances where one or more parties to a construction project are domiciled outside Australia, the parties will usually select arbitration over court proceedings for dispute resolution. This is primarily due to the easier enforcement of arbitral awards around the world, but also because arbitrators with specific industry or technical expertise can be selected.

5. Arbitration

The consortia engaged to design or construct very large projects often include parties domiciled in countries other than Australia. As it is easier to enforce international

21 www.supremecourt.vic.gov.au/home/lists+and+sittings/specialist+lists/technology+engineering+and+construction/.

22 Supreme Court (Miscellaneous Civil Proceedings) Rules 2008 (Vic), Rule 3.01.

23 www.supremecourt.lawlink.nsw.gov.au/agdbasev7wr/supremecourt/documents/pdf/supremecourt annualreview09.pdf#xml=http://PRODMWI15-0/isysquery/fdd7eaf3-11d2-4d9c-a099-8cdf3d66ca12/7/hilite/; see also, Uniform Civil Procedure Rules 2005 (NSW), Rule 45.7.

24 Supreme Court of Victoria website: www.supremecourt.vic.gov.au/home/lists+and+sittings/specialist+lists/technology+engineering+and+construction/.

arbitration awards in other countries than judgments of local Australian courts, because of the Convention on the Recognition and Enforcement of Foreign Arbitral Awards 1958 (New York Convention), the contracts associated with these large projects typically include arbitration agreements. This section considers the legal landscape of arbitrations seated in Australia. However, where an Australian seat is not an option owing to neutrality issues, Singapore is often chosen as the seat of arbitration.

International arbitration and domestic arbitration in Australia are governed by separate statutory regimes. International arbitration is governed by the International Arbitration Act 1974 (Cth), which is a federal act. Domestic arbitration is regulated by the Commercial Arbitration Acts of the states and territories.[25] As the topic of this book is international construction disputes, the focus of this chapter is on international arbitration. That said, the domestic and international regimes are similar in many respects, so cases interpreting the Commercial Arbitration Acts are relevant to certain provisions of the International Arbitration Act.

Australia has ratified both the New York Convention[26] and the Convention on the Settlement of Investment Disputes Between States and Nationals of Other States 1965 (ICSID Convention).[27] The International Arbitration Act is the implementing act for these two conventions, both of which are included as schedules to the act.

The International Arbitration Act incorporates the UNCITRAL[28] Model Law on International Commercial Arbitration, which is therefore the basis of the Australian law of international arbitration. The model law was developed to establish uniform international standards for commercial arbitration. At the time of writing, legislation based on the model law has been enacted in 66 countries.[29] This chapter focuses on aspects of Australian international arbitration law that are specific to this jurisdiction.

The model law was revised in 2006 and the International Arbitration Act was updated in 2010 to include those amendments, among other things. This makes Australia one of the few jurisdictions to have adopted the latest revision of the model law. The key changes contained in the 2006 amendments to the model law were an expansion of the definition of 'agreement in writing' and detailed rules for the granting of interim measures of protection.[30]

For arbitrations seated in Australia, the key features of the International Arbitration Act are that:

- pursuant to Australia's obligations under the New York Convention, when the parties have made an arbitration agreement the court must, at the request of one of the parties, refer the parties to arbitration, unless it finds that the

---

25 Commercial Arbitration Act 2010 (NSW); Commercial Arbitration Act 2011 (SA); Commercial Arbitration Act 2011 (Vic); Commercial Arbitration (National Uniform Legislation) Act 2011 (NT); Commercial Arbitration Act 2011 (Tas); Commercial Arbitration Act 2012 (WA); Commercial Arbitration Act 1986 (ACT); Commercial Arbitration Act 1990 (Qld).

26 Ratified on March 26 1975.

27 Ratified on May 2 1991.

28 United Nations Commission on International Trade Law.

29 www.uncitral.org/uncitral/en/uncitral_texts/arbitration/1985Model_arbitration_status.html

30 The 2006 amendments included Articles 17B and 17C, which provided for the issuance of preliminary orders in support of interim measures on an *ex parte* basis. These provisions were *not* adopted in the amended International Arbitration Act (see Section 18B).

arbitration agreement is null and void, inoperative or incapable of being performed;[31]

- it contains optional provisions addressing matters such as court support for the taking of evidence, confidentiality of information disclosed as part of arbitral proceedings and consolidation of related proceedings; and
- in respect of international arbitration awards made in Australia or overseas, there is no provision for appeals regarding the substance of an award.

As noted above, the International Arbitration Act contains a number of optional provisions, some of which apply unless the parties otherwise agree ('opt-out' provisions) and others which apply if the parties agree ('opt-in' provisions).[32] These are discussed further below.

5.1 Formal requirements for counsel and arbitrators

There are no formal restrictions in relation to appearing as counsel or arbitrator in international arbitrations in Australia. Accordingly, parties can be represented by and have their dispute decided by whoever they consider appropriate.

5.2 Interim measures

Interim measures are temporary orders to preserve the status quo between parties during the term of the arbitral proceedings prior to the final issuance and enforcement of any award. Interim measures are similar in effect to a restraining order or an injunction and are used to prevent a party to the dispute from taking actions during the dispute that could frustrate the effect of a potential award against it. Articles 17–17J of the model law provide concurrent jurisdiction to both arbitral tribunals and the courts to order a mix of interim protection measures. Interim measures issued under these model law provisions will be enforceable throughout Australia, as well as other jurisdictions that have incorporated Articles 17H and 17I of the model law into their domestic law.

5.3 Reasonable opportunity to present one's case

Article 18 of the model law requires the tribunal to give each party a full opportunity to present its case. This has sometimes been found to be problematic, as it makes it difficult for a tribunal to limit the extent to which a party can make submissions in relation to a matter. In extreme circumstances, this enables a recalcitrant party to delay proceedings by insisting on the right to make further and lengthy submissions on any and all issues. Accordingly, Section 18C of the International Arbitration Act reduces the burden on the tribunal by requiring only that each party be given a reasonable opportunity to present its case.

31 Section 7 of the International Arbitration Act; Article II(3) New York Convention.

32 Pursuant to Section 30 of the International Arbitration Act, these provisions do not apply to arbitration agreements that were concluded before the start of Part III of the International Arbitration Act (ie, before June 12 1989) unless otherwise agreed by the parties.

5.4 Evidentiary issues

Tribunals in international arbitrations in Australia are not bound by the usual evidence laws applicable to court proceedings in Australia. Instead, arbitral tribunals are empowered to "determine the admissibility, relevance, materiality and weight of any evidence".[33]

Article 27 of the model law allows an arbitral tribunal, or parties with the permission of an arbitral tribunal, to request assistance from a court in taking evidence. This general provision has been augmented with specific provisions in the International Arbitration Act (IAA) dealing with court assistance in taking evidence. Section 23 allows parties to obtain subpoenas from the court ordering any person to attend for examination before an arbitral tribunal or to produce documents specified in the subpoena to the arbitral tribunal.

Furthermore, in circumstances where a person involved in arbitral proceedings refuses or fails to attend for examination before an arbitral tribunal when required by subpoena or when required by the tribunal,[34] produce documents required by subpoena or required by the tribunal,[35] take an oath, make an affirmation or answer a question that he is required to answer[36] or do anything else which a tribunal may require to assist it in its functions,[37] the International Arbitration Act allows parties to apply to the court to make an order compelling that person to comply with a subpoena or a requirement of the tribunal,[38] as long as that person would have been required to do the same in a proceeding before the court.[39] The court may also make consequential orders for the transmission of evidence or other documents to the tribunal.[40]

If the person that is the subject of the order is not a party to the arbitral proceedings, the court must ensure that he is given an opportunity to make representations to the court before the order is made, and that the making of the order is reasonable in all the circumstances.[41] As with all court orders, a person who refuses to comply with an order issued under these provisions is likely to be in contempt of court.

In the event that a party to the arbitration agreement defaults by refusing or failing to comply with a subpoena or requirement of the tribunal, the tribunal may continue with the arbitral proceedings and make an award on the evidence before it.[42]

Sections 23, 23A and 23B are all 'opt-out' provisions, which means they will apply unless the parties agree otherwise.

The International Arbitration Act also empowers a tribunal to make an order allowing itself, a party to the proceedings or an expert to inspect, photograph, observe, conduct experiments on or sample evidence in the possession of a party to

---

33 Article 19(2) of the model law, as reproduced in Schedule 2 IAA.
34 Sections 23A(1)(a) and 23A(1)(b) IAA.
35 Sections 23A(1)(c) and 23A(1)(d).
36 Section 23A(1)(e).
37 Section 23A(1)(f).
38 Section 23A(3)(a).
39 Section 23A(4).
40 Section 23A(3)(b).
41 Section 23A(5).
42 Section 23B.

the proceedings.[43] Again, this provision is an 'opt-out' provision, which means that it will apply unless the parties agree otherwise.[44]

Article 24(1) of the model law allows an arbitral tribunal to decide whether oral hearings should be held for the presentation of evidence or whether the proceedings should be conducted on the basis of written materials alone.

5.5 Confidentiality

The question of whether information disclosed as part of arbitral proceedings is confidential in the absence of agreement between the parties has received significant judicial consideration in Australia.

The High Court of Australia (Australia's highest court) in *Esso Australia Resources Ltd v Plowman*[45] distinguished the concept of confidentiality from that of privacy. In that case the High Court found that privacy, in the sense of arbitral proceedings not being open to the public, is inherent in the subject matter of an agreement to submit disputes to arbitration.[46] However, the court held that under Australian law there is no implied term imposing a general duty of confidentiality in an arbitration agreement. Accordingly, information disclosed as part of arbitral proceedings will only be confidential if the parties expressly agree to that.

Since that decision, Sections 23C to 23G have been incorporated into the International Arbitration Act to provide a comprehensive statutory regime in respect of confidentiality. Those provisions provide that the parties and the tribunal must not disclose confidential information relating to arbitral proceedings, except in specified circumstances. Those exceptions are distributed between general circumstances when information may be disclosed and circumstances when information may be disclosed only upon the authority of the tribunal or the court.

The general circumstances include when the disclosure is:[47]

- consented to by all the parties to the arbitral proceedings;
- to be made to a professional or other advisor of any of the parties;
- necessary to ensure that a party has a full opportunity to present its case;
- necessary for the establishment or protection of the legal rights of a party;
- necessary for the purpose of enforcing an arbitral award;
- necessary for the purposes of the International Arbitration Act (and the model law), depending on whether the arbitration is domestic or international;
- in accordance with an order made or a subpoena issued by the court; or
- authorised or required by another state or territory law, Commonwealth law or law of a foreign country (in the case of international arbitration), or is required by a competent regulatory body.

The tribunal has discretion to permit the disclosure of confidential information

43 Section 23J.
44 Section 22(2).
45 (1995) 183 CLR 10.
46 *Ibid*, at [27].
47 Sections 23D(2)-23D(9) IAA.

in circumstances other than those listed above.[48] When a tribunal permits a disclosure and a party to the proceedings is dissatisfied with that decision, that party may apply to the court for an order preventing the disclosure.[49] The court may also, upon application by a party, allow confidential information to be disclosed when it has been prohibited by the tribunal or the tribunal's mandate has been terminated.[50] Similarly, unless the tribunal's mandate has been terminated, the tribunal must first make a ruling on an application made by a party to the proceedings before the court can consider the matter.[51] In both cases the court is required to weigh the public interest in disclosure against that for non-disclosure.[52]

This confidentiality regime will apply only if the parties agree in writing that it will apply.[53] Accordingly, when negotiating a contract, the parties to an arbitration agreement should consider whether they want the confidentiality regime to apply to any subsequent arbitration.

5.6 Consolidation of arbitral proceedings

The International Arbitration Act allows a tribunal to consolidate two or more separate arbitration proceedings upon application by a party to any of those proceedings if:[54]

- a common question of law or fact arises in all those proceedings;
- the rights to relief claimed in all those proceedings are in respect of, or arise out of, the same transaction or series of transactions; or
- there is another desirable reason specified in the party's application.

In addition to allowing consolidation orders to be made, the act allows for related proceedings to be heard jointly or for related proceedings to be stayed pending the determination of any other related proceedings.[55] Given the undesirability of related proceedings being conducted separately and in parallel,[56] as well as the benefits that consolidation attracts in terms of avoiding inconsistent decisions being made,[57] the act confers a wide range of procedural powers on tribunals to optimise the handling of multiple related proceedings.

The International Arbitration Act also expressly permits parties to related proceedings to agree on any consolidation and any steps necessary to effect that consolidation.[58]

---

48 Section 23E.
49 Section 23F. The court may order that confidential information must not be disclosed pending the outcome of the application (Section 23F(4)).
50 Section 23G(3).
51 *Ibid.*
52 Sections 23F(1) 23G(1).
53 Section 22(3).
54 Section 24(1).
55 Section 24(2).
56 See, for example, *Taunton-Collins v Cromie* [1964] 1 WLR 633 and *Abu Dhabi Gas Liquefaction Co Ltd v Eastern Bechtel Corp* [1982] 2 Lloyd's Rep 425.
57 UNCITRAL, Note by the Secretariat: "Possible Future Work in the Area of International Commercial Arbitration", UN Doc A/CN.9/460 (April 6 1999).
58 Section 24(8) IAA.

Again, this provision is an 'opt-in' provision, which means that it will not apply unless the parties agree in writing that it will apply.[59]

5.7 Security for costs

The International Arbitration Act permits arbitral tribunals to order a party to the proceedings to pay security for costs at any point between the start of the arbitration and the issue of a final award.[60] This is effectively an interim measure, so the provisions of the model law applying to interim measures will also apply.[61] While the tribunal's discretion is quite broad in this regard, it cannot base its decision to order security for costs against a particular party purely on the fact that that party is not ordinarily resident in Australia, is a corporation incorporated or an association formed under the laws of a foreign nation, or is a corporation or association the central management or control of which takes place in a foreign nation.[62]

This provision is an 'opt-out' provision, which means that it will apply unless the parties agree otherwise.[63]

5.8 Interest and costs

The International Arbitration Act gives arbitral tribunals discretion to order interest up to the making of an award. Tribunals may choose to make an award for interest on the entire money or any portion of it payable under an award at a reasonable rate, as determined by the tribunal.[64] This is an 'opt-out' provision, which means that it will apply unless the parties agree otherwise.[65]

The International Arbitration Act also allows the tribunal to direct a party to pay interest on any unpaid portion of an award sum that has not been paid on or before the due date.[66] This is also an 'opt-out' provision.[67]

5.9 Challenging the award

The International Arbitration Act and the model law contain very limited grounds for challenging an award. These grounds are limited to cases where the most basic notions of procedural fairness and morality would be offended by the enforcement of an award, namely that:

- a party to the arbitration agreement was under some incapacity or the arbitration agreement was invalid under the law to which the parties have subjected it;
- the party was not given proper notice of the appointment of an arbitral tribunal or of the arbitral proceedings, or was otherwise not able to present its case;

59 Section 22(5).
60 Section 23K(1).
61 Section 23K(3).
62 Section 23K(2).
63 Section 22(2).
64 Section 25(1).
65 Section 22(2).
66 Section 26.
67 Section 22(2).

- the award relates to a dispute that is non-arbitrable under the arbitration agreement or decides on matters beyond the scope of the dispute submitted to arbitration;
- the procedure for the appointment of arbitrators or the arbitral procedure itself conflicted with a prior agreement between the parties;
- the subject matter of the dispute was not capable of resolution by arbitration under Australian law; or
- enforcement of the award would contravene Australian public policy.[68]

The public policy ground has been construed quite narrowly in Australia. In *Traxys Europe SA v Balaji Coke Industry Pvt Ltd*,[69] it was held that awards should be set aside only where their enforcement would "violate the forum state's most basic notions of morality and justice". Further, the court held that "it is only those aspects of public policy that go to the fundamental, core questions of morality and justice" which may be considered in setting aside an award on the grounds that it contravenes public policy.[70]

As noted above, there is no provision for appeals in respect of the substance of an award.

6. Expert determination

Expert determination originally developed as a quick and inexpensive method of resolving discrete technical or valuation disputes, such as the quality assessment of a shipment of wheat or the valuation of a parcel of real estate or shares. However, recently parties in Australia have used expert determination to resolve entire disputes, rather than narrowly defined issues of the kind described above.

This has been done in response to a perception that arbitration has come to mimic court procedure; it has ceased to be a cheaper and more efficient alternative to litigation. While courts were initially reluctant to enforce expert determination agreements, they are now placing increasing importance on giving effect to the parties' agreed method of dispute resolution. As a result, an increasing body of Australian law makes it clear that expert determination agreements are enforceable and that the courts will generally give effect to the third-party decisions made under them.[71]

Unlike arbitration or adjudication under the various security of payment acts (discussed above), contractual expert determination is not supported by legislation. In their contract, if the parties fail to address a fundamental matter, such as the process by which the expert will be appointed, then there is no legislation to fill the gap as there is in arbitration. In that circumstance, the parties would need to reach further agreement in order for their expert determination clause to be operable.

---

68 Article 34(2) of the model law.

69 *Traxys Europe SA v Balaji Coke Industry Pvt Ltd (No 2)* [2012] FCA 276, following *Parsons & Whittemore Overseas Co, Inc v Société Générale De L'Industrie Du Papier (RAKTA)* 508 F 2d 969 (2d Cir 1974).

70 *Ibid.*

71 See, for example, *Savcor Pty Ltd v State of New South Wales* (2001) 52 NSWLR 587, 597; *Public Authorities Superannuation Board v Southern International Developments Corporation Pty Limited* (NSWSC, October 19 1987, unreported); *The Heart Research Institute Limited v Psiron Limited* [2002] NSWSC 646; *Shoalhaven v Firedam* [2011] HCA 38; *Biosciences v Plenary* [2012] VSC 249.

As expert determination is based purely on contract, the procedure to be followed by the expert is entirely a matter for the parties or, failing such an agreement, the expert. As noted above, expert determination began its existence as a very informal procedure in which an expert in a relevant field made a decision on a narrow dispute. The expert could receive submissions from the parties, but would usually make enquiries and come to a conclusion based on individual expertise. Accordingly, the traditional approach was to leave the procedure up to the expert. However, parties are becoming more prescriptive in their expert determination agreements, specifying matters such as the number of, and time limits for, submissions from the parties, whether oral hearings or cross-examination will be allowed, and the time limit for the expert's determination.

Expert determination is not suitable for all disputes. It is best suited to single-issue disputes that can be resolved by reference to a body of expertise. These include:

- questions as to value;[72] and
- questions as to the quality of work done.[73]

However, expert determination is less suited to disputes:

- where there are mixed questions of fact and law;
- that involve the expert deciding or having to decide issues beyond his technical qualifications; or
- where a more formal process in the manner of a judicial inquiry would be more appropriate in the circumstances – for instance where discovery or production of documents in response to a subpoena is appropriate or necessary.

In those circumstances parties should choose arbitration. This is because the expert determination process is likely to get so complex that it resembles an arbitration, so the parties may as well enjoy the benefits of the procedural safeguards that apply to arbitrations.

7. Conclusion

Australia's arbitration legislation has undergone significant change over the past five years. First, the International Arbitration Act was amended to include the 2006 revisions to the UNCITRAL Model Law. Secondly, the commercial arbitration acts of the states and territories were replaced with modern versions based on the model law. The amendments to the International Arbitration Act and the commercial arbitration acts also included specific changes directed at old case law that was inconsistent with best practice. These amendments – particularly the incorporation of the model law into domestic arbitration – will assist Australia to develop an arbitration culture that is of a uniformly high standard in both the domestic and international contexts and is consistent with best practice.

---

72 *Public Authorities Superannuation Board v Southern International Developments Corporation Pty Limited* (NSWSC, October 19 1987, unreported), at 7; *The Heart Research Institute Limited v Psiron Limited* [2002] NSWSC 646, at [25].

73 *Ibid.*

In future, more reliance will be placed on DRBs in Australian projects, consistent with the trend internationally. This will have a positive effect on the dispute level in construction projects across the country.

Finally, there is cause for optimism about the future of formal litigation in Australia. The courts in Australia are highly competitive among themselves and with regard to arbitration. This competition is healthy, as all courts are anxious to improve their procedures to stay competitive internationally and against one another. The judiciary is actively engaging with court users to understand their needs, is questioning whether its procedures remain appropriate to satisfy those needs, and is willing to innovate to further improve.

While there remains room for improvement (as is the case in all dispute resolution systems), the Australian courts' commitment engenders confidence that they have embarked on a process of continual improvement, which will see good processes get better.

China

William G Kelly
Goldberg Segalla LLP

1. Introduction

On December 3 2010 the Supreme People's Court of China allowed (for the first time) the public to see how the court functioned. At the same time the court displayed Xiezhi, a mythical animal who had the ability to determine right from wrong. Xiezhi was symbolic of the court's attempt to demonstrate that it is prepared to protect the rights of litigants and determine right from wrong.[1]

As the court system struggles to provide more transparency and thus garner more credibility, it must still deal with its past practice of favouritism. In a formal report by Wang Shengjun, President of the Supreme People's Court, he stated that in 2011 a total of 77 judges and court staff were prosecuted for embezzlement, bribery or favouritism.[2]

These actions by judicial personnel have a chilling effect on foreigners, especially as there is no jury system in China. Judges decide not only the issues of law, but the facts as well; they even have the right to conduct their own investigations.

The goal of the judicial system in China is to determine the truth through an analysis of the facts. The Law of Civil Procedure of the People's Republic of China was adopted in April 1991[3] and was amended with effect from January 1 2013.

In China there are thousands of local courts, several hundred intermediate courts, 32 provincial-level courts and one Supreme Court. There is one single system as there is no division between state and federal courts as is the case in the United States, for example.[4]

China's legal system encourages negotiation and mediation but when negotiation between the parties and mediation fails, they have the option of resorting to arbitration or litigation, which are both acceptable means of resolving disputes in China.

In this chapter we will discuss the construction industry and then explore dispute resolution procedures in China.

2. The construction industry

China has just embarked on its 12th five-year plan, for the period 2011–15. These

1 *China Daily*, December 4 2010, Zhang Yan.
2 *People's Daily Online*, March 11 2012
3 The Law of Civil Procedure of the People's Republic of China, most recently amended with effect from January 1 2013.
4 MoZhang, "International Civil Litigation in China: A Practical Analysis of the Chinese Judicial System", 25 *B.C. Int'l & Comp L Rev* 59 (2002).

five-year plans, developed and published by central government, are a blueprint for social and economic development initiatives. Some of the goals in the plan are binding while others are expectations.[5] For example, it is binding that over this five-year period 36 million affordable apartments for low-income citizens will be constructed or renovated. In addition it is binding that in any land assigned for new housing no less than 10% must be used for affordable housing, either new or renovated.

To fully appreciate the dynamic nature of China's construction activity one only needs to watch the opening scene of the James Bond movie, *Skyfall*, with the camera providing a bird's-eye view of the Pudong side of Shanghai highlighted by the Oriental Pearl Building. Less than 20 years ago most of those buildings did not exist. At the Urban Planning Museum on the Pusi side of Shanghai there is a diorama of Shanghai in the future, which is stunning in its scope. China joined the World Trade Organization in 2001 and has become more open to foreign investments. Two of the investment vehicles in China are the China-foreign equity joint-venture contract and the China-foreign cooperative joint-venture contract.

A China-foreign equity joint venture is a joint venture between a Chinese and a foreign company within China.[6] This joint venture can acquire land, hire Chinese workers and construct buildings. The distribution of profits is based on the capital contribution.

A China-foreign cooperative joint venture usually involves the foreign company providing capital and technology while the Chinese company provides the land and the labour.[7] In these agreements the parties decide how profits will be divided as well as each party's contribution to the project.

These joint ventures with a Chinese company are subject to the jurisdiction of the Chinese courts and are governed by Chinese law. However, these matters can be arbitrated instead of litigated.

Entering into the construction industry in China requires careful analysis, planning and guidance, but there is vast scope for future and ongoing construction projects.

An initial investigation will reveal some inherent problems, which China is attempting to resolve. An investor needs to make sure that its investment is protected and will be profitable. In the United States, contracts and the courts provide that protection. In China the basis of many business dealings used to be *guanxi*, which means 'relationships'.[8] Such relationships comprise networks of individuals who work together and support each other. In these relationships there are no formal contracts and no litigation. These networks of relationships still exist and must be understood. However, understanding and cooperating is not sufficient

---

5 US–China Economic and Security Review Commission, June 24 2011, www.uscc.gov/researchpapers/2011/12th-FiveYearPlan_062811.pdf.

6 The Law of the People's Republic of China on Chinese-Foreign Equity Joint Ventures, most recently amended on March 15 2001.

7 The Law of the People's Republic of China on Chinese-Foreign Contractual Joint Ventures, adopted on April 13 1988.

8 Christopher Warren-Gash, "Want to Capitalize on China? You Better Have Good Guanxi", *Forbes*, March 15 2012.

and a contract is now a necessity and must provide for a dispute resolution method (either litigation or arbitration).

Relationships with Chinese counterparts must be continually nurtured and developed and are key to creating a successful outcome.

One of the concerns with the Chinese construction industry was discussed by Professor Vaughn of Tsinghua University in a speech in 2007. In that speech, he spoke about the do-and-fix (DAF) method of Chinese construction where there is minimal planning resulting in the need for multiple fixes. He also noted that during this method of construction all employees are present throughout the construction. He compared the DAF system to a structural methodology where the project moves from analysis to design to develop to deliver. Professor Vaughn emphasised the need for construction projects to move in line with a structured methodology.[9]

In the cited article the author discusses a study by Professor Wang ShouQing of Tsinghua University that highlights the strengths, weaknesses, opportunities and threats facing foreign contractors who seek to operate in China.[10]

China continues to welcome and encourage foreign investment albeit with significant restrictions and inherent limitations which it is working to overcome. The goal is that eventually the transparency, quality and consistency of the court system will be improved and the confidence of the foreign investor will be enhanced.

One of the essential systems that China continues to rework with the aim of acquiring international credibility is the litigation system. As it stands now, arbitration rather than litigation is still the preferred method of dispute resolution.

3. Arbitration

Arbitration is the preferred and most credible method of dispute resolution in China. It is quicker, less costly regarding legal expenses and management time and, most importantly, the resulting judgments are enforceable in China.

China is one of the 148 members of the United Nations that has signed the United Nations Convention on the Recognition and Enforcement of Foreign Arbitral Awards, known as the New York Convention.[11] China became a signatory in 1987.[12] Under the New York Convention an arbitral award rendered, pursuant to a written agreement, in any of the signatory countries is enforceable in any other signatory country.

The governing law for arbitrations in China is the Arbitration Law of the People's Republic of China, adopted in 1994.[13] Arbitration hearings held in mainland China must be administered by an arbitration commission in order for the award to be enforceable by Chinese courts.

---

9 Professor Hubert Vaughn at the Institute of International Project Management at the Department of Construction Management at Tsinghau University on July 20 2007, as cited in the working paper "Construction Market & Construction Firms in China; Strengths, Weaknesses and Development Trajectory" by Vishnu Sridharan September 24 2007, Collaboratory for Research on Global Projects.

10 *Ibid*, 27–29.

11 9 USC §§201–208 (US enabling legislation).

12 United Nations Commission on International Law, "Status of 1958 Convention on the Recognition and Enforcement of Foreign Arbitral Awards", www.uncitral.org/uncitral/en/uncitral_texts/arbitration/NYConvention_status.html.

13 Arbitration Law of the People's Republic of China, adopted 1994, www.cietac.org/index/references/Laws/47607b540fddd47f001.cms.

Although arbitration commissions can be set up in any municipality, the most notable arbitration commission is the China International Economic and Trade Arbitration Commission (CIETAC).[14] CIETAC is associated with the China Council for the Promotion of International Trade (CCPIT).[15]

In April 2012, the American Bar Association and CCPIT held a joint conference and seminar in Beijing, China, to discuss litigation in the United States as well as international arbitration and issues regarding the enforcement of litigation and arbitration judgments. A principle that was emphasised at the conference was that foreign arbitration awards rendered pursuant to a written arbitration agreement are enforceable in China, as long as the arbitration is held in a country that is a signatory to the New York Convention.

The China Arbitration Association consists of all the arbitration commissions.[16] An arbitration commission is composed of 10 to 15 members who are experts in law, economy and trade with practical work experience.[17] An arbitrator must have at least eight years' experience as an academic, lawyer, judge or arbitrator.

An arbitration agreement must include an agreement to arbitrate, the matters for arbitration and the chosen arbitration commission.[18] If the agreement does not specify the choice of commission or the matters to be arbitrated, the agreement will be void unless the parties subsequently agree to insert those provisions.[19]

Any issues concerning the validity of the arbitration agreement must be raised before the first hearing.[20]

An application for arbitration must be submitted to an arbitration commission which then has five days to accept or reject the application. If the application is rejected, it must be in writing with the reasons for the rejection.[21]

The application for arbitration must contain:

- the underlying arbitration agreement;
- the name, sex, age, profession, employer and residence of each party and organisation and their legal representatives;
- the nature of the claim and the facts and evidence on which the claim is based; and
- the evidence and the sources of evidence, including the names and residences of witnesses.[22]

If there is a valid arbitration agreement in the contract between the parties, then the people's court will not accept the case for litigation. However, if one party files a suit in the people's court then the other party must produce the agreement to arbitrate before the first hearing or the objection will be waived.[23]

---

14 China International Economic and Trade Arbitration Commission, www.cietac.org.
15 See www.cietac.org/index/aboutUs/47601fd516b2517f001.cms.
16 Arbitration Law of the People's Republic of China, Article 15.
17 Articles 12–13.
18 Article 16.
19 Article 18.
20 Article 20.
21 Article 24.
22 Article 23.
23 Article 46.

If a party to an arbitration requires an immediate order to preserve evidence or property, it can apply for this relief to the people's court where the evidence or property is located. These property and preservation laws went into effect on January 1 2013. Prior to then the parties had to apply to the relevant arbitration commission, which would then apply to the intermediate people's court.[24]

In order to obtain pre-arbitration relief, the party seeking the preservation of evidence must demonstrate that the evidence may be destroyed or hard to locate later. It must apply to the court sited where the evidence is located or where the respondent resides, and must post security.[25] Where property must be preserved, the party seeking the relief must demonstrate irreparable harm and must post security.

The court has 48 hours to issue its ruling. If it grants the application, then the petitioner must file for arbitration within 30 days thereafter or the preservation order will be void.[26] Once a claim is accepted by an arbitration commission, the respondent has the opportunity to file a counterclaim.[27]

The parties are then provided with the rules of the arbitration as well as a list of arbitrators. The arbitration tribunal consists of either one or three arbitrators. If there is only one arbitrator, then the parties will either jointly appoint him or defer to the chairperson of the arbitration commission. When the parties decide on three arbitrators, each side picks one and the third is selected the same way that a single arbitrator is selected.[28]

An arbitration is conducted in private unless the parties agree to open the session to the public.[29] An arbitration tribunal has the option of collecting its own evidence or having an appraisal.[30] The parties have the right to submit evidence and cross-examine the witnesses.[31] They also have the right to debate and the right to give final statements.

The written record of the hearing shall be signed by the arbitrators, parties and minute keeper.[32] If the parties reach an agreement at any time before the award is made, the agreement will be documented and is equally binding legally.[33]

A foreign-related party can apply to the intermediate people's court to overturn an arbitration award. There are six grounds on which an award can be overturned:

- There is no agreement for arbitration.
- The matters ruled are out of the scope of the agreement for arbitration or the limits of authority of an arbitration commission.
- The composition of the arbitration tribunal or the arbitration proceedings violate the legal proceedings.
- The evidence on which the ruling is based is forged.
- Things that have an impact on the impartiality of the ruling have been discovered to have been concealed by the opposite party.

---

24 The Law of Civil Procedure of the People's Republic of China, Article 258.
25 Arbitration Law of the People's Republic of China, Article 46.
26 The Law of Civil Procedure of the People's Republic of China, Article 101.
27 Arbitration Law of the People's Republic of China, Article 25.
28 Articles 30–32.
29 Article 40.
30 Article 43.
31 Article 45.
32 Article 48.
33 Articles 51–52.

- Arbitrators have accepted bribes, resorted to deception for personal gains or perverted the law in the ruling.[34]

Chinese will be the contract's governing law unless one of the parties is not Chinese or is incorporated outside mainland China. In that situation the parties can choose to be governed by another country's laws, except where there is a joint venture with a Chinese company or an individual incorporated in China.

Arbitration awards conducted under the New York Convention that do not violate China's laws will be enforced under the New York Convention of which China is a signatory. Thus, an arbitration conducted under the New York Convention held in Singapore, which is not in violation of Chinese law, will have its award enforced in China under the New York Convention.

This is the key difference between litigation and arbitration in a foreign country. A judgment obtained by litigation in a foreign country will not be enforced in China unless there is a specific treaty between the two countries. There are only a few countries that have such a bilateral treaty with China for the enforcement of commercial judgments.

(a) Arbitration by CIETAC

If the arbitration is to take place in mainland China, then the most recognised arbitration commission is CIETAC. CIETAC has published its own arbitration rules which conform to the Arbitration Law of the People's Republic of China. Any party choosing CIETAC as its arbitration commission is deemed to have agreed to its rules.[35] However, if the parties have agreed to a modification of these rules, then CIETAC will abide by that agreement unless this is contrary to Chinese law.[36] The validity of an arbitration clause will not be affected by modification or termination of the contract.[37]

If the parties choose a location for the arbitration, that choice will prevail.[38] Once a party agrees to participate in an arbitration, it has waived any objections to the arbitration.

A party applying for arbitration under the CIETAC rules submits a request for arbitration in writing signed and/or sealed by the claimant or its authorised representative(s), which shall include:

- the names and addresses of the claimant and the respondent including the zip code, telephone number, fax number, email address, or any other means of electronic telecommunications;
- a reference to the arbitration agreement that is invoked;
- a statement of the facts of the case and the main issue in dispute;
- the claim of the claimant; and
- the facts and grounds on which the claim is based.[39]

34 Article 58.
35 CIETAC Arbitration Rules (CIETAC), effective March 1, 2012, Article 4(2).
36 CIETAC, Article 4(3).
37 Article 5(4).
38 Article 7(1).
39 Article 12(1).

If the application is accepted, CIETAC will send out a notice of arbitration to both parties together with a copy of the rules and a list of arbitrators.[40]

The respondent must file a statement of defence within 45 days from receipt of the notice of arbitration. The statement of defence must be signed by the respondent or its representative and include:

- the name and address of the respondent, including zip code, email address and telephone number;
- the defence to the request for arbitration setting forth the facts and grounds on which the defence is based; and
- the relevant documentary and other evidence on which the defence is based.[41]

The respondent must also file any counterclaim within the same 45-day period.[42]

The arbitration tribunal consists of one or three arbitrators. With three arbitrators each party nominates one and then they jointly nominates the presiding arbitrator. If they fail to do so the chairperson of CIETAC will appoint the presiding arbitrator.[43] If the parties have agreed to nominate arbitrators outside CIETAC's panel, then this is allowed.[44] If there is only one arbitrator, the parties will jointly nominate or defer to the chairperson.[45]

When appointing arbitrators, the chairperson must take into consideration:

- the law applicable to the dispute;
- the place of arbitration;
- the language of arbitration (the parties can choose this language in their agreement);
- the nationalities or the parties; and
- any other factors the chairperson considers relevant.

The arbitrators have broad latitude in conducting the hearings. If the parties agree on a procedure, then the arbitrators will follow that procedure. The arbitrators can conduct hearings, undertake investigations, consult with experts, collect evidence or just rely on written submissions. Any investigation results or other evidence obtained by the arbitrators must be disclosed to the parties.

The arbitral tribunal will give 20 days' notice before any hearing and must render a decision within six months from the date the tribunal was formed. The award will be by a vote of the majority of the arbitrators but if a majority cannot be obtained the award will be based on the presiding arbitrator's decision.

The award is final and binding on both parties. No application may be made to any court for its revision. However, if one party fails to carry out the award, the other party may apply to the appropriate court for enforcement.

---

40 Article 13(2).
41 Article 14.
42 Article 15.
43 Articles 23–24.
44 Article 24(2).
45 Article 25(3).

Under the recent amendments to the Civil Procedure Law of the People's Republic of China, effective from January 1 2013, the courts' latitude to reject domestic arbitration awards are reduced considerably. In addition to three procedural grounds (no arbitration clause in the agreement; the matters decided fell outside of the arbitration agreement; the composition or procedure of the tribunal violates existing law) and one misconduct ground (bribes, embezzlement or perversion of the law) there are two substantial grounds. Prior to the amendments those two grounds were that the main evidence for ascertaining the facts was insufficient or there was a definite error in the application of the law. Those sections have now been deleted and replaced with a requirement that the evidence that forms the basis of the award is fabricated or there was concealment of evidence by a party that affects the impartiality of the award.[46]

CIETAC also has a proceeding with only one arbitrator where the procedures are the same with some reduction in the timeframes, including a limit of three months to issue the award.

4. Litigation

Only lawyers qualified in China can practise in its courts. No foreign lawyers can appear before a Chinese court. China does not use a jury system. Further, there are many levels in the Chinese court system that have appellate review status as well as original jurisdiction, depending on the nature of the claim.

If you choose to litigate the matter in a foreign court, your judgment will not be enforceable in China unless there is a treaty in existence between that country and China that provides for the mutual enforcement of foreign judgments. Very few countries have such a treaty with China. This is why it is noteworthy that China became a signatory to the New York Convention, which provides that all signatories must mutually enforce arbitration awards from foreign arbitrations.

If you decide to litigate a matter, you can choose a foreign venue where your resulting judgment will not be enforced unless China has a treaty with that country for mutual enforcement of judgments or you can choose to litigate in mainland China where there is no jury system and finality is an elusive goal.

The resolution of disputes via negotiation or mediation is viewed very favourably by Chinese citizens as well as the judiciary. Mediation has been specifically recognised by the Supreme People's Court of China as an appropriate dispute resolution method.

China is a civil law jurisdiction where the various laws are set out in codes. For example, there is a code written for each of contract law, copyright law and patent law. Thus, unlike common law there is no advantage to be had from relying on case precedent.

China's civil procedure law has four parts:

- Part one contains the general provisions.
- Part two contains the trial procedure.
- Part three contains the procedure for execution of judgments.

---

46 Arbitration Law of the People's Republic of China, Article 58.

- Part four contains special provisions for civil proceedings of cases involving a foreign element.

The Supreme People's Court issued an opinion in July 2009 stating that mediation agreements are enforceable by the local courts.[47] Prior to this decision a mediation agreement had to be converted into an arbitration award in order to be enforceable in the courts.

In 1985 China enacted the Foreign Economic Contract Law.[48] This particular law recommends that any foreign-related contract dispute should be resolved through mediation or consultation and only if that effort fails should the matter proceed to litigation or arbitration.[49] Most construction disputes in China are similar to construction disputes elsewhere and relate to delay claims, payments and quality, according to a 1998 study.[50]

Recently there has been discussion about the use of dispute boards in construction claims in China and the Ministry of Construction has recently approved their use.

The Chinese aim to resolve disputes through consultation and negotiation but the problems that face foreign parties is the enforceability of those resulting agreements. If the agreements reached through negotiation are not enforceable, then foreign parties are left no choice but to seek litigation or arbitration.

All Chinese courts provide the same litigation rights and obligations to foreign litigants as are offered to its own citizens.[51] The only exception is if the foreigner's country of origin restricts the civil litigation rights of Chinese citizens, in which case the foreigner's rights will be limited within China.[52] Citizens of all nationalities have the right to use their own language in court as well as on written documents.[53]

There are four levels of Chinese courts. The first level is composed of the basic people's courts, which have jurisdiction over all civil cases unless otherwise provided. The next level is the intermediate people's courts, which have jurisdiction over all major cases involving foreign elements (foreign citizens, foreign corporations). These intermediate courts also have jurisdiction over any cases that they decide have a major impact on their area of jurisdiction. The third level, the high people's courts, have original jurisdiction over civil cases that will have a major impact on the province. The final level is the Supreme People's Court which will have jurisdiction in the first instance over cases that have a major impact on the entire country as well as cases that the court decides it should try.[54]

As noted, where a foreign element is involved the court that has original jurisdiction is not the basic people's court but rather an intermediate-level court.

---

47 Sarah E. Hilmer, "Mediation in the People's Republic of China: History and Recent Developments", 21 *Australasian Disp. Resol. J.* 104 (2010).

48 "People's Republic of China Foreign Economic Contract Law", 6 *Berkeley J Int'l L* 50 (1988).

49 Foreign Economic Contract Law, Article 37.

50 M. Kumaraswamy and K. Yogeswaran, "Significant Sources of Construction Claims", 15 *Int'l Construction L. Rev.* 144, 144–60 (1998).

51 The Law of Civil Procedure of the People's Republic of China, Article 49.

52 Article 5.

53 Article 11.

54 Articles 18–21.

All of these courts have appellate review over the court below them. Thus, the intermediate courts, the high people's courts and the Supreme People's Court all have original jurisdiction over certain cases as well as appellate jurisdiction.[55]

The venue for a lawsuit against a Chinese citizen will be the defendant's domicile unless this is different from his habitual residence, when the venue will be at the habitual residence.[56] If the suit is brought against an organisation, the venue will be the domicile of that organisation. If the dispute is a contract action, the venue can be the defendant's domicile or where the contract is performed. Parties to a contract can select a venue which can be where either party, including the plaintiff, has domicile, or where the object of the action is located.[57]

An insurance contract dispute will be brought in the venue where the defendant has his domicile or where the insured object is located.[58] A lawsuit brought as the result of a dispute over real estate will be under the jurisdiction of the people's court at the place where the real estate is located.[59] Where there are multiple possible venues, the court that first receives the first lawsuit will have jurisdiction. If a party objects to the jurisdiction of the court, it must raise that jurisdictional defence within the time period it has to submit its answer to the complaint.[60]

The people's court tries civil cases by a collegial panel which is composed of both judges and judicial assessors or judges alone. The collegial panel must have an odd number of members.[61] The decision of the people's court is rendered by a majority vote. Judicial assessors can only sit on the lowest level of the people's court.

After a decision is rendered, if one of the parties does not accept the judgment it has 15 days to appeal the matter to the next-higher level.[62] The appeal court, which is the next-higher-level court, will form a collegial panel and conduct a trial. This collegial panel can decide that it is not necessary to conduct a trial and it may make a judgment on the papers submitted alone. This higher-level court has the right to conduct a full trial similar to the trial that was conducted in the first-level court.[63]

All evidence submitted to the courts must be verified. China classifies evidence as documentary evidence, material evidence, audiovisual material, testimony of witnesses, statements of the parties, expert's conclusions, and records of inspection. The people's court has the right to investigate and collect any evidence that it sees fit.[64]

The parties are entitled to cross-examination but the court will accept documents that are properly notarised as evidence.[65]

Any document that is submitted in a foreign language must have a Chinese translation attached.[66]

---

55 Article 147.
56 Articles 22–23.
57 Article 25.
58 Article 26.
59 Article 34.
60 Article 38.
61 Article 40.
62 Article 147.
63 Article 152.
64 Articles 63–64.
65 Article 67.
66 Article 68.

The courts will provide immediate relief to preserve property upon receipt of an application and will respond to a request within 48 hours. However, if the applicant fails to then bring an action within 30 days, the property preservation order will be void.[67] As of January 1 2013, the court also has the right to enjoin someone from any particular action or order someone to take a particular action.

The plaintiff must set down all the claims, facts and causes. The claim must set out the facts and grounds on which the suit is based as well as the evidence for the suit and its source, and the names and addresses of witnesses.[68] The defendant submits its defences and also has the right to submit a counterclaim.[69] The defendant has 15 days after receipt of the complaint from the people's court to file its answer and any counterclaim.[70]

All civil cases are to be tried in public unless Chinese state secrets or personal privacy are an issue.[71]

During the trial the parties may put questions to witnesses, expert witnesses and those that conducted inspections.[72] The court clerk is required to make a written record of the entire court proceedings.[73]

The people's court should try a case and conclude the matter within six months after docketing the case.[74] However, where necessary the president of the people's court can allow a six-month extension. Any further extensions would require approval from the court at the next-higher level.[75]

Once that decision is rendered, the other party has the right to appeal within 15 days to a higher level and then that court has the right to conduct a full retrial of the matter.[76]

With respect to foreign joint ventures, the Civil Procedure Law of the People's Republic of China specifically states:

> *Actions brought on disputes arising from the performance of contracts for Chinese-foreign equity joint ventures or Chinese-foreign contractual joint ventures or Chinese-foreign cooperative exploration and development of the natural resources in the People's Republic of China shall fall under the jurisdiction of the People's Court of the People's Republic of China.*[77]

5. Conclusion

In the normal construction setting where a joint venture is entered into with a Chinese partner, the Chinese courts have jurisdiction over the matter. However, that matter can be arbitrated and as long as the arbitration is based on a written agreement and is held in a country that abides by the New York Convention, China will enforce the resulting judgment.

67 Article 92.
68 Articles 108, 110.
69 Article 113.
70 Article 113.
71 Article 120.
72 Articles 124–125.
73 Article 133.
74 Article 135.
75 Article 135.
76 Article 147.
77 Article 246.

An arbitration held in a foreign country can be administered by any arbitration forum and will be enforceable in China as long as the arbitration agreement was in writing and the country where the arbitration is held is a signatory to the New York Convention.

An arbitration held in mainland China must be administered through one of the arbitration commissions in order for the award to be enforceable in the Chinese courts. These arbitration commissions are located in most municipalities; the most noted commission is CIETAC.

A matter litigated in a foreign court will result in a judgment that will probably not be enforceable in Chinese courts. Initially you will have to determine whether there is a bilateral treaty with the foreign country which provides for the enforcement of foreign judgments in China. Most countries, including the United States, the United Kingdom and Japan, are not parties to such a treaty with China. A review of the treaty will be necessary in order to determine the various limitations and requirements.[78]

If the matter is litigated in China, the people's court is instructed to attempt conciliation first. Specifically, the Civil Procedure Law of the People's Republic of China states that the people's court must distinguish between right and wrong on the basis of the facts being clear, and must conduct conciliation between the parties on a voluntary basis. If conciliation is successful, the conciliation statement will be signed by the judge and becomes legally effective.[79] If conciliation is unsuccessful, the court will enter a judgment, which, if not appealed, will be enforceable.

As it stands today, there are several key factors that anyone seeking to participate in the construction market in China must know about. As recently as March 2013 there have been numerous articles as well as television documentaries on the residential real estate market in China. In a recent documentary, miles and miles of newly constructed uninhabited ghost towns containing residential and commercial properties were shown. According to the documentary the Chinese have limited investment vehicles as they are not allowed to invest overseas, their internal vehicles – including the stock market – are too risky, and the banks provide miniscule returns. Thus, a large number of Chinese turned to investment in housing stock when China permitted people to own more than one residential property. This permission was granted around 1999. The documentary discussed how developers had started to drop their prices and how this could lead not only to a financial crash but possibly social unrest.[80]

This real estate bubble and housing crisis in the outlying areas is in sharp contrast to the real estate markets in the first-tier cities, including Shanghai and Beijing, where the landscape is crowded with cranes and prices are constantly moving upwards.

The construction industry in China could have large rewards, but also major failures. It is extremely important to undertake detailed research and to team up with

---

78 Article 266.
79 Articles 85–89.
80 *60 Minutes*, March 3 2013, CBS-TV.

a knowledgeable and sophisticated local partner. In addition, it is very important to understand and prepare for any disputes and this preparation must include an understanding of the local law, which litigation vehicles will be used to resolve disputes and an awareness of the difficulties in enforcing any resulting judgments.

Hong Kong

David Bateson
King & Wood Mallesons

1. Introduction

1.1 Nature of the industry

The construction industry is an important contributor to Hong Kong's economy. Annually, it has a major impact on gross domestic product (GDP) and is one of Hong Kong's main drivers of economic growth and development. The three areas that comprise the majority of the market for construction in Hong Kong are public sector works and public housing projects, both of which are commissioned by the Hong Kong government and its authorities, and private development projects.

The government is the largest commissioner of construction and infrastructure projects in Hong Kong. As it is well funded, public-private partnerships (PPPs) are relatively few. In 2007, the government announced 10 major public infrastructure projects for economic growth, resulting in significant increases in GDP by construction from 2009.[1] The annual actual expenditure on capital works for 2012–13 was announced by the government to be HK$62.3 billion.[2]

The government commissions work through various public authorities. The major infrastructure projects announced in 2007, most of which are presently being carried out by or on behalf of the government, revolve around three major themes: transport infrastructure, cross-boundary infrastructure and new urban development areas.[3] These projects are causing a boom in construction activity, which will be sustained for at least the next 10 years.

The second-largest commissioner of construction projects is the Mass Transit Railway (MTR), which was solely owned by the government until June 2000, when it sold 23% of its share capital to private investors. The company became publicly listed on the Hong Kong Stock Exchange later in 2000. Following the merger with the Kowloon–Canton Railway Corporation in 2007, the MTR controls an extensive network of operations (including the entire urban railway network in Hong Kong and a substantial number of private-housing projects, generally sitting above most MTR stations), paving the way for large-scale projects, particularly in the areas of

1 HKEx News, "Industry Overview", at www.hkexnews.hk/listedco/listconews/sehk/2011/1229/01315_1232959/E113.pdf
2 Hong Kong Government 2012–13 Budget, www.budget.gov.hk
3 West Island Line and South Island Line, Sha Tin to Central Link, Tuen Mun Western Bypass & Tuen Mun-Chek Lap Kok Link, Guangzhou–Shenzhen–Hong Kong Express Rail Link, HK-Zhuhai–Macao Bridge, HK–Shenzhen Aiport Co-operation, HK–Shenzhen Joint Development of Lok Ma Chau Loop, West Kowloon Cultural District, Kai Tak Development Plan, New Development Areas.

network extension and improvement. The MTR is currently constructing an extension to its railway network, with the Southern and Western lines, and the Sha Tin–Central link.

The contracting services industry in Hong Kong comprises relatively few large local contractors, and a substantial number of subcontractors. Numerous overseas contractors are also present in the Hong Kong market. As a result of Hong Kong's open market, the industry is highly competitive. In order to bid for government projects, accreditation is required.

Both foreign and local companies can bid for public and private projects in Hong Kong. However, given the increasing complexity and size of construction and infrastructure projects, particularly those commissioned by the government, the trend has been for such projects to be awarded to larger, multi-service companies that provide expertise across a range of disciplines (usually joint ventures).

Although the construction industry is financially healthy, there is room for improvement. The culture within the industry and the relationship between contracting parties tends to be acutely adversarial and lacking in trust. This has resulted in a high number of disputes occurring on construction projects as compared with other industries. Overall, it is likely that the industry would benefit from a more collaborative approach, better contracting practices and increased project management skills within the workforce, in order to reduce the number of disputes. These issues will be discussed in further detail below.

1.2 Standard contractual forms

Standard forms of contract are commonly used on construction projects in Hong Kong. There are two particular types, the first being those generally used by the government for public works projects, and the second being those used on private projects.

The Government of Hong Kong General Conditions of Contracts (1999 edition) is a set of conditions that is broadly accepted internationally for the purpose of civil engineering, building, electrical and mechanical projects. This includes a design-and-build contract. The MTR uses its own set of pro-forma contracts, which are largely based on the government form of contracts but with a greater focus on project management and dispute resolution. The MTR's three standard forms of contract are Standard Conditions of Contract (ie, D&C, Engineer's Design, E&M, Major Works), Target Cost and Maintenance contracts.

The standard forms have long been subject to criticism, mainly because the parties will often modify the terms, which can lead to difficulties in interpretation and a consequent increase in disputes. This problem is exacerbated by the often complex and technical nature of construction projects, which is especially the case for the MTR, where projects often involve complex and incomplete interfaces. Discussions regarding options for reform of the standard contractual forms have been ongoing in Hong Kong since around 2005.

In 2005 and 2006, the Hong Kong Institute of Architects, in collaboration with the Hong Kong Institute of Surveyors and the Hong Kong Institute of Construction Managers, overhauled the 1986 Standard Forms of Building Contract (with and without quantities) for private projects and the standard forms for the nominated subcontract and nominated supply contract. It remains to be seen whether these new forms will be as popular as the old ones (that were amended twice), which a number of private developers are still keen to use.

1.3 NEC suite of contracts

The New Engineering Contract (NEC) was first published in 1993, with the latest revision, known as the Engineering and Construction Contract (ECC), published in 2005. Use of this form of contract in Hong Kong has been limited so far: however, in 2012 there were approximately 10 projects trialling contracts from the NEC suite, mostly involving the government. It is expected that use of this form of contract will increase in Hong Kong in the future.

A main objective of the drafters of the NEC suite was to develop a form of contract that would remedy the rigidity and overly legalistic nature of traditional forms of construction contract, with a focus on improving project management practices. The NEC was intended to provide a more simplified approach that could be used universally, and whereby risk would be identified early in the project in order to reduce the time and cost implications of unforseen problems and delays.

The nature of the NEC, and its focus on early identification of risk, requires a management-heavy approach, which naturally means more project management and staff resources than might otherwise be engaged. It requires all parties to the contract to exchange specific information and participate in regular decision-making processes. As a result, the NEC may not be suitable for those projects where the parties are not prepared to invest in project management and staff resources necessary to administer the NEC properly. This assumption accords with the research that suggests the NEC works better on larger projects.[4]

The NEC provides for the quick resolution of disputes through negotiation and adjudication. The key characteristic of the NEC dispute resolution process is that it allows for disputes to be formally and quickly resolved while the works are still in progress, as opposed to the traditional approach whereby disputes are usually resolved at the end of the project. This is considered to be an advantage as the NEC promotes a more collaborative approach, rather than allowing disputes to remain at large in the longer term.

Whether the NEC will become the contract of choice in Hong Kong is not yet clear. Those sceptical about the introduction of the new suite of contracts suggest that the Hong Kong construction and infrastructure industry may not be inclined to develop the necessary resources to ensure that the system works as designed, perhaps mainly due to fear of increasing the project's administration costs. Furthermore, it requires a collaborative approach between the parties in terms of project management, which is presently not the way most projects in Hong Kong are carried out.

One also needs to consider whether the NEC has any persuasive advantages over

4 Keith Keown, "Is Hong Kong ready for the NEC?", paper prepared for the Society of Construction Law Hong Kong, November 2011.

other forms of contract presently in use in Hong Kong. The central mechanisms of the NEC include early warning notifications, risk reduction meetings, a focus on the importance of the programme, compensation events and accelerated decision making. Some of these features are already present in Hong Kong construction contracts, while others may require some degree of learning and training before being capable of successful implementation.

Most Hong Kong construction contracts already require early-warning notifications and risk-reduction meetings to take place. However, these notifications and meetings will often relate to difficult and complex issues that the project management team considers incapable of rapid resolution.[5] It may be unlikely that the NEC is capable of bringing any real change to the reluctance of Hong Kong project managers to speed up the process, particularly in relation to complex issues.

The Hong Kong construction industry is highly competitive. Usually, the contractor who prices the lowest wins the tender. The tendency of contractors to under-bid in order to win the tender often causes an increase in claims for additional payment during the course of the contract, in order to make up for the winning bidder's shortfall. Of course, Hong Kong contractors could use the early-warning and compensation-event procedures in the NEC for this purpose as well.

Regularly updating the accepted programme is of central importance to the NEC. In the Hong Kong context, the necessary focus on the programme might assist employers by requiring a greater level of detail and transparency from contractors.[6]

Despite some doubts, the NEC nevertheless has proven success in Hong Kong, following the completion of the government's first pilot NEC project. The HK$96 million Fuk Man Road drainage project was completed six months ahead of target and 5% below its final target cost.[7] Further investment in developing project management skills, a more collaborative approach to the project and a move away from purely price-based strategies for winning tenders is needed in order for the NEC to work regularly in practice.

2. Construction dispute resolution

Construction projects in Hong Kong tend to have a high incidence of disputes, which is unsurprisingly one of the main causes of project failure. Many disputes relate to complex issues, such as delay and/or disruption, which are difficult for the parties to resolve alone. The costs of litigation not only have an impact on construction projects in terms of legal costs, but also through the hidden cost of a dispute, which may include damage to personal and commercial relationships and time spent by staff addressing the dispute. Unresolved and ongoing disputes are obviously counterproductive to progress.

Hong Kong has long been established as a premier international venue for dispute resolution in the Asia–Pacific region, particularly with arbitration, and is therefore the preferred venue that is often specified in construction and

5 Keith Keown, *ibid*, citing Paragraph 20.7 of The Grove Report.

6 Stuart Catchpole, "The NEC3 Form – A Success?", October 8 2012, p.12.

7 NEC Users Group, "Hong Kong set to build on success of first NEC trial", October 2012 www.neccontract.com

infrastructure contracts for the resolution of disputes. The range of alternative dispute resolution methods available is discussed in this section. No form of dispute resolution is forbidden or excluded by law in Hong Kong.

2.1 Arbitration

Hong Kong can rightly regard itself as a pioneer of arbitration in Asia, being the first to adopt the UNCITRAL Model Law in 1990. It has since developed an advanced arbitral regime, which was further enhanced in 2010 by the adoption of the new Arbitration Ordinance. Prior to 2010, Hong Kong had two separate regimes for international and domestic arbitration. The 2010 Arbitration Ordinance merged the two regimes, so that a unitary system of arbitration based on the Model Law was created. This has made it easier for foreign practitioners and their clients to use the Hong Kong arbitral system due to universal familiarity with the Model Law, while opt-in provisions from the previous domestic regime remain for parties wanting to retain features of the old system (ie, appointment of a sole arbitrator, consolidation of disputes and the right to appeal on questions of law). This retention was driven by the construction industry itself. As such, the Hong Kong arbitral regime differs from the UNCITRAL Model Law by reason of the fact that it provides for both a domestic and international regime.

One of the central objectives of the 2010 Arbitration Ordinance is to minimise the intervention of the Hong Kong courts in the arbitration process by limiting the parties' rights to challenge an arbitral award. The right of appeal on a point of law has been removed and no right of recourse to the courts on a preliminary point of law is allowed. These changes, however, do not apply if the opt-in provisions to the previous domestic regime are exercised. In fact the ordinance actually extends the grounds of challenge relevant to the domestic regime, so that a challenge on the basis of serious irregularity is now available. The ordinance also enables the Hong Kong courts to grant interim measures applying to arbitration proceedings in Hong Kong and, in certain circumstances, arbitration proceedings that are commenced outside Hong Kong. However, the courts are unlikely to intervene if interim measures are more appropriately dealt with by the arbitral tribunal.

Apart from the usual arguments in favour of arbitration, such as reducing legal costs and allowing the parties greater flexibility and autonomy, arbitration is particularly suited to the construction industry because the parties may choose specialised arbitrators skilled in the particular area relevant to the dispute. This is desirable given that construction disputes are often highly technical. Resolution of a technical dispute by an arbitrator already well versed in a particular technical area has its obvious advantages. This benefit is especially advantageous in Hong Kong, where many highly skilled arbitration practitioners focus on construction. In addition, enforcement of awards in foreign jurisdictions is easier under the New York Convention than enforcing a court judgment that depends on reciprocity of treaties.

The decision of an arbitral tribunal will be kept confidential, which is another attractive feature in the Hong Kong construction environment where reputation is extremely important. In addition, the 2010 Arbitration Ordinance provides that court proceedings commenced in relation to arbitration proceedings (such as for interim measures) must also be confidential. This prevents the publication of any decision of the court in relation to arbitral proceedings, unless the court finds that the public interest in publication is greater than the need to protect the confidentiality of arbitral proceedings (a rare and difficult hurdle to surpass).

The arbitration process in Hong Kong is nonetheless not without criticism. One such criticism presently being levied is that it may have become too expensive. Ultimately arbitration is still less expensive than litigation, but the gap between the comparative costs of the two methods of dispute resolution may be narrowing. The professional costs of lawyers, barristers and experts engaged on the dispute are unlikely to differ much between litigation and arbitration, particularly if the dispute is complex. Furthermore, the costs of the arbitration will include the arbitrators' fees, which can be substantial depending on the length of time that the arbitration runs. As the parties bear the costs associated with the arbitration, parties that cannot financially sustain extended court proceedings may not be able to financially sustain arbitration proceedings either, although arbitration should be quicker. In order for Hong Kong to remain a preferred venue for arbitration, it may be that greater focus needs to be placed on controlling the costs incurred during the arbitral process.

In this respect, the Hong Kong International Arbitration Centre has taken steps to address the issue of costs, as demonstrated by the draft revised Arbitration Rules issued in late 2012, which among other things proposed to introduce new caps on arbitrators' fees. The new rules are scheduled to come into effect on November 1 2013. They will also allow the parties to choose how the arbitrators' fees are calculated, either by reference to a percentage of the sum in dispute or on the basis of an hourly rate. If the parties choose the latter option, a cap of HK$6,500 ($838) per hour will apply.

Even with the rising costs, parties may still choose arbitration over litigation, finding that the benefits of having a decision maker with a clear understanding of the complex nature of the dispute, confidentiality and easier cross-border enforcement outweigh the costs of arbitrators.

Another criticism of arbitration is that it is no less adversarial than court proceedings, doing little to maintain the commercial relationship between the parties. As a consequence, which is discussed further below, the prospect of maintaining and preserving a commercial relationship is one of the main advantages that other forms of alternative dispute resolution may have over arbitration.

2.2 Mediation/conciliation

Unlike in civil law countries, the terms 'mediation' and 'conciliation' are generally used to describe the same thing in Hong Kong. For the purposes of this section, the term 'mediation' will be used to describe both. As in other jurisdictions, mediation is voluntary and confidential. It serves a useful purpose for the resolution of construction disputes in Hong Kong, particularly where the parties are unable to resolve a dispute due to a communication breakdown, but at the same time do not want the expense of arbitration/litigation or desire limited disruption to a project in progress. Hong Kong has a large number of trained and qualified mediators, making it a particularly suitable place for mediation to be conducted.

The mediator appointed should be neutral and independent. A mediator's role is to assist the parties to a dispute to reach a negotiated settlement. A mediator cannot impose judgment or enforce a particular outcome and no outcome will be binding unless the parties agree. To be effective, mediation usually needs to take place at a high level, such as at CEO level, to ensure that the parties have the authority to resolve and settle the dispute.

Since its introduction, mediation has become a successful means of dispute resolution in Hong Kong. Mediation was introduced in Hong Kong by way of a trial scheme in 1984, to apply to selected civil engineering contracts.[8] Revised mediation rules were introduced in 1991. The government first introduced compulsory mediation into a government contract for the construction of the new international airport in Hong Kong in the 1990s. It was reported that the mediation process had a 79% success rate during the life of a project.[9] Since that time it has been used by the government and the MTR as a second step in usually three-tier dispute resolution provisions (after an internal/contract administration review and before seeking to arbitrate the dispute).

In 2008, a working group on mediation was set up by the government to consider and report on ways to enhance and develop the use of mediation in Hong Kong. In June 2012, the Hong Kong Mediation Ordinance was enacted, which provided a statutory framework for mediation. The ordinance came into effect on January 1 2013 and the provisions of the ordinance are retrospective. On April 2 2013, the Hong Kong Mediation Accreditation Association Ltd (HKMAAL) commenced operation as the single accreditation body in Hong Kong for mediation. The HKMAAL is responsible for a range of matters referred to in the ordinance, including the appointment of a mediator when the parties cannot agree.

In addition, the civil justice reform that took place in Hong Kong in 2009 emphasised the role of the courts in promoting early settlement of disputes, predominantly through court-referred mediations. In accordance with Practice Direction 31, from 2010 onwards practitioners have been required to file a mediation certificate asserting whether a dispute undergoing court proceedings is suitable for resolution by way of mediation. Whilst mediation is not compulsory, unreasonable refusal to participate in mediation will be frowned upon by the courts and may result in adverse cost orders.

Mediation is more widely used in the construction industry than in any other industry. Now, almost all government construction contracts require referral to mediation before other avenues of dispute resolution are explored. The advantages of mediation include confidentiality and quick resolution, but, above all, the likelihood of maintaining the commercial relationship between the parties, due to the non-adversarial nature of the process. All documents and information must be disclosed on a without-prejudice basis. The procedure is quick, economical, flexible and designed to be non-confrontational.

However, the decision of the mediator is not binding and will not work if one or

---

8 Colin J. Wall, "The Framework for Mediation in Hong Kong", *Arbitration*, February 2009, p78.
9 Colin J. Wall, *ibid*, p79.

both of the parties are inflexible and not taking part in the mediation in good faith. As each party bears its own costs, there is the potential for unfairness if one party obstructs the mediation. As such, it may not be suitable for complex disputes where numerous parties are involved.

One of the main reasons that mediation sometimes fails in Hong Kong is because of the stubborn position of the parties, as opposed to the actual issues in dispute.[10] Unless the parties are genuinely willing to compromise in order to resolve the dispute, mediation will have little use. Unfortunately in Hong Kong, a lack of trust between the parties to construction contracts, particularly in the private sector, has been a common cause of failure of mediation.

2.3 Mediation-arbitration

The 2010 Arbitration Ordinance allows a hybrid form of mediation-arbitration to take place in Hong Kong, where the arbitrator may also first act as the mediator. This type of dispute resolution is common in China. If this arrangement is agreed to, the arbitration proceedings must be stayed.

There are a number of criticisms levied at this approach because of the potential for bias. One possible danger is that mediation-arbitrations may force the parties to disclose their bottom lines in the mediation process, prejudicing future arbitration. In addition, as the mediator/arbitrator will be privy to confidential information whilst also being required to meet privately and separately with each party, there is the potential for bias and uncertainty as to what is being revealed to the opposing side.

In 2011, a Hong Kong court refused to enforce an arbitral award issued in China on the basis that it conflicted with public policy.[11] When asked to enforce the arbitral award in Hong Kong, the court refused because of conduct by the mediator-arbitrator that could give rise to an implication of bias, who was privy to confidential information provided by both parties. However, this decision was overturned on appeal, sparking further debate about the ability of an arbitrator who also acts as a mediator to remain neutral.

Many believe that the 2010 Arbitration Ordinance has enough safeguards to ensure that arbitration-mediation is conducted properly. These are set out in section 33 of the 2010 Arbitration Ordinance as follows:

(3) An arbitrator who is acting as a mediator—

(a) may communicate with the parties collectively or separately; and

(b) must treat the information obtained by the arbitrator from a party as confidential, unless otherwise agreed by that party or unless subsection (4) applies.

(4) If –

(a) confidential information is obtained by an arbitrator from a party during the mediation proceedings conducted by the arbitrator as a mediator; and

---

10 K Chau, "Insight into resolving construction disputes by Mediation/Adjudication in Hong Kong", *Journal of Professional Issues in Engineering Education and Practice*, April 2007.

11 See *Gao Haiyan and Xie Heping v Keeneye Holdings Ltd and New Purple Golden Resources Development Ltd* [2001] HKE 514, Court of First Instance, April 12 2011.

(b) those mediation proceedings terminate without reaching a settlement acceptable to the parties,

the arbitrator must, before resuming the arbitral proceedings, disclose to all other parties as much of that information as the arbitrator considers is material to the arbitral proceedings.

(5) No objection may be made against the conduct of the arbitral proceedings by an arbitrator solely on the ground that the arbitrator had acted previously as a mediator in accordance with this section.

These provisions appear to guard against the risks associated with mediation-arbitration. However, as this form of alternative dispute resolution is not that common in Hong Kong, the adequacy of these provisions has probably not been sufficiently tested.

2.4 Adjudication

Adjudication is a binding dispute resolution procedure designed to facilitate the quick resolution of disputes, usually while the works are in progress. An adjudicator will be appointed to assess the evidence in relation to the dispute within a tight time frame and will reach a decision that is binding, unless the matter is thereafter referred to arbitration or litigation or is otherwise settled between the parties. In practice, however, most decisions handed down by an adjudicator will achieve final resolution of the dispute.

Unlike other jurisdictions, Hong Kong has no statutory adjudication scheme. Adjudications taking place on government projects are governed by the Hong Kong Government Special Administrative Region Construction Adjudication Rules (2004) and administered by the Hong Kong International Arbitration Centre (HKIAC). The HKIAC later developed a set of rules applicable to adjudications (HKIAC Adjudication Rules 2009).

One of the main advantages of adjudication is that it imposes a strict timetable within which the adjudicator must reach a decision (usually 56 days within receipt of referral submissions by the adjudicator), facilitating a quick resolution. Although still an adversarial process, adjudication allows for early payment and for the works to continue, and it can minimise the impact of the dispute on the project. Adjudication is not as common in Hong Kong as in other jurisdictions (eg, the United Kingdom), but as it is the main mechanism for dispute resolution in the NEC suite of contracts, it may increase in popularity should the NEC also do so.

2.5 Expert determination

Determination of disputes by an expert has long been common in the construction industry in Hong Kong. This occurs where the parties agree to appoint an independent person in the capacity of expert as opposed to in the capacity of judge, arbitrator or mediator to resolve disputes as they arise. The appointment of an independent expert is usually allowed for in the governing contract, or may be introduced by the parties by agreement.

While there is no ordinance in Hong Kong that governs the appointment of independent experts, various professional bodies have published rules that relate to their appointment and practice, for example rules published by the Royal Institute of Chartered Surveyors Hong Kong Dispute Resolution Professional Group or CEDR Asia Pacific (part of the Centre for Effective Dispute Resolution). Best practice would see the parties contracting prior to the dispute to be bound by a particular set of rules.

It is imperative that the expert appointed to resolve the dispute has the knowledge and skills that would be expected of an expert in the particular area that the dispute relates to. Furthermore, the expert must be impartial, and therefore if the parties cannot agree on the appointment of an expert, their agreement to be bound by a set of rules published by a professional body will also bind them to acceding to the appointment of an expert chosen by the relevant professional body.

The expert's role is to make an independent decision, which is reasonable by reference to industry standards and professional opinion, made without the assistance of outside parties. The expert may make a decision completely free of reference to any submissions or evidence served by the parties, although the expert is required to allow the parties the opportunity to have their say. The expert owes a duty to both parties to act with reasonable care and skill when reaching a decision. The expert's determination will be binding, although the contract may allow for the decision to be challenged on certain grounds.

Expert determination is used regularly in Hong Kong for the purpose of resolving technical disputes. Again, it has similar advantages to other alternative dispute resolution procedures in terms of efficiency, avoiding adversarial confrontation and allowing finality to be introduced in relation to the dispute.

2.6 Dispute adjudication boards

Dispute adjudication boards (DABs) (or dispute review boards), while not yet common in Hong Kong, provide another means of alternative dispute resolution. DABs were successfully used by the Provisional Airport Authority when the Chep Lap Kok Airport was built. This method is well suited to the construction industry because it allows for quick, informal and cost-effective dispute resolution. The process tends to be non-confrontational and as such may assist to preserve the working relationship between the parties. There is a suggestion that the appeal of DABs in Hong Kong may be on the rise, having already been used on several large government projects.

A DAB will usually comprise a panel of three independent and impartial persons who are appointed at the outset of a project to resolve disputes as they arise. Generally, the persons appointed to act on the panel will have been involved on various aspects of the project – for example, they may be engineers, architects, quantity surveyors or lawyers working in some capacity on the project. Recourse to a DAB will be governed by the contract, whereby the terms will provide that the parties agree to establish a DAB to hear and advise on the resolution of disputes. The contract will provide for the quick resolution of disputes by the DAB which the parties cannot resolve, and require quick publication of the decision and recommendations.

Whether a decision of the DAB will be binding is dependent on the terms of the contract. Sometimes the contract will provide that the decision will only become binding if it is not disputed by either party, which lessens the effectiveness of the process. Alternatively, an immediately binding decision may be issued. However, most contracts allow recourse to arbitration if the DAB process does not work.

While recourse to arbitration/litigation will usually remain available, parties tend to respect the decisions of experienced experts involved on the project. Accepting a decision of a DAB will often be in the parties' best interests to preserve and maintain personal and commercial relationships, particularly in the context of large, unfinished commercial construction projects. Arbitration/litigation thereby becomes a last resort.

As far as negatives are concerned, the appointment of a DAB may result in quick and potentially unjust decisions. In addition, the process can be costly if industry-leading and expensive panel members are appointed. Unlike an arbitral award, the decision of a DAB is unlikely to have the same enforcement potential, nor be protected by law or legislation. For example, parties will not be able to rely on the New York Convention in order to enforce a decision of the panel. This presents a potential risk for the parties, as the decision will not have the potential to be enforced by the courts.

There are nevertheless ways that parties to construction contracts can protect themselves, such as ensuring that decisions will be final and binding, requiring implementation without delay and inclusion of a right for the contractor to suspend the works if the employer does not comply with a decision of the DAB, and for either side to be able to terminate the contract if the decision of the DAB is not complied with. At this stage, it is safe to say that, in the Hong Kong context, DABs as an alternative option for dispute resolution require further consideration.

2.7 Partnering and alliancing

'Partnering' and 'alliancing' (the ultimate form of partnering) are terms used to describe a contractual relationship where two or more parties work together for the purpose of achieving a shared goal. An alliance will remove the confrontational parts of a subcontracting relationship between the main contractor and the subcontractor, create risk sharing and align the parties' project systems so that they work together as part of one team. The terms of the alliance contract do not need to be particularly detailed: the document simply needs to clearly outline the parties' respective scopes of work and address how the fee is paid.

Alliancing/partnering is intended to have the overriding benefit of removing the adversarial aspects of the contractual relationship by virtue of the fact that neither party is liable to the other, except with respect to wilful default. As discussed above, there is a pervasive adversarial culture in Hong Kong within the construction industry, which could potentially be addressed in part by wider use of the partnering approach.

When an alliance or partnering agreement is in place, the risk of disputes, claims and subsequent litigation lessens, as the parties must engage in dialogue and work together to resolve issues as they arise. It implies a focus on problem solving in a non-adversarial environment for the purpose of mutual benefit. This in turn means that, theoretically, there should be greater flexibility in dealing with problems as they arise and responding urgently when required.

Although more than 50 projects have adopted the partnering approach in Hong Kong, it is not, however, in widespread use.[12] While the Hong Kong government has used the approach, some issues prevent its widespread adoption by both domestic and international players in the Hong Kong construction industry.

Alliances require significant up-front investments in terms of resources and money, which may be a deterrent for investors not wanting to make a long-term commitment to other stakeholders. From a brief survey, use of the partnering approach is presently restricted to large-scale projects such as major civil engineering works.

3. Conclusion

The construction industry in Hong Kong uses a broad range of different procedures for the resolution of disputes. Often, a multi-tiered approach to dispute resolution will be embraced, particularly on larger projects. While multi-tiered dispute resolution may ultimately cost more, this approach should increase the chances of resolving disputes at an early stage and will be particularly useful when the parties require resolution during the course of the works.

Arbitration remains the preferred method of dispute resolution for the construction industry in Hong Kong. This jurisdiction is well placed to provide arbitration services to both domestic and international parties, particularly because of the depth of experience of arbitrators and practitioners. However, while arbitration has the potential benefit of being generally quicker than litigation, the recent developments in cost control will need to be closely monitored to ensure that they will successfully rein in the growing problem of cost. In the future it is likely that Hong Kong will see greater use of the NEC suite of contracts and of the dispute resolution procedures associated with these forms of contract. Adjudication and use of DABS are yet to take off, although they have been successfully utilised on some government and airport contracts, and are likely to increase along with use of the NEC. Whether partnering will become more common in Hong Kong may depend on whether the construction industry remains fundamentally adversarial in nature over the coming years, or whether the market opens up to alternative forms of risk sharing. For now, at least, the industry has a number of dispute resolution measures available to deal reasonably with its disputes.

The author would like to extend thanks to Eve Ormond for her assistance in preparing this chapter.

---

12 Wong, Siu-yue, Patrick "Partnering in Hong Kong Construction Industry"', The University of Hong Kong, 2005.

India

Sumeet Kachwaha
Kachwaha & Partners

1. Introduction

Construction has been a rapidly growing sector in India for the past 15 years. This growth is fuelled by a large infrastructure building task that the country has undertaken. After liberalisation of the economy (from the early 1990s) came the realisation that India needed to upgrade its infrastructure rapidly. Infrastructure (and thereby construction) leads to economic growth, which in turn attracts investment. Hence the priority given to this sector.

Currently, construction is the second-largest employer in the country (after agriculture). According to the Planning Commission of India, the construction industry employs approximately 45 million people with more than 85% serving as workers. The country's main international trading partners in this sector are the Middle East, Africa and Malaysia. The use of various new technologies and the deployment of project management strategies has recently made it possible to undertake large-scale projects.[1]

The current 12th Five-Year Plan (2012–17) envisages an investment of US$1 trillion in infrastructure and that the private sector will share 47% of the investment required. (Over the past 10 years private investment in infrastructure has steadily grown from 25% to 35%.) Private investment is largely through tax-free bonds and the public-private partnership (PPP) route.

India has emerged as a leading PPP market in the world. As a result, a proper PPP ecosystem of developers, financiers, equity providers, policies and procedures has matured.[2] The 2012–13 Annual Report of the Ministry of Finance reported that at mid-2013 there are more than 900 PPP projects, with a total project cost (TPC) of Rs5.4 trillion (about $90 billion) as compared with around 600 projects with a TPC of Rs3.3 trillion at end-March 2010. The projects are at different stages of implementation, ie, are at the bidding, construction or operational stages.[3]

On a PPP basis, roads have taken the lion's share, accounting for 53.4% of the total number of projects and 46% by value. Ports come second with 8% in terms of number of projects but a more significant contribution of 21% in terms of value. The table overleaf gives the sector-wise figures published by the Department of Economic Affairs, Ministry of Finance dated July 31 2011.

1 IHS Global Insight. www.ihsglobalinsight.com/gcpath/India_Construction_1-7.pdf
2 "Accelerating Public Private Partnerships in India", Ernst & Young Publications.
3 PPP India Database as of July 31 2011; and Ernst & Young Publications, *supra*.

Sector-wise	Total number of projects	Of value less than Rs1 bn (Rs bn)	Of value Rs1 bn to Rs2.5 bn (Rs bn)	Of value over Rs2.5 bn up to Rs5 bn (Rs bn)	Of value over Rs5 bn (Rs bn)	Total (Rs bn)
Airports	5	–	–	3.0	188.1	191.1
Education	17	4.2	3.7	4.6	6.0	18.5
Energy	56	3.4	9.3	30.8	628.9	672.4
Health Care	8	3.1	3.4	2.8	9.0	18.3
Ports	61	0.9	17.5	43.0	749.0	810.4
Railways	4	–	1.0	8.7	6.0	15.7
Roads	405	43.6	117.0	385.2	1.221.4	1,767.2
Tourism	50	11.4	15.0	8.0	10.5	44.9
Urban Develop-ment	152	28.1	31.4	66.9	168.4	294.8
Total	**758**	**94.7**	**198.3**	**553.0**	**2,987.3**	**3,833.3**

2. Sector-wise snapshot

Some major highlights of India's various industry sectors are as follows.

2.1 Road construction

The road sector was the first to take off and the procurement and execution models have reached a certain level of maturity. The target here is to accomplish an average of 20 km (kilometres) of road every day or about 7,300 km a year. A specialised authority called the National Highways Authority of India has been set up under the Ministry of Roads, Transport and Highways to administer this vast task at the central level. (Various states have their own set-up relating to state roads and highways.)

2.2 Ports

The year 2013 will see the establishment of two new major ports on the eastern coast (within the states of Andhra Pradesh and West Bengal), which will add 100 million tonnes of capacity. Additionally a new outer harbour will be developed in South India (in the state of Tamil Nadu) through a PPP with an estimated cost of $1.5 billion. When completed, this will add 40 million tonnes of capacity.

2.3 Industrial corridors

An ambitious project has been under way for some time to create an industrial corridor between Delhi and Mumbai, and work is expected to start in the near future. The plan is to have seven new cities and two industrial smart cities en route. The project includes a mega power plant and other dedicated infrastructure units required for an industrial corridor. This project is supported by the Government of Japan. There are also plans for further industrial corridors, including ones connecting Bangalore and Chennai and Bangalore and Mumbai.

2.4 Airports

The airport sector has seen a somewhat bumpy ride. Four airports have been privatised so far: two in the greenfield sector (Bangalore and Hyderabad) and two in the brownfield sector (Mumbai and New Delhi). These were signed off between 2004 and 2006 and account for over 60% of the market. Thereafter there was a long lull owing to the policy framework for airport privatisation not being in place (and some glitches in the existing models had surfaced). Also the regulatory system had not been worked out. Now these issues have been addressed and airport privatisation seems set to progress again.

Recently the government announced, in principle, clearance to privatise 14 airports in the greenfield sector on a PPP basis. In the airport sector, privatisation is on a revenue-sharing basis. The concessionaire is allotted the right to develop 5% of total airport land for commercial exploitation and development (ie, the non-aeronautical side). Considering the enormous value of land, this essentially takes care of the development costs and also gives the government a very healthy return (through revenue sharing). In its first five years of existence, the Delhi airport has returned over half a billion dollars to the government by way of revenue sharing (and the return is expected to grow exponentially as the non-aeronautical side develops).

2.5 Railways

India has the third-largest rail network in the world in terms of size and is the largest passenger carrier in the world but is far from efficient. It has remained a government monopoly for far too long. After some resistance, this important sector is opening up to private participation. The government issued a press release dated May 10 2012 announcing certain projects for execution on a PPP basis, as follows:

- a high-speed corridor (Mumbai–Ahmedabad);
- an elevated rail corridor in Mumbai's suburban section;
- the redevelopment of stations;
- logistics parks;
- wagon leasing and other freight schemes;
- port connectivity projects;
- dedicated freight corridors;
- loco and coach manufacturing units; and
- captive power generation renewable energy and other energy-saving projects.

Contemporaneously, the government also announced a draft policy for private participation in capacity augmentation and connectivity projects.

Investors' enthusiasm is not lacking. According to one press report,[4] "Within two months of the government issuing a note allowing companies to own and operate private railway lines to transport goods, Indian Railways has received investment proposals worth [Rs13.6 billion (around US$230 million)], mostly from logistics companies and ports."

Besides, metro projects are an ongoing activity in Delhi, Chennai, Hyderabad, Kochi, Jaipur, Pune and Kolkata.

2.6 Incentives to attract investment

There have been some recent government incentives to attract investment in infrastructure:[5]

- A number of institutions would be authorised to issue tax-free bonds. The government hopes to raise US$10 billion from this incentive in 2013–14.
- Infrastructure debt funds will be encouraged. These funds will be used to provide long-term debt for infrastructure.
- India Infrastructure Finance Corporation Limited in partnership with the Asian Development Bank will offer credit enhancement to infrastructure companies that wish to access the bond market to tap into long-term funds.

3. Impediments and obstacles

Despite the government's commitment to boost infrastructure, there have been several impediments. The biggest challenges lie in land acquisition, removal of encroachments, shifting of utilities and getting clearances from forest and environment departments. These usually meet with resistance from activists and the local population. Often government bodies overlap (and indeed may act at cross purposes). One major impediment in recent years has been the forest rights laws of 2006 under which all construction projects (even where there may only be a passage involved) have to obtain approval from local village councils. This has led to corruption and hold-ups. The government is taking steps to address all this but it will take a while for qualitative changes to happen.

4. Dispute resolution methods accepted and used in India

Indian litigation unfortunately suffers from court delays and the virtual absence of case management. The regular courts are quite choked with the backlog and it can take anything up to 20 years (or more) for a civil matter to be resolved.[6] According to a 2008 World Bank estimate, more than the equivalent of US$12 billion is locked up in the courts due to construction disputes. More recent estimates put this figure at US$25 billion.[7]

Against this background, the various dispute resolution methods prevalent in India are described below.

---

4 *Economic Times*, January 4 2013.

5 Speech of Finance Minister dated 28th February 2013 while presenting the Union Budget in Parliament.

6 Speech of Law Minister dated 20th December 2011 in Parliament while tabling 114th Amendment Bill at page 7543.

7 Press Report (Mint) dated 17th May 2013.

4.1 The engineer

India mainly follows the Fédération Internationale Des Ingénieurs-Conseils (FIDIC) Red Book for construction contracts. This is for historical reasons and prompted by international lending institutions (chiefly the World Bank and the Asian Development Bank). Although the FIDIC Red Book assigns a significant role to the engineer in dispute resolution, in practice this rarely carries the confidence of the contractor as the engineer is perceived as the employer's agent. Hence the engineer has a rather limited role in dispute resolution in India.

4.2 Dispute review boards (DRBs)

The World Bank has made DRBs mandatory in all high-value contracts that it funds. These have been adopted in India in other contracts as well.

All over the world, DRBs have been very beneficial in construction contracts. Their role goes beyond dispute resolution as they have been proved to facilitate the contract's smooth implementation. Essentially the boards try to ensure that 'differences' do not escalate into 'disputes' and are nipped in the bud, thus saving the parties' relationship. DRBs are able to achieve this as they keep abreast of the project. They deal with and address developments as they evolve and have a practical, contract-friendly approach.

Indian contracts incorporate the model terms published by FIDIC for the appointment of the DRB (unlike under the International Chamber of Commerce, DRBs are not divided into three types).[8] Each member of the board is required to be, and must remain so throughout appointment, independent of the parties. The board is required to act impartially and in accordance with the contract. The board members have a contractual agreement that they will not be held liable for any act or omission in discharging their functions (unless vitiated by bad faith). Board members are remunerated equally by both parties. In the event of failure to agree upon a sole member or to appoint a party-nominated member, the appointment shall be made by the appointing body or the official named in the contract. When a dispute is referred to the DRB, a copy is sent to the relevant engineer for information. The board has full power to:

- establish the procedure to be applied in deciding the reference;
- decide upon its own jurisdiction and the scope of any dispute referred to it;
- take the initiative in ascertaining the fact and matters required to take the decision;
- make use of its own personal knowledge or expertise, if any;
- decide on the issue of provisional relief, including interim or conservatory merits;
- decide the issue of payment of interest in accordance with the contract; and
- open up, review and revise any opinion, instruction, determination, certification or valuation of the engineer related to the dispute.

The board is expected to give its decision within 84 days of receiving the referral. However, in practice this time limit is often exceeded.

8 ICC Dispute Board Rules 2004.

Any party dissatisfied with the board's decision must notify the other party and the engineer of its dissatisfaction within 28 days of the receipt of notice. The DRB agreement provides that if notice of dissatisfaction is not given then the board's decision will become final and binding on the employer and the contractor. Although the courts have not yet issued a decisive pronouncement on the subject, it is doubtful whether such a stipulation will be upheld by Indian courts. It is most likely to be seen as an agreement in restraint on legal proceedings and therefore void.[9]

(a) Working of DRBs

DRBs have met with only partial success in India. This is for several reasons:

- DRBs are often not constituted contemporaneously with contract signing. Often there is a delay in forming the board, and parties end up completing the formalities only when a dispute arises. While the contract has progressed, disputes may have arisen but remained hidden, and all this comes up as a prelude to arbitration, thus in effect bypassing the DRB mechanism.
- The DRB board is made up of retired government officials. Coupled with the fact that they look for repeat government appointments, the perception is that they have a pro-government leaning.
- The government is the largest employer and drives almost all large construction projects. Sadly it has not developed any culture for accepting an alternative dispute resolution (ADR) method which is voluntary in nature. The government agencies are answerable to multi-layered internal and external oversight bodies which perhaps have a blinkered approach to the whole issue. This generates a climate of fear and no one wants to be seen as having favoured another. Thus the unwritten management rule is to try every available avenue before an adverse order is accepted. The tendency is to let matters take their logical legal course: arbitration followed by court challenge to the extent possible.

According to a 2008 World Bank report, DRB recommendations were not accepted in 80% of cases involving the government and the chief reason for this was fear of being investigated and audit questions (should the case involve a decision against the government).

India's Planning Commission is actively considering some sort of mechanism where adverse DRB recommendations can be accepted by government agencies. To begin with, the proposal is simply to accept DRB recommendations where the amount involved is US$2 million or less. For larger amounts the recommendation is

---

9 Section 28 of the Indian Contract Act, in material part states:
'28. Agreements in restraint of legal proceedings void: Every agreement-
(a) by which any party thereto is restricted absolutely from enforcing his rights under or in respect of any contract, by the usual legal proceedings in the ordinary tribunals, or which limits the time within which he may thus enforce his rights; or
(b) which extinguishes the rights of any party thereto, or discharges any party thereto from any liability, under or in respect of any contract on the expiry of a specified period so as to restrict any party from enforcing his rights, is void to that extent.'

to put in place high-powered bodies which would examine the reasonableness of a DRB recommendation and in turn recommend to the government whether or not it can be accepted. An interesting reason given by the Planning Commission for accepting DRB recommendations below US$2 million (and not those involving higher amounts) is that it was found that the higher the amount the greater the tendency in the arbitral tribunals or courts to interfere with the sum awarded. In cases where the amount awarded by the DRB exceeded US$20 million it was found that, after challenge, the award could be reduced by as much as 50% in favour of the government. Apparently there is a tendency in judicial bodies to subject the DRB recommendations to stricter scrutiny when the amounts are high (and be more indulgent when the same are low). It could also be a reflection of a difference in approach between a legal body and a lay body such as a DRB.

Another important move is to have an increased window in the contract of 60 days to enable parties to decide whether or not to accept the DRB's recommendations. The World Bank contracts provide for 14 days and the Red Book for a 28-day window to protest the decision. This is considered to be too narrow by the Indian governmental authorities to take a decision and this could well be a factor leading to defensive rejections of DRB recommendations (even though they may otherwise merit acceptance).

It remains to be seen whether or not these initiatives are implemented both in letter and spirit.

5. Arbitration

Considering the inadequacies of the regular courts in dealing with commercial disputes, the government has focused on giving arbitration a boost. In 1996 (by way of an ordinance, followed by an act of Parliament) the government passed a new act.[10]

5.1 Scheme of the act

The act is a composite piece of legislation. It provides for domestic arbitration, international commercial arbitration, the enforcement of foreign awards, and conciliation (the last being based on the United Nations Commission on International Trade Law (UNCITRAL) Conciliation Rules of 1980).

The more significant provisions of the act are to be found in Part I and Part II thereof. Part I contains the provisions for domestic and international commercial arbitration. Any arbitration to be conducted in India is governed by Part I, irrespective of the nationality of the parties. Part II essentially provides for enforcement of foreign awards.

Part I is more comprehensive and contains extensive provisions based on the Model Law and the UNCITRAL Rules of 1976. It provides for: the arbitrability of disputes; non-intervention by courts; composition of the arbitral tribunal; jurisdiction of the arbitral tribunal; conduct of the arbitration proceedings; and recourse against arbitral awards and enforcement. Part II is largely restricted to enforcement of foreign awards governed by the New York Convention of 1958.

---

10 The Arbitration and Conciliation Act, 1996 (Act 26 of 1996).

5.2 **Salient features of the act**

The Act applies to all types of arbitrations, statutory or non-statutory, institution-administered or *ad hoc*. The only qualification is that the dispute must be arbitrable.

5.3 **Appointment of arbitrators**

Where the parties fail to agree upon a mechanism for appointment or if there is a disagreement relating to this, the appointment is to be made by the Chief Justice of the High Court in the case of a domestic arbitration, or the Chief Justice of the Supreme Court in the case of an international commercial arbitration.

The issue of whether the Chief Justice, in making the appointment, would be performing a judicial function or an administrative one has led to controversy. If the role is administrative in nature, it is capable of being challenged and set aside in subsequent proceedings; but this is not so if it is a judicial role. The Supreme Court settled this issue in 2005 when it held the role to be a judicial one.[11] The Court did not stop there. It went on to hold that when its jurisdiction was invoked, it may well have to decide preliminary issues which may arise as to the validity of the arbitration agreement, including whether the claim is a live one, or whether it has met with an accord or satisfaction, or whether it is time barred, etc. Any decision of the court would be conclusive and binding on the parties and on the tribunal.

This decision has proved to be retrograde because the simple process of forming an arbitral tribunal (which obviously needs to be accomplished as soon as possible) can (at times) take years to get over preliminary issues or objections. Moreover the role which the court has now taken for itself is meant to be performed, according to Section 16 of the act (equivalent to Article 16 of the Model Law), by the arbitral tribunal. This is thus an erosion of the *kompetenz-kompetenz* jurisdiction of the arbitral tribunal and unnecessarily gives the court an interventionist role in arbitrations, which leads to delays and frustration of the arbitral process.

5.4 **Governing law**

In determining the rules applicable to the substance of the dispute, the law makes a distinction between international commercial arbitration and arbitration between Indian parties.

In international commercial arbitration the arbitral tribunal decides the dispute in accordance with the rules of law designated by the parties as applicable to the substance of the dispute and, failing any such designation, the rules of law that the tribunal considers appropriate given all the circumstances. Indian courts have long since accepted that in the absence of express or implied choice, the arbitrators would apply the law that has the closest and most real connection with the contract.

In an arbitration between Indian parties, however, the tribunal is obliged to apply the substantive law in force in India.

5.5 **Recourse against awards**

A domestic award (ie, a Part I award) can be challenged and set aside only on the

---

11 *SBP & Co. v Patel Engineering* (2005) 8 SCC 618.

grounds specified under Article 34 of the Model Law and this does not permit a challenge on merits. However, here again there has been a more interventionist role created by the courts than envisaged under the act. This was in the case of *ONGC v Saw Pipes*.[12] In this case the Supreme Court held that an award can be challenged on merits if the court finds it to be contrary to the substantive law governing the parties or to be against the terms of the contract. This judgment applies only to domestic awards, since foreign awards continue to be governed by an earlier decision of the Supreme Court which narrowly construed the public policy ground under the New York Convention to exclude any challenge on merits.[13]

In so far as enforcement of foreign awards is concerned, this is governed by Part II of the act (ie, subject to the New York Convention grounds) and thus cannot be challenged on merits.

Athough India has tried to put in place an efficient and modern law of arbitration and Indian courts do not suffer from any arbitration bias, many international arbitrations are getting seated outside India. Owing to geographical proximity, Singapore is turning out to be a favourite venue and the Singapore International Arbitration Centre (SIAC) has seen a significant workload from India.[14]

6. Mediation and conciliation

Mediation and conciliation have not taken off in India as there is no incentive for the defendant or the weaker party to agree to a reasonable settlement. The litigation process is slow and costs awarded are nowhere near compensatory in nature. (They are essentially tokenism and a pittance compared with the real costs.) Accordingly, it is rare for parties to agree voluntarily to a settlement. Largely as a result, mediation is not considered to be a fruitful activity. The winds of change started to blow in 1996 when the new Arbitration and Conciliation Act was enacted and further in 2002 by way of an amendment to the Code of Civil Procedure (the code) by the introduction of Section 89.

The Arbitration and Conciliation Act 1996 contains a chapter (Part III) entitled 'Conciliation'. It is essentially based on the UNCITRAL Conciliation Rules 1980. If a settlement is arrived at and it is authenticated by the conciliator, it is final and binding on the parties and the persons claiming. Section 74 of the act provides that such a settlement agreement has the same status and effect as if it were an arbitral award on agreed terms on the substance of the dispute rendered by an arbitral tribunal. This, for the first time, gives a statutory framework for parties to arrive at a voluntary settlement (other than through a court/arbitration mechanism), which would have legal effect and, once entered into, cannot be retracted from.

Section 89 of the code states that when it appears to the court that there is an element of a settlement which may be acceptable to the parties, the court will formulate the same and, subject to the parties' observations, refer the dispute to

---

12 2003 (5) SCC 705.

13 1994 Supp (1) SCC 644; Renu Sagar II.

14 According to the Annual Report of the SIAC for 2012, a total of 42 cases involving Indian parties were filed in 2012, making it the second-highest overseas source for SIAC arbitrations – China with 44 cases was the leading source.

arbitration, conciliation/mediation or judicial settlement. This statutory initiative (it was felt) would become the backbone of India's foray into mediation. Section 89 of the code came up for judicial consideration in the *Salem Advocates Bar Association* case,[15] where the court held:

> *It is quite obvious that the reason why Section 89 has been inserted is to try and see that all the cases which are filed in court need not necessarily be decided by the court itself. Keeping in mind the law's delays and the limited number of Judges which are available, it has now become imperative that resort should be had to alternative dispute resolution mechanisms with a view to bringing to an end litigation between the parties at an early date.*

However, there was a setback in the case of *In Re: Afcons Infrastructure Ltd.*[16] Here the issue concerned a works contract and whether a court could refer the parties to arbitration under Section 89 of the code in the absence of the defendant's consent. Overruling the decision of the lower court and the High Court (which had held that the court indeed had such powers) the Supreme Court held that an unwilling party cannot be compelled to go to arbitration in the absence of its consent or an arbitration agreement.

Notwithstanding this dampener, the green shoots of mediation have sprung. Currently, mediation is essentially confined to domestic or matrimonial disputes or disputes against state-owned utilities or insurance companies. Court-annexed mediation centres have become popular and meet with considerable success but, as stated above, these are not really used by the construction industry or for that matter by parties in high-value commercial disputes.

7. Expert determination

The concept of referring a dispute to an independent third party (an expert) to use his expertise to resolve the dispute is sometimes followed (though not often in construction contracts). Moreover, a determination by an expert is not enforceable (unlike an arbitral award). The Indian Supreme Court in the case of *KK Modi v KN Modi*[17] had occasion to consider the distinction between an expert determination and arbitration. The court concluded that, by and large, there were no conclusive tests one could follow to determine whether the agreement was to refer an issue to an expert or whether the parties had in fact agreed to resolve disputes through arbitration. It held:

> *therefore our courts have laid emphasis on (1) existence of disputes as against intention to avoid future disputes; (2) the tribunal or forum so chosen is intended to act judicially after taking into account relevant evidence before it and the submissions made by the parties before it; and (3) the decision is intended to bind the parties. Nomenclature used by the parties may not be conclusive. One must examine the true intent and purport of the agreement.*[18]

---

15 2003 (1) SCC 144.
16 2010 (8) SCC 24.
17 1998 (3) SCC 573.
18 *Supra* at p585.

8. Regulator

A regulator is considered (the world over) to be critical for infrastructure growth. For some time, Indian policymakers have also considered the option of a regulator (including in relation to dispute resolution). However, this has largely remained on paper only, because the government has taken time to conceptualise the mechanism. In September 2008 the Planning Commission published a comprehensive paper titled, "Approach to Regulation of Infrastructure". This gave an overall framework to put in place the regulatory regime. Some issues considered in the paper included: (i) the scope of the regulator's powers, (ii) the regulator's independence and autonomy, and (iii) accountability. The recommendations and proposals can be summarised as set out next.

8.1 Scope of the regulator's powers

The paper, spanning virtually every segment of the infrastructure sector, proposed a powerful and independent regulator. It recommended that the regulator be empowered to make regulations, issue licences, set performance standards and determine tariffs. It should also have the power to enforce its regulations, licence conditions and orders by imposing punitive measures, including suspension or cancellation of licences. It should be able to adjudicate disputes amongst the licensees, and between the licensees and the government, subject to review on appeal before a specialised appellate tribunal. The regulator should act as a quasi-judicial authority.

8.2 The regulator's independence and autonomy

The basic rationale for setting up a regulator is to create a 'level playing field'. As the government is a major player, independence and autonomy received special attention in the paper.

The selection, appointment and removal of the chairperson and the members should be insulated against any perceived interference or manipulation that may influence the outcome. A selection committee would shortlist two or three names and, from these, the appointment would be made by the President of India on the recommendation of the Prime Minister. Similarly, removal of the chairperson or a member can only be on defined grounds, such as insolvency, physical or mental incapacity, conviction for an offence, etc. The removal of a chairperson or a member can take place only with the approval of the President of India on the recommendation of the Prime Minister.

8.3 Accountability of the regulator

As the regulator should be independent of government control, it was important to make it accountable through various processes. The Planning Commission paper suggested that accountability be largely achieved through transparency. Accordingly, any regulation made by the regulator must be published in advance with sufficient time for notice and comments. The regulator is obliged to respond to any comment received before any regulation enters into force. The regulator's activity is subject to parliamentary scrutiny. The regulator must table all regulations made before

Parliament. Further, the regulator is obliged to submit a full report to Parliament setting out the approach that it proposes to adopt in the forthcoming year and the outcome it hopes to achieve. At the close of the year, the regulator must present a report to Parliament assessing its success in achieving the objectives set out in the annual plan. Finally, the regulator is accountable to a specialised judicial body, which shall be set up as an appellate authority.

8.4 Airport/roads regulator

Parliament moved ahead in putting in place (in the first instance) a regulator in relation to airports. The Airports Economic Regulatory Authority of India Act 2008 was passed constituting the airport regulator and an appellate judicial forum in relation to any dispute between two or more service providers or between service providers and a group of consumers. The Appellate Tribunal has been given appellate jurisdiction to hear appeals from any order of the regulator. The tribunal is headed by senior judicial officers, and the chairman must be a current or former judge of the Supreme Court of India or the chief justice of a high court.

Following the airport regulator's appointment, on February 28 2013 the government announced that it would also set up a roads regulator. The government is hopeful that this would address several bottlenecks in road construction.

9. Dispute resolution methods forbidden in India

The general philosophy of Indian law is that any dispute resolution method is acceptable as long as a party is not restricted absolutely from enforcing its rights by the 'usual legal proceedings in the ordinary tribunals'.[19] (An exception has been carved out by the section in relation to arbitrations.) Hence, recourse to courts or judicial review cannot be precluded.

Further, under Indian law a non-compoundable criminal offence cannot be settled or compromised through the parties' private agreement. This, it has been held, is in violation of public policy.

10. Conclusion

India is a commercially vibrant jurisdiction. Currently it is the tenth-largest economy in the world and in the next five years is predicted to become the eighth- or perhaps the seventh-largest economy.[20] Moreover, India's growth is premised on the rule of law, democracy, a strong and independent judiciary, and a free and vibrant press.

At the same time it is clear that India needs to focus more intensively and with greater imagination on dispute resolution in construction and infrastructure contracts, focusing in particular on reducing court delays. This will provide a great impetus to construction activities in India.

---

19 See note 8 (Section 28 of the Indian Contract Act).

20 Speech by the Finance Minister while presenting the Union Budget on February 28 2013.

Singapore

Philip Jeyaretnam
Melvin See
Rodyk & Davidson LLP

1. Introduction

As a small (714.3 square metres) and highly urbanised (100%) country, it is no wonder that the construction industry is a key component of Singapore's gross domestic product (GDP). After a trough of 6.23% in 2004 – the cumulative effect of the terrorist attacks, the Iraq war and the outbreak of severe acute respiratory syndrome (SARS) – the construction industry has been steadily increasing its share of GDP, standing at 11.19% in 2010 (at 2005 market prices). In dollar terms, this translates to an output of S$27.34 billion for the construction industry.[1]

Public sector construction demand is significant and in recent years (2008 to 2010) accounted for 31% to 61% of total demand. All public sector construction projects utilise the public sector standard conditions of contract (PSSCOC). The PSSCOC for Construction Works was first published in 1995 and the latest iteration is the sixth edition (December 2008); the PSSCOC for Design and Build was first published in 2011 and the latest iteration is the fifth edition (December 2008).

The PSSCOC forms provide that disputes are to be resolved by arbitration, with a non-binding option for parties to refer the disputes for mediation prior to arbitration. If the disputes involve a payment claim or payment response to which the Building and Construction Industry Security of Payment Act (BCISPA) applies, the contractor is entitled to make an adjudication application.

The BCISPA was enacted in November 2004 after multiple contractors encountered financial difficulties and eventually had to pull out of various public sector projects, delaying them and inconveniencing the public. Therefore, the BCISPA sought to improve contractor's cash flow by giving the contractor the right to seek progress payments for work done and goods and services supplied, and to have a quick and low-cost resolution of payment disputes through adjudication.

Unlike the public sector, the private sector does not utilise a uniform standard form of contract. The common forms are the Singapore Institute of Architects (SIA) Articles and Conditions of Building Contract ninth edition (August 2011) (either lump sum or measurement) or the Real Estate Developers Association of Singapore (REDAS) Design and Build Conditions of Contract third edition (October 2010). The SIA and REDAS forms both provide for disputes to be resolved by arbitration. The SIA form provides that parties may refer disputes to mediation but a prior reference to mediation is not a condition precedent to arbitration. Although the REDAS form

1 Building Control Alliance Annual Report 2010/11.

provides that parties should endeavour to settle any dispute through direct negotiations and, if negotiations fail, refer the dispute for mediation, it goes on to provide that prior reference to mediation is not a condition precedent to arbitration. Finally, both forms also provide that a contractor is entitled to make an adjudication application if the BCISPA applies. This is not surprising as any attempt to contract out of the BCISPA is void.

Singapore is not new to the concept of a public-private partnership (PPP) and its purpose – to combine the expertise and resources of both public and private sectors to provide services to the public at the best value for money. However, only eight projects have been awarded since the first project in 2003 for a desalination plant. Five projects have been for infrastructure works (two desalination plants, two waterworks, one incineration plant), one information technology project, one school and one sporting facility.[2] Given the varied nature of PPP projects, there is no standard form of contract. However, the PPP Handbook (second edition, March 2012) published by the Singapore Ministry of Finance mandates that every PPP contract must contain an alternative formal dispute resolution procedure to court proceedings. This is most likely to be arbitration, with an option for mediation.

Finally, a unique feature of Singapore's construction industry is the push to build underground. Underground space has been named a strategic resource by Singapore's Economic Strategies Committee. In 2006, the Common Services Tunnel was built in Marina Bay to house utility service pipes for easy access and maintenance without disruption to traffic above ground. There is also the Deep Tunnel Sewerage System, between 20 and 60 metres deep, that delivers wastewater across the span of Singapore from the main industrial area in the west to an underground water treatment plant in the east. At 150 metres deep, the Jurong Rock Caverns will house an underground liquid hydrocarbon storage facility. The local standard forms are not usually used for such projects as they cater for simpler substructure and superstructure works. Nevertheless, the contracts for such deep-underground works would usually provide for an alternative formal dispute resolution procedure, such as arbitration.

2. Dispute resolution methods

In the Singapore High Court decision of *The Oriental Insurance Co Ltd v Reliance National Asia Re Pte Ltd* [2009] 2 SLR(R) 385, four principal modes of dispute resolution – where disputants submit their dispute to a neutral third party that has and exercises the authority to hear their respective positions and make a decision binding on them – were enumerated and their key characteristics identified.

The four principal modes are as follows:

- Litigation – a process administered through the courts. A judicial officer of the court makes a binding decision on the dispute.
- Administrative or statutory tribunals – adjudication by a tribunal established by statute to determine statutory issues. In the context of the construction industry, the most visible statutory tribunal is that of an adjudicator appointed under the BCISPA to deal with payment claims for progress made.

2 Ministry of Finance website: www.mof.gov.sg

- Arbitration – a procedure usually governed by arbitration rules laid down by statute or imposed by an arbitral organisation. A neutral third party privately chosen and paid by the disputants makes a binding decision.
- Expert determination – parties appoint their own expert to consider the disputed issues and make a binding decision, without necessarily having to conduct a full enquiry following the usual adjudicatory rules (eg, rules of court in litigation, formal arbitration rules and general rules of natural justice). The role of the expert is to undertake an investigation of the facts and to determine a dispute using his expertise. The expert's power and jurisdiction is derived solely from the terms of the contract.

Quite apart from the four modes above where the outcome is decided by a third party, a further mode of dispute resolution, namely mediation, is recognised and commonly in use. The resolution of a dispute through mediation is voluntary and parties do not risk having the matter decided against them by a judge, arbitrator, adjudicator or expert. Mediation is also informal and flexible, saving time and costs.

2.1 Litigation

This is no longer the default mode of dispute resolution for the construction industry in Singapore given that all the common forms of construction contracts (PSSCOC, SIA, REDAS) contain arbitration clauses.

However, if disputants opt to litigate their dispute, the Singapore High Court (which hears disputes valued at S$250,000 or greater) clears 85% of its writ cases (which most construction disputes are) within 18 months.

Disputants will also benefit from a recent change announced by the Singapore Chief Justice in January 2013: a modified docket system of litigation is to be implemented in the Singapore High Court. This means that cases will be assigned, at an early stage, to specific judges and registrars who will manage and prepare them for trial, enabling a degree of judicial continuity, with each judge being assigned to specific lists. Although this new system has already been informally used for some construction disputes, its formal introduction has, at July 2013, yet to occur. When it does, it will benefit all construction disputants.

2.2 Adjudication

The statutory adjudication regime set up by the BCISPA aimed to solve a common problem in the construction industry of contractors (especially subcontractors) going unpaid for work done or materials supplied. To help facilitate the cash flow of contractors, the BCISPA sought to establish a fast and low-cost adjudication system to resolve payment disputes.

A claimant begins by making a payment claim. The respondent has to reply with a payment response. If the response is not satisfactory, the claimant may lodge an adjudication application. The respondent has to reply with an adjudication response and the adjudicator will then make an adjudication determination.

The adjudication process is characterised by strict time lines and the adjudicated sum has to be paid within a short time; it is enforced through various means to help the contractor's cash flow. However, the adjudication outcome can be disputed (and any errors as to the amount payable accounted for) at a later arbitration or litigation that finally determines the parties' contractual rights. To protect contractors, any attempt to contract out of the statutory adjudication regime is void.

The Singapore Court of Appeal had the opportunity in *Lee Wee Lick Terence (alias Li Weili Terence) v Chua Say Eng (formerly trading as Weng Fatt Construction Engineering) and another* appeal [2013] 1 SLR 401 to clarify certain aspects of the statutory adjudication regime under the BCISPA. The court was given to understand by counsel for both parties that the two judicial approaches had created difficulties among adjudicators on the proper approach to adopt, and that it was desirable for the court to express its views on the state of the law, even though it would not affect the parties as the parties had settled their disputes in the meantime.

First was whether the court had power to review issues arising in relation to the validity of the adjudicator's appointment. The court answered in the affirmative as this was essential to the adjudicator's jurisdiction.

Second was whether the adjudicator has competence to decide whether he was validly appointed to adjudicate the matter. The court answered in the negative. Any jurisdictional challenge should be made to the court when applying to set aside the adjudication determination.

Third was whether, if a payment claim satisfies all the requirements of a payment claim, it is a valid payment claim. This overruled previous decisions where the court considered whether the subjective intention of the claimant in relation to a payment claim was communicated to the respondent. It is now clear that the claimant's subjective intention is irrelevant. The emphasis is on the respondent being given notice of certain information about the claim (such as the amount claimed, the contract under which the claim is made and a breakdown of the items constituting the claim).

The court disagreed with a previous case where it was held that a payment claim expressly stated not to be a payment claim prevented the adjudication from proceeding. However, the court declined to address and decide on this issue as it did not arise in the case. If the occasion should arise, it is likely that the court will maintain its tentative view that the claimant in such a situation should not be allowed to rely on a payment claim that is expressly stated not to be a payment claim to avoid prejudice to the respondent.

Fourth was whether there was no limitation period preventing a payment claim from being lodged for work done more than a month ago. In a previous case, it was held that as the scheme contemplated monthly payment claims, each payment claim could only address the work done in the month in question and not before. The court explained that the scheme merely limited the maximum frequency of payment claims to a month and that contractors were free to make less-frequent claims if their cash flow permitted.

2.3 Arbitration

Arbitration is the most common form of dispute resolution for the construction industry, not least because it is the default mode in the common local standard forms.

Even when the contract terms are specially negotiated, parties (especially foreign parties) tend to opt for arbitration in Singapore. The reasons are that Singaporean arbitral awards are enforceable in more than 140 countries worldwide as Singapore is a party to the 1958 Convention on the Recognition and Enforcement of Foreign Arbitral Awards.

Singapore is seen as an independent neutral country, perceived to be the fifth least corrupt country in the world after Denmark, Finland, New Zealand and Sweden (according to the 2012 Corruption Perceptions Index 2012). Parties are free to choose whom they wish to represent them; there is no restriction on the nationality of the law firm advising and representing parties in an arbitration.

The Singapore courts offer judicial support for arbitration and keep their interventions in the arbitration process to a minimum, especially for international arbitrations.

(a) Setting aside arbitral awards on the ground of public policy

International arbitral awards issued by tribunals seated in Singapore may be set aside on the ground that it is contrary to public policy of Singapore.

In *PT Asuransi Jasa Indonesia (Persero) v Dexia Bank SA* [2007] 1 SLR(R) 597, the Court of Appeal sketched an outline of when an international arbitration award might be said to be contrary to the public policy of Singapore:

> *Although the concept of public policy of the State is not defined in the Act or the Model Law, the general consensus of judicial and expert opinion is that public policy under the Act encompasses a narrow scope. In our view, it should only operate in instances where the upholding of an arbitral award would 'shock the conscience'... or is 'clearly injurious to the public good or... wholly offensive to the ordinary reasonable and fully informed member of the public'... or where it violates the forum's most basic notion of morality and justice... This would be consistent with the concept of public policy that can be ascertained from the preparatory materials to the Model Law.*

This exception is a narrow one. The Court of Appeal explained that even if an arbitral tribunal's findings of law and/or fact are wrong, such errors would not *per se* engage the Singapore's public policy.

This general principle was clarified by the Court of Appeal in *AJU v AJT* [2011] 4 SLR 739, where it held that the Singapore's public policy was a question of law and that if the tribunal had made an error of law in relation to what constituted public policy, an arbitral award could be set aside.

2.4 Expert determination

Expert determination is not a mode of dispute resolution commonly used in the construction industry, not least because the standard forms of building contract do not feature it.

The distinguishing characteristics of an expert were described in *Evergreat Construction Co Pte Ltd v Presscrete Engineering Pte Ltd* [2006] 1 SLR(R) 634. Thus, an expert has a discretion to adopt an inquisitorial function and has complete discretion to arrive at his determination without being hamstrung by procedural and evidential intricacies or niceties. He is permitted to inject into the process personal expertise and to make his inquiries without any obligation to seek the parties' views or consult them. The expert is also not obliged to make a decision on the basis of the evidence presented to him and can act on his subjective opinion.

Such a mode should theoretically be fairly attractive to disputants in the construction industry, given the technical nature of most disputes. However, acceptance could be curtailed because the court cannot interfere with the expert's determination in the absence of fraud or corruption. Errors of fact or law would not vitiate his determination and the expert does not have to observe due process by granting both parties the right to be heard on all issues to be determined. Only a breach of an expert's terms of appointment would suffice to set aside a decision.

If parties wish to exploit expert determination and safeguard themselves they will have to consider adding the procedural safeguards they wish (eg, requiring the expert to hear parties before deciding) to the expert's terms of appointment. The prescription will have to be done with a light touch: overly restricting the expert's discretion may lead a court to treat the expert as an arbitrator.

2.5 Mediation

Mediation, as a mode of dispute resolution, receives a broad level of support from Singapore's courts.

In *HSBC Institutional Trust Services (Singapore) Ltd v Toshin Development Singapore Pte Ltd* [2012] 4 SLR 738, the Singapore Court of Appeal held that there is no good reason why an express agreement between contracting parties to negotiate in good faith should not be upheld. First, such an agreement is valid because it is not contrary to public policy. Parties are free to contract unless prohibited by law. The court was of the view that negotiate-in-good-faith clauses are in the public interest as they promote the consensual disposition of any potential disputes and that it is a fairly common practice for Asian businesses to include similar clauses in their commercial contracts. The court also observed that there is no difference between an agreement to negotiate in good faith and an agreement to submit a dispute to mediation. Such agreements serve a useful commercial purpose in seeking to promote consensus and conciliation in lieu of adversarial dispute resolution and are values that Singapore's legal system should promote.

In the subsequent case of *International Research Corp plc v Lufthansa Systems Asia Pacific Pte Ltd and another* [2013] 1 SLR 973, the Singapore High Court applied *HSBC v Toshin* to hold that an obligation to negotiate in good faith that is part of a broader contractual framework, which is expressly made a condition precedent to resolution of a dispute by arbitration, is enforceable. This means that if there is a failure to comply with the obligation to negotiate in good faith before proceeding to arbitration, then it would be defective to proceed to the jurisdiction of the arbitral tribunal and the tribunal would have no jurisdiction to resolve the dispute. Any award made by the tribunal is liable to be set aside on that basis.

All the common local standard forms of construction contract suggest mediation as an option before arbitration without going as far as making mediation a condition precedent to arbitration. Given the emphasis of mediation on consensus building, that this is more likely to help preserve the commercial relationship between the parties, and the relatively low cost of mediation compared with arbitration, it may be time for the drafters of the local forms to consider making mediation a mandatory step in the dispute resolution process. Alternatively, more progressive parties may decide to modify the standard form to do so.

2.6 Dispute adjudication boards

None of the local standard forms refer disputes to a dispute adjudication board as an initial step, with arbitration being resorted to only if there is dissatisfaction with the decision of the dispute adjudication board. It is for this reason that there have been only two reported decisions in Singapore (one of the High Court and the other of the Court of Appeal), involving the same parties, concerning dispute adjudication boards.

Not surprisingly, the contract under consideration was not a local standard form but the 1999 FIDIC Conditions of Contract, and it related to a construction project in Indonesia, the parties to which had chosen Singapore as the seat of arbitration.

The Court of Appeal described the nature of a dispute adjudication board thus in *CRW Joint Operation v PT Perusahaan Gas Negara (Persero) TBK* [2011] 4 SLR 305:

> *[it] is not bound by any fixed rules of procedure, and is able to adopt the most appropriate method in making its determination (such as conducting a hearing or undertaking an inquisitorial process), subject to the general requirements of: (a) acting fairly and reasonably; and (b) giving each party a reasonable opportunity to advance its case and to respond to the other party's case. Indeed, [it] may even do without an oral hearing if it believes that such a hearing is unnecessary, unless one or both of the parties request for it.*

Given that there is now a statutory adjudication process applicable to all construction projects in Singapore, it is likely that the use of dispute adjudication boards in Singapore will remain infrequent. Singapore's experience of dispute adjudication boards will continue to be largely limited to the situation where Singapore is the seat of arbitration for a regional construction project to which one of the FIDIC forms applies.

3. Party autonomy and hybrid processes

As can be seen from the approach taken by the Singapore courts from the cases mentioned above, the courts respect party autonomy, especially in how they wish disputes between parties to be resolved – be it litigation, arbitration, expert determination or mediation.

This was articulated in *Evergreat Construction Co Pte Ltd v Presscrete Engineering Pte Ltd* [2006] 1 SLR(R) 634, where the Singapore High Court observed that parties that wished to have an alternative mode of dispute resolution may draw on the different principles, attributes and procedures in each of the alternative modes, and devise an agreed method or approach which fits their particular needs and circumstances. In choosing their alternative mode of dispute resolution, the parties are not constrained by any mode or particular set of attributes or procedures. Therefore, hybrid processes may be contractually formulated by the parties themselves to resolve a particular dispute in a manner considered most appropriate by them. The choice is basically that of the parties.

In fact, respect for party autonomy is so entrenched that the Singapore High Court observed in *Bovis Lend Lease Pte Ltd v Jay-Tech Marine & Projects Pte Ltd and another Application* [2005] SGHC 91 that arbitral rules that sought to take precedence over any and all provisions in a party's underlying contract relating to dispute resolution by arbitration may be an unwarranted limitation on party autonomy.

The reasoning in *Bovis v Jay-Tech* was approved by the Singapore Court of Appeal in *Insigma Technology Co Ltd v Alstom Technology Ltd* [2009] 3 SLR(R) 936, where the court upheld the parties' agreement to have an arbitration conducted under the International Chamber of Commerce Rules of Arbitration but administered by the Singapore International Arbitration Centre instead of the International Court of Arbitration.

Thus, parties are free to construct their own dispute resolution scheme, subject to any public policy reasons against upholding the parties' choice.

4. Conclusion

Dispute resolution activity in Singapore is on the rise overall, driven in part by the growth of arbitration and its incorporation into all local standard forms of construction contracts. From 99 new cases in 2008, the Singapore International Arbitration Centre handled 235 new cases in 2012. The value of the disputes arbitrated in 2012 was S$3.61 billion, more than the combined value of disputes arbitrated in 2011 and 2010 of S$1.32 billion.[3]

This growth is underpinned by the key features of Singapore's legal system: the strong rule of law, an independent judiciary, a robust arbitration framework, party autonomy to fashion their own dispute resolution scheme and to be represented by counsel of their choice. The last feature is an important consideration for multinational construction entities – there is no restriction on foreign law firms advising on or engaging in arbitration proceedings in Singapore.

As Asia's top arbitration venue in 2010,[4] Singapore is constantly looking to enhance its legislative framework for arbitration. On June 1 2012, Singapore became one of the first countries to expressly legislate support for the emergency arbitrator, instead of the court, to provide urgent interim relief prior to the constitution of a tribunal, by making it clear that such orders made would be enforceable.

Singapore's legal system looks to continue its growth and innovation in the years ahead, in tandem with that of one of its major users, the construction industry.

---

3 Ministry of Law, Singapore, press release, February 13 2013.

4 "2010 International Arbitration Survey: Choices in International Arbitration", Queen Mary University of London.

Belgium

Sophie Bourgois
Diederik De Block
Benoît Kohl
Rony Vermeersch
Stibbe

1. Introduction

The construction sector in Belgium accounts on average for 5% of the country's total GDP each year. When all the other activities directly linked to this sector are taken into account, this figure is almost 11%. The sector employs 200,000 workers from a working population of approximately 5 million people. The construction sector thus constitutes an important part of the Belgian economy.

Statistics show that the construction sector is mostly active in the residential market. In 2010, Belgian authorities delivered 27,054 building permits for the construction of new residential buildings. These permits authorised the construction of 49,701 new housing units, of which 25,599 were apartments and 24,102 were single family homes. Likewise, in the same year the authorities delivered 4,747 permits for industrial and commercial (non-residential) buildings.

The 2010 figures confirm the two main trends witnessed by the Belgian construction sector during the past 15 years:

- a steady decrease in the construction of industrial buildings (with the number of industrial building permits decreased by approximately 35% between 1996 and 2010 – that is, from 7,238 permits in 1996 to 4,747 in 2010); and
- a steady increase in the construction of new apartments as opposed to new, single family homes (with the number of permits for new apartments having increased by 51% and the permits for single family homes having decreased by 24% between 1996 and 2010).

Despite the slowing down of the non-residential market, the construction industry remains solid.

The Belgian economy is open to foreign lenders, investors and contractors. There are no specific restrictions on foreign investments and ownership. On the contrary, Belgian legislation contains certain advantages that should attract foreign investment, such as the 'deduction for risk capital' (also known as the 'notional interest deduction'), which is a tax incentive to reinforce Belgium as an attractive location for investors.

As to licensing, contractors should be registered with the Belgian authorities as builders because under certain circumstances this could lead to a reduced VAT rate (6% instead of 21%).

In relation to public works licensing, it is essential that both national and foreign contractors are 'licensed to build' or are able to prove that they have the equivalent experience and skills to entitle them to a licence. These licences are granted in different grades according to the size of the construction works, and in different categories and subcategories.

As Belgium has an open economy, there are no real currency controls that would make it difficult or impossible to change operating funds or profits from one currency into another, nor any controls or laws that restrict the removal of profits and investments.

2. Construction law and related legislation

Belgian legislation has very few rules that apply specifically to construction contracts.

The Belgian legal system is based on civil law traditions. A construction contract is considered a contract for hire of work and is thus governed by the rules of employment law and the general rules of contract. The Civil Code does not contain any specific comprehensive legislation on construction contracts.

Only four articles of the Civil Code deal specifically with construction contracts: Article 1792 (decennial liability), Article 1793 (modifications and additions in the framework of lump sum contracts), and Articles 1798 and 1799 (subcontracting). These four articles were introduced in the Civil Code in 1804 because of public mistrust towards construction professionals, who often took advantage of the ignorance of their co-contracting parties. Since then, the aforementioned shortcomings of the Civil Code have never been remedied. No new comprehensive legislation has been adopted regarding construction contracts, except for the law of July 9 1971 that deals with the specific issue of the promotion and the construction of dwelling houses. Article 1798 of the Civil Code was nonetheless modified by the law of February 19 1990, which aimed to increase the protection of subcontractors in the case of a contractor's bankruptcy (subcontractors are granted a right to direct action against the owner).

Parties to a construction contract enjoy an extended contractual freedom. However, this freedom is somewhat restricted as there are a number of specific public policy rules that restrict the parties from enjoying such freedom. For instance, the profession of 'contractor' is governed by certain rules on the admission to the profession, registration, and accreditation requirements for public works. Architects' contracts are also influenced by mandatory professional rules: for example, the Law of February 20 1939 grants architects a monopoly over the drawing of plans and the control of works for which a building permit is required; and under Article 6 of this Law, an architect's profession is incompatible with that of a constructor. In addition, architects must abide by a code of ethics and professional conduct which has been rendered obligatory by Royal Decree of April 18 1985; in that respect, architects must be and remain independent in the performance of their work.

In addition, public works are subject to specific legislative instruments, including the *Règles générales d'exécution* (RGE; Royal Decree of January 14 2013), which regulates the performance of public works. Derogations from the RGE are possible but must be rendered necessary by the specific characteristics of the tender. Some derogations must, moreover, be formally motivated. The RGE contains rules on price, terms of payment, guarantees, modifications of the work, liability of the contractors, default, liquidated damages for delay, termination of the contract, etc. The RGE replaced the former *Cahier général des charges* (CGC; annex to the Royal Decree of September 26 1996) as from July 1 2013.

Finally, the European legislation on consumer protection, such as the directive on unfair business-to-consumer commercial practices, generally applies to construction contracts between professional builders and private individuals. The consumer protection legislation restricts the contractual freedom of the professional party by banning certain contractual provisions that are considered abusive.

In other words, Belgian construction law itself has evolved little over the past few years. As to practice, the most important trend is the continued rise of integrated contracting, and in particular the boom of public-private partnership (PPP) and private finance initiative contracts. These days, few large public works contracts are tendered that are not some type of integrated contract.

3. Dispute resolution

3.1 Introduction

Construction contracts are particularly prone to disputes. The main factors that increase the risk of disputes are the long-term nature of the contracts, the large number of intervening parties on a single project, the complexity of the building works and the often high financial value of the contracts. Construction disputes usually relate to the quality of the works, time and cost overruns, payment defaults and contract documentation.

Construction disputes are technically complex and are often multi-party:

- First, these types of disputes are rarely exclusively contractual. Complex technical issues are either at the core of the dispute or underlie the contractual matters. Resolution of construction disputes therefore requires intensive fact and technical investigations. Parties (or alternative dispute resolution (ADR) providers) will usually need to have recourse to one or several technical experts to support their case or resolve the dispute.
- Secondly, the execution of construction contracts always involves many parties. An average construction contract involves at least an owner, contractors and subcontractors, suppliers, insurers and financing institutions. Each party has a direct contractual relationship with one or a few of the other intervening parties. The chains of contracts linked to construction projects mean that disputes are regularly multi-party.

Arbitral tribunals have limited power to order the joinder of third parties to proceedings and consolidation of multiple arbitral proceedings. In most instances, joinder or consolidation will require the consent of the parties (unless the contracts and arbitration rules contain appropriate provisions or unless joinder and consolidation can be ordered by state courts). Where joinder or consolidation cannot be achieved, it will almost invariably multiply the number of procedures and increase the risk of inflated costs and inconsistent decisions. Moreover, Belgian courts have not yet accepted that a company can be bound by an arbitration agreement entered into by another company of the same corporate group.

As a consequence, even if the use of ADR in the Belgian market is increasingly popular, its market share is still limited, and disputes regarding projects (including infrastructure and PPP projects) or construction are usually dealt with by the courts, quite often combined with expert advice to the courts.

In a commercial context, the use of arbitration precedes mediation or any (other) ADR method. The governing legislation as to both (international and domestic) arbitration and mediation can be found in the Judicial Code. The general rules on arbitration can be found in Part 6 of the Judicial Code (Articles 1676 to 1723), whereas the rules on mediation constitute Part 7 (Articles 1724 to 1737).

Expert determination in construction contracts is quite common, in particular regarding large or long-term projects, requiring an efficient settlement of certain categories of disputes. In general, the use of expert determination is limited to technical issues. Dispute resolution or adjudication boards are still rare.

In particular regarding public contracts or strictly national transactions, ADR is only applied occasionally.

As PPP projects in Belgium are structured as public contracts, one can conclude that the same reluctance towards introducing ADR methods also applies to PPP projects. Indeed, until approximately three years ago, a standard PPP project in Belgium only provided for standard proceedings before the civil courts. For more information on proceedings before the Belgium civil courts, see below.

Occasionally, certain of those PPP projects also provided for a consultative structure. Such a structure is still provided for in most PPPs today, mainly as a first step. In practice, such a structure involves a cool-down period, combined with a forced/organised consultation between (high-level) representatives of the parties to the contract. Such a structure does not imply the intervention of external parties.

In recent PPP projects, however, ADR methods have started to appear although, in practice, only in the form of dispute boards, expert determination or a mix of the two. For more information on dispute boards and expert determination in Belgium, see below.

The international influence on the structures used for these PPPs, the influence of international funders and the standardisation in this field explains why such ADR methods have appeared. The contracts underlying the PPP projects in Belgium were mainly inspired by precedents from the Netherlands and the United Kingdom. Hence, as those international reference contracts often provide ADR methods, and lenders and equity providers are familiar with those documents, the need for bankable projects stimulated the Belgian tendering authorities and their advisors also to provide ADR methods in Belgian design-build-finance-maintain contracts, in order to remain market standard.

However, the actual use and structuring of the ADR methods (dispute boards, expert determination or a mix of those) is not yet standardised in Belgium. In fact the method differs according to the relevant tendering authority or its advisors.

In addition, the ADR procedures are not always 'final'. Some contracts provide that decisions made by the dispute board or the expert(s) are final, whereas in other contracts the ADR procedures only act as an intermediate procedure, prior to falling back on (mainly) the courts or (in rare cases) arbitration.

Yet in the meantime only a few Belgian PPP projects have been faced with problems requiring the use of dispute resolution methods. Hence, so far there is not much experience in the market as to the actual use and functioning of the methods provided for in the contracts. Nevertheless, as more and more projects come into the market, the next few years might provide more opportunities to test these dispute resolution methods in practice.

3.2 Proceedings before the civil or commercial courts

(a) Civil or commercial courts versus administrative courts

In Belgium, there are no separate courts or tribunals dealing exclusively with project finance transactions or construction contracts. Depending on the specific circumstances, disputes fall under the jurisdiction of the civil or commercial courts.

Nevertheless, two administrative courts are important to note in a project finance context: the Council of State at the federal level and the Board of Permit Appeals in the Flemish region. The latter is competent to rule on appeals against building permits in the Flemish region, and the former is competent to rule on administrative decisions taken by any public authority.

The Council of State plays an important role in the disputes concerning public procurement for construction works: the suspension or annulment of the tender decisions taken by contracting authorities are brought before the Council of State except in cases where the contracting authority is not a public authority in the sense of the legislation. In this case, the suspension or annulment actions are brought before the civil courts. Applications for review do not have an automatic suspensive effect.

The civil courts have the exclusive competence for damage claims and for all disputes concerning the execution of private and public construction contracts.

(b) Highlights of the judicial procedure before civil or commercial courts

Interlocutory proceedings: In cases of urgency, a party may apply to the president of the Tribunal of First Instance or of the Commercial Court to obtain interim measures and/or injunctive relief. The requesting party must establish that an order is required due to the risk of major harm or serious inconvenience.

Summary proceedings: A matter may be settled by summary proceedings if this is requested jointly by the parties or if it concerns collection of uncontested debts, interim measures or preliminary measures such as the designation of a judicial expert.[1] 'Summary proceedings' means that the exchange of written submissions will be limited in the strictest possible way and the matter will be pleaded at and decided after an introductory hearing only.

---

1 Article 735 of the Judicial Code.

Intervention: Third-party intervention is largely accepted under Belgian Law.[2] A third party may be forced to intervene in order either to assert a claim against the plaintiff or the defendant, or to safeguard the intervener's or one of the party's rights. There are thus four kinds of permissible intervention: voluntary or compulsory offensive intervention, and voluntary or compulsory conservatory intervention.

Compulsory offensive intervention aims at obtaining a judgment ordering a party to do or refrain from doing something, and is allowed only if introduced in the first instance. Conservatory intervention aims only at obtaining that a judgment that will be rendered between two parties can be opposed by a third party; such conservatory intervention can be formed either in the first instance or in appeal. The admissibility of compulsory intervention depends on the timing of the request: the third party must still be able to exercise its rights of defence. A voluntary intervention, be it offensive or conservatory, is admissible up to the closing of the proceedings, provided that the intervener accepts all the acts already taken, that it does not delay the proceedings and that the other parties can still fully exercise their rights of defence.

Evidentiary measures: The court or tribunal may order a wide range of evidentiary measures, such as document production, the examination of witnesses or of the parties, a site visit, etc. In construction matters, the most common evidentiary measure is the designation of an expert. The duration and the scope of the expert's assignment are determined by the judge. The expert first renders a preliminary report, on which the parties have the right to comment, and then submits its final report.[3] The expert report is not binding on the judge, but he or she must give a reason for not following the expert's conclusions.[4]

Penalty: Under Articles 1385*bis* to 1385*nonies* of the Judicial Code, the court may, upon the plaintiff's request, impose a penalty against the defendant in case the latter does not comply with the judgement. The court determines the amount of the penalty and the condition of application: fixed or periodic sum, capped amount, etc. A penalty cannot be granted by the court when the defendant has been condemned to the payment of a monetary sum.

Legal fees and costs of the proceedings: The losing party must bear the costs of the proceedings and the legal costs of the counterparty.[5] The amount of the legal fees is fixed at a flat rate and varies according to the amount of the claim. It ranges between €82.50 and €33,000.[6]

---

2 Article 812 of the Judicial Code.
3 Article 976 of the Judicial Code.
4 Article 962 of the Judicial Code.
5 Article 1017 of the Judicial Code.
6 Royal Decree, October 26 2007.

3.3 Arbitration and ADR

(a) Arbitration

The Judicial Code incorporates into Belgian Law the Model Law annexed to the European Convention on Arbitration signed in Strasbourg on January 20 1966. Any arbitration seated in Belgium is governed by Articles 1676 to 1723 of the Judicial Code.

According to Article 1677 of the Judicial Code, an arbitration agreement needs to be contained in a written document, signed by the parties, or in other documents binding on them and showing their intention to refer their dispute to arbitration. For the arbitration agreement to be valid and enforceable, no elements are required other than those the parties wish to refer to arbitration. Nevertheless, it is advisable to define the arbitration agreement in further detail.

The Belgian courts adopt a rather neutral approach towards arbitration, neither favouring arbitration nor showing a particular bias against it. Provided they are valid, the Belgian courts enforce arbitration agreements (and if relevant decline jurisdiction accordingly).

Tax disputes or criminal matters are excluded from arbitration. When an individual is concerned, caution is required because use of arbitration in consumer, insurance and labour matters is restricted. Automatic domestic arbitration does not exist in Belgium.

Arbitration law in Belgium is quite standard compared with those in other European countries; it does not contain any particularly notable features. The parties are free to determine the rules of the arbitral proceedings as long as the fundamental principle of fair and equitable treatment is respected (Articles 1693 and 1694 of the Judicial Code). According to Article 1696-2, the arbitral tribunal has a discretionary authority to assess the admissibility and weight of the evidence submitted by the parties. Unless the parties agreed differently, the arbitral tribunal is not bound by the rules of evidence applicable in court proceedings. Arbitration proceedings should respect the fundamental principle of non-discrimination between the parties, which must be granted the same possibility to assert their rights and put forth their arguments (Article 1694-1). Beyond this basic principle, which cannot be waived by any of the parties, it is up to the parties to determine the rules of the arbitral proceedings, including the seat of the arbitration (Article 1693). Failing agreement between parties, the arbitral tribunal is entitled to determine the rules of procedure. Article 1695 allows an arbitral tribunal to conduct proceedings by default if a party fails to appear or present its arguments.

The Judicial Code does not distinguish between the rules that apply to domestic or international arbitration. However, Article 1717-4 allows the parties to exclude the right to apply for the setting-aside of an arbitral award if none of the parties is a Belgian citizen or resident, or a corporation with its registered office or a branch office in Belgium.

Arbitral awards may only be appealed if the parties have expressly provided for it in the arbitration agreement – which is rarely the case. Setting-aside proceedings can be commenced before the Belgian Court of First Instance in a limited number of specific circumstances, enumerated in Article 1704 of the Judicial Code. In addition, the courts must examine whether an award is contrary to public policy and whether the dispute is arbitrable. Setting-aside proceedings must be brought within three months after the award has been notified to parties.

The New York Convention entered into force in Belgium in 1975. Upon ratification Belgium declared that it will only apply the Convention to recognition and enforcement of awards made in the territory of another contracting state. If an award is contrary to public policy or the dispute was not arbitrable, enforcement will be refused. Enforcement of a foreign award will also be refused if one of the grounds for setting aside the award exists.

Belgium ratified the ICSID Convention in 1970 and has signed a large number of bilateral investment treaties, providing for either *ad hoc* or ICSID arbitration. Until now, no proceedings have been brought under the ICSID Convention against Belgium; however, Belgian investors have initiated proceedings against foreign countries.

(b) Mediation

Mediation was neither recognised nor regulated in Belgium until 2001. The law of February 19 2001 first introduced mediation in the field of family law matters. Eventually, by a law of February 21 2005, mediation was extended to all civil matters. The Judicial Code now contains a chapter dealing exclusively with mediation (Chapter 7, Articles 1724 to 1737).

This does not mean that mediation was not used in Belgium before 2001 or 2005; it was, however, a purely informal process. The law of February 21 2005 intends to develop the practice of mediation by giving guarantees as to the qualification of mediators and the confidentiality of the process, on the one hand, and introducing the possibility of a judicial approbation of the agreements reached in mediation, on the other hand.

Article 1724 of the Judicial Code provides that any dispute regarding negotiable rights can be referred to mediation. However, the code restricts the power of legal persons under public law to have recourse to mediation. Such persons may only take part in mediation if so duly authorised by a law or a Royal Decree. In the field of construction, this restriction is significant given that public works form an important part of the activity.

The Judicial Code foresees three kinds of mediation:

- voluntary mediation, which takes place independently of any judicial procedure and follows the rules of the Judicial Code;
- judicial mediation, which is ordered by a judge upon the parties' request or consent; and
- 'simple mediation', which takes place outside the legal framework set by the Judicial Code.

The procedure is identical for voluntary and judicial mediation. The parties and the mediator must sign a mediation protocol and decide freely upon the organisation and duration of the mediation. Any agreements reached between the parties during mediation must be made in writing. Since 2005, parties opting for judicial mediation must select an accredited mediator (except when no accredited mediator has the required qualification to help solve the dispute). In voluntary mediation, the parties are free to choose a non-accredited mediator but cannot thereafter submit their agreement to judicial approbation.

The confidentiality of the procedure is guaranteed. All documents and communications made during mediation are confidential. They cannot later be used or produced in judicial or arbitral proceedings and are not admissible as a means of evidence or as acknowledgement of a claim. Both the parties and the mediator are bound by the confidentiality obligation.

An agreement reached between the parties in mediation has the same legal value as a contract. The Judicial Code allows the parties to increase the binding force of their agreements. Whether mediation is voluntary (with an accredited mediator) or judicial, parties can submit their agreements to judicial approbation in order that it be recorded in a consent judgment.

(c) Other ADR methods

In Belgium, as in many countries, other types of ADR methods can also be used for the resolution of disputes. For instance, expert determination and dispute boards are sometimes foreseen in multi-stepped dispute resolution clauses.

These ADR methods are not subject to any specific legislation. Rules of contract law apply to them. Parties may of course refer to the rules of specific ADR institutions such as the International Chamber of Commerce (ICC) or the Belgian Centre for Arbitration and Mediation (CEPANI).

3.4 Belgian arbitration and ADR institutions interested in construction disputes

There are several arbitral and ADR institutions in Belgium. CEPANI is the best known and is widely used; it deals with all kinds of cases. Other smaller institutions specialise in certain kinds of disputes. There are three main institutions that deal exclusively with construction and real estate disputes, namely the Chambre de Conciliation, d'Arbitrage et de Médiation en matière immobilière (CCAI), the Commission de Conciliation Construction (CCC) and the Centre Scientifique et Technique de la Construction (CSTC).

(a) CEPANI

CEPANI (www.cepani.be) is the most prominent arbitration institution in Belgium. It was created in 1969 by the Belgian Business Federation and the Belgian national committee of the International Court of Arbitration.

CEPANI offers arbitration and mediation services as well as mini-trials, technical expertise and contract adaptation services. It is a non-specialised arbitration/mediation institution, which means that its scope of activity is not restricted to any specific type of dispute on the basis of its subject matter or the capacity of the parties.

CEPANI statistics indicate that construction arbitration forms an important part of its activity. The total number of arbitration cases relating to construction matters represented 16.7% of all cases in 2004, 4.3% in 2005, 13.7% in 2009, 9.0% in 2010 and 15.0% in 2011. These statistics are largely similar to those of the International Commercial Court, where construction cases have represented between 14% and

17% of all cases since 2005. CEPANI deals mostly with national cases, but about one-third to one-half of all cases involves a foreign party.

In 2000, CEPANI set up a working group to examine the possibility of promoting arbitration in the construction sector. The working group noted that the use of arbitration could be increased in the Belgian construction sector, as shown by the international and Dutch traditions to refer construction cases to arbitration. Belgium is indeed far away from the quasi-systematic recourse to arbitration that exists in the Netherlands and for international contracts.

(b) CCAI

The CCAI was created in 2005 by various local associations of notaries, lawyers, architects, land surveyors and expert architects. The association of owners and the association of lenders later joined the CCAI as institutional members. It was created in response to the perceived inadequacy of ordinary judicial proceedings for the settlement of real estate disputes due to their high costs and duration. The aim of the CCAI is to offer mediation, conciliation and arbitration services for the resolution of real estate disputes. The CCAI brings together lawyers and technical experts who are supposed to complement and assist each other for the purpose of resolving disputes in a fast and cost-effective manner.

The CCAI has the broadest jurisdictional scope of all ADR institutions specialising in construction and real estate disputes. Any real estate dispute can be referred to the CCAI. This covers disputes relating to leases, building works, real estate sales, leasing, neighbourhood nuisance, urbanism, environment, etc. Private individuals and professionals can refer their disputes to the CCAI.

One of the distinct features of the CCAI procedure is the collaboration that exists between legal and technical experts for the resolution of disputes. The CCAI Rules provide that mediations and conciliations must be conducted by a panel composed of one technical expert and one lawyer. In the case of arbitration, the CCAI Rules provide that a three-member arbitral tribunal must, as a general rule, include at least one technical expert and one lawyer. Disputes will be resolved by single arbitrators in exceptional cases only or upon the request of both parties.

The collaboration between the legal and the technical ADR experts increases the understanding of the dispute and the chances of an amicable settlement between the parties. However, in purely legal disputes (such as rent issues or financing of leasing, for instance) having two mediators or conciliators seems redundant. Unfortunately, the CCAI Rules do not provide for any exceptions with regard to the number or qualification of mediators and conciliators.

Over the past two years, the CCAI dealt with about 100 cases, 75% of which were resolved amicably. The number of arbitration cases is still limited (about 10 cases every year). This could be explained by the novelty of the institution and also by the fact that the CCAI Rules do not allow the parties to nominate their own arbitrators.

(c) CCC

The CCC was set up in 2001 by four institutions: the Confédération de la construction (an organisation of employers comprising about 15,000 businesses in the field of construction); the consumers' association Test-Achats; the Bouwunie (formerly known as Nacebo, the Flemish federation of small and medium-sized enterprises in construction); and the Royal Federation of Architects in Belgium. The Flemish architects' organisation (the NAV) joined the CCC in 2005.

Article 7 of the CCC's Procedural Rules sets forth a model clause that the parties can insert into their contracts. It obliges the parties to insert the CCC's model clause into all the contracts they conclude with third parties for the execution of a project's works. Consequently, all the contractors, subcontractors and architects working on that project should in principle be bound by the same conciliation clause. This guarantees that any interested party in the resolution of the dispute will be present at the conciliation proceedings, which at the same time can be a disadvantage where a party would seek to settle its disputes through arbitration, exactly in order to prevent multi-party disputes. It is important to remember that the objective of conciliation is the conclusion of a final and binding settlement agreement.

The jurisdiction of the CCC is limited and well-defined. First, the dispute must relate to defects of a technical nature and any related dispute arising from it. Secondly, a consumer must be a party to the dispute; disputes exclusively between professionals are expressly excluded from the CCC's jurisdiction. Finally, the works must have been ordered or purchased off plan by the consumer for his personal needs.

While the CCC does not deal with purely legal cases, the Procedural Rules allow the expert-conciliator to submit a non-binding opinion on the technical liabilities of the parties, if one party so requests.

The CCC-nominated conciliator has in fact a dual mission. On the one hand, he must try to make the parties come to an agreement during the entire duration of the mission. On the other hand, the conciliator must observe and consider all the necessary elements regarding the technical defects. The combination of conciliation and expertise makes sense in the framework of construction disputes. A conciliator will indeed need to have a good understanding of the dispute in order to present the parties with acceptable proposals. The Procedural Rules also provide that the technical conclusions of the expert-conciliator are considered to be made contradictorily and bind the parties. Thus, even if the conciliation were to fail, the court would be able to rely on the conclusions of the expert-conciliator and would not necessarily have to order a preliminary judicial expertise.

According to the CCC's statistics, an average of 69 cases are handled by it every year. In the great majority of the cases (80%), disputes are submitted by consumers. The CCC has a relatively high success rate: an average of three out of four cases are settled amicably by the parties. In terms of time and costs, the CCC's annual statistics show its time and cost-efficiency. In most cases (80% on average), the procedure does not cost more than the basic fixed rate i.e. €200 for each party (increased by €200 when a specialist is appointed to assist the expert-conciliator with the dispute). The low fees can be explained by the fact that a great majority of disputes are resolved during the first site visit. The duration of procedures is usually less than 12 weeks.

(d) *CSTC*

The CSTC (www.cstc.be) is a research institute created in 1960. The CSTC has 70,000 members representing the entire construction sector (eg, contractors, plumbers, glaziers, roofing contractors). CSTC members are mostly small and medium-sized businesses. The CSTC is not *per se* an ADR service provider. It pursues scientific and technical research for the benefit of its members, gives information, assistance and technical advice, and tries to contribute to the innovation and development of the construction sector.

With regard to technical advice, the Technical Advice Division of the CSTC (ATA) answers any technical questions relating to construction works. Technical advice can be requested before, during or after the execution of the works. Preliminary advice aims to limit the risk of errors during the conception stage of the works, while *ex post* advice aims to identify and resolve any defect at any stage of the works. Technical advice from the ATA is always made in consultation with the contractors concerned.

The services of the ATA are exclusively available to professionals and judicial experts. Requests to the ATA, and the resulting technical advice, can be made either orally (by phone) or in writing. Upon the express request of a contractor, the ATA can also visit the construction site and submit a written report containing an analysis of the technical problem and possible remedies. The technical advice of the ATA is generally free – a fee will only be due if a written report is requested by the parties, if the ATA acts upon the request of a judicial expert, or if analyses, measurements, calculations etc are needed. These fees, however, are quite low: €125 for a written report and €625/day for tasks related to judicial expertise.

4. Outlook

Construction law has evolved little since the adoption of the Civil Code in 1804. Nevertheless, some changes can be expected in the coming years. Three issues are of particular note, and these are outlined next.

4.1 The architect's monopoly

As mentioned in briefer form above, according to Article 4 of the 1939 Act on Protection of Title and Profession of Architects, Belgian owners are under a duty to engage an architect registered at the Tableau de l'Ordre whenever building activities that require a building permit start. As a consequence, the architect's function is protected in Belgium. Moreover, the architect's monopoly does not only cover the design of the building works for which a building permit is required, but also the control of the performance of such building works. This makes the monopoly one of the widest in Europe. This monopoly is regularly contested, under the pressure of the European Commission. As a result of past legislative action, several building activities have already been placed outside the scope of the architect's monopoly, such as infrastructure or civil engineering works (in Flanders) or minor renovation works.

4.2 Professional liability insurance

In Belgium, only architects are under a duty to cover their professional liability by insurance. The absence of any such mandatory insurance for the others professionals involved in a construction project (notably the building contractors) has been held contrary to the Belgian constitution by the Constitutional Court. As a consequence, a bill is currently before the Belgian Parliament. It aims at imposing the requirement to have professional insurance on building contractors. This would impose the same duty on building contactors as is currently on architects (which have to prove they are covered by a professional liability insurance in order to be registered with the Architects' Bar).

4.3 Impact on the building industry of the evolution of European contract law

On October 11 2011, the European Commission published its "Proposal for a Regulation of the European Parliament and of the Council on a Common European Sales Law". This proposal suggests adopting an optional instrument in European sales law. It constitutes a significant step in the process of harmonising contract law in the European Union. Even if this remains largely unknown, the European harmonisation of contract law will have an impact on the building industry – for instance, the sale of building materials is already included in the proposal's field of application. Moreover, this regulation would also apply to a contract of related services so it could be rendered entirely applicable to contracts dealing with the installation of goods into a pre-existing building. Consequently, certain activities in the real estate industry – in particular those related to the renovation, installation or improvement of a pre-existing building, like plumbing, roofing, grouting, and so on – could be included in the scope of the draft instrument since they involve both the sale of materials, the building elements and the installation of these into a pre-existing building.

With regard to dispute resolution, no notable changes are foreseen in the near future. The caseload of Belgian judicial courts will, in all probability, remain high (in certain jurisdictions it takes two to four years to get a final decision). In this context, ADR methods should become progressively more attractive to construction professionals. The growing number of specialised institutions already offers convenient fora for the resolution of construction disputes. Professionals are, however, yet to be convinced of the cost and time efficiency of these alternative procedures. The promotion of ADR by public authorities and private bodies should help to achieve this goal.

Finland

Tuomas Lehtinen
Castrén & Snellman Attorneys Ltd

1. Introduction

The judicial background to construction disputes in Finland may be examined from the legislative standpoint and the contractual standpoint.

The contractual aspect of construction projects is not strictly regulated in Finland, although construction itself in Finland is regulated quite strictly. Construction regulation relating to disputes is most commonly conducted in relation to public authorities, whereas straightforward contractual disputes usually occur between the contractual parties – one of which, of course, may be a public authority.

Two of the main codes for construction projects are the Land Use and Building Act (132/1999, amendment 222/2003) and the Act on Public Contracts (348/2007). The objective of the former is to ensure that the use of land and water, as well as the building activities on land and water, create the necessary preconditions for a favourable living environment and promote ecologically, economically, socially and culturally sustainable development. The latter, in turn, regulates how the state, municipal authorities and other contracting authorities put their contracts out to tender. The act should be kept in mind when cooperating with public authorities on construction projects. The purpose of the act, framed in 2007, is to facilitate more efficient use of public funds, promote high-quality procurement and safeguard equal opportunities for companies and other communities in offering supply, service and public works contracts under competitive bidding for public procurement.

The judicial background of construction disputes nevertheless leans quite heavily towards contractual law, as most of the issues concern contractual differences in opinion. The standard contractual conditions for construction projects, drafted in 1998, are widely used. These conditions apply particularly in domestic construction projects, to the extent that they have occasionally been compared with dispositive legislation. Consequently, the contractual stipulation is quite established, in spite of the lack of legislation.

Judicial principles and other non-statutory rules also play a significant role. These principles are mainly discretionary and may be excluded by contractual stipulations. There are, however, principles that are mandatory in a way that prohibits their total exclusion. Limitation of risk, for example, is not binding by internationally established custom if the damage has been caused by wilful misconduct (intentionally) or by gross negligence. However, the legal definitions of these terms are widely debated in Finland and no precise definition can be given.

Similarly, it may be contested whether contractual relations without any form of fidelity-related requirements can exist. The standard contractual conditions for construction projects include several fidelity-related clauses, thus providing further arguments in support of fidelity as an inseparable part of construction contracts in Finland. The significance of the issues touched upon here is discussed in more detail below (see section 3).

Furthermore, even the parties to a dispute are not always unambiguous. The formal requirement for raising claims based on contractual damage is generally that the claimant is the contractual party of the respondent, whereas the general rule is that tort claims cannot be raised based on contractual damages. Recently, however, there has been discussion in the legal literature about both the possibility of a third party invoking a contract and the eventual expansion of tort law with respect to contractual damages. There have been arguments in support of deviating from the privity of contract under certain conditions, on the one hand, and for tort claims being raised based on contractual damages, on the other. In large construction project disputes – and especially subcontracting arrangements – these questions may cause inconvenience to the parties involved. These issues are also covered in more detail in section 3 below.

As the construction dispute field is generally governed more by contractual principles than by legislation, construction disputes in Finland rarely concern absolute legislative questions but, rather, those differences of opinion on more relative issues. This makes the solution more complex than a simple 'yes' or 'no', and could allow more room for arguments.

1.1 Construction project outlook

The Finnish construction sector is becoming increasingly diverse. For example, public-private partnerships (PPPs) are becoming increasingly popular in Finland. The first PPP project in Finland – the Lahti highway – was completed in 1999. Recent examples of significant state-driven PPP projects include the expansion to the E18 highway between Koskenkylä and Kokkola, and the railway enhancement between Kokkola and Ylivieska. PPP projects have also been favoured in the municipalities: for example, the city of Espoo intends to carry out the construction of a service centre for the elderly costing €200 million in Puolarmetsä as a PPP.

The Finnish energy sector is also highly active. The government is currently constructing a new nuclear plant, Olkiluoto 3, which constitutes the largest single investment in Finnish industrial history to date. Olkiluoto 3 is being implemented on a turnkey basis by a French-German consortium formed by AREVA NP and Siemens AG. The net electrical output of the unit will be approximately 1,600 megawatts (MW). Once finished, Olkiluoto 3 will provide permanent employment for 150 to 200 people, and about 1,000 additional people will be employed during maintenance outages. Finnish wind power construction also took a leap forward recently as Kiinteistö-Tapiola Oy established a property fund with the target of investing approximately €100 million in wind power. The investments are to be made in cooperation with TuuliSaimaa Oy, which is seeking to construct a 200 MW wind power plant in Finland. Finnish wind conditions and technical requirements make Finland less suited to wind power than the other Nordic countries, but the future potential is nevertheless considerable.

Furthermore, the recently initiated construction of the Helsinki West Metro is currently the largest infrastructure project in Finland. The project includes, among other things, the construction of two parallel, 14-kilometre (km) long tunnels and seven new stations. The construction of the West Metro has similarly had a strong impact on the surrounding areas. The regeneration of Tapiola, a central city area along the West Metro route, is developing quickly and most of the building stock is to be torn down and rebuilt. Complete reconstruction will facilitate rapid enhancements to the energy efficiency of the building stock. The covering structures of public areas will also be renewed in their entirety.

Finally, the focal areas for new offices are the business parks of Leppävaara and Keilaniemi, and two major office headquarters close to Helsinki's central business district (CBD) are being constructed. The Helsinki CBD has had very few office vacancies, indicating almost chronic scarcity, which will be somewhat relieved when the headquarter buildings are completed. Completion of the West Metro will shift the focal centre from the CBD to sub-centres along the new metro line.

2. The status of dispute resolution in the construction field

2.1 Public dispute resolution options

In large part due to the development of the construction sector and the general economy as described above, the significance and popularity of alternative dispute resolution (ADR) has increased in recent years, both in Finland and in the other Nordic countries. The ADR methods presented here differ from regular court proceedings, and are divided into those provided by the public sector on the one hand, and the private sector on the other.

Ordinary courts in Finland provide for two ADR methods, both of which strive to facilitate an amicable settlement of the dispute:

- settlement promotion during the course of civil proceedings; and
- judicial court mediation.

These options are described further below, together with brief mention of a third (rarer) approach.

(a) Settlement promotion during the course of civil proceedings

The purpose of settlement promotion in civil court proceedings is, as its name suggests, to explore how parties can reach an amicable settlement during court proceedings. Settlement during proceedings mitigates procedural costs and promotes economic efficiency.

The legislative basis for settlement promotion during the course of civil proceedings is the Code of Judicial Procedure (4/1734; amendments up to 718/2011 included). According to Chapter 5(19) of the code, the possibility of a settlement is determined during the preparation of the case. Furthermore, pursuant to Chapter 5(26), in a case that is amenable to settlement the court will endeavour to persuade the parties to settle the case. When the court deems it expedient to promote a settlement, while considering the wishes of the parties, the nature of the case and the other circumstances, it may also propose that the parties settle the case amicably. However, the court must not promote settlement too actively as this could be seen as favouring one party over the other. The court must rather promote a justified resolution of the case.

Reaching an amicable settlement during the course of civil court proceedings may differ from settling the dispute informally. In dispositive matters, the freedom to reconcile prevails regardless of the case having been taken to court or not; the parties are free to settle the case independently of the legal proceedings stage. However, in non-discretionary matters, the freedom of reconciliation may under certain preconditions be more extensive during civil proceedings as opposed to the parties settling the case informally, as the freedom of reconciliation is restricted in these matters. This will be covered in more detail later.

(b) Court-annexed mediation

According to Chapter 1(1) of the Act on Court-Annexed Mediation (663/2005), civil matters and contested petitionary matters before the general courts may be mediated as provided in the act. Pursuant to Chapter 1(2), the objective of court-annexed mediation is to reach an amicable settlement. The purpose of mediation is to help the parties to a dispute find a solution that is acceptable to both. Mediation may thus favour what is reasonable under the circumstances over the strict application of law (in contrast to settlement promotion described above). The administration of justice is slowly shifting from the idea of material justice in ordinary court proceedings to the idea of negotiations and pragmatic compromises.

The commencement of court-annexed mediation requires the consent of all parties. One or both of the parties to a dispute may request the initiation of mediation, regardless of whether the case is already subject to court proceedings, and the court may also suggest mediation in a pending case. The court will decide whether a mediation procedure should be initiated. The matter must also be amenable to mediation, and mediation must be appropriate in view of the claims of the parties.

Pursuant to Chapter 2(5) of the act, a mediator will be designated for the dispute. The mediator must be a judge in the court in which the case is pending. However, the mediator may not continue to judge the dispute if the mediation does not succeed and the dispute continues. The mediator will hear the parties and consult with them, assisting them in their endeavours towards agreement and an amicable settlement. At the request or with the consent of the parties, the mediator may, pursuant to Chapter 2(7) of the act, make a settlement proposal. The mediator may make the proposal *ex aequo et bono* (ie, according to what is right and good). A settlement accepted by the parties has the effect of concluding the mediation and may be certified in court-annexed mediation.

Subject to Chapter 3(12) of the act, the mediation, the related documents and the settlement are subject to the provisions of the Act on the Publicity of Court Proceedings (945/1984), "in so far as appropriate". Court mediation in Finland is, thus, in principle open to the public, unlike in Norway and Denmark. The general public is not, however, admitted to the negotiations between the mediator and one of the parties (a session referred to in Section 6(3)). Other phases of the mediation process may also be closed to the general public at the request of a party, on the grounds that the achievement of a settlement would otherwise be jeopardised and that the credibility of the mediation or some other significant reason requires that the proceedings be closed to the public.

The status of court-annexed mediation in Finland is strong in principle, but in reality its popularity varies greatly from court to court. Around 100 to 150 cases annually are processed via court mediation, which is about 1% of disputed civil cases. In practice, parties to disputes rely on ordinary court proceedings (subject to settlement promotion during their course, as described above) or arbitration (which is covered below). One general criticism of court-annexed mediation has been its tendency to lean on the authoritative administration of justice instead of flexible, party-based dispute resolution. Thus, the Finnish parties to a dispute have often engaged in lengthy negotiations prior to the case appearing in court. There have usually been several settlement proposals, as well as party-based and private mediation proceedings between the parties, prior to the court hearings. In this environment, the Finnish parties are not keen on using the court-annexed mediation when discussions and negotiations have been unsuccessful.

(c) *Public boards and committees*

The public dispute resolution boards and committees relevant to the Finnish construction sector may be divided into two categories: boards and committees with actual jurisdiction and those that issue recommendations only. The differences between committees with jurisdiction and special courts are mainly formal and administrative. The Labour Council is one of the former and is touched upon briefly here, as it is occasionally relevant from a labour law perspective.

The Labour Council is governed by the Act on the Labour Council and Derogation Permits Concerning Labour Protection (400/2004). The Labour Council is an independent specialised authority subject to the Ministry of Labour, which issues opinions on the application and interpretation of acts falling within the sphere of labour legislation (eg, the Occupational Safety and Health Act (738/2002)), and on whether the Act on Cooperation within Undertakings (725/1978) applies to a particular company. The Labour Council functions as an appeal body for the decisions of industrial safety districts. When it is addressed as an appeal body, the Labour Council's statements have formal validity; more generally, however, its statements are recommendations only.

2.2 Private dispute resolution mechanisms

(a) *Arbitration*

Arbitration is a relatively popular ADR method in Finland. Arbitration is governed by the Arbitration Act (967/1992; amendments up to 460/1999 included). Certain parts of the act apply only to an arbitration taking place in Finland, and certain parts only to the effects in Finland of an arbitration agreement concerning arbitration in a foreign state, as well as to the recognition and enforcement in Finland of an arbitral award issued in a foreign state.

Pursuant to Section 2 of the act, any dispute in a civil or commercial matter that can be settled by agreement between the parties (ie, other than non-discretionary matters) may be referred for final decision by one or more arbitrators. It may also be agreed that any disputes that arise in future from a particular legal relationship specified in the agreement will be finally decided by one or more arbitrators, unless otherwise provided in statutory law. Pursuant to certain legislation (eg, Chapter 16(13) of the Companies Act, where arbitral proceedings are the default dispute resolution method), parties do not always separately have to agree on arbitration.

The arbitration agreement must be in writing, which will be the case if it is contained in a document signed by the parties or in an exchange of letters between the parties. An arbitration agreement is also in writing when the parties, by exchanging telegrams, telexes or other such documents, agree that a dispute will be decided by one or more arbitrators, and if an agreement that has been made in such a manner refers to a document containing an arbitration clause.

Unless otherwise agreed by the parties, there will be three arbitrators. In principle, anyone who is not bankrupt and whose competence has not been restricted may act as an arbitrator. The parties are free to choose their arbitrators, although it is important to consider the competence of the arbitrators and their objectivity. Arbitrators are generally appointed based on their experience and expertise, particularly taking into account the key qualifications required by the parties and the specific subject matter of the dispute. Recently, the president of the Supreme Court of Finland made a statement to the chancellor of justice on the current legal status of judges used for arbitration and how they should be developed. Currently, judges and state officials are allowed to act as arbitrators (in a prerequisite position) subject to licence. It is accustomed practice that a judge acts as an arbitrator only when he is either chair of the arbitration tribunal or a sole arbitrator. In principle, a judge may act as an arbitrator in only one dispute at a time. According to the Supreme Court's statement, the current regulation of participation by the judiciary in arbitration is inefficient, especially with regard to transparency and public confidence. However, incompetence due to the likelihood of bias is, according to the statement, an issue that should not be addressed out of context but, instead, from the perspective of transparency and public confidence.

Arbitration may be arranged by institutes or on an *ad hoc* basis. When a person is approached in connection with possible appointment as an arbitrator, he must, unless he refused the appointment, immediately disclose any circumstances that are likely to give rise to justifiable doubts as to his impartiality and independence. An arbitrator may be challenged by a party if he is disqualified to handle the matter as a judge, or if there are circumstances that give rise to justifiable doubts as to impartiality or independence.

The Arbitration Institute of the Finland Chamber of Commerce (FCC), a popular arbitration institute, administers arbitrations conducted under its rules and can also act as an appointing authority under the UNCITRAL Rules. The institute appoints arbitrators and conciliators to domestic and international cases, without, however, having any list of frequently used arbitrators. If the parties have not agreed on the number of arbitrators, the rules of the institute provide that there will be three. In this case, each of the parties appoints one arbitrator and the institute appoints the chair of the arbitral tribunal. If there are more than two parties involved in the arbitration, the institute may appoint all the arbitrators. In expedited arbitrations, the dispute is always decided by a sole institute-appointed arbitrator. In 2011, the institute received 66 disputes referred to arbitration, 20% of which concerned *ad hoc* arbitration and most of which were handled by sole arbitrators. The median duration of arbitration under the FCC rules was 10 months. The institute has appointed a working group to revise its rules, and the new FCC rules entered into force on June 1 2013.

The variety of ADR methods used in PPPs is in practice the same as that in traditional construction contracts. However, some public sector representatives might be more inclined to look more favourably on ordinary court proceedings in comparison with private construction sector companies. In practice, PPP dispute resolution often appears to require multi-party requirements and this trend leads to dispute resolution clauses that tend to favour institutional arbitration.

Dispute resolution boards and committees have rather complex procedures. The common experience, however, is that these procedures are not that strictly followed, but instead are used as flexible guidelines and applied quite freely in order to ensure that the process progresses quickly. Boards are seen as encouraging the parties to negotiate, which is positive.

In general, dispute boards are rarely used in both private and public projects in Finland. Different kinds of consultation procedure are commonly used in both, and as far as actual dispute resolution goes, ordinary court proceedings and different forms of arbitration and mediation are still the most common forms of action.

(b) Expert determination

As for dispute resolution by expert determination, Finnish RIL Conciliation, in particular, should be mentioned. RIL Conciliation – which operates alongside RIL, the Finnish Association of Civil Engineers – focuses on the dispute resolution and risk management of construction projects. Its services include contract reviews, dispute resolution boards, mediation and expert opinions, with a particular focus on resolving disputes that arise in construction processes. The operations of the company are undertaken by a network of technical and legal professionals, and focus on both private and public sector companies and organisations. Cases cover domestic, commercial and industrial building projects, infrastructure projects, as well as water and waste water projects.

2.3 Forbidden dispute resolution methods

In principle, all methods compliant with non-discretionary legislation are allowed. Settlement in non-discretionary matters is, however, restricted. Some legal relationships regarding a specific public interest prevent the parties from settling the case independently, but are subject to civil court proceedings. Agreements that are contrary to mandatory legislation (eg, competition provisions) may lead to significant sanctions or even criminal liability. One example of the restrictions is recorded in the Consumer Protection Act. According to Chapter 12, Section 11d of the act: "A term in a contract concluded before a dispute arises, under which a dispute between a business and a consumer shall be settled in arbitration, shall not be binding on the consumer."

Moreover, all contractual conduct must comply with the Contracts Act (228/1929; amendments up to 449/1999 included). The invalidity and adjustment of contracts are governed by Chapter 3 of the act. Pursuant to this act, a transaction into which someone has been coerced is not binding (subject, naturally, to certain preconditions). Moreover, a transaction that would otherwise be binding is generally not enforceable if it was entered into under circumstances that would make it incompatible with honour and good faith. Finally, if a contract term is unfair or if its application would lead to an unfair result, the term may be adjusted or set aside. The threshold for applying these provision is rather high.

3. Construction case law updates

3.1 Privity of contract

In 2008, the Supreme Court of Finland set out a clear definition of policy regarding the privity of contract in Decision KKO 2008:31. Previously, the prerequisites for deviating from the privity of contract – that is, allowing non-contractual parties to invoke a contract – were energetically debated in legal literature. The conclusion reached was that liability in a chain of contracts could indeed be accepted under certain circumstances. A chain of contracts may be formed (eg, in a construction project), when the owner purchases from a supplier, which in turn purchases parts of the supply from sub-suppliers. In this context, liability in a chain of contracts would mean that, under certain circumstances, the owner could make claims directly against the sub-supplier instead of claiming against the supplier, which in turn would claim against the sub-supplier. However, Decision KKO 2008:31 stated, in a setting very much resembling a chain of contract, that liability overstepping the privity of contract could not generally be accepted, unless expressly stipulated by law.

3.2 Rules that prevail irrespective of contractual obligations

Another decision, KKO 2009:92, further confirmed the policy defined in KKO 2008:31 regarding liability in a chain of contracts. The dispute involved a chain of contracts, and deviation from the privity of contract was not accepted unless, again, expressly stated by law. Instead, the Supreme Court introduced the possibility of applying tort law to what in this case appeared to be a contractual violation. A boat manufacturer had neglected certain safety regulations, which had caused the boat to sink. As the manufacturer had violated public safety provisions and expectations, it was concluded that the damage should be compensated for based on tort law regardless of the damage itself having been contractual and the contractual liability having expired.

3.3 Judicial implication of prerequisites

The Supreme Court's decision KKO 2012:1 has a bearing on the contractual aspects of construction case law. The central question concerned the judicial implication of prerequisites, and was grounded not on specific legislation but on legal principles. The case thus reflects construction case law quite well – as described earlier, construction is a field of law that is quite heavily biased towards contractual relations.

The case concerned a real property transaction, in which the seller had undertaken to remedy contaminated soil at the property. The parties had referred to the seller's soil testing and restoration plan in the deed of sale. After the transaction, however, the environmental authorities required further soil testing before approving the seller's initial restoration plan. These further tests revealed that the soil was significantly more contaminated than the parties had expected: the estimated restoration costs were many times more than the transaction price and the restoration costs according to the initial restoration plan.

The Supreme Court assessed the legal validity of the seller's undertaking under the circumstances. The essential question was whether the condition should be considered as binding, as the basis of it turned out to be fundamentally incorrect and consequently caused the condition itself to be significantly disproportionate to the parties' initial understanding.

The foundation of contractual relations rests on the parties' liability for their own intentions, commitments and expressions. A party is generally responsible if its own prerequisites later fall through or prove incorrect. A false or expired prerequisite may nevertheless affect the legal validity of the agreement, provided that the prerequisite was of significant importance to the party and a determinant in the conclusion of the agreement and that the counterparty was aware of both the prerequisite and its significance to the other party. Moreover, the party that presumed incorrectly should have acted diligently.

The Supreme Court considered the initial soil testing and restoration plan both significant and determinant as a prerequisite to the transaction at hand. Since neither the seller nor the purchaser had or should have had any reason to suspect the initial prerequisites to be incorrect, the agreement was considered to differ substantially from the initial understanding between the parties. Thus, the Supreme Court did not find the seller's undertaking legally valid.

3.4 The validity of a limited liability clause

Decision KKO 2012:72 concerned the validity of a limitation-of-liability clause. According to a clause in a contract of sale between two entrepreneurs, the buyer accepted "responsibility for all possible actions and costs thereof required for repairing or demolishing the building irrespective of whether they had been taken into account in the cost estimate, and whether they were at the date of sale hidden defects or whether they had harmful effects on health or the environment". The buyer claimed a price reduction and damages based on defects in quality found after the date of sale. The case dealt with whether the limitations of liability were valid.

It was concluded that, when signing the contract of sale, the buyer had taken a conscious business risk that the need to repair the buildings would turn out to be greater than predicted. Despite these predictions, the repair costs were over €2.5 million. The fact that the seller possibly did not adequately account in its own price estimate for other repair needs was of no relevance in assessing whether the condition was binding. The effects of the limitation-of-liability clause could not be considered surprising or unreasonable from the seller's perspective; therefore, the limitation-of-liability clause was deemed binding upon the association.

4. Conclusion

The Finnish construction sector is growing steadily, and the size and variety of projects have increased. There are several current interesting construction projects under way in Finland and more in the pipeline. Unfortunately, however, many projects have suffered from delays and other circumstances that could give rise to major disputes. The Helsinki West Metro has suffered from delays and is finishing behind schedule, and the Olkiluoto 3 nuclear plant has yet to be finished, despite originally being planned to start commercial operations in 2009. Some PPP projects have also been rather demanding contractually.

The Finnish construction dispute field is generally governed more by contractual principles than by legislation as such. This provides for an interesting setting and new challenges for dispute resolution. This is well illustrated by the cases discussed in section 3 above. Moreover, in Finnish construction projects there are more options for dispute resolution in contractual matters. This is advantageous to the Finnish construction industry and bodes well for future projects.

Germany

Rouven F Bodenheimer
Claus H Lenz
Lungerich Lenz Schuhmacher Rechtsanwälte

1. Current highlights

Several construction projects in Germany have been attracting regular media attention – especially where public alarm has been raised due to questions about whether they are in fact necessary, due to environmental issues or, mostly, due to cost concerns. Such projects can create all kinds of problems and disputes which need to be resolved.

1.1 Berlin-Schönefeld Airport

The reconstruction of Berlin-Schönefeld Airport was originally budgeted at €1.7 billion, with the opening scheduled for 2007. However, due to numerous problems both in the design phase and during construction, several delays were incurred. The latest postponement came just three months prior to proposed completion, when severe deficiencies in the fire protection system came to light. According to current estimates, completion is now expected in 2014 or even 2015. So far, costs have soared to €4.3 billion and are likely to rise further still.

In July 2012 the airport company filed an action against the architects, claiming that the delays were caused by their poor planning. Air Berlin also filed suit against the airport company in November 2012, alleging losses of several million euros due to the delays. Both disputes are pending. Lufthansa is additionally considering legal action.

1.2 Stuttgart 21

The railway terminal in Stuttgart is being replaced by an underground through station. Costs were initially estimated at €2.5 billion, to be shared among the federal government, the state of Baden-Württemberg and Deutsche Bahn. The project has proved highly controversial from the outset.

Since the commencement of construction works in 2010, opponents have demonstrated almost continuously in the square in front of the station. When their protests became increasingly violent in September 2010, it was decided to appoint a former minister to mediate between both sides and prevent future violence.

After eight sessions, the mediation ended with a recommendation from the mediator that the project continue, but with revisions to reflect some important concerns. Half a year later, having conducted studies to investigate possible compromises, the mediator submitted a proposal to amend the project and build a small new underground station while keeping part of the old station. However, Deutsche Bahn rejected this proposal.

Following further unforeseen complications which led to cost increases and delays, it now appears that the federal government might well have a claim against Deutsche Bahn. Costs have thus far amounted to €4.3 billion; an estimation of total costs suggests they are more likely to reach €5.3 billion. However, the federal government and the state of Baden-Württemberg have agreed to a cap of €4.5 billion, with Deutsche Bahn having to bear any additional costs by itself.

1.3 *Elbphilharmonie*

In 2001 the City of Hamburg, through a special purpose vehicle, contracted a joint venture between construction company Hochtief and finance company CommerzLeasing to build the city's new concert hall, the *Elbphilharmonie*. According to calculations, the project would cost €186 million and be completed by 2010. However, after several problems arose, leading to delays and massive cost hikes, it began to look as though Hochtief was not taking the city council seriously. In 2011 the city council applied for a declaration that Hochtief was not entitled to delay the project any longer than February 2012, and was liable for any damages arising from the delay. The court dismissed the first application as inadmissible. Regarding damages, the parties reached a settlement in December 2012. Hochtief will bear all future costs itself, while the City of Hamburg will remain principal of the project. However, the city must still meet the existing costs of €575 million. Takeover is now scheduled for late 2016.

1.4 Freight vehicle toll system

A company called Toll-Collect was appointed to launch a highly technical and complicated new freight vehicle toll system in 2003. The commissioning date was pushed back several times. The system was eventually launched at the beginning of 2005, but it took another year before it was operating flawlessly. The federal government commenced arbitration against Toll-Collect due to lost toll earnings, claiming damages amounting to €3.5 billion as well as a €1.6 billion contractual penalty, along with interest at a rate of 9%. Toll-Collect counterclaimed to recover the 15% of its contractual annual payment that the government had decided to retain. Together, both claims are worth some €7 billion. Toll-Collect denies any blame for the delay, alleging that this was down to the usual 'innovation risk' of any new system. The government claims that Toll-Collect was grossly negligent due to defective risk management.

Proceedings were adjourned when the chairman of the arbitral tribunal resigned due to illness in March 2012, and resumed only in the following December. The government has recently considered waiving a major part of its claim. As at July 2013, a conclusion to the proceedings remains eagerly awaited.

1.5 Conclusion

What the above large-scale projects have in common is that in each case a public body acted as principal, and in each case the project ended disastrously – at least from a financial perspective. That said, in recent years Germany has seen similar problems arise in the private sector, where delays and changes in the scope of projects have caused huge cost overruns. In most cases deficiencies in the planning phase were the cause of the problem, rather than sloppy performance by the contractors. However, the insolvency of contractors or subcontractors can also be a contributing factor.

Such problematic projects invariably end up with disputes between the principal and contractor, and/or between the main contractor and subcontractors, most of which can be resolved only after lengthy proceedings (often by way of more or less 'forced' settlements).

2. Dispute resolution methods in common use

2.1 Litigation

In the German construction industry, disputes are often finally resolved by litigation before the ordinary courts.

For those who are unfamiliar with the German legal system, it may be helpful to highlight some features of German civil litigation:

- No pre-trial discovery – unlike in other jurisdictions, German law does not provide for pre-trial discovery. Litigation in Germany relies on an elaborate system of allocating the burden to submit and to prove the facts, in which the parties have very limited rights to request information from the other side and confidential information is extensively protected.
- Comprehensive pleading – unlike in other jurisdictions, where a statement of claim might only outline the dispute, in Germany litigation begins with a detailed statement of claim which provides a complete and concise description of the relevant facts, including the evidence on which the plaintiff relies and an exact specification of the relief it seeks. If the court finds the statement of claim insufficient, the case may be dismissed even before the defendant has submitted its statement of defence.
- Costs – in Germany, the costs of litigation (ie, court fees and statutory attorneys' fees) are borne by the losing party. As long as the attorney representing the winning party charges based on the statutory fees, there will be full reimbursement of costs to the winning party. Contingency fees and fee agreements are generally not allowed.

Besides some fundamental procedural guarantees enshrined in the German Constitution – such as the right to be heard by the court, the right to legal recourse, the right to be heard by a lawful judge, the right to a fair trial according to the rule of law, the right to be treated equally by the court and the commitment of the courts to follow the law – the main statute governing German civil litigation is the Civil Procedure Code.[1]

The Civil Procedure Code sets out some basic principles, including:

- the principle of party control of the subject matter of the lawsuit;

1 An English translation of the German Civil Procedure Code is available at www.gesetze-im-internet.de/englisch_zpo/index.html.

- the principle of party control of allegations and proof;
- the principle of oral procedure – that is, the court decision may be based only on statements made by the parties or reiterated orally;
- the principle of publicity;
- the principle of immediacy – that is, the proceedings must be conducted before the court;
- the principle of expediting proceedings; and
- the right to be heard by the court.

The German court structure is as follows:

- Courts of first instance – these are local (lower district) courts that hear claims for up to €5,000 or regional (district) courts, which would be the normal entry level for construction disputes. The regional courts are organised in chambers, usually consisting of three professional judges (although it has become common practice for a single judge to hear and decide the case). A number of regional (district) courts have chambers which also regularly deal with construction disputes and which may be regarded as more specialised.
- Courts of second instance (appellate level) – appeals against regional court decisions are handled by the higher regional (district) courts, usually before a panel consisting of three professional judges. Again, some of the higher regional courts have specific panels experienced in construction disputes.
- Further appeal – under certain circumstances, judgments on first appeal may be further appealed to the Federal Court of Justice, which is organised in panels of five professional judges.

Unless otherwise agreed by the parties, jurisdiction of the courts is determined either by the seat of the defendant or by the location where the defendant has assets. Construction contracts in Germany normally contain a jurisdiction clause.

The length of proceedings is commonly cited as an argument against litigation. However, the German court system is quite efficient: the average time frame between commencement and conclusion of first-instance proceedings is usually less than one year, subject to the complexity of the matter and, in particular, any need for expert opinion, which is often required in construction cases. Consequently, it cannot be ruled out that first-instance proceedings in some cases can take up to six or even eight years, particularly where preliminary proceedings to preserve evidence are initiated before the actual litigation. When deciding whether to litigate or arbitrate, the potential for appeal must also be considered.

Arguments relating to expert knowledge often used in favour of arbitration over litigation do not necessarily apply where courts with experienced chambers or panels have jurisdiction.

The Civil Procedure Code contains specific provisions relating to independent evidentiary proceedings.[2] Such proceedings are widely used in the construction industry in order to preserve evidence and to enlist an expert to determine the status

2 2nd Book, Title 12, Sections 485 and following.

of the construction site, in particular with regard to alleged defects at an early stage (ie, before evidence might be destroyed by further ongoing activities). Once a corresponding petition has been filed, the court may direct (in the course of litigation or outside the proceedings) that visual evidence be taken onsite, that witnesses be examined or that an expert prepare a report, provided that the opponent consents or there is concern that evidence might be lost or become difficult to use.[3] These independent evidentiary proceedings might also drag on for a long time (sometimes several years) if the issues are complex and the expert must render one or several reports, which might be contested by the parties in hearings at which the parties bring along their own experts. Preserved evidence can be used in subsequent litigation.

Overall, litigation is a viable option for parties to resolve domestic construction disputes, particularly when the court with jurisdiction has a chamber or a panel with judges experienced in construction cases. Where there is a foreign element, litigation might be less favourable – particularly if, for example, correspondence and documentation are primarily in a foreign language, since in principle all documents presented to the German courts must be translated into German (commercial courts may exceptionally allow submissions in English, albeit that judgments are still delivered in German).

One advantage of litigation is the relative efficiency of the German court system, given its limited discovery and the fact that the parties can rely to a certain extent on precedents set by other courts.

The disadvantages include that parties might end up before judges who have limited technical understanding and the fact that ordinary court proceedings are not confidential.

2.2 Arbitration

Arbitration is a major form of alternative dispute resolution (ADR) in Germany.

German arbitration law in its current form came into force on January 1 1998, after a lengthy reform process in the late 1980s and early 1990s, when the regime was modernised to ensure compatibility with the United Nations Commission on International Trade Law (UNCITRAL) Model Law of 1985.

German arbitration law is set out in the Civil Procedure Code.[4] In principle, the provisions of the 10th Book apply to both *ad hoc* arbitration and institutional arbitration, as long as the seat of arbitration is in Germany, irrespective of whether the dispute is international or domestic. Only a few provisions of German arbitration law will apply to arbitrations where the place of arbitration is in a different country; these basically concern the enforcement of arbitration agreements and awards, as well as judicial support.

German arbitration law recognises and supports party autonomy as a general principle, with few exceptions. It affords the tribunal wide discretion in the conduct of the proceedings and allows only limited court intervention.

Of major importance in German arbitration proceedings (as in litigation in the

3 Section 485, para. 1.
4 10th Book, Sections 1025 to 1066.

ordinary courts) is the promotion of amicable solutions with the help of the arbitrators, who play an active role in this process.

It has been estimated that approximately two-thirds of domestic arbitrations in Germany result in an amicable settlement. Such settlements may be recorded in the form of an arbitral award on agreed terms, which has the same effect as any other award on the merits of the case and is thus enforceable to the same extent.

Arbitration proceedings are subject to a valid and binding arbitration agreement between the parties, which under German law needs to satisfy relatively few formal requirements.

The arbitral tribunal is constituted in accordance with the agreement between the parties, which are free to determine the number of arbitrators and the procedures for their appointment. In the absence of agreement, three arbitrators will be appointed, with each party appointing one arbitrator and the third appointed by the higher regional court in the jurisdiction of the seat of the arbitration. German arbitration law allows limited scope for challenging and substituting the appointment of arbitrators, but arbitrators must disclose all circumstances that could give rise to justifiable doubts as to their impartiality or independence.

In *ad hoc* arbitrations, a separate arbitrators' agreement must be concluded between the parties and the arbitrators, in particular with regard to payment of the arbitrators' fees and reimbursement of their expenses. This is not necessary in institutional arbitration, where such issues are already dealt with in the rules of the relevant institutional arbitration.

Of course, as a German concept, the principle of *Kompetenz-Kompetenz* applies, meaning that the arbitral tribunal is permitted to rule on its own jurisdiction. A relatively new feature of German arbitration is the tribunal's authority to order protective interim measures, although these might require enforcement to be granted by the courts.

The conduct of the proceedings is relatively flexible. Section 1042 of the Civil Procedure Code expressly states that, subject to mandatory provisions of the law, the arbitral tribunal shall conduct the proceedings according to the rules determined by the parties; in the absence of such agreed rules, the arbitral tribunal shall conduct the proceedings in a manner that it considers appropriate. German arbitration law *per se* does not dictate that continental European-style proceedings be chosen over Anglo-American-style proceedings, but leaves this to the parties' autonomy.

Nevertheless, discovery in German arbitration proceedings will normally be limited in line with the Civil Procedure Code, which allows the court to order the production of documents which are in the possession of a party or a third party only if one party has made specific reference to them or has given a specific reason for the need to disclose such documents. The International Bar Association Rules on the Taking of Evidence in International Commercial Arbitration (2010) are often used as a guideline, particularly in cases where foreign parties are involved.

The advantage of arbitration compared with litigation before the ordinary courts is the freedom of the parties to agree on the appointment of the arbitrators, the seat of arbitration and the language of the proceedings.

Difficulties arise, however, with regard to multi-party issues. German law has no explicit provisions on the appointment of arbitrators where multiple parties are involved. However, the arbitration rules of the Deutsche Institution für Schiedsgerichtsbarkeit eV (DIS) – the most widely recognised arbitration institute in Germany – contain relevant provisions (as do the International Chamber of Commerce Rules).[5]

The taking of evidence and the appointment of experts are also subject to the parties' agreement or to the wide discretion of the tribunal.

With regard to the confidentiality of proceedings, German arbitration law does not expressly impose a confidentiality obligation on the parties, although this is usually expected as one of the key advantages of arbitration proceedings. In fact, arbitration proceedings are held in confidence and awards are normally not published and do not become public knowledge, except in subsequent court proceedings.

Where arbitration is chosen by the parties, this will usually be institutional arbitration, in which case the institution will also provide a model arbitration clause/agreement.

For *ad hoc* arbitration, careful drafting of the arbitration clause/agreement is necessary. It will almost always be executed in writing. At a minimum, the agreement should determine: the seat of the arbitration; the number of arbitrators (which sometimes depends on the sum in dispute); the appointment procedure; the qualifications of the arbitrator(s) (eg, at least one lawyer); and, if a foreign element is present, the choice of law and language of the proceedings.

With regard to available institutional arbitration in the construction industry, three organisations and their rules should be mentioned.

(a) Deutscher Beton- und Bautechnik-Verein eV/Deutsche Gesellschaft für Baurecht eV

The Deutscher Beton- und Bautechnik-Verein eV/Deutsche Gesellschaft für Baurecht eV recently issued a completely new set of rules, the ADR Rules for the Construction Industry, which allow disputing parties to choose between four different dispute resolution proceedings. These proceedings may be selected individually or cumulatively.[6]

(b) ARGE Baurecht

The Working Group for Construction and Real Estate Law of the German Lawyers' Association has issued rules which basically cover a sort of mediation, as well as arbitration proceedings. The rulebook also has a chapter on isolated proceedings for the purpose of securing evidence. The rules are not available in English.[7]

---

5 The DIS website is very informative, with all of its institutional rules also available in English: www.dis-arb.de.

6 The objective of mediation is to support the disputing parties through the help of a mediator to reach a mutually amicable solution. Conciliation may result in an award, whose effectiveness is subject to the acceptance of the disputing parties. Arbitration decisions regarding disputes are legally binding. Arbitration now provides for and decides upon third-party notices and the intervention of third parties, and upon the nature of this intervention. Adjudication was introduced after a call from the construction industry to make available assertive, temporarily binding resolutions of disputes during the planning and construction stages. The rules are available in English at http://dg-baurecht.de/fileadmin/user_upload/ downloads/sl_bau_englisch.pdf.

7 The German version can be obtained at www.arge-baurecht.com/rechtsuchende/sobau/schiedsordnung.

(c) *Deutsche Institution für Schiedsgerichtsbarkeit*[8]

The DIS covers the entire range of commercial arbitration (including, most recently, sports arbitration), and is not specifically relevant only to the construction industry. Accordingly, no qualification requirements for arbitrators are specified. The DIS now also offers rules on conciliation, conflict management, mediation, expert determination and adjudication.

3. Mediation

While mediation has had a comparatively short history in Germany, its use as a dispute resolution mechanism in the commercial context is growing. Indeed, disputes in the construction industry are considered particularly well-suited to ADR.[9] Awareness and understanding of mediation, especially in the construction industry, have been steadily increasing since 2002.[10] In construction disputes in particular, the advantages are evident: even with Germany's relatively time- and cost-effective judicial system, litigation before the state courts often leads to protracted procedures with significant costs – not forgetting the indirect costs incurred in the conduct of ordinary proceedings.[11]

In Germany, two recent developments can be considered 'German specialities': the implementation of court-associated mediation and mediation by judges.

3.1 *Gerichtsnahe* mediation

The concept of *gerichtsnahe* mediation enables the parties to refer a dispute to mediation even once a claim has been filed. Mediators are appointed from among a pool of local registered and properly qualified mediators. The *Projekt Anwaltsmediation* proceedings in the Higher Regional Court of Cologne represent a good example;[12] in that case, the court proceedings were interrupted and the official court file was submitted to the mediators, who called a meeting between the parties and their counsel in a timely manner. Mediation always foresees co-mediation, matching different levels of experience and – if possible – different genders of the mediators. The mediators themselves commit to fixed fees for the first four hours, which encourages the parties to choose mediation. Once these four hours have elapsed, the parties can continue on the basis of an individual agreement with the mediators. Once a settlement has been reached, this settlement can be recorded by the court and then becomes enforceable between the parties. The advantage of this process is that it allows for the appointment of experienced practitioners in the field of construction law. If mediation fails, the court file is resubmitted to the court and the court proceedings continue as if the mediation had never taken place.

3.2 *Richter* mediation

In other regions of Germany, the civil courts themselves are trying to incorporate

---

8 See n5.
9 See Frickell, ZKM 2000, 158.
10 See Wagner, Mediation im Privaten Baurecht: Eine Alternative zum Bauprozess, BauR 2004, 221 and following.
11 See Wagner, BauR 2004, 222, 223.
12 See http://projekt.anwaltmediation.de.

mediation procedures into court proceedings. The concept of *Richter* mediation foresees mediation executed by a state judge (*Richter*). Support for mediation is reflected in the fact that mediation has been part of the mandatory training for German judges since 2003.[13] Mediation is also incorporated into court proceedings: where a case is considered to be appropriate for mediation, the presiding judge will – with the parties' approval – refer it to another judge within the court who is trained in mediation. The mediator judge will then try to mediate the case before him without conveying any confidential information to the presiding judge. Again, if the mediation is successful, an enforceable settlement agreement will be recorded by the presiding judge. If the mediation fails, the file is resubmitted to the court and the ordinary proceedings continue.[14]

3.3 Standby mediation or short mediation

The parties to a construction project have a strong interest in ensuring its continuation, given that the biggest cost escalator will be any stoppage due to unresolved disputes. This is where the concept of short mediation comes into play. Short mediation is in no way less valuable than ordinary or long-term mediation; but it is conducted under increased time constraints. It therefore requires greater levels of concentration and planning, especially with regard to time management.

Most construction projects will fulfil the criteria for short mediation, which are as follows:[15]

- There is a limited conflict;
- There is a limited budget;
- A solution can be achieved within a short time frame;
- The parties are geographically distant; or
- Only limited time is available.

Short mediation effectively merges the concepts of mediation and of a permanent dispute board.

Practical experience indicates that it might be advisable to identify and isolate key problems between the parties in advance of short mediation. This enables the parties to achieve a result on crucial issues, thereby facilitating the continuation of the project while also preserving the relationship between the parties and ensuring that no party feels unduly pressurised by time constraints.

In the construction industry in particular, there are always downsides to considering ADR mechanisms when a dispute has already become complex. There may be a steadily increasing list of defects and deficiencies for which damages or compensation is being claimed on different legal grounds. Without general

---

13 See Judiciary Employment Act, Paragraph 5a(3).

14 For example, in Lower Saxony, six courts are participating in a model project to gain experience with court-annexed mediation.14 One of these courts is the Regional Court of Göttingen. In 2003 the court referred 600 out of 2,000 cases to mediation (see court-annexed mediation project at www.mediation-in-.niedersachsen.de/english.html). In about 75% of the cases both parties agreed to choose a judge as mediator. Similar projects have been started in other parts of Germany such as with the Regional Court of Frankfurt am Main (see www.lg-frankfurt.justiz.hessen.de).

15 See *Krabbe, Kurz-Mediation – die Kunst der Gesamtmediation in einer Sitzung*, ZKM 2004, 72 and following.

agreement between the parties on how to deal with these defects, a position-by-position approach would not be possible in short mediation. A prerequisite to the parties consenting to such an abbreviated procedure is that both parties have made a realistic assessment of their chances of establishing such claims in court. If these assessments differ too widely, the process will lack an objective common basis. In such cases, ADR mechanisms which allow for assessment by a third party should be used. Even then, however, mediation may still be not off the table. The process can still be worth considering when a precise assessment of every position would be too cost-intensive, or in order to establish future proceedings; or once again, after an expert opinion or adjudicator's decision has been obtained, the parties could use mediation to agree on conclusions and practical steps forward based on that third-party input. What is paramount is the sincere intention of both parties to achieve a win–win solution. In construction disputes, this often acts as a block: the principal will enjoy more bargaining power than the contractor; while the contractor will enjoy more bargaining power than its subcontractors.

3.4 Practical recommendations

Mediation in construction disputes can be an effective alternative to court proceedings or arbitration. The German courts offer a very effective and mediation-friendly system, which allows the parties to attempt mediation even if court proceedings have already been initiated. Because of the nature of the construction industry, parties should consider a multi-tier approach whereby mediation is followed by arbitration or court proceedings. In other words, the parties should bear mediation in mind as a useful tool throughout the different stages of a dispute to help reduce costs and keep the project going without interruption. It might be worth considering a standby mediation 'board' consisting of two core mediators to assist the parties over the course of the entire project.

The (increased) use of mediation in Germany has been confirmed by a 2008 survey.[16] Nine-hundred completed questionnaires (12%) were returned. Forty per cent of the principals that responded considered mediation a preferred method for settling disputes, giving mediation number-1 ranking, above adjudication. Of the contractors that responded, 48% preferred mediation.

3.5 The 2012 mediation law

The Act on the Promotion of Mediation and Other Alternative Dispute Resolution (The Mediation Act) came into force on July 26 2012. It is divided into two parts: the first short part covers mediation, while the second part contains changes to the codes of procedure. The Mediation Act is based on EU Directive 2008/52/EC.

The core provision of the Mediation Act is Article 1, which defines 'mediation' as a confidential and structured proceeding whereby the parties, with the assistance of one or more mediators, try to resolve their dispute amicably in a voluntary, self-

16 Information taken from *Vogt, Mediation in der Praxis – Teil II: gesetzliche Regelungen zur Mediation und typischer Anwendungsfelder*, DS 2009, 263. Survey conducted at the German Construction Court Day, June 2008.

responsible manner. A 'mediator' is defined as an independent, neutral party with no decision-making powers, who guides the parties through the mediation. These definitions have been criticised as somewhat circular.[17] The question further arises as to whether duties as outlined in the law do not apply if the parties mutually agree to waive confidentiality; or what structural procedures must be in place in order for the Mediation Act to apply. These questions may become relevant if the parties have not initially agreed to mediation and agree on an *ad hoc* procedure, and therefore lack any detailed rules on aspects of the process. It would certainly be advisable to consider these details carefully, to ensure confidentiality in particular.

Article 2 deals with the proceedings and the duties of the mediator. The mediator is obliged to ensure that the parties understand the basic principles of mediation and are participating voluntarily. Again, due to a lack of further detail, the question arises as to what needs to be done in order to avoid claims against mediators for damages in respect of their conduct of the process. When mediating in Germany, it appears to be both necessary and sufficient to ask the parties whether the above requirements are fulfilled and to record this in a protocol. According to the Mediation Act, third parties can participate only with the consent of the parties, which is intended to cover legal counsel and other representatives of the parties.[18] As in most construction disputes the parties will always be represented by third parties, it is highly recommended that parties agree upfront that representation by third parties is admissible.

Article 3 deals with conflicts of interest of the mediator. No special points for the construction industry arise here. However, the legislature has explicitly specified that a party cannot act as mediator where an adviser or third party from the same law firm has represented one of the parties on the same matter in the past (thus explicitly excluding those legal counsel who have acted on one party's side and might be tempted to try to find a mutual solution by changing hats and acting as mediator).

Article 4 deals with the duty of confidentiality. This provision is of practical relevance in so far as it contemplates that confidentiality is now implemented by the Mediation Act. However, the act does not fully implement confidentiality: it remains necessary to agree in detail the duties of confidentiality between the parties and the mediator. The duty in question applies to the mediator and his assistants; third parties such as legal counsel are not covered by the provision.

There is another practical risk: the legislature has consciously decided not to privilege mediators in relation to criminal proceedings. Therefore, the mediator's duty of confidentiality will not apply where criminal proceedings arise – with the exception only of specific professions such as members of the bar who are exempt. This, at least in practice, has the effect of making lawyers more attractive as mediators, especially in circumstances where criminal issues may arise.

The Code of Civil Procedure has also been amended to require claimants, when filing claims, to indicate whether mediation has taken place or whether there are any reasons against considering mediation. Here again, the intent of the legislature is expressly pro-mediation.

17 See further *Risse, Das Mediationsgesetz – eine Kommentierung*, SchiedsVZ 2012, 244.
18 Reasoning of the government draft of the Mediation Act BT-WRS. 17/5335, Section 15.

Especially from an international perspective, having legislation on mediation might appear odd – perhaps even worrying. After all, why should a state pass legislation on a subject which, by its nature, is a mechanism for settling disputes outside the facilities provided by the state? The tool of mediation has now been partially incorporated into the state system of settling disputes. In passing the legislation, Germany has complied with its obligations to transpose EU Directive 2008/52/EC. Even though the act remains vague in many respects, certain criteria need to be observed when considering mediation in Germany in order to avoid formal deficiencies or even potential claims for damages against the mediator. While the act lacks any provisions on the enforceability of mediation agreements, there are other efficient means within the German system that cover enforceability.

Once mediation has been successfully concluded, a settlement agreement can become enforceable by submitting it to a notary, who will notarise the agreement; or by being exchanged and approved by two legal counsel/lawyers *(Anwaltsvergleich)*. It is also widely understood that no enforcement mechanism is in fact required, as mediation agreements are based on the parties' own will and should therefore be complied with. However, given the complex nature of construction disputes, it might be helpful – or sometimes necessary – to try to ensure the enforceability of the agreement nonetheless, and various practical means are at parties' disposal in Germany to achieve this. The Mediation Act should further promote mediation as a tool for resolving disputes.

3.6 Institutional mediation rules

Across the European and international markets, the number of institutions offering mediation and ADR services continues to grow.

Two sets of institutional mediation rules should be mentioned in this regard:

- the DIS Mediation Rules;[19] and
- the ADR Rules for the Construction Industry (SLBau/ADR Construction).[20]

An interesting feature of the DIS rules is the opportunity they afford to continue the process with follow-on arbitration. At any time, the parties can choose to mandate the mediator as arbitrator under the DIS Arbitration Rules.

A special feature of the ADR Rules for the Construction Industry is the explicit inclusion of certain qualification criteria. Depending on the subject matter in dispute, the mediator must have knowledge of construction technology, construction management and/or construction law, as well as extrajudicial dispute resolution.[21]

The ADR Rules for the Construction Industry also explicitly entitle the mediator to conduct individual discussions with the parties, as long as the other party is informed of this prior to such discussions.[22] It can generally be said that these mediation rules are of a rather more fragmentary character. Some of the provisions appear odd from a practical perspective, and some issues which often cause problems in practice are not addressed, such as the appointment of a mediator.

19 Available on the website www.dis-arb.de, see also n 5.
20 See n 6.
21 Article 11(3) SL-Bau.
22 Article 12(4) SL-Bau.

3.7 Conflict resolution under the Construction Tendering and Contract Regulations

Whenever public authorities act as principal, they are obliged to incorporate into their contracts with contractors the Construction Tendering and Contract Regulations (*Vergabe- und Vertragsordnung für Bauleistungen Teil B* (VOB/B)), which provide for a multi-tier dispute resolution method.[23]

4. Rarely used ADR methods/adjudication

Statutory adjudication does not (yet) exist in Germany.

For a number of years, the ARGE *Baurecht* in particular has worked on legislative drafts in relation to statutory adjudication, but without much success. An initiative of *Deutsche Baugerichtstag*, a working group of construction lawyers and judges, came to an end in November 2011 when another working group (of the Federation and the Federal States, acting on behalf of the Ministry for Justice) closed the file on this initiative.

What remains is adjudication as a means of dispute resolution on the basis of party autonomy.

Although there was allegedly great demand for adjudication in the construction industry (which led to various associations and organisations developing adjudication rules), in reality adjudication plays almost no role at all in the German domestic market.

At the same time, a number of the bigger players in the construction industry and the industrial plant sector use dispute boards as a means of adjudication on international projects.[24]

It remains to be seen whether adjudication will find a place as a preferred means of dispute resolution in the domestic construction industry.

4.1 Institutional adjudication rules

(a) ADR Rules for the Construction Industry

Adjudication under the ADR Rules for the Construction Industry aims to facilitate the swift resolution of disputes. Decisions are temporarily binding on the disputing parties, and can later be revised by arbitration or accord. Section 1 of the ADR Rules

---

23 Paragraph 18(2) VOB/B reads as follows:
1. In case under a contract a dispute arises with authorities the Contractor shall in first place address its issue to the immediately superior authority. The superior authority shall give the contractor the opportunity for an oral exchange of views and shall make a decision thereafter feasibly within two months in written form whereby it should mention the potential consequences according to sentence three of this provision. The decision is to be deemed accepted if the Contractor does not object with the Principal within three months upon receipt of the written decision provided that Principal has indicated the exclusive character of the deadline.
2. With receipt of the written request for conducting a proceeding according to 1 ... the limitation period of all claims submitted is time-barred. In case Principal and Contractor do not want to continue the proceedings, they inform the party accordingly. The time-bar of the claims ends three months after receipt of a written decision or an information according to sentence 2 of this provision.
3. Besides this a proceeding for dispute settlement can be agreed upon by the Parties. The agreement shall be concluded at the time when the contract is concluded.

24 A good example is provided in the publicised clear preferences of Siemens AG (*Hobeck/Mahnken/Koebke, Schiedsgerichtsbarkeit im internationalen Anlagenbau – Ein Auslaufmodell?*, in SchiedsVZ 2007, 225 and following, including excerpts from Siemens's internal dispute resolution circular), as well as Bombardier's declared willingness to consider adjudication as a preferred method of dispute resolution.

for the Construction Industry sets out general provisions which apply to the various ADR methods covered by the rules. The initiation of regular court proceedings or arbitration proceedings is excluded from the date on which the parties enter into an agreement to undertake adjudication until the conclusion of such proceedings (except for legal detention, injunction or independent proof-of-evidence procedures).

The adjudicator is paid on the basis of hourly or daily rates, to be agreed between the parties and the adjudicator. The adjudicator's remuneration and all necessary expenses are borne equally by the parties, unless otherwise agreed. The adjudicator's liability is restricted to cases of intent and gross negligence, except in case of injury to life, body or health.

The ADR Rules for the Construction Industry provide that the parties should agree on who should serve as the adjudicator or adjudicators.[25] They do not specify the appointment procedure where there are to be several adjudicators, but merely provide for a nominating authority in case of non-agreement (the Deutscher Beton- und Bautechnik-Verein eV).

Adjudication proceedings are initiated by one party informing the adjudicator of the dispute and petitioning him to decide the matter. The applicant should deliver an application letter to the respondent within a time frame specified by the adjudicator, who will also set a time frame within which the respondent should provide its response.

The rules afford the adjudicator wide discretion with regard to accessing information. Accordingly, he is permitted to participate in project meetings, inspect documents and visit the construction site. The adjudicator is also entitled to call upon competent third-party experts, subject to the parties' agreement. The adjudicator must discuss the issues and status of the dispute with the parties prior to issuing any adjudication decision.

The adjudicator's decision is to be made "immediately" – which generally means within two weeks of discussing the status of the dispute with the parties (subject to agreed extensions).

The adjudicator will issue a provisional, binding decision, which might variously include payment orders, acceleration measures, a ban on the cessation of works or determinations on the acceptability of completed works.[26] The interim nature of the adjudicator's decision is supported by the fact that a precondition of the decision is that the claim be highly viable according to the status of the dispute and, further, that the benefiting party provide adequate security as instructed by the adjudicator. The security required is determined pursuant to the provisions of the VOB/B,[27] taking into account any disadvantages that a party might suffer if the adjudication decision is subsequently amended (in the course of arbitration or court proceedings).

The adjudication decision should be reasoned and in writing, and should further outline the legal consequences of the decision. A party that has an obligation imposed upon it under the decision may be required to fulfil this within six working days of

---

25 Article 22(1) of the ADR Rules for the Construction Industry.

26 Article 25(2) of the ADR Rules for the Construction Industry.

27 *Ibid.*

notification of the decision. The rules further provide for the possibility of sanctions, in particular financial penalties, should the party fail to fulfil this obligation.[28] Ultimately, the benefiting party should have the right to discontinue the services or terminate the contract, provided that the adjudicator has informed the sanctioned party of the legal consequences of breach at the time of determining the penalty.

The adjudication decision will become final and binding unless one of the parties objects within one month of notification of the decision by filing a written declaration with the adjudicator.

If a party files an objection, the adjudication decision may be reviewed only following either the acceptance of all services, following the final rejection of acceptance or following the conclusion of the service contract between the parties. Otherwise, the adjudicator's decision will become final and legally binding within six months, at the latest, unless an action is filed with an (arbitration) court following the acceptance of all services, the final rejection of acceptance or the conclusion of the service contract.[29]

A loophole may be found in the provisions on the legal validity of an adjudication decision in cases where the acceptance of all services, the final rejection of acceptance or the conclusion of the service contract does not occur within six months of the adjudicator's decision. The practical application of this article is as yet unknown and developments in this regard will be of interest.

Finally, with regard to the statute of limitations, the limitation period is suspended from the time of filing of an application with the adjudicator until conclusion of the proceedings, either by declaration of conclusion by the parties presented to the adjudicator or by a joint written settlement agreement between the parties or an adjudication decision.[30] The limitation period is also suspended from the time of filing of an objection against the adjudicator's decision until the institution of legal proceedings.[31]

(b) *DIS Adjudication Rules*

The DIS describes its DIS Adjudication Rules as 'project-accompanying' – implying that adjudicators should be appointed at the beginning of a project rather than *ad hoc* once a dispute has arisen – and as producing preliminary binding decisions. The DIS recommends including a combined adjudication and arbitration clause in agreements between the parties.[32]

If the parties do not agree on the number of adjudicators, the dispute adjudication board (DAB) shall consist of three adjudicators. Only natural persons may serve as adjudicators. The chairman of a DAB or a sole adjudicator must be a lawyer. The appointment of the sole adjudicator or of two adjudicators of a DAB must be arranged jointly by the parties. In the case of a DAB, the two adjudicators nominated by the parties must agree on the chairman within 30 days, failing which

28 Article 26(2) of the ADR Rules for the Construction Industry.
29 Article 28(2) of the ADR Rules for the Construction Industry.
30 Article 29 of the ADR Rules for the Construction Industry.
31 *Ibid.*
32 See DIS Adjudication Rules, at www.dis-arb.de.

the DIS will, at the request of one party, nominate the chairman of the DAB. The DIS rules require regular meetings between the adjudicators and the parties at six-monthly intervals, unless otherwise agreed.

Each party is entitled to institute adjudication proceedings by making a request to the adjudicator or to the chairman of the DAB, who must inform the parties of the commencement of proceedings without undue delay. The opponent must reply to the request in writing within six weeks of commencement of the proceedings. The applicant may then comment on the reply within three weeks of receipt. The opponent may answer the comment within another three weeks.

An oral hearing will be held if requested by a party; otherwise, it is left to the discretion of the adjudicators to decide whether an oral hearing is necessary. In general, adjudicators have broad discretion in organising the proceedings.

Decisions of the DAB or the sole adjudicator must be issued as quickly as possible – normally within four weeks of the oral hearing or receipt of the last brief, and at the latest five months after commencement of the proceedings, unless both parties have agreed to an extension.[33]

Adjudicators may issue preliminary rulings in some cases.[34]

Decisions of the DAB or the sole adjudicator are binding on the parties. However, this binding effect will cease if they are set aside or altered by decision of a court or an arbitration tribunal. The binding effect of a preliminary ruling also ceases in cases where it is set aside by decision of the adjudicators.

Non-observance of a decision constitutes an intentional and severe breach of contract. With regard to the consequences of this breach, the rules refer to the main contract between the parties. Such a breach of contract persists irrespective of whether the decision is subsequently declared to be justified or unjustified by a court or an arbitration tribunal.[35] In the event that non-observance of a decision leads to a delay in the relevant project, the contractual party which is obligated to perform is in default, even if a court or arbitral tribunal subsequently confirms that the party had a right to refuse performance.[36]

On the other hand, no intentional or severe breach of contract will be assumed if the adjudication suffered from a procedural defect which, in corresponding arbitration proceedings, would lead to the award being set aside.[37] The rules further clarify that any party which carries out, or refrains from carrying out, legal acts in accordance with the decision and in reliance on the binding effect of that decision has no obligation to pay damages to the other party.

If a party wishes to have a decision reviewed in either arbitration or court proceedings, it must notify the other party in writing within one month of receipt of the decision by way of a so-called 'declaration of non-recognition'; otherwise, the decision becomes final and binding.[38] If one party issues a declaration of non-

---

33 Section 17.6 of the DIS Adjudication Rules.
34 Section 20 of the DIS Adjudication Rules.
35 Section 22.2 of the DIS Adjudication Rules.
36 *Ibid.*
37 Section 22.3 of the DIS Adjudication Rules.
38 Section 23.2 of the DIS Adjudication Rules.

recognition, both parties are entitled to file a claim in arbitration or before a court.[39] Section 23.5 of the DIS rules provides that if the binding effect of the decision under Section 23.2 is not observed, the party so entitled may seek performance of the obligation established by the adjudicators through court proceedings, even if an arbitration agreement exists.

The limitation period is suspended for claims which are subject to adjudication from the commencement of adjudication proceedings until six months after the end of the month in which the proceedings are terminated.[40]

Adjudicators are liable only for intentional misconduct.[41]

With regard to costs, the DIS rules provide for a monthly base fee and a variable hourly fee for the adjudicators. Unless otherwise agreed, Appendix 1 ("Table of costs for DIS adjudication proceedings") applies. The table foresees an hourly rate of €300 and a monthly base fee of eight times the hourly rate. The DIS's fees are negligible (€250 for the nomination per adjudicator if this is conducted by the DIS appointing committee).

The adjudication proceedings terminate according to the provisions of the adjudication service agreement or, where the dispute relates to a project based on a contract for work and services, one year after acceptance within the context of the main contract ('provisional acceptance').

The DIS rules also include a model adjudication services agreement at Appendix 2.

5. Outlook

Most disputes in the construction industry are due to (alleged) changes in the scope of the works, delays or issues with the quality of the works or of specific performance, and usually result in monetary claims or remediation. There is limited scope to avoid such disputes in advance. Proper planning before the start of the project can assist in this regard, but is often overlooked due to cost and time constraints – even though this may exacerbate any problems further down the line. Securing a better cash flow for contractors is another option – the German legislature has recently passed new legislation which is intended to improve contractors' position in this regard, thus helping to prevent delays and disruption due to the liquidity problems of contractors.[42]

That said, while these options may reduce the potential for disputes arising, they cannot guarantee a dispute-free project. Therefore, dispute resolution in the construction industry will always be a hot topic.

The choice between one or several of the various dispute resolution methods available will depend on the individual circumstances. Today, multi-tier dispute resolution clauses are most commonly found in larger contracts.

If the dispute concerns isolated technical questions, reference to an expert may suffice; such an expert determination could then be used as evidence in further proceedings, if necessary. Expert determination is regularly used in Germany within

---

39 Section 23.4 of the DIS Adjudication Rules.

40 Section 27 of the DIS Adjudication Rules.

41 Section 29 of the DIS Adjudication Rules.

42 The Act to Combat Delayed Payments in Business Transactions came into force in March 2013. The new law should benefit the construction industry by forcing clients to pay contractors' invoices more quickly.

separate proceedings to preserve evidence as part of the litigation or arbitration process.

While litigation and arbitration remain the ultimate dispute resolution methods, it appears that project-accompanying early settlement procedures are becoming increasingly popular, due to the ever-increasing costs and protracted timescales associated with the established procedures.

Mediation and (contractually agreed) adjudication are thus on the rise, although the introduction of statutory adjudication (as in the United Kingdom) is currently on hold.[43]

The advantages of these ADR methods are clear: the early resolution of minor disputes during the project enables the parties to carry on with their respective obligations without any risk of deadlock arising, and might even allow for adjustments to the project to ensure its success. The potential downside is that recommendations or decisions might not be finally binding and could still become the subject of subsequent litigation or arbitration proceedings.

That said, however, the success rate of ADR – that is, the rate of acceptance, with protracted litigation or arbitration avoided – is extremely high.[44] ADR is thus being promoted increasingly enthusiastically, as is reflected by the introduction of new rules by some institutions, and awareness among players in the construction industry is growing.

While mediation is now taught as a separate subject at a number of German universities and other educational institutions, no such educational initiatives are currently in place for adjudication.[45]

Only time will tell whether the construction industry will embrace the full range of ADR methods outlined in this chapter, to ensure more effective dispute resolution in Germany.

43 Even if the current discussion on whether the introduction of mandatory adjudication is constitutional is resolved, there are other factions (including established arbitrators) which do not supporting this relatively new method of dispute resolution.

44 Reported to be at 90–95%.

45 Programmes are offered by foreign institutions such as the Dispute Resolution Board Foundation (DRBF: www.drb.org) or the Dispute Board Federation (DBF: www.dbfederation.org).

Greece

Ioannis Vassardanis
Alexander Vassardanis & Partners

1. Introduction

The construction sector is one of the most important sectors of the Greek economy. However, since 2009 it has suffered a continual decline, as publicly funded and private projects have ground to a halt and unemployment rates have soared. Data produced by the Association of Greek Contracting Companies demonstrates how the sector's contribution to Greek gross domestic product (GDP) has shrunk over the last decade:[1]

- In 2000–01 the construction sector's contribution to national GDP was significant and on the rise. It reached its highest level in the fourth quarter of 2001, accounting for 9% of GDP.
- A period of stabilisation followed from the first quarter of 2002 to the fourth quarter of 2008. On average, construction accounted for 6.7% of GDP (reaching its highest level of 8.8% in the fourth quarter of 2006).
- This period of stability was followed by a rapid decline. The sector's contribution to GDP shrank from 7% in the fourth quarter of 2008 to 4.1% in the second quarter of 2012.

The construction sector is crucial to the national economy, as it contributes to the country's overall development and maintains strong links with key industries and other sectors (eg, metallurgy, non-metallic minerals, electrical equipment, wood and metal products, transport and the commercial sector).

Despite this decline, however, there are promising signs that the current situation may improve. Construction projects are being restarted and a wave of privatisations has been launched within the context of the austerity plan agreed between the Greek government and the European Union, the European Central Bank and the International Monetary Fund. The construction industry should experience a boost from this wave of privatisations; it is hoped that this will also help to overcome investors' caution.

In this regard, the Ministry of Development has announced that four stalled highway construction projects are due to restart. The aim is to complete the highways by the end of 2015, in order to prevent the loss of EU subsidies and create new jobs. Agreements have been signed with the four contractors – Olympia Odos, Aegean Motorway, Nea Odos and Kentriki Odos. According to these agreements, the

1 www.sate.gr/nea/press/FINAL_7_2012_A.pdf.

contractors will receive a total of €353.3 million in compensation from the state due to town-planning issues, archaeological excavations and other problems. The minister of development has explained that these funds will come from the Public Investment Programme.

According to the minister: "The restarting of the four highways symbolizes the restarting of the Greek economy with the creation of 25,000 new jobs... This is exceptionally positive news, particularly at the current juncture, and constitutes a vote of confidence in the Greek economy."[2]

There are also plans for the privatisation of the Egnatia Motorway, which crosses Northern Greece, extending from the western port of Igoumenitsa to the Greek-Turkish border at Kipoi.

The state is also in the process of evaluating the most appropriate method for exploiting a portfolio of ports, which will subsequently be privatised through a series of transactions. This portfolio comprises 12 ports, incorporated in the form of *sociétés anonymes*: Piraeus, Thessaloniki, Volos, Rafina, Igoumenitsa, Patras, Alexandroupoli, Iraklio, Elefsina, Lavrio, Corfu and Kavala. It also includes several other small ports and marinas.[3]

The privatisation programme also extends to the country's international airport and regional airports. The state is seeking to extend the concession agreement for the Athens International Airport and to transfer part of its shares. There are also plans to privatise 37 airports, including the airport in Thessaloniki – the second-largest Greek city – and those of Rhodes, Corfu, Chania, Kos, Zakynthos, Santorini, Mytilini, Samos and Mykonos, which attract tourists from all over the world.[4]

2. Public and private construction contracts

2.1 Private construction contracts

The execution of private construction contracts is regulated by the Civil Code. A separate chapter of the Civil Code (Articles 681 to 702) is dedicated to contracts for works. Several articles of the Civil Code of the Law of Obligations, which regulate contractual relationships and general principles of contract law, additionally apply to private construction contracts.

Article 681 of the Civil Code provides that: "in a Contract for Works the contractor has the obligation to execute the work and the owner to pay the agreed remuneration." The articles which follow outline the parties' obligations, responsibility for defects, works approval, prescription of claims, payment of remuneration, contract price modification, guarantees and termination of contracts.

The contractor undertakes to execute the work in time and without delay, using with care the materials supplied by the owner. If a contractor fails to complete or delays in completing the work, the owner may withdraw from the contract and/or claim damages.

---

2 www.ekathimerini.com/4dcgi/_w_articles_wsite2_1_12/04/2013_493558.
3 www.hradf.com
4 *Ibid.*

If work defects are identified, the owner may request the contractor to repair them. If a contractor fails to repair the defect, the owner may do so at the contractor's expense, reduce the contractor's remuneration, withdraw from the contract or claim damages.

The contractor is paid upon completion of the work. In cases of destruction or deterioration of the work due to the owner's fault, the contractor may request payment for the work performed, provided that it has informed the owner of possible dangers.

The owner may terminate the contract without providing any reason at any time prior to completion. In case of termination, the contractor is entitled to receive the contract price, reduced by any costs saved due to termination or any other benefit obtained through other work.

In addition to the special provisions of Chapter XIX of the Civil Code on contracts for works, the following provisions of the Civil Code – especially its general principles – apply to construction contracts:

- Articles 173 and 200 on the interpretation of contracts;
- Article 281 on the abuse of rights; and
- Article 288 on the performance of obligations in accordance with good faith and sound business practices.

Moreover, the general provisions of the Civil Code on the law of obligations – which regulate default, remedies for breach of contract, obligations from bilateral contracts, penalties and so on – are also applicable to private construction contracts.

2.2 Public works contracts

The construction of public works is regulated by Law 1418/1984 and Presidential Decree 609/1985. Over the years, these laws have been repeatedly amended and additional laws have entered into force. In 2008, the Public Works Act (3669/2008) codified the various laws, presidential decrees and ministerial decisions, in force since 1984, governing the award and implementation of public works contracts. The Public Works Act implements EU rules on the award of public works contracts and also governs public works contracts without an EU dimension. However, public works contracts that fall within the scope of application of Presidential Decree 59/2007, which transposed the EU Utilities Directive (2004/17/EC) into Greek law, or Law 3978/2011 on public works contracts in the field of defence and security, are exempt from the application of the Public Works Act. Special rules on works concessions are also included in the Law on Public-Private Partnerships (PPPs), which applies in addition to the Public Works Act.

Several state agencies have their own additional regulations governing the award and execution of works contracts, where the value of the contract falls below the thresholds set out in the EU procurement directives.

The Public Works Act is divided into the following chapters:

- Chapter I governs pre-contractual issues and the award procedure.
- Chapter II deals with the works contract (works management, payments, additional works, termination, works delivery, dispute resolution).

- Chapter III concerns contractors and registries.
- Chapter IV regulates the award of works that fall within the scope of European law. Its provisions are in line with EU Directive 2004/18/EC and Presidential Decree 60/2007, which transposed the EU directive into Greek law.
- Chapter V includes special provisions.

As stipulated in Article 1 of the Public Works Act, its provisions apply to all works scheduled and executed by public sector bodies, as defined in Article 14 of Law 2190/1994. These are:

- the Greek state;
- regional and local public authorities;
- legal entities of public or private law which are controlled or financed by the state; and
- public companies.

'Public works' are defined as infrastructure works which contribute to the growth of productive capacity and are generally for the benefit of the nation.

Following publication of a contract notice, the procedures for the award of public works contracts without an EU dimension are as follow:

- open procedure (Article 22) – any interested party may submit tenders;
- restricted procedure (Article 23) – any economic operator may participate but, following a preselection stage, only invited participants may submit tenders; and
- direct award (Article 28) – in specific cases justified by reasons of urgency, the procedure is held between a restricted number of economic operators.

The works contract is drafted in accordance with the terms of the call for tenders and the tender documents and design. Specific articles in Chapter II govern the parties' obligations, project defects, variations, risk insurance, payments, subcontracting, dissolution and termination of the contract.

For any issue not covered by the specific provisions of the Public Works Act, the relevant provisions of the Civil Code apply. Moreover, for the execution of public works that are co-financed by structural funds, Law 3614/2007 and other provisions that aim to simplify and accelerate the contracts' implementation are also applicable.

3. Works concession contracts and public-private partnerships

The lack of a clear and distinct legal framework for the award of works concession contracts has created a degree of uncertainty for stakeholders. The distinction between concession contracts and standard public contracts lies in the concessionaire's right to exploit the works as a means of obtaining payment for their execution. This transfers to the concessionaire an economic risk: the possibility that it may not recoup the investments made and the costs incurred in operating the works. Works concession contracts are not subject to Presidential Decree 60/2007. However, Presidential Decree 60/2007 contains certain provisions which deal with public works concession contracts (Articles 67 to 76, mirroring Articles 56 to 65 of EU Directive 2004/18/EC). In all cases, general EU law principles of equal treatment, non-discrimination and transparency apply to works concession contracts.

Concession contracts for large infrastructure projects are subject to notification requirements and normally – on an *ad hoc* basis and as a matter of parliamentary practice – are ratified by law, which typically includes the concession agreement and sets out the rights and obligations of the contracting parties.

Acknowledging the importance of PPPs to the development of the Greek economy and to the prompt and efficient delivery of necessary infrastructure, the state has developed a well-defined legal framework governing PPPs. The main law in this regard is the PPP Law (3389/2005, subsequently amended by Laws 3483/2006, 3375/2009, 3746/2009, 3840/2010, 3982/2011 and 4013/2011).

The PPP Law defines a 'PPP' as a cooperation contract, with pecuniary interest, between public and private sector entities for the construction of a facility or the provision of services in areas of responsibility of the public sector partners. Under the PPP Law, PPPs can be contractual only, and the law applies only to projects with a budget below €200 million.

Central administrative support and guidance for the implementation of PPPs is provided for public authorities through the establishment of the Inter-ministerial Committee for PPPs and the creation of a Special Secretariat for PPPs (located within the Ministry of Development).

According to the PPP Law, any legal entity that is fully controlled by public authorities can participate as a public sector partner in PPPs. Private sector partners conclude contracts through a special purpose company (ie, a company governed by Greek law and established exclusively for the purpose of a PPP).

The private sector partner is responsible for the execution of the works and assumes the risks associated with financing, construction and availability of necessary infrastructure, against consideration paid by the public entity or end users of the service. The project is financed by the private entity, whether partially or wholly.

Once a PPP project has been approved by the Inter-ministerial Committee for PPPs, the Special Secretariat for PPPs initiates the tender procedure to select the private sector partner. Articles 7 to 16 of the PPP Law set out the basic principles, criteria and tendering procedures for the selection of private sector partners. The advantages of the PPP Law include the following:

- a special tax regime for both public and private sector partners;
- provision for accelerated issuance of necessary administrative permits;
- provision for prompt responses from the archaeological authorities;
- provision for early approval of environmental studies; and
- provision for expropriation and constitution of property rights.

The state is investing a great deal of effort in promoting the PPP project and services delivery scheme, in order to reduce public debt in both the short and long term. The legal framework for PPPs has evolved significantly since the introduction of the PPP Law.

Both before and since the law's introduction, numerous projects have been executed through concession agreements which were also ratified by law. It is considered that both private and state needs can be satisfied through this process, which has proved successful in practice.

4. Dispute resolution methods for construction activities

The dispute resolution methods used in Greece are litigation, arbitration, mediation and a complex mechanism foreseen for major projects/concession agreements.

4.1 Litigation

As far as litigation is concerned, the civil or administrative courts have jurisdiction, depending on the legal nature of the parties to the dispute.

If the parties to the dispute are private legal entities and Greek law is the applicable law, the Civil Code applies and the civil courts have jurisdiction to hear the dispute. Several claims can be raised, including:

- the contractor's right to payment upon completion of the works;
- the contractor's right to payment upon termination of the contract; and
- a party's right to compensation if the contractor is in default.

The time limits for raising the relevant claims vary, depending on the nature of the claim. For example, a contractor's claim for payment is subject to a five-year limitation period, starting from the end of the year in which the claim arose. An employer's claim against a contractor for failure to perform expires after 20 years.

The Code of Civil Procedure sets out the procedure to be followed in such disputes, which relies mostly on briefs and supporting documentation, as well as on oral testimonies. At first instance, this procedure takes place before the justice of the peace or the single-member or multi-member court of first instance. At second instance, the relevant procedures take place before the court of appeal, and any request for cassation is filed with the Supreme Court.

If one of the parties to the dispute is a public sector entity, then the Public Works Act applies. This provides for contract administration and dispute resolution, and the administrative courts have jurisdiction. However, contracts governed by this law are also subject to the Civil Code, and in case of a conflict with the Public Works Act, the latter usually prevails.

According to Article 77 of the Public Works Act, any dispute that arises from a public construction contract is resolved by filing a recourse or an action with the competent court, in accordance with either the Code of Civil Procedure or the Code of Administrative Procedure. The competent court is either the administrative court of appeal or the civil court of appeal in the district where the project is being carried out. If the project is carried out in several districts or areas, the chairman of the Council of State or of the Supreme Court will determine the competent court of appeal.

A specific procedure must take place before filing a recourse or an action with the court of appeal, and in particular before filing a remedy request. The right to file a recourse expires within two months of the date on which the decision on the remedy request is communicated to the person or entity filing the remedy request, or upon the expiration of the three-month time limit specified in the act within which the competent authority must respond to the remedy request.

A request for cassation may be filed against court of appeal decisions, but only for specific reasons clearly stipulated by law and relating to the procedure which the court followed in reaching its decision. If it is deemed likely that enforcement of the decision would cause damage which could not easily be restored, enforcement may be totally or partially suspended at the request of a party.

A party may also submit an application for interim measures pursuant to Law 3886/2010 on judicial protection in public contract procedures. This law governs disputes that arise during the pre-contractual phase for the award of public contracts for the provision of works, supplies and services, if the contract falls within the scope of EU Directives 2004/18/EC and 2004/17/EC, or within the scope of the provisions through which these directives were incorporated into Greek law. It also determines the conditions for annulling a public contract.

All disputes that fall under the scope of this law fall under the jurisdiction of the administrative court of appeal at the place where the registered seat of the appointing authority is located. Decisions cannot be appealed. However, disputes that involve concession agreements for public works or services, contracts that fall under the scope of Directive 2004/17/EC or contracts with a budget that exceeds €15 million including value added tax (VAT) fall under the competence of the Council of State.

4.2 Arbitration

Arbitration is regulated by the Code of Civil Procedure (Articles 867 to 903, codified in Book VII) and the Law on International Commercial Arbitration (2735/1999).

All private law disputes may be submitted to arbitration, provided that the parties to the arbitration agreement may freely dispose of the subject matter of the dispute. However, some disputes are exempt from arbitration, such as matrimonial and personal status matters, and labour disputes. An agreement to submit a dispute to arbitration should be made in writing. The terms of the agreement will need to be interpreted in order to determine whether a dispute falls within its scope.

The parties may agree on the method of appointment of the arbitrators. However, if they have made no such agreement or have referred to no specific arbitration rules, the relevant provisions of the Code of Civil Procedure will apply in domestic arbitrations. The Law on International Commercial Arbitration also contains detailed provisions for the appointment of arbitrators in international commercial arbitrations. Once again, these provisions apply where the parties have not agreed themselves on the method of appointment of the arbitrators.

Unless the agreement specifies otherwise, the arbitrators may rule on their jurisdiction, the validity of their appointment, the validity of the main contract and the validity, scope and interpretation of the arbitration agreement.

A party may request that an arbitral award be set aside under specific circumstances. The domestic courts may review an arbitral award only for the reasons set out in Article 897 of the Code of Civil Procedure, as follows:

- The arbitration agreement is null.
- The arbitral award was issued after the arbitration agreement ceased to have effect.
- The arbitrators were appointed in violation of the arbitration agreement or the law; their appointment was revoked by a party; or they ruled on a dispute even though a challenge had been submitted and granted against them.
- The arbitrators acted beyond the scope of the powers granted to them by the arbitration agreement or by law.
- Article 886(2), Article 891 or Article 892 of the code was breached.
- The award is contrary to the rules of public policy or good morals.
- The award is incomprehensible or contains contradictions.
- There are grounds to review the decision pursuant to Article 544 of the code.

An arbitral award may be set aside pursuant to the Law on International Commercial Arbitration only in the following circumstances:

- The party making the application furnishes proof that:
  - a party to the arbitration agreement referred to in Article 7 was in some way incapacitated;
  - the arbitration agreement is invalid under the governing law or, failing any indication of the governing law, under Greek law;
  - the party making the application was not given proper notice of the appointment of an arbitrator or the arbitral proceedings, or was otherwise unable to present its case;
  - the award deals with a dispute not contemplated by or not falling within the terms of the arbitration agreement, or contains decisions on matters that are not arbitrable. If the decisions on matters that fall within the scope of arbitration can be separated out, only that part of the award containing decisions on matters that are not arbitrable may be set aside; or
  - the composition of the arbitral tribunal or the arbitral procedure did not accord with the agreement of the parties, unless such agreement conflicts with a provision of law from which the parties cannot derogate; or, failing such agreement, did not accord with the law.
- The court seized by an application to set aside shall also decide, by operation of law, whether:
  - the subject matter of the dispute is arbitrable under Greek law; or
  - the award conflicts with international public policy, as defined in Article 33 of the Civil Code.

Arbitration in Greece has been boosted through the enactment of the PPP Law, which provides that any dispute arising from the implementation, interpretation or validity of PPP agreements must be resolved through arbitration (Article 31) – although some academics have raised objections as to the compulsory nature of this clause. The relevant PPP agreement will determine, among other things:

- the method for appointment of the arbitrators;

- the applicable arbitration rules;
- the seat of the arbitral tribunal;
- the arbitrators' fees; and
- the language of the arbitration.

Further, in accordance with the Public Works Act, an arbitration clause may be approved and included in an invitation to tender or in the agreement for performance of a project. Approval of the arbitration clause and the terms of the arbitration will be determined by joint decision of the minister of environment, physical planning and public works, the minister of economics and finance, and the competent minister for each project.

4.3 Mediation

Mediation is gradually being developed in Greece. Specifically, in 2010 Law 3898/2010 was adopted, transposing EU Directive 2008/52/EC on mediation in civil and commercial cases. Law 3898/2010 applies to cross-border disputes and internal mediation processes. It further sets out the guidelines for mediation and determines, among other things, the following:

- the scope of the law;
- the process for submitting a dispute to mediation;
- the organisations with competence to accredit and train mediators;
- the accreditation process;
- the mediation process;
- confidentiality in mediation;
- the effects of mediation on limitation periods; and
- the mediator's fees.

All types of private dispute may be settled by mediation upon the parties' agreement, provided that they may freely dispose of the subject matter of the dispute (Article 2 of Law 3898/2010). An agreement to submit a dispute to mediation may be proved through written documentation or court transcripts.

According to Article 3 of Law 3898/2010, mediation may take place in the following cases:

- The parties agree to mediate before or while a case is pending before the courts.
- The court before which a case is pending invites the parties to attempt mediation in order to settle their dispute.
- The court of another EU country orders the parties to attempt mediation.
- Mediation is compulsory by law.

The mediator will determine the mediation process in consultation with the parties. The parties may terminate the mediation process if they wish. However, if the process leads to a settlement, the mediator will draw up a mediation transcript. Once the mediation process has ended, the mediation transcript will be signed by the mediator, the parties and their lawyers. The mediator can submit the original agreement to the secretariat of the court of first instance in the local jurisdiction where the mediation took place upon the request of one of the parties. Once the agreement has been submitted, it becomes an enforceable title, provided that it contains an enforceable claim.

4.4 Concession agreements

Reference should also be made to the dispute resolution methods provided for in several concession agreements, which mainly relate to the construction of motorways. Concession agreements have been executed in Greece since 1991, when the process for the tender of Sparta Airport was initiated.

As a result of the economic crisis that has beset Greece in recent years, projects relating to the construction of motorways were suspended. However, they now seem to be restarting. To this end, concession agreements have been executed and relevant laws have been drafted. These project agreements relate to:

- the concession agreement for the design, construction, financing, operation, maintenance and exploitation of the Elefsina–Korinthos–Patra–Pyrgos–Tsakona Motorway Project (Law 3621/2007);
- the concession agreement for the design, construction, financing, operation, maintenance and exploitation of the Central Greece Motorway Project (E 65) (Law 3597/2007);
- the concession agreement for the design, construction, financing, operation, maintenance and exploitation of the Korinthos–Tripoli–Kalamata Motorway Project and the Lefktro–Sparti section (Law 3559/2007);
- the concession agreement for the design, construction, financing, operation, maintenance and exploitation of the Ionia Odos Motorway Project from Antirio to Ioannina (Law 3555/2007); and
- the concession agreement for the design, construction, financing, operation, maintenance and exploitation of the Maliakos–Kleidi section of the Patra–Athens–Thessaloniki–Euzoni Motorway (Law 3605/2007).

The relevant laws also include sophisticated dispute resolution methods – identical for each project – which provide for the swift resolution of complex disputes.

From the date on which the concession agreement is signed to the commencement date of the concession, all disputes between the contracting parties regarding the implementation, interpretation or validity of the agreements are resolved by the competent courts in Athens.

After the commencement date of the concession, a compulsory technical dispute resolution procedure is foreseen for all technical disputes between the contracting parties.

Non-technical disputes, and disputes involving the following issues, may be resolved through arbitration:

- the allocation of liability;
- financial issues; and
- the allocation of the cost of proceedings to the parties, in so far as the findings of an adjudication panel for technical disputes are concerned.

The laws all provide that arbitration is unavailable while technical dispute resolution proceedings are ongoing. Technical dispute resolution proceedings are conducted by three experts, who must have the necessary training and experience. These experts constitute a three-member adjudication panel. Two of the experts are appointed by the parties to the dispute, who must then appoint the third expert within a certain period from the appointment of the second expert. If no agreement can be reached within this period, either party to the dispute can request the appointment of the third expert, who shall be appointed by the International Centre of Technical Exports Appraisement of the International Chamber of Commerce (ICC) in Paris. The laws further contain certain provisions on the procedure to be followed, as well as the time limits for each procedural step.

If the adjudication panel decides that the dispute is not a technical one, it will immediately notify the parties so that they may refer it to arbitration. The panel's findings with regard to the technical nature of the dispute are binding on the parties.

If a dispute is not first dealt with under the technical dispute resolution procedure, but is directly referred to arbitration, and one party claims it is a technical dispute, the arbitral tribunal will decide on the nature of the dispute within a specific period from the raising of the claim. Its decision is final and binding. If the arbitral tribunal finds that the dispute is a technical one, the parties will refer it to technical dispute resolution. Following the findings of the technical dispute resolution proceedings, the dispute shall be referred to arbitration.

The arbitration proceedings are governed by the International Chamber of Commerce (ICC) Rules of Arbitration, subject to the variations provided in the specific laws.

The arbitral tribunal is also composed of three arbitrators. Two of the arbitrators are appointed by the parties to the dispute and the third is appointed by the two arbitrators. If the two arbitrators fail to agree on the third arbitrator, the third arbitrator shall be appointed by the International Court of Arbitration of the ICC in Paris.

5. Conclusion

Several methods are used in Greece to resolve disputes in the construction industry: litigation, arbitration, mediation, other specific dispute resolution methods and amicable settlement procedures before state-owned or partly state-owned entities (eg, the Public Power Corporation). The dispute resolution method adopted will often depend on whether the parties are foreign or domestic companies, and whether the projects are private or public.

In Greece, parties mainly resort to litigation and arbitration. As far as litigation is concerned, a reduction in the number of parties submitting applications for interim measures in relation to public tenders and supplies is likely, due to a recent change in legislation. According to Law 4111/2013, a party that submits an application for interim measures must pay a fee corresponding to 1% of the estimated value of the tender, including VAT. This fee cannot exceed €50,000. However, in a recent decision the Council of State held that this provision is unconstitutional. In particular, it ruled that this fee should be paid only by a party whose application for interim measures is rejected.

Regarding mediation, Law 3898/2010 should hopefully further promote mediation as an alternative dispute resolution method. However, in the author's view the enactment of a law alone may be insufficient to change a culture which is not positive towards mediation and inclined more towards binding court decisions and arbitral awards.

Finally, activity in the construction sector may be stimulated following the enactment of Law 3894/2010 (the 'Fast-Track Law') to facilitate licensing for large-scale investments. These investments concern the industrial, energy, tourism, transportation, telecommunications, health services, waste management, high-technology and innovation sectors, and are crucial to the Greek economy. The law should facilitate not only the licensing, but also the implementation of strategic investments, provided that they meet certain conditions and criteria in terms of size and anticipated economic effect.

Ireland

Rory Kirrane
Mason Hayes & Curran

1. Introduction

Ireland has no specialist construction or civil engineering court. Parties to a construction dispute are typically free to choose the manner in which they resolve their dispute. Disputes can be resolved either through litigation or alternative dispute resolution (ADR) methods. Over the past five years Ireland has experienced an evolution in the use of arbitration and other forms of ADR. Conciliation and arbitration are the most common methods of dispute resolution as they are endorsed in contracts involving works funded or part-funded by the state, following revised public works contracts issued in 2007. Most standard forms and bespoke construction contracts provide for some methods of dispute resolution that involve the dispute being referred to an expert in the construction industry. This approach ensures that those dealing with the dispute are conversant with the finer details in dispute. Mediation and expert determination are specified in numerous standard-form contracts. In addition, for payment disputes, adjudication is soon to become mandatory when the Construction Contracts Bill 2010 is enacted.[1]

2. Dispute resolution methods

2.1 Litigation

While parties have a right to bring disputes to the civil courts, most standard-form construction contracts specify some form of ADR, ensuring that construction disputes rarely end up before the courts unless parties avail themselves of the limited instances permitted under the Arbitration Act 2010, which are discussed below.

As Ireland does not have a specialist construction court to hear construction disputes when parties choose to litigate, they do so in the ordinary civil courts. The level of the court is determined by the monetary value of the claim:

- district court – less than or equal to €6,348.69;
- circuit court – greater than €6,348.69 but less than or equal to €38,092.14;
- High Court – greater than €38,092.14; and
- Commercial Court – greater than €1 million (commercial disputes only).

The Courts and Courts Officers Act 2002 contains a provision that will increase the monetary jurisdiction of the district and circuit court up to €20,000 and

1 The bill is due to be enacted in the coming months.

€100,000 respectively; however the relevant provisions of the legislation have yet to be enacted.

The High Court has a separate division, known as the Commercial Court, which can handle disputes in excess of €1 million provided one party to the dispute is a commercial business. This route is a fast-track procedure and cases are typically concluded within six to nine months of starting. Cases that proceed in the High Court can take more than two years to proceed to hearing. The Commercial Court operates on a case management basis and actively encourages the resolution of disputes by mediation. In most cases the managing judge will adjourn proceedings to allow mediation take place. Parties who refuse to pro-actively engage in the mediation process can be penalised by way of costs orders. The Commercial Court has been widely applauded for its efficiency in resolving large-scale commercial disputes. Cases that proceed in the High Court can elect case management but this is a voluntary practice and requires the consent of both parties. Very often in disputes where an arbitration clause exists, the parties will enter a post-dispute submission agreement agreeing not to go to arbitration and to proceed in the Commercial Court instead.

Unfortunately, the efficiencies of the Commercial Court are not replicated in the appellate courts. Ireland has only one civil court of appeal, the Supreme Court, and parties can find themselves waiting two or three years before an appeal hearing is heard. This is a widely criticised aspect of Irish court proceedings and hinders parties proceeding in this manner.

Where there is an issue of EU law, parties can also refer their dispute to the European Court of Justice provided they meet the standing criteria.

(a) Jurisdiction and enforcement

In resolving a construction dispute a court may award damages or issue an order requiring one of the parties to refrain from doing a certain action or requiring specific performance. As Ireland is a member of the European Union, judgments and orders of Irish courts are enforceable in all member states of the European Union, as well as the European Economic Area and Switzerland under the Brussels Regulations (Council Regulation (EC) 44/2001), Brussels Convention (1968) and Lugano Convention (1988). Outside these jurisdictions enforcement will depend on local courts and whether there are any specific bilateral agreements in respect of enforcement of judgments.

Note that alterations to the Brussels Regulations (44/2001/EC) are under consideration following a series of decisions of the European Court of Justice which call into question the basic principle that a defendant is entitled to be sued in its home jurisdiction in the absence of an agreement to the contrary. In *Owusu v Jackson* (C-281/02) the court decided that a member state court on which jurisdiction is conferred by Article 2 of the Brussels Regulation (44/2001/EC) cannot decline jurisdiction on the ground that the court of a non-member state would be a more appropriate forum, even if the jurisdiction of no other member state was in issue, or the proceedings involved no factors connecting the situation with another member state. In the case in question, this resulted in Jamaican defendants being sued in the

English courts in tort by virtue of one of their co-defendants being properly sued in England and Wales, and so conferring jurisdiction on the English courts.

The *Owusu* decision along with the decision in *Gasser v Misat* (C-116/02), otherwise known as the 'Italian Torpedo case', has left uncertainty about what is the most suitable jurisdiction to bring a case involving parties from multiple jurisdictions. Defendants are now capable of bringing an action in member states which may not be the proper jurisdiction. Member states may also have a relatively (and in some instances very) slow legal process, which can effectively stop a dispute being resolved for so long that, even if ultimately successful for the plaintiff, the outcome may be of little practical benefit because of delay. The rules of EU law dictate that if a case is brought in one jurisdiction, it cannot be heard elsewhere until that member state rules on the jurisdiction issue. Until the Brussels Regulations are clarified and recast, the resolution of a preliminary issue of jurisdiction where parties from multiple jurisdictions are involved can be a lengthy and complex process.

2.2 Arbitration

(a) Arbitration clause

The vast majority of construction contracts in Ireland include a referral to arbitration as the final forum of dispute resolution. The following standard building and construction contracts are most frequently used in Ireland. They include an arbitration clause for dispute resolution either as a stand-alone form of dispute resolution or as part of a multi-tiered dispute resolution clause with arbitration as the final means of resolution:

- Engineers Ireland conditions of contract;
- FIDIC contracts;
- Institute of Civil Engineers contract;
- public works contracts (also known as the GCCC contracts);
- Royal Institute of Architects of Ireland (RIAI) (blue, yellow and short forms);
- Construction Industry Federation (CIF) subcontract forms for use with RIAI forms;
- CIF subcontract forms for use with public works contracts; and
- RIAI/Construction Industry Federation/Society of Chartered Surveyors collateral agreement.

(b) Arbitration Act

Arbitration in Ireland is governed by the Arbitration Act 2010 that applies to both domestic and international arbitrations in Ireland. The act is based on the United Nations Commission on International Trade Law (UNCITRAL) Model Law and stipulates that the High Court and circuit court must adjourn court proceedings when an agreement to refer disputes to arbitration or mediation exists. Arbitrations that started before June 8 2010 are governed by the pre-existing Arbitration Acts 1957–1998. These pre-existing acts have separate rules for domestic and non-domestic arbitration.

(c) Arbitration and court interaction

Irish courts are only permitted to intervene in an arbitral reference in limited circumstances. These circumstances are those set out in Article 5 of the UNCITRAL Model Law, and provided the applications are brought within the time period permitted the court may do any of the following:

- deal with applications in relation to jurisdiction under Article 6(3) of the Model Law;
- stay litigation pending arbitration in accordance with Article 8 of the Model Law;
- order an interim measure of protection in relation to an arbitration or an intended arbitration under Article 9 of the Model Law;
- appoint an arbitrator as permitted under Article 11(3)(a)–(b) of the Model Law;
- take necessary measures in the event of failure to act, inability to reach agreement or failure to perform a function under an appointment procedure agreed upon by the parties under Article 11(4) of the Model Law;
- decide on a challenge to an arbitrator under Article 13(3) of the Model Law;
- decide on a mandate to terminate an arbitrator under Article 14(1) of the Model Law;
- recognise and/or enforce an interim measure issued by the arbitral tribunal under Article 17H of the Model Law;
- issue an interim measure in relation to the arbitration proceedings under Article 17J of the Model Law;
- make an award following an application under Article 34 to set aside an arbitral award;
- enforce an award under Article 35 of the Model Law;
- give leave to enforce or enter judgment on foot of an award under section 23(1) of the Arbitration Act 2010;
- enforce pecuniary obligations imposed by an award under section 25 of the Arbitration Act 2010; and
- adjourn any proceedings to allow the dispute be referred to arbitration under section 32 of the Arbitration Act 2010.

In line with the UNCITRAL Model Law, the Arbitration Act 2010 specifies that there can be no appeal from a court's decision on an application to stay litigation pending arbitration. This highlights the legislative preference for the arbitral process where it has been chosen by the parties. The courts will honour such preference.

(d) Arbitration awards and enforcement

Arbitration awards are final, binding and enforceable in the same manner as a judgment or order. Ireland is a signatory to the New York Convention on the Recognition and Enforcement of Foreign Arbitral Awards 1958, ensuring that an arbitration award handed down in Ireland is enforceable in over 144 countries.

(e) ***Arbitration and third-party involvement***

Agreements to refer a dispute to arbitration only apply to the parties to the specific agreement. Circumstances where third parties can be involved in arbitration are extremely limited. There are no statutory restrictions on multi-party arbitration but parties must expressly agree to join the arbitration process. Arbitrators are only permitted to make awards against the original parties to the agreement. However, construction contracts in Ireland sometimes include a joiner provision that permits subcontractors to be included in an arbitral reference between the main contractor and the client. This approach ensures that multiple arbitrations against related parties on similar facts are not conducted, incurring additional cost and delaying resolution of the dispute.

(f) ***Arbitration procedure***

Under the Arbitration Act 2010, parties are free to set the rules and procedures to govern their arbitration. There is a wide range of organisations available in Ireland to assist parties by providing industry-specific rules and procedures for conducting the arbitration process. These include:

- Chartered Institute of Arbitrators of Ireland;
- Dublin International Arbitration Centre (Bar Council);
- Engineers Ireland (formerly the Institute of Engineers of Ireland) (IEI);
- International Centre for Dispute Resolution, a division of the American Arbitration Association;
- International Chamber of Commerce;
- Law Society of Ireland; and
- RIAI.

(g) ***Arbitration and public works forms of contract***

In Ireland, there are 10 different forms of contract for publicly funded works, each of which is appropriate in different circumstances. The public works forms of contract provide for dispute resolution initially by negotiation between the employer's representative (named in the contract) and the contractor. The dispute resolution provisions allow either party to the contract to refer a dispute to conciliation in the first instance, with disputes being finally determined by arbitration.

This multi-tiered dispute resolution process mandated in public works contracts reflects the broad approach adopted in the Irish construction market. The IEI and RIAI standard-form construction contracts have similar multi-tiered dispute resolution clauses that provide for disputes to be referred to conciliation/mediation and eventually arbitration.

Arbitration under public works contracts is governed by a specific set of arbitration rules called the Public Works and Services Arbitration Rules 2008 (AR 1), which form part of the Capital Works Management Framework. These rules can be located on the government's construction procurement website (www.constructionprocurement.gov.ie).

Separately, Ireland is also a signatory to the 1965 Washington Convention, relating to the settlement of investment disputes between states and citizens of other countries.

The Washington Convention created the World Bank's arbitration centre, the International Centre for Settlement of Investment Disputes (or ICSID). Compared with other arbitration institutions, relatively few awards have been rendered under ICSID. However, important infrastructure projects frequently require international financing and investment under public procurement contracts where state bodies are contracting with nationals of other states. Following *Lanco International Inc v The Argentine Republic*, ICSID Case No. ARB/97/6, it has been widely discussed whether disputes relating to large-scale public procurement contracts involving an international investing party, whose state is a signatory to the Washington Convention, might be amenable to arbitration under the Washington Convention. Parties who are able to proceed under the Washington Convention have the added advantage of any award issued by ICSID being self-enforcing once it is registered with ICSID.

2.3 Conciliation

Where a dispute is referred to conciliation under a public works contract, the conciliator's terms of appointment shall be those set out in the works requirements that forms part of the contractual documentation. If there are no terms set out in the contract, the parties will agree terms with the conciliator at the beginning of the process. Disputes not resolved by conciliation can be referred to arbitration. The short form of contract (applying to contracts with a value of less than €500,000) does not provide for a reference to arbitration following conciliation. That contract provides that where a resolution cannot be reached the dispute is at an end and therefore the parties are free to litigate in the civil courts.

If the dispute is not resolved by agreement between the parties during the course of the conciliation, the conciliator will issue a recommendation. If either party rejects the recommendation, they must issue a notice of dissatisfaction within 45 days of the date of the conciliator's recommendation. If neither party issues a notice of dissatisfaction within that time, the recommendation will become final and binding. Where a notice of dissatisfaction is issued by one party and they proceed to arbitration, the conciliator's recommendation will remain binding until ruled upon by the arbitrator.

Parties must comply with any payment provisions contained in the conciliator's recommendation pending determination by an arbitrator. However, in order for a party to secure payment on foot of the recommendation, the paying party must provide a bond as prescribed in the works requirements. Such bonds are difficult to obtain in the current environment and therefore it is extremely difficult to obtain payment pursuant to a conciliator's recommendation. If the recommendation is overturned, the paying party is entitled to repayment of the amount paid plus interest.

(a) Risk assessment

In all public works contract disputes, a risk assessment must be carried out by the public body and any proposed settlement figure or conciliator's recommended settlement figure must be compared with a range, following the assessment, to establish whether a settlement can be justified as offering better value for money than proceeding to arbitration. This risk assessment must also be carried out after an arbitrator's award is handed down. This assessment must evaluate the quantum of the award against the costs of an appeal to the High Court, and whether there is any reasonable prospect of success. The assessment should also take into account the costs of the appeal and the interest on the award which will accrue during the appeal proceedings.

(b) ***Settlement***

Prior to entering into any settlement or accepting a conciliator's recommendation for settlement, approval is required from the relevant government department for any project funded or part-funded with public finances.

2.4 Mediation

The use of mediation has grown significantly in construction disputes despite the fact that it is only formally stipulated under one standard form building contract, the Construction Industry Federation subcontract for use with public works contracts. The form of mediation, however, is very similar to the conciliation process except that there is no recommendation issued where parties fail to agree.

The Irish Law Reform Commission in its "Report on Alternative Dispute Resolution: Mediation and Conciliation" published in 2008, and the draft Mediation and Conciliation Bill appended to it, proposed an express obligation on solicitors to advise their clients of the option of conciliation/mediation prior to starting any proceedings. In March 2012 a general scheme for a Mediation Bill was published by Ireland's minister for justice but as at July 2013 has yet to pass into law. This Mediation Bill expands on current court procedure rules (Rules of Superior Courts Order 56A) which encourage disputing parties involved in litigation to engage in ADR. Any refusal to consider this approach could result in the courts making an adverse costs order against the refusing party.

The Mediation Bill proposes to place a statutory obligation on solicitors and barristers to inform parties to disputes, prior to commencing court proceedings, about the possibility of using mediation as a means of resolving the dispute, and as far as possible to provide an estimate of the legal costs in the event of court proceedings and an estimate of the likely duration of court proceedings.

The Mediation Bill will require parties who proceed to issue proceedings to certify that they have been informed of, and have considered using, mediation as a means of resolving the dispute, and of the potential costs and duration of court proceedings. The Mediation Bill requires that in the event that mediation is refused by one of the parties, the court should consider the following factors in determining whether refusal to consider mediation is unreasonable and whether any cost implications can be determined upon:

- whether the costs of mediation would have been disproportionately high;
- whether any delay in setting up and attending mediation would have been prejudicial to a party; and
- the overall circumstances relating to the proceedings and the conduct of the parties.

In light of the proposed duties to be imposed on solicitors and barristers under the Mediation Bill, it will therefore be imperative that all parties to civil litigation, and their legal advisors, properly consider whether mediation or conciliation is appropriate, or risk facing adverse costs implications for their clients, and possibly themselves, if they do not.

In addition to promoting the use of mediation, the Mediation Bill places mediation on a statutory footing, permitting a government-approved code of practice for the conduct of mediation by qualified mediators to be published. Once enacted, the Mediation Bill will ensure the systemisation of mediation in Ireland which is widely included in multi-tier dispute resolution clauses for standard-form construction contracts.

In addition to the arbitration procedures highlighted above, Engineers Ireland has developed a mediation procedure available free of charge for use in commercial disputes. The procedures are not confined to construction disputes, but they are widely used in assisting in the resolution of such disputes.

2.5 Adjudication

Despite a decline in the level of construction activity in Ireland, there has been a sharp rise in the number of construction disputes. Parties are increasingly looking for quick and cost-effective means of settling their disputes in an effort to free up cash flow. Subcontractors have traditionally refrained from bring actions against the main contractor, but due to tighter budgets and increased financial hardship there has been an increase in the number of subcontractors bringing claims in respect of outstanding payments.

The Construction Contracts Bill 2010 has been introduced to assist in creating cash flow in the construction industry. The bill, when passed, will provide a fast-track adjudication process for the resolution of payment disputes. The process set out in the Construction Contracts Bill provides that either party may issue a notice of dispute at any time during the contract. The party issuing the notice must refer the dispute to adjudication within seven days of issuing the notice. The adjudicator's determination must be made within 28 days of appointment, or longer if the parties agree. A major flaw in the draft legislation is that the adjudicator's decision is not binding if either party refers the dispute to arbitration or other proceedings. This is currently under discussion.

The legislation will apply to all construction contracts whether they are oral or written. Contracts that are not capable of being performed within a year and those relating to the sale of property are required, amongst other types of contract detailed in the Statute of Frauds 1695, to be evidenced in writing. Outside this statutory requirement, any construction contract can be orally agreed between the parties. This can, however, create an evidentiary requirement as to the exact terms of the contract; it can be difficult to prove that the terms included a notice to refer to arbitration or some other ADR method. As currently drafted, the legislation only applies to private construction contracts with a value in excess of €200,000 and public contracts in excess of €50,000. Again this has been widely criticised and is currently under discussion. Contracts relating to residential dwellings are excluded from the legislation unless the value of the contract is in excess of €200,000.

The Construction Contracts Bill prohibits the use of pay-when-paid clauses. These clauses have typically been used in subcontracting arrangements in the construction industry in Ireland and have been a major problem, particularly for subcontractors. The Construction Contracts Bill provides a statutory right to suspend works pending resolution of a dispute, but the Construction Contracts Bill in its current form limits this period of suspension to 14 days. This has been the subject of much criticism and is currently under discussion.

The Construction Contracts Bill as currently drafted does not provide for a proper mechanism for enforcing the decision of the adjudicator in Ireland. Accordingly, the only way of enforcing a decision will be to go to the High Court or circuit court, which is a long and expensive process. A proper enforcement mechanism, preferably by way of a dedicated construction court list, is essential if this legislation is to achieve its stated aims of ensuring timely payment in construction contracts and introducing a mechanism for the swift resolution of disputes.

At present, Ireland has no rules surrounding the use of adjudication or the adjudication process as a means of dispute resolution. Adjudication is, however, used on a contractual basis and some National Road Authority contracts include a multi-tiered dispute resolution clause that provides for disputes to be referred to adjudication and arbitration on an escalated dispute resolution procedure.

2.6 Expert determination

While expert determination is not regulated in Ireland by legislation, parties are free to appoint an expert to determine a matter of fact, valuation or law, in a final and binding manner. If the agreement does not stipulate that the expert's determination is to be binding, the decision will be merely advisory. This process is known as 'expert evaluation'. Experts are not permitted to rule on their own jurisdiction and have no authority to summon a witness or state a case on a point of law to the High Court.

Where an expert's decision is stated as being final and binding on the parties, the dispute resolution clause contained in the contract should also provide for a time frame following the determination by the expert within which one party, if it wishes to, must formally reject, in writing, the determination. If there is no rejection within this time frame then the determination will be final and binding on the parties. If there is a rejection of the determination then the parties may wish to refer the matter to arbitration or litigation. Parties may also specify in an expert determination clause the time frame for the expert to make a determination.

Where experts have acted fairly and within the scope of their jurisdictions, it is difficult to get the Irish courts to overrule the determination. Case law has suggested that even where experts have answered the right question the wrong way, their decision will still be binding and the court will not overrule the determination. Despite the lack of legislation governing the use of expert determination, Irish courts are unwilling to overturn an expert determination unless there is evidence of fraud or collusion or the expert has acted beyond his powers.

Parties should be mindful when drafting an expert determination clause in a contract to ensure that it is not so wide as to oust the jurisdiction of the courts. This will be discussed further below.

There is no international convention for the recognition or enforcement of expert decisions abroad, so they may not be particularly appropriate for international contracts.

2.7 Dispute boards

The FIDIC contracts provide for preliminary adjudication of disputes by dispute boards. While FIDIC contracts are widely used in Ireland for large-scale construction projects, the standard clause providing for adjudication of disputes by reference to a dispute board is frequently amended by contractors where they wish to choose their own dispute resolution procedures. The dispute board approach has nonetheless been adopted on a number of Irish projects including the building of Dublin's Light Rail System, the Luas.

Dispute boards conducted in Ireland are typically run in accordance with the ICC dispute board procedures but largely depend on the drafting of the dispute resolution clause. The clause should stipulate the constitution of the board and whether the board can make a temporarily binding determination similar to that of an adjudicator or merely make a recommendation that the parties are free to reject pending final resolution of the dispute.

The FIDIC Orange Book form of contract used in public water projects by the Department of Environment has recently been amended to remove reference to dispute boards in favour of conciliation, in line with the standard dispute resolution clauses contained in public works contracts.

3. Costs

In relation to costs, the standard rule typically applies to court and arbitration procedures, that costs follow the event. Most ADR forums such as conciliation, mediation and adjudication require each party to bear their own costs irrespective of the outcome of the dispute.

It should, however, be noted that in September 2011 the public works contracts were amended so that each party to a contract, funded or part funded by the government, is now required to cover its own costs for any arbitration entered into, save for circumstances where a sealed offer is submitted and the contractor does not exceed it in any ultimate arbitration award. In such circumstances the contractor will be liable for both parties' costs: however, if the contractor beats the offer it is still not permitted to recoup its costs. This amendment is seen as excessively harsh on contractors in the Irish construction industry as it deprives the arbitration process of any value from the contractor's perspective.

4. Limitations of dispute resolution methods

Parties are free to agree among themselves the method of dispute resolution they wish to use. While there are no laws prohibiting any specific dispute resolution methods in Ireland, there are some limitations to parties' freedom when choosing an ADR method.

Projects that are funded or part-funded by public finances are subject to the public works contracts dispute resolution clauses and ancillary procedures. Outside of this, parties to construction and building contracts are free to choose any method of dispute resolution provided they do not offend public policy. When drafting a dispute resolution clause, parties should be mindful not to expel the jurisdiction of the courts to hear disputes as they run the risk of having their dispute clause rendered invalid on grounds of public policy.

When drafting an expert determination clause, parties should ensure that the provision is not drafted so widely that it will apply to all and any dispute with final and binding effect. While there is no case on this point in Ireland a recent English Court of Appeal case and two English High Court decisions can be used as a guide when drafting an expert determination clause. Generally, courts will not intervene in matters which fall within an expert's jurisdiction, but when a question of law is at issue and the clause is drafted so that the determination is final and binding, the expert's decision could be challenged for being outside his mandate and ousting the jurisdiction of the court. Careful contract drafting is recommended to ensure that the expert determination clause is not too wide.

While parties are free to choose their own method of dispute resolution, it is necessary to be wary if any party wants to pick a faith-based body of law such as Sharia law or ancient Brehon law to resolve legal disputes. Ireland does not have any laws or authority that prevents the use of Sharia law for solving construction disputes but a number of English cases have examined the issue and these cases would be viewed as favourable precedents if the issue came before an Irish court. When choosing a body of law to govern a dispute resolution procedure in construction contracts, the parties should focus on choosing a regulated body of law that will not fall foul of the Irish courts' rules on certainty and upholding public policy.

5. Conclusion

The removal of dispute boards from the FIDIC Orange Book form of contract used in public water projects by the Department of Environment appears not to have been particularly successful in encouraging early resolution of disputes. Particular advantages of dispute boards include speed, cost, binding nature until overturned, and the ability to refer to the decision in any subsequent arbitration. Conciliator's recommendations on the other hand have no effect if rejected.

While the Irish construction market has suffered a dramatic decrease in activity levels following the 2008 economic crash, investment in wind farm development has helped to maintain some level of construction activity in the country. Ireland is on track to meet its 2020 EU renewable-energy requirements and has recently signed a memorandum of understanding to export wind-generated energy to the United Kingdom. This will see the construction of more than 700 wind turbines on around 40 different clusters of wind farms across Ireland. The FIDIC design-and-build (Yellow Book) form of contract is consistently used on wind farm projects in Ireland. Parties appear to favour an amended dispute resolution provision where disputes that are not capable of settlement amicably are referred to mediation and ultimately arbitration.

Italy

Giuseppe Broccoli
BDA – Studio Legale

1. General overview

Compared with other EU countries, Italy has some gaps in its infrastructure which can cause delays and create higher costs for energy, transport and supplies. Furthermore, according to the ANCE (the Italian Association of Contractors) investment in the construction industry decreased by 30% between 2008 and 2013. Investment in the non-residential sector dropped by 31.6% and in infrastructure by around 42.9%.

The ANCE has suggested various solutions to attempt to lessen the effects of these shortcomings as quickly as possible, in order to try to reduce the gap between Italy and the other EU member states. Some of those solutions relate to:

- timing of payments from public authorities;
- insolvency procedures and making available alternatives to insolvency to companies in financial stress; and
- the financial support available to the industry.

At the same time, the National Strategy on Energy (recently approved by the Italian government) has set out some objectives and targets in respect of energy efficiency. It has also made proposals on the following:

- developing gas production (with suggestions for improving Italy's place as a European hub for gas distribution);
- developing renewable energy;
- restructuring the oil-refining industry; and
- achieving sustainable production of energy from Italian fossil sources.

The Italian judicial system does not provide for dedicated special courts for construction disputes. The complexity of construction disputes means that the courts sometimes struggle in terms of relevant industry expertise – or, at least, whereas it may be relatively easy to find judges experienced in civil works and residential construction issues, it can be more difficult to bring disputes on more technical matters in respect of industrial or power-producing plants.

There is no widespread take-up of internationally recognised standard contracts (such as FIDIC, ICC, LOGIC and the like) in Italy, even though the Italian market can be seen to have become increasingly sophisticated in recent years, especially when lenders with international exposure are involved in projects. It is common for parties, even including small power-producing plants (eg renewable power plants), to make use of available well-structured contracts based on international standards, even where the contracts are in fact entirely subject to Italian law.

This absence of specialised courts, in addition to the unfortunate well-known tardiness of the judicial system in Italy, makes the availability of alternative dispute resolution methods crucial to the construction industry. Construction disputes are indeed rarely brought before the state courts.

Under Italian law there are basically four alternative dispute resolution instruments:

- arbitration;
- mediation;
- *arbitraggio*; and
- *perizia contrattuale.*

Another could be added – 'non-judicial settlement' (*arbitrato irrituale*). Dispute boards are not used at present in Italy unlike in other jurisdictions.

The use of arbitration in Italy has increased in the last 15 years or so, with this trend certainly fuelled by the slowness of civil proceedings in the state courts. Italian culture is therefore improving in relation to its uptake of alternative dispute resolution methods, albeit at present they are limited mainly to arbitration and, very recently, mediation.

The 2006 Italian arbitration law and, more importantly, the current level of sophistication and professionalism of certain Italian arbitral institutions make Italy an attractive seat for arbitration.

According to a highly regarded authority,[1] the use of alternative dispute resolution methods in Italy can be divided into three main categories:

- where the parties themselves reach a settlement of their dispute without the intervention of an independent third party: mainly by non-judicial settlement and waiver (of the claim);
- where the parties settle their dispute through the intervention of an independent third party: mainly via arbitration and mediation; and
- where there is no actual dispute between the parties but a conflict of interest exists: *arbitraggio* and *perizia contrattuale.*

The most common dispute resolution method in the Italian construction industry is arbitration. According to a report by the Chamber of Arbitration of Milan[2] in the period between 2007 and 2011, approximately 18% of the arbitration proceedings administered by the chamber were construction-related.

Compulsory arbitration or conciliation is included in certain specific contracts (such as the so-called *subfornitura*, a particular kind of construction contract) and voluntary ADR is possible in public works' contracts.

This chapter describes the general system of arbitration law and practice in Italy with reference to private construction works, and highlights issues relevant to public

1 Rubino Sammartano, *Il diritto dell'arbitrato*, I, p4.
2 The report can be found at www.camera-arbitrale.it/Documenti/arbitration_stat_2006-2011_it.pdf.

works where special legal provision exists. We then go on to consider other alternative dispute resolution mechanisms recognised and used in Italy.

2. Dispute resolution methods

2.1 Arbitration

Italian arbitration legislation has changed significantly since 2006 when the state saw reforms to make Italy more attractive as a seat of arbitration both for national disputes and in cases where one of the parties is a foreign entity. The current system is certainly closer to the standard set by the international principles contained in the UNCITRAL Model Law, albeit that many believe the Italian legislature could have gone further towards improving the system.[3] In any case, there is no longer any distinction between domestic and international arbitration, and it would seem that the Civil Procedure Code also applies to public-private partnerships (PPPs) unless specific rules in the Code for Public Contracts apply.

Another main feature of the reform is that arbitral awards are now binding on the parties and have the same effect and force as decisions of the state court: in other words, arbitration now has the same weight as judicial proceedings in Italy. This also has the effect of differentiating arbitration from the other dispute resolution methods based on negotiated settlement[4] – in line with other jurisdictions.

Arbitration proceedings with seats in Italy are governed by Articles 806 to 840 of the Civil Procedural Code, which grant significant autonomy to the parties and apply where the parties have not agreed that any other rules will govern the arbitration proceedings. The underlining principle is that it is up to the parties to decide how the arbitration ought to be conducted, as long as this complies with public-policy and due-process[5] rules. If the parties have not agreed on the rules of arbitration, the arbitrators will decide on the procedural matters. The process can also be governed by arbitration rules established by an arbitrational institution – again, as long as these comply with the rules of public policy and due process (Article 832, Civil Procedure Code).

As the provisions on arbitration in the Civil Procedure Code do not regulate all aspects of the arbitral process (as is common in many jurisdiction where the mandatory rules on arbitration are rather broad), the tendency in Italy is to refer to the Civil Procedure Code governing ordinary court proceedings. In Italy, domestic arbitration also tends to follow the structure of court proceedings, sharing almost all of the stages and formalities.[6] In fact, even when the parties or arbitrators have established specific provisions for the arbitration (in *ad hoc* arbitration) they rarely provide for rules that differ substantially from the Civil Procedure Code. This is

---

3 Bernardini, *L'arbitrato nel commercio e negli investimenti internazionali*, p3.

4 Redfern and Hunter, *International Arbitration*, 1.75, p27.

5 The principle of 'due process', also known as the principle of equal treatment, as accepted in Italy, is not really different from what is well established in Article 18 of the UNCITRAL Model law on Commercial Arbitration ("The parties shall be treated with equality and must be given full opportunity to present their case").

6 Rubino-Sammartano, *L'appalto di opera e contratti di servizi*, p791.

referred to as the 'judicialisation'[7] of arbitration – a risk that may also arise in the international context.[8]

Another distinction recognised by the Italian system is between *ad hoc* arbitration and institutional arbitration. In Italy there are well-known and professional arbitration institutions of high international standing, including the Milan National and International Chamber of Arbitration[9] and the Italian Arbitration Association (AIA),[10] whose rules are much more detailed than those of the Civil Procedure Code.

(a) Arbitration agreements

The arbitration agreement must be in writing – in the case of both arbitration clauses and submission agreements.

The Civil Procedure Code sets out only the broad, non-specific rule that the parties should come to some agreement either by reference to institutional rules or independently by themselves. In *ad hoc* arbitrations, parties should include terms determining the following issues (among others):

- the seat of arbitration;
- jurisdictional powers of the arbitrators;
- rules for the appointment of arbitrators and any necessary qualifications;
- how costs should be allocated; and
- provisions on confidentiality.

The well-known principle of autonomy of the arbitration clause seen in the UNCITRAL Model Law[11] (and also known also as 'separability') is also recognised in Italy. Any agreement to arbitrate is autonomous and independent of any underlying contract, the enforceability and validity of which will not affect the validity of the arbitration clause.

The 2006 Italian arbitration reform could certainly have gone further with regard to the provisions on multi-party arbitration proceedings. The Civil Procedure Code provides that all parties must agree on the appointment of the arbitrators. Each party may start proceedings against one or more of the other parties bound by the arbitration agreement.

(b) The arbitral tribunal

The agreement to arbitrate should contain a term providing for the manner of appointing the arbitrators. The arbitral panel will be composed of three members unless the parties agree on a different number. Under Italian law, the number of arbitrators must be uneven.

The first party appoints its choice of arbitrator and invites the other party to do the same. If the latter party fails to appoint an arbitrator, the selection is made, upon

7 By 'judicialisation' we mean that, despite the less formal and more flexible process in arbitration proceedings, arbitration tends still to be conducted with the procedural formality typical of litigation in the national courts.

8 See Redfern and Hunter, *International Arbitration*, 1.115, p40.

9 www.camera-arbitrale.it/index.php?lng_id=14.

10 www.arbitratoaia.org/?page_id=291&lang=en.

11 Article 16 of the UNCITRAL Model Law on International Commercial Law.

the request of the first party, by the president of the tribunal of the place of arbitration. Where the parties have failed to designate that place of arbitration, the tribunal of the place where the arbitration agreement was entered into will select the arbitrators. If the arbitration agreement was entered into outside Italy, the president of the Tribunal of Rome has competence to appoint the arbitrators.

Any person with legal capacity may be appointed as arbitrator, and it is now possible to appoint an arbitrator whose nationality is not Italian. Apart from a general duty to act impartially, the Civil Procedure Code does not prescribe any other specific duty that an arbitrator must comply with nor any obligation to disclose conflicts of interest. However, some rules are imposed on arbitrators either by their professional body (if they belongs to such a body), or by the rules of the institutional arbitration bodies. The IBA Rules on Conflict of Interests, for example, are followed by the National and International Arbitration Chamber of Milan but are not commonly used in domestic arbitrations where the arbitrators and counsel do not have international experience.

The Civil Procedure Code provides for specific circumstances in which an arbitrator may be challenged, broadly where:

- the arbitrator fails to meet the requirements agreed upon by the parties;
- the arbitrator (or a company of which he is a director) has an interest in the dispute;
- there is a parental relationship between the arbitrator and a party or an authorised officer of a party or its lawyers;
- the arbitrator has a pending litigation or serious dispute with one of the parties, or its authorised officer or one of its lawyers;
- the arbitrator is employed by or regularly advises one of the parties, the person or body that controls it, or a company controlled by it; or is in another relationship that affects his independence; or
- the arbitrator has given advice or assistance to one of the parties in a previous stage of the dispute or has been a witness in those proceedings.

Any arbitrator who fails to act or delays undertaking any act he should perform under the appointment may be revoked by the parties or by decree of the president of the state court upon request of one of the parties. Any arbitrator is also generally liable for wilful misconduct and/or gross negligence.

The principle of *Kompetenz-Kompetenz*, as spelled out in the 1961 Geneva Convention[12] and in the UNCITRAL Model Law,[13] is also applied in Italy. This has two main aspects:

- The arbitral tribunal has power only to decide on its own competence and on the existence and validity of the agreement to arbitrate.
- If, despite the presence of an arbitration clause, one of the parties initiates a

12 Article V(3) of the Geneva Convention 1961: "Subject to any subsequent judicial control provided for under the *lex fori*, the arbitrator whose jurisdiction is called in question shall be entitled to proceed with the arbitration, to rule on his own jurisdiction and to decide upon the existence or the validity of the arbitration agreement or of the contract of which the agreement forms part."

13 Article 16 of the UNCITRAL Model Law on International Commercial Law.

legal action before a state court, the other party is entitled to raise an objection for lack of competence of the court as a first reaction in defence. Failure to raise a timely objection would be deemed an acceptance of the state court jurisdiction and deemed a waiver of the arbitration clause.

(c) *Arbitral proceedings*

Under Italian law, parties have freedom to select the place of arbitration and the language of the proceedings.

Under the Civil Procedure Code, the arbitration commences upon serving a request for arbitration to the other party. The request for arbitration contains the names of the party-designated arbitrators and a brief description of the dispute. The request must also contain: a statement of intent to start the arbitration (because the request for arbitration will suspend any applicable limitation period under the Civil Procedure Code); sufficient details in respect of the subject of the dispute; and the relief claimed. The arbitral proceeding will be considered to have started as of the date of acceptance of the appointment of all the arbitrators. The rules of arbitration institutions provide details about what the minimum content of the request for arbitration and the time frame for the response should be.

While the Civil Procedure Code does not set out specific rules to be followed in the proceedings, it is more or less standard to have a first hearing following the setting-up of the arbitral tribunal, during which the arbitrators formally accept their appointment. During the same hearing the arbitral tribunal usually rules on the timing of the exchange of the various pleadings. The proceedings generally end with a final hearing.

(d) *Evidence*

Italy has a civil law system which recognises the central role of a judge and his powers, especially in connection with the taking of evidence.

In general terms, the principles regulating evidence in arbitration are the same as those provided for in state court proceedings, and in particular they try to safeguard:

- that due process is fully respected; and
- that proof can be made available to the parties (which basically means that the arbitrators are bound to limit the taking of evidence to the evidence offered by the parties).

That said, the principle of availability of proof may be derogated from by the parties themselves, in line with the rules of the main arbitration institutions.[14]

The arbitral tribunals have some limited powers of inquiry, such as the power to order:

---

14 Under Article 25 of the Italian National and International Chamber of Arbitration of Milan Rules: "The Arbitral Tribunal leads the case by taking all the evidence deemed relevant and admissible. (2) The Arbitral Tribunal shall freely evaluate all evidence, with the exception of that which constitutes legal proof under mandatory provisions applicable to the proceedings or to the merits of the dispute." Under Article 26(1) of the AIA Rules: "The arbitral tribunal, *ex officio* or upon request of the parties, may ... take any evidence."

- site access and inspections;
- a request for information to public bodies in relation to their acts and documents if these need to be considered in the arbitral proceedings;
- the exhibition of documents where there is clear proof that they exist and are relevant; and
- the appointment of technical experts.

In respect of witnesses of fact, the Italian legal system (as with many civil law jurisdictions) tends to give greater weight to witnesses as opposed to written documents. The provisions relating to examination of witnesses (which, however, can be derogated from by the parties) therefore derives directly from that approach, with the Civil Procedure Code providing that a witness must be examined only by specific questions. The concept that a witness 'pertains' to a party and can therefore be freely examined by the counsel of the party itself is alien to the Italian legal system.[15] This is one of the main reasons why in purely domestic arbitration proceedings cross-examination is rare and witness examination is led by the arbitrators. It is standard practice for the arbitrator who questions a witness to allow counsel (as a sort of concession)[16] to ask some questions of that witness also. The Civil Procedure Code provides that any person who has an interest in the dispute which could enable him to take part in the proceeding cannot be a witness. It follows that the parties themselves cannot be examined as witnesses.

The Civil Procedure Code introduced the possibility of receiving written replies from witnesses to specific questions (replicating some provisions in respect of state court proceedings). This is not really quite the same as the procedure on witness statements used in international arbitrations, but it could be considered as an improvement in Italian arbitration practice.

The arbitrators do not have powers to summon any witness who fails to attend or appear to be examined; but the arbitrators may, after evaluating all the circumstances and if they believe it is appropriate, apply to the court to obtain an injunction to order a witness to appear.

(e) Interim measures

Despite the reasonably clear provisions of Article 818 which prevent arbitrators from granting interim measures, this is still a grey area. Article 818 provides that the arbitral tribunal cannot grant "seizure orders and any other precautionary measures". This derives from the Italian legislator's historical preference for litigation over arbitration.

There are precautionary measures which affect third parties and which therefore could cause prejudice to third parties that are not involved in the arbitration. But there are also precautionary measures which are directed only to one of the parties of the arbitration and there would be no reason to prohibit the granting of precautionary measures against them. The fact that the arbitrators do not have

15 Rubino Sammartano, *Il diritto dell'arbitrato*, p845.
16 *Ibid.* p846.

enforcement powers will certainly jeopardise (some) precautionary measures eventually granted by the arbitrators. An additional distinction has then to be made in respect of precautionary measures which require by their nature enforcement, or at least a judicial modification of the *status quo*. Having said that, we tend to agree with the authority[17] which holds that the arbitrators are entitled to grant all precautionary measures addressed to one of the parties if they can be voluntarily complied with, or those measures which do not imply in themselves any judicial modification of the *status quo*. Failure to comply voluntarily with measures adopted by the arbitrators can be sanctioned with monetary fines, and this is indeed exactly the approach adopted by most Italian arbitral institutions.[18]

We agree with those authorities[19] who suggest that the Italian legislator should have provided arbitrators with the power to grant interim measures, as happens in many other jurisdictions and is provided for in the UNCITRAL Model Law. Also, adopting the provision in the Model Law on security for interim measures would limit any potential negative impact. The Civil Procedure Code could perhaps have included provision for a second level of control to be carried out by the state courts – possibly similar to the provisions contained in the Model Law.

(f) *Awards*

The Civil Procedure Code provides that an award must be rendered by arbitrators within 240 days of their accepting appointment, unless the parties have agreed differently. That term may be extended by agreement between the parties or upon request to the president of a competent state court if supported by good reasons. The term may also be extended (but for no more than 180 days) in the following cases:

- where there are specific needs in respect of the taking of evidence;
- where an expert witness is appointed by the arbitral tribunal;
- where a partial award is rendered; or
- where the composition of the arbitral tribunal needs to be challenged.

The award must be rendered following a majority decision of the arbitrators and will be valid even if signed by only a majority, provided that it is specified that all the arbitrators took part in the decision-making process and that the missing signature is from an arbitrator who has not been able to sign or dissent.

The award must be rendered in writing and must contain certain minimum details such as:

- the names of the arbitrators;
- reference to the seat of the proceeding;
- reference to the parties;
- reference to the arbitration agreement and the parties' requests for relief;
- a brief statement of the decision;

---

17 Rubino Sammartano, *Il diritto dell'arbitrato*, pp791, and following.

18 Italian National and International Chamber of Arbitration of Milan Rules and AIA Rules.

19 Bernardini, *L'arbitrato nel commercio e negli investimenti internazionali*, p72, who believes also that the lack of such power on the arbitrators will cause some problems in attracting international arbitration proceedings to Italy.

- relevant decisions; and
- the date of signature.

The arbitral tribunal can make:

- partial awards (when deciding only partly on the merits of the dispute);
- interim awards (when deciding preliminary matters but not the merits); and
- final awards.

An award by consent is not excluded by law and is therefore possible. The rules of the AIA expressly provide that the parties are entitled to apply to the arbitral tribunal for an award based on their own agreement.

The enforcement of a domestic award is made through a court proceeding. The party must file the award and the arbitration agreement with the competent court, which will simply check that the award is correct as to formalities (not looking at the merits of the dispute). The court will either recognise or refuse enforceability by issuing a decree which can be challenged by application to the Court of Appeal.

(g) Correction and challenge of awards

The Civil Procedure Code provides that the award may be amended by the arbitrators and upon the request of one of the parties but only in respect of omissions, errors or miscalculations.

In addition to this, the award can be:

- set aside;
- revoked; and/or
- challenged by a third party.

Challenging the award on the basis that it violates any substantive law applicable to the case is clearly excluded (unless this was expressly agreed to by the parties or by law).

The Civil Procedure Code provides for specific causes which allow the setting-aside of the award, including the following:

- The arbitration agreement is invalid (a party is entitled to set aside the award only if the invalidity issue was raised in a timely manner during the arbitration proceedings).
- The arbitrators were not properly appointed (this objection must also be raised in a timely fashion during the arbitration).
- The award was rendered by a person who has no legal capacity and therefore should have not been appointed as arbitrator.
- The award exceeds the limit set by the arbitration agreement (and this objection must also be raised in a timely fashion during the arbitration).
- The final award fails to decide the merits of the case, which the arbitrators should have decided.
- The award lacks details of the reasons for the decision or is missing the signature of the majority of the arbitrators.
- The award is rendered after the expiry of the prescribed time limit (as long as

that objection was notified before the award).

- The formalities requested by the parties under penalty of nullity were not observed and the nullity was not cured.
- The award is contrary to a previous award or judgment which has the force of *res judicata* between the parties, provided that such award or judgment was on the record of the arbitration proceedings.
- The principle of due process has been violated.
- The award contains contradictory provisions.
- The award fails to decide any of the issues submitted to arbitration.

Set-aside proceedings are brought before the Court of Appeal which, if it proceeds to set aside the award, has powers to decide the merits of disputes in limited cases (in particular the situations described in the last seven bullet points above) – provided that, if the arbitration is a purely domestic arbitration, the parties have not agreed otherwise, or, if one of the parties is domiciled or has its registered headquarters abroad, the parties have expressly agreed to obtain from the Court of Appeal a decision on the merits. If the Court of Appeal does not have competence (because of the terms of the parties' express agreement), a new arbitral tribunal can decide on the merits.

The revocation of an award is generally possible in the following cases:

- where there has been a finding of fraud (committed by the parties and/or by the arbitrators);
- when the award has been made on the basis of evidence found later to have been false; or
- where additional evidence is discovered after the award was made.

The revocation action must be submitted to the Court of Appeal within 30 days of the discovery of the fraud (or of the judicial decision ascertaining the fraud) or of the discovery of decisive proof.

The award is subject to third-party challenge only in cases where the award itself has affected third-party rights or if the award has been the result of fraud or collusion between the parties, and the third party (being a successor to or a creditor of one of the parties) is prejudiced.

(h) *Enforcement of foreign award*

A foreign award can be enforced in Italy following a procedure instigated before the competent appeal court. The appeal court will only check the formalities of the award (not the merits) and will make a ruling on the enforceability of the award as long as the award does not conflict with public policy rules and the subject matter was arbitrable under Italian law.

Italy has been a contracting state of the 1958 New York Convention since 1969 (Law 62/1968). The Civil Procedure Code has almost exactly replicated the provisions of Article V of the 1958 New York Convention, giving the grounds for the Italian courts to refuse to recognise or enforce a foreign award.

2.2 Mediation

The statement that "agreements resulting from mediation are more likely to be complied with voluntarily and are more likely to preserve an amicable and sustainable relationship between the parties"[20] would seem to be correct.

Italy has implemented Directive 2008/52/EC of the European Parliament of 21 May 2008 on Certain Aspects of Mediation in Civil and Commercial Matters via Legislative Decree 28 of 2010. However, in a recent decision the Italian Constitutional Court has declared the decree partially invalid.

The kind of mediation set out in the decree (in compliance with the Directive) is the procedure pursuant to which the mediator aims to facilitate agreement between the parties. The mediation is carried out by an independent third party who assists the parties in settling their dispute or, where no settlement is reached or where the parties have expressly requested this, in proposing a settlement.

Unfortunately, the chance was missed, in implementing the EC Directive, to make changes to ensure Italy enjoyed a really effective alternative dispute resolution scheme. In addition, despite the decree initially providing for mandatory mediation before the instigation of any other kind of proceeding (either in court or in arbitration), the Constitutional Court has ruled that provision was enacted in violation of the law, so mediation is no longer compulsory.

As a result of that decision of the Constitutional Court, the current decree provides that if the parties have agreed to carry out mediation prior to any legal proceeding or arbitration but the mediation is not actually carried out (or is still in process), the judge or the arbitral tribunal can suspend the legal proceeding or the arbitration until the mediation is completed. And any pending mediation procedure will not prevent the parties from applying to the court to obtain interim measures.

The decree also provides that the mediation procedure can last for up to four months (maximum). It is instigated by a written request, which must specify the specific mediation institutions that will administer the procedure, the parties, and a description of the dispute. Those mediation institutions can be only those enrolled in a special register kept by the minister of justice.

One of the most significant provisions of the Italian decree is that which expressly provides that if the parties have reached a settlement agreement (either on their own or by signing the mediator's proposal), then that agreement must be incorporated in a set of minutes to be ratified by the competent court (which will check only the formalities of the agreement and make sure it is not contrary to public policy). On receiving such court ratification, the minutes then entitle the party to enforce the agreement.

Italy's mediation law represents a positive development and should prove to be an effective ADR instrument (albeit that the system could have been improved still further had mediation been made compulsory). That said, a settlement reached by parties through the support of (or proposed by) an independent third party can be actually more meaningful than a simple amicable settlement.

---

20 Directive 2008/52/EC of the European Parliament of 21 May 2008 on Certain Aspects of Mediation in Civil and Commercial Matters.

2.3 ***Arbitrato irrituale***

The Civil Procedure Code also provides for a proceeding called *arbitrato irrituale* (roughly translated as 'non-ritual arbitration'). This was a customary Italian form of arbitration that has more recently been criticised by Italian scholars. The 2006 reform resolved the issue, retaining the traditional form of arbitration but giving it a clearer structure. It remains a common part of Italian procedure. In substance it can be seen as a non-judicial agreement reached by the parties based on a compromise acceptable to both.[21]

The *arbitrato irrituale* is really no more than an amicable settlement (with a contractual value) or a contractual determination which leads to a contractual award. In essence the difference between a pure arbitration (*arbitrato rituale*) and *arbitrato irrituale* is that the latter does not have the force and effect of a court decision. It should not be confused with an 'award by consent', which is a consensual arbitration in respect of the award itself only.

An award rendered as a result of an *arbitrato irrituale* can be challenged by applying to the competent state court on the following grounds only:

- The arbitration agreement is void or the arbitral tribunal exceeded the scope of the arbitration agreement and this issue was raised as an objection during the arbitral proceedings.
- The arbitrators were not appointed in accordance with the provisions of the arbitration agreement.
- The arbitrators should not have been appointed to act.
- The arbitrators breached the procedural rules agreed by the parties.
- There was a violation of the due-process rules.

The Civil Procedure Code is clear in providing that if the parties have not expressly agreed to an *arbitrato irrituale*, the arbitration will be deemed an *arbitrato rituale*.

2.4 ***Arbitraggio* and *perizia contrattuale***

Two other forms of amicable dispute resolution methods should be mentioned: the *arbitraggio* and the *perizia contrattuale*.

Scholars rightly point out that the *arbitraggio* is not a dispute resolution method *per se*, since it does not require the existence of a 'dispute' but simply of a conflict of interest between the parties.[22] The parties in fact decide to have an independent third party to settle a single aspect of their contractual relationship (when it is still in progress) and to consider such a settlement as their own settlement and to be bound by it. The process may apply also in cases where the parties are not capable of (or are not willing to) reach an agreement on specific issues of a contract or agreement.

The *perizia contrattuale* is similar to the *arbitraggio* in the sense that it does not actually require the existence of a dispute. It tends to be used by parties to settle technical issues that the parties are not capable of settling by themselves.

---

21 It is really no more than an amicable settlement of a dispute: see Redfern and Hunter, *International Arbitration*, 1.75, p28.

22 Rubino Sammartano, *Il diritto dell'arbitrato*, p21; and Punzi, *Disegno sistematico dell'arbitrato*, p14.

According to one authority, ultimately the distinction between arbitration and other means of dispute resolution is to be found in the fact that with arbitration the decision has the same effect as a court decision, whereas all other processes are based on the agreement of the parties.

Italian law does not provide for the concept of a dispute resolution board, although some authorities believe that it can be construed under the scheme of the *perizia contrattuale*.

3. Public-private partnerships

3.1 General overview and legislation

Despite the fact that participation of the private sector in public infrastructure and services projects is a relatively recent development, these days Italy has an established track record in PPP and other forms of public service contracting.

The term 'private-public partnership' (PPP) is generally used to define various forms of cooperation between the public and private sectors aimed at combining respective skills in order to carry out and manage infrastructure works in the most economically efficient manner.

Most of the Italian PPP contracts have been in the power sector and have been structured on a concession-style basis. Other projects have been seen in the roads, light railway and health service sectors.

The basic Italian rules governing PPP projects are contained in Legislative Decree 163/2006 (Code of Public Contracts) and Legislative Decree 267/2000 (Consolidated Act on Local Authority Government).

3.2 Public contracts

There are no specific courts in Italy specialised in or dedicated to construction disputes and this applies also in respect of public works and PPP disputes.

For disputes arising during the tender phase, a method alternative to ordinary court proceedings is set out in (a) below. For disputes arising during performance of the works, the Code of Public Contracts provides for ADR methods set out in (b)–(d) below.

(a) Opinion of the supervision authority for public contracts

Pursuant to the Code of Public Contracts, the supervision authority for public contracts, upon request of one of the parties to such a contract, may give a non-binding opinion on certain issues – but only if court proceedings have not already been instigated. An opinion will not be available if there is no dispute between the parties.

Since the procedure is not compulsory, parties can withdraw at any time before the opinion is issued (but with the consent of both parties if the opinion has been requested jointly by the parties).

The opinion of the supervision authority is not binding, so the party who requested the opinion can still apply to the courts after the opinion is issued.

(b) *Amicable settlement*[23]

Amicable settlement is a viable route for disputes in respect of variations (resulting during construction) which may affect the price if the sum in dispute is not lower than 10% of that price. If the sum is indeed lower, the parties should have recourse to the settlement procedure (see (c) below). Parties must try to resolve their dispute via this process prior to commencing any ordinary court proceeding.

The amicable settlement procedure comprises the following steps:

- The contractor notifies its objections/reservations to the person responsible for the procedure,[24] together with a report describing and evaluating those objections.
- The person responsible for the procedure examines the admissibility of the objections.
- For works valued at or above €10 million, the person responsible for the procedure is obliged to set up a special commission which, after examining the documentation, will make a proposal for amicable settlement.
- For works worth less than €10 million the person responsible for the procedure will himself propose an amicable settlement.
- In either case, the proposed amicable settlement will be sent to the contractor (which has submitted its reservations and/or objections). If the proposal is accepted, the person responsible for the procedure shall prepare a minute of the agreement to be signed by the parties.

(c) *Settlement agreement*[25]

This can be either an alternative to amicable settlement, or can be used where the dispute cannot be settled through amicable settlement.

In terms of procedure, the opinion of the person responsible for the procedure must be obtained, and the mechanism can be started by either party. A settlement agreement is not really different from an amicable settlement: it basically consists of a settlement through mutual waiver by the parties and has mainly a contractual value.

(d) *Arbitration*

The Code of Public Contracts provides that disputes concerning the execution of public contracts for works, services and furniture, as well as disputes not resolved through amicable settlement, may be referred to arbitration. Even in cases where such arbitration is 'special' arbitration, the proceedings for public works are regulated by the general provisions of the Civil Procedure Code, unless otherwise specifically provided for by the Code of Public Contracts. Therefore arbitration for public works is substantially carried out pursuant to the Civil Procedure Code rules with some additional applicable rules contained in the Code of Public Contracts. The latter provides also for an Arbitration Chamber for public works. The main role of the

---

23 *Accordo bonario*, as set out in Article 240 of the Code of Public Contracts.

24 The 'person responsible for the procedure' means the public officer appointed to supervise the entire construction phase.

25 *Transazione*, as set out in Article 239 of the Code of Public Contracts.

chamber is the appointment of the chairman of the arbitral panel in cases where the parties do not reach agreement on that appointment.

The awarding party must indicate whether or not the contract should contain an arbitration clause. The party who has been awarded the contract has the power to reject the arbitration clause (and therefore arbitral jurisdiction) by communicating its decision to the awarding party within 20 days of the date of it being awarded the contract.

The arbitration panel must be composed of three arbitrators, one for each party (chosen from a pool of subject experts) and a third, independent chairman, also selected from a pool of experts.

In addition to the challenge causes provided by the Civil Procedure Code, it is not possible to designate as arbitrators individuals who have prepared the design or issued an opinion in respect of the project, or supervised or tested the works disputed, or who have in any way been involved in giving an opinion on the matter.

With reference to evidence, all the means of proof established by the Civil Procedure Code (except for taking an oath) apply.

The enforcement procedure mainly follows the rules provided by the Civil Procedure Code, but the Code of Public Contracts expressly provides that the award becomes effective only once filed with the Arbitration Chamber.

The Code of Public Contracts provides that the award can be set aside. The general provisions on the challenge of the award under the Civil Procedure Code also apply to public works.

The Court of Appeal is the competent forum for challenging awards. The award may be challenged not only for reasons of invalidity but also on grounds of violation of the legal rules applicable to the substance of the dispute. Any challenge must be mounted within 90 days of the notification of the award and cannot be made after 180 days have passed from the date of filing the award with the Arbitration Chamber.

As to the Arbitration Chamber, it is set up at the supervision authority on public contracts for works, services and furniture even if it is an autonomous and independent body in respect the supervision authority above.

The main role of the Arbitration Chamber is to supervise the arbitration procedure. To make sure everything is correctly followed, the Chamber must set up and maintain the bar of arbitrators, technical experts and secretaries; draft the arbitrators' code of conduct; and establish rules for the appointment and functioning of the arbitration panels.

4. Conclusion

Italian arbitration law, as recently revised, has improved and it is now closer to international practice. The aim of the reforms was to render arbitration an effective dispute resolution mechanism as an alternative to state court proceedings. National legislation on mediation has also been implemented, driven by problems deriving from the slowness of litigation in Italy and from obligations percolating down from the European Union.

Improvements are still needed, however, in several areas. Most crucially, the construction industry would benefit if arbitrators were to be given powers to grant interim measures. Arbitration proceedings (despite the recent reforms and the high level of sophistication of certain Italian arbitral institutions) are still considered to be both expensive and sometimes slow. The tendency of Italian arbitrators and counsel (with no experience in international arbitration) to judicialise arbitration proceedings also needs to change.

The mediation procedure, as implemented in Italy, seems to represent a forward step but it needs further improvement (ie, it should be made compulsory).

Other ADR mechanisms widely used in international practice should also be admitted as alternatives by Italian policymakers for the benefit of the industry as a whole.

Spain

Alfonso Iglesia
Cuatrecasas, Gonçalves Pereira

1. Introduction

The construction industry[1] has historically been one of the drivers of the Spanish economy. Until 2007, turnover in the construction industry grew annually, reaching its historical highest that year. From 2008, when the recession started, turnover in this industry started to fall, as the sector entered a recession from which it has not yet recovered.[2]

The Spanish construction companies compensated for this loss of activity with increasingly greater international activity. In 2007, the international turnover of the six largest Spanish construction companies[3] represented approximately 35% of the total. Currently, these companies' average international turnover represents close to 80%. Thus, the largest Spanish construction companies currently carry out more than two-thirds of their activity outside Spain.

This internationalisation process of Spanish companies is, logically, accompanied by the internationalisation of their disputes, so Spanish construction companies are increasingly involved in disputes relating to international contracts. So far, arbitration is the main dispute resolution method that these companies use in international spheres.

This chapter focuses on giving a general view of the dispute resolution methods used by companies operating in the construction sector in Spain.

2. Commonly used dispute resolution methods: litigation

In Spain, almost all disputes arising in the construction sector are resolved through court (the majority) or arbitration proceedings.

Although those operating in the construction sector are aware of standard[4] alternative dispute resolution (ADR) methods, these are not frequently used in Spain (see section 4). In this section, we focus on resolving disputes in the construction sector through litigation.

Regarding disputes submitted to the courts for resolution, in Spain, as in many other countries in continental Europe with a civil law system, there is a civil

1 In this chapter, we use the term 'construction' to refer collectively to the construction, infrastructure and public-private partnership sectors.
2 In 2007, the construction activity represented 12.3% of Spanish gross domestic product. In 2012, that percentage had fallen to 9.3%.
3 Acciona, ACS, FCC, Ferrovial, OHL and Sacyr.
4 Disputes resolved through direct negotiation with those in charge of the works or company management are not considered.

jurisdiction and a contentious-administrative jurisdiction. Thus, which construction disputes are resolved by civil courts and which ones by contentious-administrative courts must be clarified.

2.1 Resolving construction disputes in the civil jurisdiction

(a) Power of the civil courts to resolve construction disputes

The civil courts generally have the power to hear construction disputes, unless these disputes are to be expressly heard by the courts of a different jurisdiction.[5] This means that the civil courts have the power to hear disputes arising from construction contracts subject to civil law when the parties to these are private parties (whether individuals or legal entities).

Judicial proceedings at the civil courts are procedurally governed by the Code of Civil Procedure. With regard to the substantive law, these disputes are mainly governed by the Civil Code and the Construction Act of 1999.[6]

Once it has been established that a construction case is to be heard by a civil court, the case is usually assigned to the court corresponding to the defendant's residence. There are no courts specialising in construction.

The Spanish civil jurisdictional system establishes a two-instance procedure, with extraordinary recourse to the Supreme Court:

- first-instance proceedings before the courts of first instance (single-judge courts);
- second-instance proceedings before the courts of appeal (bench of judges);
- judgments issued by the courts of appeal can be appealed before the Supreme Court, but only in specific circumstances and subject to strict legal requirements.

(b) Proceedings

First-instance proceedings: The Spanish civil proceeding is a complicated process that is started by filing a lawsuit in which the claimant can exercise an action for a declaratory judgment (requesting the court to declare that the claimant is the holder of a right), an action requesting the court to order the defendant to pay a sum of money or to carry out or not to carry out an action, or an action for a constitutive judgment (requesting a judgment implying a legal change, eg, a declaration of ownership).

Depending on the value of the claim, the proceeding can be conducted through oral proceedings for claims of up to €6,000 or through ordinary proceedings for claims over €6,000. These proceedings are conducted differently; oral proceedings for claims of up to €6,000 are short and simple.

As disputes arising from construction contracts tend to exceed €6,000 in most cases, these disputes follow ordinary proceedings.

---

5 Section 9 of the Judicial Power Act (the LOPJ) grants civil courts the power to hear "all matters under the scope of their powers, as well as any matters not under the scope of the powers of the courts of another jurisdiction".

6 Construction Act 38/1999 of November 5 1999.

Below we summarise the main steps of the ordinary proceedings:

- The claim is filed.
- The court gives permission to proceed (or refuses to give permission to proceed if the lawsuit does not meet the formal requirements under the Code of Civil Procedure) and process is served on the defendant.
- Declinatory plea: the defendant can plead lack of jurisdiction, and lack of objective and territorial powers.
- The defendant submits answer to the claim. The defendant can:
  - answer the claim objecting to the claimant's allegations;
  - answer the claim, fully or partially accepting liability; or
  - not answer, in which case the defendant would be declared in contempt of court.

  In addition, the defendant could file a counterclaim against the claimant. In this case, the claimant would have 20 days to answer the counterclaim.
- Pre-trial hearing: once the period for answering the claim (or the counterclaim) has elapsed, the court will announce the date of the pre-trial hearing. The pre-trial hearing is a hearing before the judge in which:
  - the judge will try to encourage an agreement or settlement between the parties;
  - procedural issues that could impede the process will be examined;
  - any additional allegations and claims will be filed;
  - any controversial facts will be established;
  - the parties will propose means of evidence and the judge will admit or reject them; and
  - the trial date will be set.
- Trial: during the trial, the evidence proposed by the parties and admitted by the judge will be presented, and the parties will give their closing arguments.
- The judgment is issued.

Ordinary proceedings in the first instance can take approximately 12 to 18 months from the date the claim is filed until the court issues its judgment.

Second-instance proceedings (appeal): An appeal against a judgment issued by a court of first instance can be filed with a court of appeal.

Second-instance proceedings involve limited appeals in which the parties cannot raise new issues. New evidence can only be presented in exceptional circumstances as follows:

- evidence that was wrongfully rejected in the first-instance proceedings (provided that motion for reversal of the rejection was brought and the appropriate objection was raised during the trial);
- evidence proposed and admitted in the first-instance proceedings which, for reasons not attributable to the person who requested it, could not be presented; and
- evidence referring to facts relevant to the decision occurring after the commencement of the period for the issuing of the judgment by the court of

first instance, or occuring before that deadline provided that the party can prove that it became aware of these facts after the said deadline.

The proceedings before the court of appeal start with the appellant filing an appeal, of which notice is served on the appellant, who can object to the appeal and, if applicable, challenge the judgment. If the appellant challenges the judgment, the appellant can object to the challenge. If evidence is to be presented, there will be a trial. The proceedings end with the court of appeal's judgment.

Second-instance proceedings can take approximately 12 months from the date the appeal is filed.

Appeals to the Supreme Court: Lastly, the Code of Civil Procedure establishes the possibility, in certain circumstances, of filing two kinds of appeals before the Supreme Court against judgments issued by the courts of appeal: cassation appeal, and extraordinary appeal on the ground of procedural infringement.[7]

To file these appeals, the criteria established in the Code of Civil Procedure[8] must be met and, in any case, the amount of the claim must be more than €600,000.

Appeals before the Supreme Court can take approximately 18 months.

(c) *Most common construction disputes subject to court proceedings*

As explained, civil proceedings relating to construction cases follow the same civil proceedings as any other issue, and the courts of first instance have the powers to hear such cases (there are no courts specialising in construction issues).

The following is a list of the most common kinds of construction claims filed with and resolved by the civil courts:

- Claims for defects:
  - Claims for defects can be based on the contracts signed and/or on the Construction Act.
  - The Construction Act regulates the liability regime of the different agents involved in the building process (developers, engineers and architects, contractors, etc) and entitles the buyers of buildings to take action against any of these agents for defects in the buildings within the time limits established.
  - Proceedings in which the buyers of buildings file claims against agents involved in the building process for defects in the buildings or developers take action against contractors, engineers and architects for not complying with a contract to execute a construction, based on defects in the works, are common.
  - In these types of disputes, the claimant can bring an action for payment (compensation for the damage suffered and cost of repairing the defects) or an action for remedy *in natura* (requesting that the defendant be ordered to repair the defects and, if applicable, to pay compensation for the damage caused).

---

7 Sections 468 to 489 of the Code of Civil Procedure.
8 Sections 469 and 477 of the Code of Civil Procedure.

- Claims relating to the cost of the works: works executed but not paid for:
    - These are proceedings started by the contractor against the developer or by the subcontractor against the main contractor claiming the cost of the works executed but not paid for.
    - In general, these are proceedings in which the contractor claims payment for works which, while not being initially included in the project, were executed following the orders of the owner or with the owner's express or tacit consent.
- Claims relating to the time for completion and delays:
    - These are proceedings that can be started both by the owner against the contractor and by the contractor against the owner.
    - In the first case, typically the owner requests a declaration of contract termination because of the contractor's breach, with compensation for damage suffered; or the application of liquidated damages established in the contract.
    - In the second case, the contractor typically claims from the owner the extra costs of speeding up the work at the owner's request to reduce the end date of the works; or the extra costs of the works taking longer to complete for reasons attributable to the owner.

(d) Importance of expert evidence

Lastly, expert evidence is particularly relevant in legal proceedings involving construction cases, because of their particularly technical and specialised nature.

The Code of Civil Procedure establishes that both parties can file expert reports issued by their own experts or request the court to appoint experts. In any case, Spanish proceedings are ruled by the principle of free assessment of the evidence; thus, the expert's opinion is not binding on the judge.

2.2 Resolving construction disputes in the contentious-administrative jurisdiction

(a) Powers of the contentious-administrative courts to resolve construction disputes

The contentious-administrative courts have the powers to hear disputes arising 'in relation to actions of the public administrations subject to administrative law'.[9] Based on this precept, the jurisdiction of the contentious-administrative courts to hear a dispute is determined according to two criteria:

- a subjective criterion: one of the parties to the dispute must be a public administration (in line with that explained below); and
- an objective criterion: the action challenged must come under the framework of a public administration's public activity.

(b) Concept of public administration for the purposes of determining the jurisdiction of the contentious-administrative courts

Act 29/1998, of July 13 1998, regulating the contentious-administrative jurisdiction

9 Section 1.1 of Act 29/1998, of July 13 1998, regulating the judicial review jurisdiction (the LJCA).

(the LJCA) does not define exactly which entities can be reviewed by the contentious-administrative courts, providing only a general indication[10] that those entities are the administrations at all levels (state, autonomous regions and local authorities) and any entities related to them.

The Public Sector Contracts Act[11] defines the entities included under the concept of public administration:

- general state administration;
- administrations of the autonomous regions;
- entities comprising the local administration;
- management entities and common services of the social security;
- regional bodies, state-owned companies, public universities, state agencies and other public law entities with their own legal personality and linked to an entity belonging to the public sector;
- companies in which the state holds a stake of more than 50%;
- consortiums assigned their own legal personality;
- foundations incorporated with a majority of state control, whether direct or indirect;
- social security insurance companies for work-related accidents and illness;
- any other entity or body with its own legal personality, specifically created to meet general interest needs not of a commercial or an industrial nature, provided that one or more entities belonging to the public sector finances most of its activity, controls its management, or appoints more than half of the members of its board of directors, or management or supervisory board; and
- associations comprising any of the entities and bodies listed.

(c) *Actions of the public administrations that are subject to the contentious-administrative jurisdiction*

The mere fact that a public administration may be one of the parties to a contract does not automatically mean that all the disputes arising in relation to the interpretation and performance of the contract will be resolved by the contentious-administrative courts. In addition, the action being challenged must have been carried out under administrative law.

Therefore, the contentious-administrative courts have the powers to hear the following:

- disputes relating to preparing, awarding, the effects of, compliance with, and termination of, administrative contracts;[12] and
- disputes relating to preparing and awarding the private contracts of the public administrations and contracts subject to harmonised regulation.[13]

---

10 Section 1.2 of the LJCA.

11 Section 3, according to the wording in Royal Legislative Decree 3/2011, of November 14 2011.

12 Section 21 of the Public Sector Contracts Act.

13 This is in line with the doctrine of separable acts, under which the acts of preparing and awarding private contracts could be considered separate from the content of the contracts, forming a kind of untouchable public nucleus, and subject to review by the judicial review courts.

The civil courts have the powers to hear the following:

- disputes relating to the effects, compliance and termination of private contracts entered into by a public administration or any other public sector entity; and
- disputes relating to preparing and awarding private contracts not subject to harmonised regulation, which were entered into by public sector entities not considered public administrations in the strict sense of the term.

Consequently, when none of the contracting parties is a public administration, or when a contracting party is a public administration but the action leading to the dispute was carried out under private law, the civil courts, and not the contentious-administrative courts, would have jurisdiction to hear the dispute.

Nevertheless, it must be highlighted that the inclusion of arbitration clauses between private contractors and public entities in order to resolve the disputes that could eventually arise from the type of contracts that we are considering is becoming more frequent.

The same dispute resolution rules apply to public-private partnerships (PPPs, a specific kind of administrative contract, as explained below).

(d) Typical administrative contracts most relevant in the Spanish legal system

The classification of contracts subject to the Public Sector Contracts Act depends on the entity that entered into the contract, and traditionally a distinction has been made between administrative and private contracts.

Based on the definition in Article 1.2.a) of EU Directive 2004/18/EC,[14] contracts in which at least one of the awarding agents is a public administration under the definition given earlier are considered administrative (or public).

Typical administrative contracts in the Spanish public sector include construction contracts,[15] public works concession contracts,[16] public service management contracts,[17] supply contracts,[18] services contracts,[19] and cooperation contracts between the public and private sectors.[20]

Regarding the construction sector, infrastructures and PPPs in the public sector, the following types of contracts used in the Spanish legal system stand out in particular.

Construction contracts: Contracts whose objective is to:

- carry out works to construct a building (with the meaning of a 'set of construction or civil engineering tasks, aimed at complying with an

---

14 This refers to "contracts for pecuniary interest concluded in writing between one or more economic operators and one or more contracting authorities and having as their object the execution of works, the supply of products or the provision of services within the meaning of this Directive".

15 Section 6 of the Public Sector Contracts Act.

16 Section 7 of the Public Sector Contracts Act.

17 Section 8 of the Public Sector Contracts Act.

18 Section 9 of the Public Sector Contracts Act.

19 Section 10 of the Public Sector Contracts Act.

20 Section 11 of the Public Sector Contracts Act.

economic or technical function, with the objective of constructing a building');[21]

- carry out the tasks listed in Annex I of the Public Sector Contracts Act; or
- carry out any works that meet the specific needs of the awarding entity.

Public works concession contracts: Under this contract, the awarding entity grants to an individual or legal entity, which will be known as the concession holder, the right to construct and/or operate the works necessary to provide public services of an economic nature or to engage in activities or services of general interest. The remuneration the concession holder receives is the right to operate the constructed works or to receive a payment.

Cooperation contracts between PPPs: The objective of this type of contract is to carry out a global and integrated action in which two elements must concur:

- The financing of immaterial investments, works and supplies must meet certain public service objectives or objectives relating to actions of general interest; and
- The contract must relate to any of the following cases:
  - the building, installation or transformation of works, equipment, systems, and complex products or goods, as well as their maintenance, updating or renovation, operation or management;
  - the comprehensive management of the maintenance of complex installations;
  - the manufacture of goods and the provision of services incorporating technology specifically developed with the aim of contributing more advanced and economically beneficial solutions than those available on the market; and
  - other service provisions relating to the administration's development of the public service or an action of general interest that was assigned to the administration.

The compensation that the cooperating contractor receives consists of an amount that will be paid throughout the performance of the contract, which could be linked to the meeting of certain performance objectives. One of the distinctive characteristics of this type of contract is that, depending on the risk distribution agreed, the payment of the amount could be linked to the effective use of the goods or services comprising its object.

The Public Sector Contracts Act places a limit on this type of contract, only allowing its use when public needs cannot be met using another type of contract (subsidiary or residual nature).

3. Commonly used dispute resolution methods: arbitration

Arbitration is a dispute resolution method widely used in Spain to resolve

21 Section 6.2 of the LCSP.

construction disputes. Given the existence of a solid regulatory framework favourable to the development of arbitration, there has been a considerable increase in the use of this dispute resolution method (in particular, regarding construction disputes) with the number of contracts with arbitration agreements having increased.

The basis of this consolidation of arbitration in Spain is the Spanish Arbitration Act of 2003[22] which, in the same way as the former arbitration act of 1988,[23] is based on the Model Law on International Commercial Arbitration adopted by the United Nations Commission on International Trade Law (UNCITRAL) on June 21 1985.

The UNCITRAL Model Law has been an essential tool in promoting the uniformity of procedural arbitration law and meeting the needs of international commercial arbitration. Indeed, the Spanish Arbitration Act opts for a substantially unified regulation of arbitration, based on the premise that if there is good regulation of international arbitration then the same must apply to national arbitration.

In addition to other rules, Section 22 of the Spanish Arbitration Act establishes the classic principle of *Kompetenz-Kompetenz*, empowering all arbitrators to rule on their own jurisdiction. This principle is complemented by the principle of the separability of the arbitration agreement, under which the validity of the arbitration agreement does not depend on the validity of the main contract in which it is incorporated.

Also, Section 23 of the act includes one of the most important developments in arbitration: the power of arbitrators to adopt preventive measures, without prejudice to their lack of executive powers and to the fact that a party in an arbitration could use an alternative direct way to ask the legal authority for the application of preventive measures.

Also, under the Code of Civil Procedure,[24] any entity that can prove it is a party to arbitration proceedings pending in Spain can request preventive measures through the courts, even before the arbitration board has been formed.

Regarding the arbitration agreement, the Spanish Arbitration Act adopts an unconventional criterion,[25] only requiring that it exists in writing, and recognises the validity and use of new forms of communication and new technology.

The Spanish Arbitration Act also establishes the positive and negative effects of the arbitration agreement, stating in Section 11.1 that "the arbitration agreement obliges the parties to submit to arbitration and prevents the courts from hearing disputes subject to arbitration, provided the interested party invokes the arbitration agreement by raising an objection to the jurisdiction (declinatory plea)". The declinatory plea enables the defendant to object to the jurisdiction of the courts inasmuch as the claim should correspond to the jurisdiction of arbitrators. To complement this, and to protect the development of arbitration in the face of obstructionist strategies, the act also establishes that the declinatory plea cannot impede the starting or continuation of arbitration proceedings.

---

22 Arbitration Act 60/2003, of December 23 2003.
23 Arbitration Act 36/1988, of December 5 1988.
24 Article 722.
25 Article 9.2.

Regarding the development of arbitration proceedings, the Spanish Arbitration Act is based on the principles of party autonomy, due process, contradiction, and equality of the parties. The act also recognises the possibility of issuing partial awards that can deal with part or the merits of the dispute, such as the jurisdiction of the arbitrators or the preventive measures. This makes it possible to apply flexible formulas to dispute resolution that are common in international arbitration practice, such as the formula permitting a decision to be taken in the first stage of arbitration on the existence of the liability of the defendant or defendants and, in the second stage, on the award amount.

Finally, regarding enforcement, awards have the same enforceability as court judgments. Spain is a signatory to the New York Convention on Recognition and Enforcement of Foreign Arbitral Awards of 1958 (the New York Convention), which has been an essential and decisive tool in the development of international commercial arbitration. This means that foreign arbitration awards can be enforced in Spain in line with the New York Convention.

In short, the existence of a regulatory framework favourable to the development of arbitration, the favourable interpretation towards the preservation of the arbitration agreements, and the enforcement regime of arbitration awards form the base of arbitration consolidation in Spain.

Based on the above, it is very common for contracts entered into with construction agents in Spain to include arbitration agreements, and construction disputes – particularly those involving large amounts – are regularly resolved through arbitration. This results from the complexity of the construction business's legal structure and the fact that the ordinary courts do not have judges specialising in this area.

By contrast, arbitrators can be experts in the subject of the arbitration; they are in a better position to understand the skills and practices involved in construction and the most common issues arising in the business.

That parties can propose legal experts specialising in construction law as arbitrators, and that they have control over the development and duration of the arbitration proceedings, which provides more flexibility than in the case of proceedings before the courts, have been decisive factors in the increase of construction disputes being resolved through arbitration in recent years.

The arbitration courts to which most disputes are submitted for the resolution of construction disputes are the Court of Arbitration of the Chamber of Commerce and Industry of Madrid (Court of Arbitration of Madrid), the Civil and Commercial Court of Arbitration (CIMA) of Madrid, and the Arbitration Court of Barcelona.

4. Less commonly used dispute resolution methods

In Spain, there are no requirements to attempt any of the dispute resolution methods before commencing judicial or arbitration proceedings, unless contractually agreed. Furthermore, ADR methods such as expert determination, mediation and conciliation have traditionally seldom been used in Spain. Nevertheless, Spanish firms use them in international contracts, particularly when they are mandatory (eg, dispute adjudication boards (DABs) in projects financed by the World Bank).

4.1 Expert determination

The Spanish Civil Code regulates three examples of the parties' agreement to resort to a third party to make determinations that resolve disputes and/or fulfil the parties' will: approval of works, determination of the price, and determination of the distribution among shareholders of the company's results). Following the principles stemming from these examples, the parties to a construction contract may agree to submit similar determinations to a third party that could be named as an adjudicator.

4.2 Dispute adjudication boards

Any decision taken by a dispute adjudication board (DAB) would probably be treated as an adjudicator's decision in Spain.

Under Spanish law, adjudicators' decisions are not directly enforceable, but can be enforced as contractual obligations. Therefore, upon non-observance of the adjudicator's decision by the defeated party, the winning party must start legal proceedings and request an order for specific performance, apart from damages.

(a) Enforcement and reviewability

It is against Spanish law to completely exclude the competent court's or arbitral tribunal's review of a DAB decision. Yet the scope of review may greatly vary depending on whether the parties have established the criteria that the adjudicator should follow when addressing disputes. In the absence of these criteria, the adjudicator's decision could only be reviewed based on evidence that he acted in bad faith. If these criteria were set out, however, the review might also focus on whether they were followed or whether the parties' consent to submit to adjudication was defective.

4.3 Mediation

Traditionally, construction industry players have rarely turned to mediation to resolve their disputes, partly because of the lack of a normative framework until very recently. It was only on July 27 2012 that Act 5/2012, of July 6 2012, on Mediation in Civil and Commercial Matters (the Mediation Act) came into force. European Union Directive 2008/52/EC was incorporated into Spanish law through Royal Decree Act 5/2012 of March 6 2012. The deadline for implementing this directive into the Spanish framework was May 21 2012, justifying the use of this legal instrument. The Royal Decree Act was then validated by Parliament, resulting in the Mediation Act, which establishes a general regulation for mediation. Mediation in construction disputes would be governed by this law.

There is a perceived interest in mediation in Spain. Public powers and institutions are increasingly supporting this mechanism as an alternative to traditional dispute resolution methods. Based on the principles of voluntarism and freedom of decision, mediation constitutes a highly creative tool for parties to resolve their disputes amicably.

In the international construction disputes forum, it is well known that mediation has become an attractive solution for the different players often involved in this type of conflict. Mediation ensures that the sessions will be conducted neutrally by an expert in the construction field, who will help the parties reach agreement. Under the Mediation Act, the parties can choose the mediator, so they are able to choose the person best suited for the task and who understands the specific interests involved. Mediation is also a good opportunity to meet all the players in an amicable environment and discuss relevant facts and matters before reaching a decision.

The main features of mediation in Spain, as provided in the Mediation Act, are summarised thus:

- Whenever an agreement in writing to submit a dispute to mediation is in place, mediation must be attempted before the parties may institute any other extrajudicial proceedings, such as arbitration, or bring an action in court. The jurisdiction of the chosen dispute resolution authority may be challenged when an agreement to refer the matter to mediation is not honoured. Once an action has been brought into court, parties can also turn to mediation by mutual agreement. This is called the mediation window, and the judge must suspend the judicial proceedings until mediation has finished, regardless of whether an amicable agreement is reached or a party requests that the suspension be lifted.
- The filing of the request for mediation suspends but does not interrupt the prescription or limitation periods in which a party may bring an action. The Mediation Act provides a general term of 15 days, from the date the request for mediation is filed, for the signature of the act of the constitutive session. If this deadline is not respected, the suspension will be lifted.
- Any person involved in the mediation (including the mediator) must keep confidential any information acquired as a result of the mediation process, and that person is exempt from giving evidence about any such information in judicial or arbitration proceedings, unless the parties agree otherwise in writing or the evidence is requested by a reasoned decision of a judge of the criminal jurisdiction.

(a) *Rules of procedure*

Once the mediation request has been filed and the informative session has taken place – unless otherwise agreed by parties – the mediation procedure will start with a constitutive session in which, among other issues, the subject matter of the dispute submitted to mediation, the procedural calendar and the deadline for completion of the procedure will be agreed by the parties and recorded in the corresponding minutes. If no agreement is reached on any of those matters, the minutes of the constitutive session must state that the mediation was unsuccessful.

The Mediation Act stresses that the procedure must be as brief as possible and the different stages must be condensed into the fewest possible number of sessions. The procedure may end without an agreement for any of the following reasons:

- One or all the parties exercise their right to terminate it;
- The time limit allocated to the mediation procedure elapses; or
- The mediator determines that the parties' positions are irreconcilable.

The final minutes executed at the end of the procedure must include any agreements reached.

(b) *Enforceability of agreements resulting from mediation*

The parties may include the terms of the agreement resulting from mediation in a public deed, thereby constituting an enforceable title.

The agreement resulting from mediation may be challenged before the courts with an action seeking annulment of the agreement based only on causes for the annulment of contracts.

When the agreement is reached as a result of a mediation process that took place after the start of judicial proceedings, the parties may request judicial approval of the agreement.

Without prejudice to the provisions of EU regulations and international conventions, a foreign agreement resulting from mediation that has not been declared enforceable by a foreign authority will only be enforceable in Spain upon its additional formalisation in a public deed before a Spanish notary public at the instigation of all the parties, or only one of them with the express consent of the others.

(c) *Mediators and mediation institutions*

Mediation institutions promote mediation and administer mediation proceedings but are not permitted to act as mediators themselves. These institutions must separate mediation and arbitration, should they be involved in administering arbitration proceedings as well.

The mediator must not incur any conflict of interest, must be impartial, must have completed specific training provided by accredited institutions and must have a civil liability insurance policy.

If the mediator fails to faithfully comply with his responsibilities, the mediator may be held liable for any damages caused by that act or omission. The damaged party will have a direct action against the mediator and, when applicable, against the mediation institution, regardless of the availability of any actions for reimbursement of the mediation institution against the mediator.

5. Conclusion

Based on what has been discussed in this chapter, it can be concluded that construction disputes arising in Spain are resolved through informal negotiation or through court or arbitration proceedings. ADR methods, such as mediation, conciliation and adjudication, are rarely used.[26]

Spanish lawyers specialising in construction law are fully aware of the advantages that ADR methods offer a sector as prone to disputes as the construction sector, and of the outstanding results these methods are having in other countries, particularly common law countries. Also, Spanish construction companies engaging in activities abroad are now more exposed to these methods.

---

26 The limited use of ADR methods applies to most of the disputes between companies.

In this context (namely awareness of the advantages of ADR methods in the construction sector and of their limited use), initiatives have sprung up to incorporate ADR methods into the resolution of disputes in the Spanish construction sector.[27]

Therefore, one of the main developments we might witness in the coming years in dispute resolution in the construction sector in Spain will be the progressive introduction of ADR methods, particularly mediation and adjudication.

The author would like to thank Maribel Rodríguez, Miguel Angel Malo, Carola García and Mónica Lasquíbar, associates at Cuatrecasas, Gonçalves Pereira, for their assistance in the preparation of this chapter.

27 The recent creation of a group specialising in construction law backed by the Court of Arbitration of the Chamber of Commerce of Madrid must be mentioned. One of the group's objectives is to promote ADR methods in the construction/engineering sector.

Switzerland

Sonja Stark-Traber
Schellenberg Wittmer Ltd

1. Introduction

In recent years, Switzerland has seen a high level of construction activities, including a number of major construction projects. In particular in the public sector, several large infrastructure projects have been realised, the highlight being the construction of the New Rail Link (NEAT) through the Alps. At the heart of this project are two base tunnels under the Ceneri and the Gotthard mountains. The Gotthard base tunnel consists of two 57-kilometre single-track tubes and is thus the longest railway tunnel in the world. With a depth of up to 2,300 metres, the Gotthard Base Tunnel is also the world's deepest railway tunnel constructed to date.[1]

In contrast, the number of public-private partnership (PPP) projects realised in Switzerland is still very low. Switzerland's first PPP project was realised in 2010 with the Neumatt Burgdorf project. The project involved the demolition of existing buildings at the site, as well as the planning, financing, construction and operation of administrative premises and a prison. It remains to be seen whether, based on the experiences of the Neumatt Burgdorf project, further PPP projects will be initiated in Switzerland.

As for the settlement of disputes arising from such construction, infrastructure and PPP projects, party autonomy is the guiding principle. Swiss law provides for a multitude of possible dispute resolution mechanisms from which the parties can choose the method best suited for their project and specific needs. This chapter gives a broad overview of the dispute resolution methods most frequently applied in Switzerland to resolve disputes arising in construction, infrastructure and PPP projects.

2. Switzerland's liberal dispute resolution regime

Switzerland has a very liberal regime for the settlement of disputes in general, and of disputes arising from construction, infrastructure or PPP projects in particular. Swiss law does not, as a general rule, prescribe any mandatory dispute resolution mechanisms nor does it prohibit any dispute settlement methods. Rather, Swiss law leaves the parties utmost freedom to tailor the methods to settle their disputes to their specific needs.

The only exception applies where the parties' relationship is not of a private law nature, but is governed by public law. This may, for instance, be the case in certain

1 See details of the New Rail Link project at www.alptransit.ch/en/project/the-project.html.

PPP projects[2] or in specific infrastructure projects, in particular in the energy sector. In such cases, jurisdiction lies with the administrative authorities and the parties are barred from resorting to dispute resolution methods available under private law. Since it is to be determined on a case-by-case basis whether a specific relationship is governed by private law or by public law, it would go beyond the scope of this chapter to go into any further details. The following text will only deal with dispute resolution methods available to settle disputes arising from projects subject to private law.

The following overview will be divided into dispute resolution methods that aim to resolve a dispute by way of party agreement (see section 3 below), and methods that aim to settle a dispute by way of a binding third-party decision (see section 4 below). Furthermore, this chapter will deal with multi-tier dispute resolution methods that combine both sorts of method (see section 5 below).

The use of the individual dispute resolution methods may vary depending on the sector and on whether the project is of a domestic or an international nature.

3. Dispute resolution methods aimed at settling disputes by way of party agreement

3.1 Conciliation

Conciliation proceedings are aimed at encouraging the parties to settle their dispute by way of negotiations with the support of a neutral third person. Conciliation is generally based on the concept of voluntariness. The parties may appoint a recognised, independent and impartial person, who is familiar with the respective industry, as a conciliator. The conciliator is not empowered to impose a solution on the parties to the dispute.[3] The conciliator may, however, present a non-binding settlement proposal to the parties.[4] When the negotiations are successful, the result is recorded in writing in a settlement agreement.

In 2007, a number of associations in the real estate and construction sector, including the Swiss Master Builder Association and the Swiss Association of Engineers and Architects (SIA), established a conciliation procedure for construction and real estate disputes, which is set out in the regulations on conciliation and arbitration for construction and real estate.[5] These regulations apply if the parties expressly agree to submit their dispute to a conciliation procedure conducted in accordance with these provisions. They provide for a cost-effective and expeditious conciliation procedure, conducted by a conciliator with the necessary expertise to facilitate a settlement. The conciliator invites the parties to a conciliation hearing, in which he gives advice to the parties and seeks to bring about a settlement between

---

2 For example, if the private partner is granted a concession by the public partner; see Thomas Müller-Tschumi, "Der PPP-Projektvertrag beim Inhabermodell", in *Aktuelles Vergaberecht 2012/Marchés Publics 2012*, Zurich 2012, p413.

3 Daniel Girsberger and Nathalie Voser, *International Arbitration in Switzerland*, second edition, Zurich 2012, note 48.

4 Urs Gloor and Barbara Umbricht Lukas, in *Schweizerische Zivilprozessordnung*, edited by Paul Oberhammer, Basel 2010, Article 197 note 2.

5 The regulations on conciliation and arbitration construction and real estate are available at www.baumeister.ch/fileadmin/media/2_Kernthemen/Unternehmerfragen/Konfliktloesungsmetoden/verm_schiedsgericht_regl_d.pdf.

them. Unless the parties agree on an extension of the term of negotiation, the conciliation procedure ends after three months if the parties are not able to reach a settlement. The parties may then choose to have their dispute resolved in arbitration or state court proceedings.

The Zurich Chamber of Commerce offers its members a conciliation procedure for the settlement of domestic disputes. The impartial conciliator is authorised to do everything which appears conducive to amicable settlement of the differences. The conciliator presents a non-binding settlement proposal to the parties.

Switzerland also has a long-standing tradition of judicial conciliation. Before bringing a claim before a state court, the plaintiff must submit the dispute to a state-appointed conciliation authority for a conciliation attempt. Such conciliation proceedings are, as a rule, mandatory and a necessary preliminary phase of civil judicial proceedings. The Swiss Code of Civil Procedure provides, however, for a number of exceptions where the claim may be filed directly with the court (Articles 198 and 199 of the Code of Civil Procedure). The conciliation authority attempts to reconcile the parties in an informal manner (Article 201(1), Code of Civil Procedure). If the value in dispute does not exceed Sfr5,000, the conciliation authority may also submit a judgment proposal to the parties (Article 210(1)(c), Code of Civil Procedure). If the parties reach an agreement or accept the proposed judgment, it will have the effect of a binding decision (Articles 208 and 211(1), Code of Civil Procedure). If no agreement is reached or the proposed judgment is rejected, the conciliation authority will grant the plaintiff authorisation to proceed with the claim before the state court (Articles 209(1) and 211(2), Code of Civil Procedure).

Conciliation may also form part of pending legal proceedings. Swiss state courts may attempt to reconcile the parties at any stage of the proceedings and Swiss judges frequently (and successfully)[6] make use of this power. Commonly, such an attempt is made in the so-called instruction hearing provided for in Article 226 of the Code of Civil Procedure. Traditionally, the Commercial Court of the Canton of Zurich even provides a without-prejudice preliminary assessment of the case in such a hearing, with the aim of furthering settlement. In domestic arbitration, the arbitral tribunal usually asks the parties if they are interested in a preliminary assessment of the case and/or a conciliation attempt.[7] In international arbitration practice, arbitrators are often reluctant to act as settlement facilitators, depending on their legal background.[8] Swiss arbitrators sitting on international arbitral tribunals will, however, frequently offer such services or even provide a preliminary assessment of the case if the parties expressly agree to such a procedure.

3.2 Mediation

Like a conciliator, a mediator is a neutral third person who assists the parties in

6 In practice, a considerable number of lawsuits are settled with the assistance of the court. In cases before the commercial courts, the rate of success is estimated to be well above 50%. See Bernhard Berger and Franz Kellerhals, *International and Domestic Arbitration in Switzerland*, Berne 2010, note 154, with further reference.

7 Berger and Kellerhals, *op. cit.*, note 156.

8 Berger and Kellerhals, *op. cit.*, note 157.

negotiating a legally binding agreement for the resolution of their dispute. The lines between mediation and conciliation are blurred and both terms tend to be used interchangeably. However, a mediator commonly plays a more active role than a conciliator. A mediator uses various techniques to encourage, facilitate and structure the dialogue between the parties. Unlike a conciliator, a mediator does not usually propose a solution to the dispute; rather, the parties develop a solution on their own with the mediator's assistance. A mediator usually has no authority to impose a solution on the parties.[9]

Mediation is a voluntary process. The parties retain full authority and responsibility to decide on the resolution of the matter in dispute and on how the mediation is to be conducted. They can also terminate the mediation process at any time.[10]

Even though experiences with mediation in construction disputes appear to be positive, parties in the construction industry still seem reluctant to settle disputes by way of mediation.[11] Mediation clauses are, however, increasingly included in standard contract forms, in particular in those issued by the Swiss Association of Engineers and Architects. Many SIA standard contract forms contain an optional mediation clause providing for the conduct of mediation proceedings prior to the initiation of court proceedings.

In an effort to promote mediation as an alternative form of dispute resolution, provisions concerning mediation in civil matters were introduced into the new Code of Civil Procedure which came into force on January 1 2011. The Code of Civil Procedure contains provisions on mediation linked to court proceedings. The respective provisions do not, by contrast, apply to mediation proceedings initiated without any link to judicial proceedings, such as mediation proceedings in the context of arbitration. Article 213(1) of the Code of Civil Procedure provides that conciliation proceedings to be conducted prior to court proceedings (see section 3.1 above) shall be replaced by mediation upon the request of all the parties. The courts may recommend mediation to the parties and the parties may make a joint request for mediation at any time during the proceedings (Article 214(1) and (2), Code of Civil Procedure). In such case, the court proceedings remain suspended until the request is withdrawn by one of the parties or until the court is notified of the end of the mediation (Article 214(3), Code of Civil Procedure). The organisation and conduct of the mediation proceedings is within the responsibility of the parties (Article 215, Code of Civil Procedure), that is the Code of Civil Procedure does not govern the mediation process itself. The mediation proceedings are confidential and kept separate from the conciliation authority and the court. Also, the statements of the parties made in mediation may not be used in state court litigation (Article 216, Code of Civil Procedure). If the parties reach an agreement in mediation, they may apply for a confirmation of their agreement, giving it the force of a legally binding decision (Article 217, Code of Civil Procedure).

---

9 Girsberger and Voser, *op. cit.*, note 38.

10 *Ibid.*

11 See Barbara Carl, "Aussergerichtliche Formen der Streitbehandlung im Bauvertragsrecht – unter besonderer Berücksichtigung des Schiedsgutachtens, der Mediation, der Empfehlung VSS 641 510 für Streiterledigung und weiterer bauspezifischer Mechanismen", Zurich 2010, notes 331 *et seq.*

There are several private organisations in Switzerland that offer mediation services. Two of the most prominent are the Swiss Chamber for Commercial Mediation (SCCM), which is dedicated to the promotion and development of mediation as a method for resolving business conflicts, and the Swiss Chambers of Commerce and Industry's Arbitration Institution, which offers services in commercial mediation based on the Swiss Rules of Commercial Mediation adopted in 2007.

3.3 Dispute Review Boards

Dispute review boards (DRBs) are still not widely used in Switzerland. However, in November 1998 the Association of Swiss Professionals for Roads and Traffic published recommendations on the resolution of disputes arising from construction contracts in connection with the realisation of major infrastructure projects, the so-called VSS Recommendation 641 510. VSS Recommendation 641 510 is based on a dispute resolution model originally devised in 1996 by a working group of the Construction Industry Standing Conference to cope with large infrastructure construction works in Switzerland (eg, NEAT, Rail 2000 and completion of the motorway network).[12] It is the express objective of VSS Recommendation 641 510 to provide a dispute resolution model geared to mutual agreement, by which conflicts among the contracting parties can be resolved from the start of construction, within short deadlines and with minimal effort.

VSS Recommendation 641 510 provides for a three-stage dispute resolution process (see section 5.1 below for details). Following a building site decision procedure (phase 1), the parties can call upon a conciliation board for the conduct of a conciliation procedure (phase 2). If the parties are not able to reach a settlement agreement in either phase 1 or phase 2, the dispute is resolved in litigation or arbitration proceedings (phase 3).

According to VSS Recommendation 641 510, the conciliation board not only conducts the conciliation procedure, but it also fulfils a similar function as a dispute review board. The conciliation board consists of three members. Both the chairman and the co-conciliators are to be appointed by the parties within 60 days from the awarding of the contract, whereby each party is entitled to nominate a co-conciliator to be agreed upon by the counterparty. The chairman may be a lawyer with experience in construction matters or a construction expert with knowledge and experience in construction law. All members of the conciliation board must be and remain independent from the parties.

The conciliation board accompanies the project from the start and may make the parties aware of any potential conflicts even without a formal conciliation procedure. To this end, the owner is required to keep the members of the conciliation board informed by regularly providing them with written reports on the progress of the works and on other important project information. The conciliation board visits the construction site on a regular basis (at least three times a year), in particular if crucial works are executed, and to meet with representatives of the owner and the contractor.

12 Roland Hürlimann, "Streiterledigung bei Grossprojekten", *Anwaltsrevue* 4/2007, p148.

These regular site visits always involve an inspection of the ongoing works and a subsequent discussion which does not need to comply with any particular form.

The conciliation board is not supposed to make any recommendations on disputes during these visits. On the contrary, VSS Recommendation 641 510 expressly prohibits the parties from seeking advice from a member of the conciliation board or even asking for an opinion during such discussions. It is only in the course of a formal conciliation procedure initiated in accordance with VSS Recommendation 641 510 that the conciliation board will make non-binding proposals as to the settlement of a dispute (see section 5.1 below for details).

3.4 Joint expert report

In construction disputes, the parties frequently agree jointly to appoint an expert to prepare an expert report on specific contentious issues. In contrast to an expert determination (see Section 4.3 below), the parties do not undertake in advance to accept the findings of the expert as binding. Rather, the joint expert report serves as a basis for settlement negotiations and facilitates a resolution of the dispute by agreement.[13]

In case the parties are not able to settle their dispute amicably, the joint expert report may be submitted as evidence in subsequent litigation or arbitration proceedings. The expert report is subject to free assessment by the court or arbitral tribunal. Its evidentiary value will largely depend on the quality of the expert's work.[14]

3.5 Mini-trial

Since 1985, the Zurich Chamber of Commerce has provided a set of mini-trial rules. The main characteristic of such a mini-trial is that the parties present their case to a panel composed of a high-ranking executive board member from each of the parties and a neutral chairperson. The proceedings are concentrated on the main issues and the parties' positions are presented in summary pleadings. The mini-trial is aimed at enabling the parties to appraise the chances and risks of potential litigation or arbitration proceedings on the basis of an assessment by a neutral third party. At the same time, the mini-trial proceedings seek to bring the parties to a settlement of their dispute. Until now, this procedure has, however, been invoked only very infrequently.[15]

4. Dispute resolution methods aimed at settling disputes by way of a binding third-party decision

4.1 Litigation

While in international construction and infrastructure projects parties regularly agree to settle their disputes in arbitration proceedings, litigation is still the preferred dispute resolution method on a domestic level, in particular in domestic

---

13 Carl, *op cit*, note 541 *et seq*.

14 Carl, *op cit*, notes 541 to 543.

15 See Carl, *op cit.*, note 564, with further references; Daniel Hochstrasser and Marc Blessing, in *Basler Kommentar, Internationales Privatrecht*, second edition, Basel 2007, "Introduction to Chapter 12 of the Private International Law Act, note" 328.

construction projects. Disputes arising from such projects are usually referred to the state courts, and less frequently to arbitral tribunals for resolution, particularly if the owner is a public entity.

Swiss civil procedure is governed by the Swiss Code of Civil Procedure, which replaced the 26 different cantonal codes formerly governing civil procedure on a cantonal level.[16] However, the organisation of the judiciary and the determination of the material and functional jurisdiction of the courts remained, in principle, in the competence of the cantons.

All cantons have established one or several court(s) of first instance and a high court that serves as an appellate court or as a court of first instance for a limited number of disputes. Switzerland's highest court is the Swiss Federal Supreme Court, which ensures both the correct application of federal substantive law by the cantonal courts and continuity of the legal practice in Switzerland.

There are no state courts specialising in construction, infrastructure or PPP disputes. A number of cantons have, however, established commercial courts – that is, specialised courts that deal primarily with commercial disputes as a court of first instance. The most prominent of these courts is the Commercial Court of the Canton of Zurich. Cases brought before this court are generally decided by a panel of five judges, two of which are professional judges and three of which are non-professional commercial judges. Commercial judges are individuals who are active as company owners or hold an executive position or who were in such a position for at least 10 years. Commercial judges are recruited from various economic sectors, in particular from the construction and architectural sector. The collaboration of professional and commercial judges results in a competent and expeditious adjudication of disputes. Due to the high quality and efficiency of its dispute resolution process, the Commercial Court of the Canton of Zurich not only hears domestic cases, but is also frequently chosen as a venue for international commercial disputes.

As mentioned above (see Section 3.1), the Code of Civil Procedure generally provides for (state) conciliation proceedings before the claim can be brought before the court. There are, however, numerous exceptions to this rule: in particular, no conciliation proceedings are conducted if a dispute falls within the jurisdiction of the commercial courts.

At the pre-trial stage, Swiss civil procedure law provides for several remedies:

- *Interlocutory injunctions:* prior to the start of the main proceedings, a party may apply for an interlocutory injunction. Such an injunction is granted if the petitioner brings *prima facie* evidence that in the absence of an injunction he would suffer irreparable harm and is likely to prevail on the merits of the case (Article 261, Code of Civil Procedure). In cases of particular urgency, especially where there is a risk that otherwise legal rights would be compromised, interlocutory injunctions may even be granted *ex parte* (Article 265, Code of Civil Procedure).
- *Attachment of assets (freezing orders):* a creditor may obtain from the court an attachment of assets in Switzerland on a limited number of grounds set out

16 Switzerland is a federal state with 26 cantons.

in Article 271 of the Swiss Federal Debt Enforcement and Bankruptcy Act. In particular, a creditor may apply for an attachment of assets if he holds an enforceable title such as a Swiss or foreign judgment.

- *Precautionary taking of evidence:* the court can take evidence on a precautionary basis at any time, even before court proceedings are pending. The court will grant a request for the precautionary taking of evidence if the law grants a corresponding right, or if the applicant shows credibly that the evidence is at risk or that it has a legitimate interest (Article 158(1), Code of Civil Procedure). In a recent decision, the Swiss Federal Supreme Court confirmed that the assessment of the prospects of a potential litigation constitutes a legitimate interest within the meaning of Article 158 of the Code of Civil Procedure.[17] Article 158 allows a party, for instance, to request that an expert report be prepared on a specific issue, that a witness be examined by the court or that the production of documents by a potential counterparty or a third party be ordered. Article 158 does not, however, allow for a US- or UK-style disclosure. Rather, the court can only compel a party to produce a document if the applicant shows on a *prima facie* basis that he has a claim and if the document is sufficiently specified. The latter is also a prerequisite for the production of documents in pending court proceedings.

The Code of Civil Procedure also provides for a number of procedural tools allowing the intervention or joinder of third parties to the proceedings. These tools are of particular relevance in construction disputes where, for example, the contractor has subcontracted part of its works to a third contractor and wants to take recourse against the latter in case a lawsuit by the owner is successful. A person alleging a legal interest that pending court proceedings be decided in favour of one of the parties can at any time intervene in such proceedings by making an application to the court (Article 74, Code of Civil Procedure). If the intervention is granted, the intervener can perform all procedural acts in support of the main party that are admissible at any given time in the proceedings (Article 76(1), Code of Civil Procedure). Furthermore, a party that intends to hold a third party liable or that fears that it might be held liable by a third party in the event that it succumbs in pending proceedings can request the third party to support it in the proceedings (Article 78(1), Code of Civil Procedure). As a general rule, any outcome of the proceedings that is unfavourable to the principal party is also effective against the intervener or third party (Articles 77 and 80, Code of Civil Procedure, with exceptions). Additionally, the Code of Civil Procedure provides for a third-party action (a party can bring a third-party action before the court dealing with an action for the eventuality of its succumbing in such action (Article 81, Code of Civil Procedure).

4.2 Arbitration

Arbitration is often the preferred dispute resolution mechanism in international construction and infrastructure disputes, whereas domestic disputes in these fields

17 Decision of the Swiss Federal Supreme Court 138 III 86, cons. 2.4.2.

are usually referred to the local courts. By contrast, disputes arising from PPP projects are frequently settled in arbitral proceedings.

The applicable legal framework varies depending on whether the dispute is of an international or a domestic nature.

(a) International arbitration in Switzerland

Switzerland is one of the traditional and most prominent venues for international commercial arbitration. Its location at the heart of Europe, an excellent business infrastructure, the well-developed legal system, high professional standards in the legal profession as well as its political stability and historical neutrality are factors that have contributed to Switzerland's success as an international arbitration location.

One of the main reasons for Switzerland's leading position in international arbitration lies, however, in its arbitration-friendly legislation. International arbitration in Switzerland is governed by Chapter 12 (Articles 177–194) of the Private International Law Act, which has been considered an advanced and modern arbitration code since its enactment in 1989. Chapter 12 of the Private International Law Act is committed to party autonomy and flexibility, giving the parties and the arbitrators within the boundaries of due process utmost freedom to tailor the arbitral proceedings to their needs. As a general rule, any dispute involving an economic interest may be settled in international arbitral proceedings in Switzerland (Article 177(1), Private International Law Act).

The legal framework assures the proper constitution and functioning of the arbitral tribunal. In particular, Chapter 12 of the Private International Law Act provides for the necessary assistance by state courts in support of arbitration. State courts may, for instance, be asked for assistance if the parties fail to agree on the procedure for the appointment of arbitrators (Article 179(2), Private International Law Act) or if such assistance is required for the taking of evidence (Article 184(2), Private International Law Act). Prior to the constitution of an arbitral tribunal, the state courts have exclusive jurisdiction to order interim relief. Following the constitution of an arbitral tribunal, a party can seek interim relief from either the arbitral tribunal or directly from the state courts, unless the parties have agreed otherwise. The arbitral tribunal can also request the assistance of the state courts if the parties do not voluntarily comply with interim measures ordered by the arbitral tribunal (Article 183(2), Private International Law Act).

At the same time, Chapter 12 of the Private International Law Act keeps judicial intervention in arbitration to a minimum. State courts must generally decline jurisdiction, where the parties have agreed to arbitrate an arbitrable dispute (Article 7, Private International Law Act). A state court seized may, in such cases, only accept jurisdiction over the merits of the case if (a) the respondent has submitted to the proceedings without reservation, if (b) the court establishes that the agreement to arbitrate is null and void, ineffective or incapable of being performed, or if (c) the arbitral tribunal cannot be constituted for reasons manifestly attributable to the respondent.

An arbitral award may be set aside only by the Swiss Federal Supreme Court as the sole appellate authority and only on a limited number of grounds. These grounds principally relate to the violation of fundamental procedural rights and are the following (Article 190(2), Private International Law Act):

- improper appointment of arbitrators;
- incorrect acceptance or denial of jurisdiction by the arbitral tribunal;
- ruling of the arbitral tribunal beyond the claims submitted, or failure to rule on one of the claims submitted;
- violation by the arbitral tribunal of the principle of equal treatment of the parties or of the right to be heard in an adversarial procedure; and
- incompatibility of the award with international public policy.

The arbitral tribunal's ruling on the merits cannot be challenged unless it violates public policy. Parties who do not have their domicile, their habitual residence or a place of business in Switzerland even have the option partially or fully to waive a petition for setting aside an arbitral award (Article 192(1), Private International Law Act).

The Swiss Federal Supreme Court has consistently exercised considerable restraint when ruling on setting aside petitions. Statistics show that only about 7% of challenges to arbitral awards have been successful.[18] Swiss law thus provides for a high degree of finality of arbitral awards rendered in Switzerland.

Moreover, since Chapter 12 of the Private International Law Act only provides for one tier of jurisdiction for the setting aside of arbitral awards, as opposed to the two or three prevalent in many other jurisdictions, challenge procedures in Switzerland are expeditious and less costly than in other countries.

(b) Domestic arbitration in Switzerland

Domestic arbitration in Switzerland is governed by Part 3 (Articles 353–399) of the Swiss Code of Civil Procedure that replaced the outdated former Swiss Intercantonal Concordat on Arbitration of 1969. The Code of Civil Procedure has strengthened the principles of flexibility and party autonomy and has thus significantly modernised and enhanced the attractiveness of the legislative framework for domestic arbitration.

The object of domestic arbitral proceedings can be any claim of which the parties can freely dispose (Article 354, Code of Civil Procedure). As in international arbitration, assistance of the state courts in procedural matters is guaranteed, while judicial intervention in arbitral proceedings is restricted.

Domestic arbitral awards can be set aside on the same grounds as international arbitral awards, except for incompatibility with international public policy (Article 393, Code of Civil Procedure). In addition, a domestic award can be challenged on the ground that the result of the award is arbitrary because it is based on findings of fact that are contradicted by the documents on record or on a manifest violation of the law or of equity, and on the ground that the fees and expenses determined by the arbitral tribunal for its members are manifestly excessive. In the latter case, the appellate authority may not set aside the award as such, but only the arbitral tribunal's decision on the costs of the arbitration.

---

18 See Felix Dasser, "International Arbitration and Setting Aside Proceedings in Switzerland – An Updated Statistical Analysis", *ASA Bulletin*, Vol. 28, No. 1, 2010, pp82–100.

The Swiss Federal Supreme Court is the sole default court for challenges against domestic arbitral awards (Article 389(1), Code of Civil Procedure). The parties are, however, free to agree that the award may instead be challenged before the upper state court of the canton where the arbitral tribunal has its seat (Article 390(1) in conjunction with Article 356(1)(a), Code of Civil Procedure).

(c) Swiss arbitration rules

Swiss Rules of International Arbitration: In 2004, six chambers of commerce and industry in Switzerland (Basel, Bern, Geneva, Ticino, Vaud and Zurich, later joined by Neuchâtel) introduced the harmonised Swiss Rules of International Arbitration (the Swiss Rules) in order to further bolster Switzerland's leading position in international arbitration. Since then, the Swiss Rules have become highly successful, with around 600 arbitrations having been conducted under the rules since their entry into force.

On June 1 2012, a revised version of the Swiss Rules came into force, creating the Swiss Chambers' Arbitration Institution and the Arbitration Court. The main goal of this revision was to bring the Swiss Rules up to date with current arbitral practice and to further enhance the efficiency of the arbitral process in terms of time and cost. The revised Swiss Rules should at the same time preserve flexibility of the proceedings, as well as the autonomy of the parties and the arbitral tribunal. The Swiss Chambers' Arbitration Institution provides domestic and international arbitration services under any applicable law, in Switzerland and in any other country. The revision will undoubtedly further increase the success of the Swiss Rules.

Arbitration rules of the Swiss construction industry: A number of institutions in the Swiss construction industry have introduced arbitration rules whereby disputes may be referred to specialised arbitral tribunals.

The already mentioned regulations on conciliation and arbitration for construction and real estate issued by a number of associations in the real estate and construction sector contain a set of arbitration rules specifically established for the resolution of disputes in the construction and real estate sector.

Furthermore, the Swiss Association of Engineers and Architects has issued a guideline for the procedure before an arbitral tribunal (SIA Guideline 150). This guideline contains a set of rules applicable to arbitration proceedings before an SIA Arbitral Tribunal, which is defined as an arbitral tribunal competent for the resolution of disputes in the fields of architecture, engineering and construction and established under SIA Guideline 150.

4.3 Expert determination

The Swiss Federal Supreme Court defines 'expert determination' as an agreement by which a neutral expert is assigned to make a binding determination of certain legally relevant facts or certain legal questions.[19] The expert decides on only individual disputed factual and legal issues, whereas a court or arbitral tribunal decides the dispute as a whole.

Expert determination is frequently used to resolve technical issues and is therefore a common dispute resolution method in construction disputes. An expert may, for instance, be appointed by the parties to make a binding determination on the technical defectiveness of works, on the causes of a disruption or on the legal timeliness of a notification.

The expert is appointed (and removed) jointly by the parties.[20] When drafting the contract for the expert, the parties should take care to describe clearly the expert competences and the procedure to be followed by the expert to make a determination on the relevant issues.[21] The parties should, in particular, clarify that the expert does not act as an arbitrator.[22]

Expert determination can take place before or during legal proceedings. The expert's determination is binding on the parties and on any state court or arbitral tribunal in any subsequent or already pending lawsuit between the same parties and concerning the same subject-matter.[23] This distinguishes the expert determination from the joint expert report described in section 3.4 above. According to Article 189(3) of the Code of Civil Procedure,[24] for the expert determination to be binding, the following requirements must be met:

- The parties must have liberty to dispose freely of the legal relationship in question (Article 189(3)(a)).
- There are no grounds for recusal against the expert (Article 189(3)(b)). The expert must in particular be impartial and independent.[25]
- The expert determination has been stated in an impartial manner and is not manifestly incorrect (Article 189(3)(c)). The expert must respect the principles of due process – in particular, equal treatment of the parties – in the course of developing his conclusions.[26] Furthermore, a court or arbitral tribunal may only depart from the expert's findings if the determination is manifestly unjust, arbitrary, flawed or inequitable to a high degree, or is based on erroneous facts, or is vitiated by lack of consent.[27]

Expert determinations are not subject to recourse. The parties may only challenge the binding nature of an expert determination in a separate lawsuit or by raising the grounds for a challenge as a defence.[28]

5. Multi-tier dispute resolution methods

In particular in complex construction projects, it has become increasingly popular to include multi-tier dispute resolution clauses in the contract, providing for distinct

---

19 Decision of the Swiss Federal Supreme Court 129 III 535, cons. 2, with further references.
20 Girsberger and Voser, *op. cit.*, note 55.
21 Berger and Kellerhals, *op. cit.*, note 142.
22 *Ibid.*
23 Berger and Kellerhals, *op. cit.*, note 145; Girsberger and Voser, *op. cit.*, note 56; Carl, *op. cit.*, note 283.
24 Even though Article 189 CCP does not apply in arbitration, legal commentators take the position that the principles set out in Article 189 CCP may be applied *mutatis mutandis* before domestic and international arbitral tribunals; see Berger and Kellerhals, *op. cit.*, note 140.
25 Berger and Kellerhals, *op. cit.*, note 145b.
26 Berger and Kellerhals, *op. cit.*, note 145c.
27 Decision of the Swiss Federal Supreme Court 129 III 535, cons. 2.1, with further references.
28 Berger and Kellerhals, *op. cit.*, note 146.

stages and involving separate procedures for the settlement of disputes. Typically, a multi-tier dispute resolution clause provides for party-led negotiations as a first tier, followed by more formal conciliation or mediation proceedings as a second tier, and litigation or arbitration proceedings as a third and last tier of dispute resolution.[29]

Such a multi-tier dispute resolution method was also introduced by VSS Recommendation 641 510 for the resolution of disputes arising from construction contracts in connection with the realisation of major infrastructure projects (see section 3.3 above for details on VSS Recommendation 641 510). This method is presented in more detail below.

5.1 Multi-tier dispute resolution according to VSS Recommendation 641 510

If the parties make their contract subject to VSS Recommendation 641 510, they are obliged to resolve their disputes in accordance with a three-stage dispute resolution process consisting of the phases described in the remainder of this section.

(a) Phase 1: Building site decision procedure

As a general rule, the parties undertake to resolve any disputes between themselves, if possible. To facilitate such internal settlement, the parties must go through a procedure of common negotiations, the so-called 'building site decision procedure', which follows precisely defined temporal milestones. This procedure is aimed at preventing the procrastination of disputes right from the outset.

The dispute resolution process starts with a notification, which must be given by the plaintiff without delay. The notification can be given orally or in writing and must summarise the main reasons for the complaint. When the parties next get in touch, for example at the next site meeting, the complaint and a summary of the reasons must be set out in writing in the meeting minutes or in a letter. The counterparty must thereafter comment on the complaint at the next meeting. Provided the counterparty does not categorically reject the complaint, the plaintiff is required to substantiate its complaint and to present evidence at the next meeting. The opposing party must then once more comment on the complaint within 10 days. If the opposing party recognises the controversial issues in its second submission or if the remaining differences can be resolved between the parties, the settlement will be laid down in writing and the procedure comes to an end.

If a settlement cannot be reached or if the opposing party categorically rejects the complaint from the outset, the plaintiff may submit the dispute to the parties' senior management for discussion. Only if the senior management cannot reach a settlement until the next site meeting can the second phase of the procedure be initiated.

(b) Phase 2: Conciliation procedure

If the building site decision procedure is unsuccessful, each party may call upon the

29 See Alexander Jolles, "Consequences of Multi-tier Arbitration Clauses: Issues of Enforcement", *Arbitration Journal of the Chartered Institute of Arbitration*, Vol 7, November 2006, p329. For issues of enforcement of multi-tier dispute resolution clauses, see also Christopher Boog, "How to Deal with Multi-tiered Dispute Resolution Clauses – Note on the Swiss Federal Supreme Court's Decision 4A_18/2007 of 6 June 2007", *ASA Bulletin*, Vol 26, No 1, 2008, pp103–112.

conciliation board for the conduct of a conciliation procedure. For details on the appointment of the conciliation board and its function during the construction process, see section 3.3 above.

The conciliation procedure is initiated by written request of one of the parties. The conciliation board is obliged to conduct a hearing, at which both parties may present their positions in a comprehensive manner. Within 14 days from the end of the hearing, the conciliation board must submit to the parties its non-binding proposals for the settlement of the dispute. Each party must declare within two weeks whether it accepts or rejects the proposals, failing which the proposals are deemed to be rejected. If a dispute remains unresolved, the parties may agree to resubmit the matter to the conciliation board for reconsideration. Alternatively, each party may initiate phase 3 of the dispute resolution process.

(c) Phase 3: Decision by an arbitral tribunal or a state court

In the case of unsuccessful conciliation proceedings, the parties may call upon the state courts or an arbitral tribunal for resolution of the dispute, depending on their agreement. VSS Recommendation 641 510 contains a set of rules for arbitral proceedings, declaring Chapter 12 of the Private International Law Act inapplicable and subjecting the proceedings to domestic arbitration law.

(d) Further competences of the conciliation board

According to VSS Recommendation 641 510, the parties may empower the conciliation board to decide disputes as an arbitral tribunal up to a defined amount in dispute. In recent years, in a number of infrastructure projects subject to VSS Recommendation 641 510, the conciliation board acted as arbitral tribunal in controversies up to an amount in dispute of SFr500,000, after the conciliation procedure had not resulted in a settlement of the dispute.[30]

Quite frequently, the conciliation board is also entrusted with the securing of evidence during the project.[31]

6. Conclusion

In the past years, alternative methods of dispute resolution such as conciliation, mediation and expert determination have become increasingly popular, in particular in large construction projects. The reasons for this development are manifold and include the considerable time and costs involved in litigation or arbitration proceedings or the desire to maintain existing business relationships. Conciliation and mediation in particular aim at finding a win–win solution between the parties, thereby often creating a new basis for a future relationship. It is to be expected that this development in favour of alternative methods of dispute resolution will continue in the coming years, not least because the foregoing reasons for using such methods will further gain importance under the current economic conditions.

It is also expected that the use of arbitration in domestic disputes will increase

30 Hürlimann, *op. cit.*, p150.
31 *Ibid.*

after the legal framework for domestic arbitral proceedings has been significantly modernised and made more attractive. As for international arbitration, it is to be expected that Switzerland will defend its position as one of the leading venues for arbitration in the future, not least because Chapter 12 of the Private International Law Act will be modernised in the near future.

United Kingdom

Lucy Goldsmith
Nicholas Gould
Fenwick Elliott LLP

1. Introduction

The construction industry in any developed country makes the largest industry-specific contribution to the gross domestic product (GDP) of that country. It also tends to provide more employment than any other industry. In 2011 the gross value added (GVA) of the construction industry in the United Kingdom was £89.5 billion, 6.7%% of total GVA. There were 2.04 million jobs in the UK construction industry in March 2012, amounting to 6.4% of all workforce jobs. The construction industry, particularly house building, has fared badly during the recession since 2009. Output in the industry fell at a faster rate than total GDP. The industry rebounded more quickly than the rest of the economy during the last three quarters of 2010, but contracted again during the third quarter of 2011 and the first quarter of 2012.[1]

Some specific and important projects include the Olympics, Crossrail, Heathrow Airport Terminal 5, and energy projects.

1.1 London 2012 Olympics

Undoubtedly the highlight of 2012 for the UK construction industry was the London 2012 Olympic Games. The 2012 Games were hailed as a huge success and silenced critics who had suggested the project would be riddled with disputes akin to those played out on Wembley Stadium with the infamous Multiplex/Honeywell litigation.[2] The London Olympics project was completed on time and within budget.[3]

Following the success of the 2012 Games, the National Audit Office (NAO) has urged the government to deploy the skills developed during the construction of the Olympic Games venues and infrastructure, particularly in respect of project management, contracting and risk management, to other public sector projects.[4]

---

1 House of Commons Library, "Construction Industry", Standard Note SN/EP/1432, August 13 2012. Author: Lucinda Maer. Section: Economic Policy and Statistics.

2 By way of illustration, reference is made to *Multiplex Constructions (UK) Ltd v Cleveland Bridge (No 6)* [2008] EWHC 2220 (TCC).

3 The Olympic stadium was completed in March 2011, under budget and ahead of schedule. The actual cost was £8.921 billion versus a budget of £9.28 billion. The National Audit Office (NAO) reported on December 5 2012 that, if no further cost pressures emerged, the cost of delivering the Olympic Games was expected to come in £377 million under its £9.3 billion budget. The NAO also confirmed that the Olympic Delivery Authority's (ODA) programme to build the Games' venues and infrastructure is expected to be around £6.7 billion, 17% lower than the £8.1 billion originally available to it.

4 Reference is made to NAO Executive Summary Report, *The London 2012 Olympic Games and Paralympics Games: Post Games Review*, dated December 5 2012.

1.2 Crossrail

Crossrail is currently the biggest engineering project in Europe, forming a major part of the mayor's Transport Strategy for London. This project is not scheduled to finish until 2018; however, 2015 will mark the completion of its first station, Canary Wharf. When it opens in 2018, Crossrail will connect 37 stations, including Heathrow Airport and Maidenhead in the west with Canary Wharf, Abbey Wood and Shenfield in the east. Large-scale stations will be built along the central route of the line at Paddington, Bond Street, Tottenham Court Road, Farringdon, Liverpool Street, Whitechapel and Canary Wharf.

As well as making travelling easier and quicker, the new Crossrail service will assist in reducing crowding on London's transport network, with each train carrying up to 1,500 passengers. The project is a key part of London's plan for growth over the years ahead and will encourage regeneration and social inclusion, creating thousands of job opportunities. Crossrail has provided a much needed boost to the UK construction industry with an estimated benefit of £42 billion to the UK economy.

1.3 Heathrow Airport Terminal 5

Heathrow Airport's Terminal 5 (T5) was one of the largest infrastructure and construction projects in Europe. It comprised a complex web of 16 major interconnecting projects and 140 sub-projects. The scope of the total project included the 270,000m^2 main terminal building, two satellite buildings (each the size of Heathrow Terminal 4) and a new 87m-high control tower to serve all of Heathrow.

Supporting infrastructure works included a major tunnelling programme to connect T5 with existing terminals, a new transport interchange, the extension of the Heathrow Express rail link and the Piccadilly tube line, two river diversions and a dedicated spur off the M25 motorway.

The works commenced in September 2002 and were completed in March 2008. The actual cost was £4.2 billion. Overall, the works were completed on time and within budget.[5]

1.4 Pembroke B Power Station

Pembroke B Power Station is a 2,000-megawatt (MW) natural-gas-fired power station located in South Wales. Construction started in summer 2009 and the power station was officially opened on September 19 2012. It cost £800 million to build and currently generates enough power to supply 3.5 million homes and businesses.

The power station uses natural gas supplied from the nearby liquefied natural gas terminals at Milford Haven rather than directly from a gas field. The gas is fed to five 400 MW modules, each with a gas turbine, heat recovery steam generator and steam turbine.

2. Procurement and standard forms

An overview of standard forms cannot be divorced from the procurement pathways used in the construction industry. The development of standard forms is historic in that the most widely recognised standard forms were developed by construction professionals, principally the Royal Institute of British Architects (RIBA) and the

---

5 www.echarris.com/PDF/7374_Case%20study_T5%20FINAL%20NO%20MARKS.pdf

Institution of Civil Engineers (ICE). However, with commercialisation of standard forms and diversity within the construction industry, not to mention its global nature, there are now a wide variety of standard forms and a large number of organisations producing them.

2.1 Traditional procurement standard forms

Traditional procurement standard forms that may be selected, for example, for traditional, employer-designed works include:

- JCT suite of contracts (for building works);
- ICE suite of contracts (for engineering works);
- NEC (for both building and engineering works);
- GC/Works; and
- minor works agreements.

Probably the most widely recognised and certainly the most widely used in the UK is the JCT 2005 family of forms (updated in 2011).[6] The ICE forms are no longer published by the Institution of Civil Engineers, but they remain popular because of their long history of use in the engineering industry.

The NEC (now NEC 3rd Edition) was produced by a private publisher in order to provide a suite of contracts for a variety of different procurement pathways.[7] The NEC approach has been the most novel, mainly because NEC has adopted a 'less is best' approach to drafting, resulting in very short clauses. NEC is an attempt to draft a simple and direct standard-form contract without trying to build upon the standard forms. The core principles of NEC may be described as flexibility, simplicity, clarity and a stimulus for good management.

The GC/Works suite of construction contracts was published in 1999 and 2000, and it is still used occasionally for public-sector or engineering projects. It is perceived as an employer-friendly suite.

Minor works contracts are available from JCT, ICE, NEC and a variety of other publishers.

In reality there has been a huge move to design-and-build contracts, together with the expansion and now retraction of the public finance initiative (PFI). This has led to a wider range of standard-form contracts, with increased design obligations being used throughout the construction industry.

2.2 Management contracting and construction management

Alternative forms of procurement, management contracting and construction management are innovations from the 1980s which largely developed from the greater

---

6 The RICS/Davis Langdon, "A survey of building contracts in use during 2010", found that over 97% of construction projects use a standard form of contract; 88% of projects used one of the JCT family of contracts, up from 79% in 2007 and 78% in 2004. The JCT Design and Build Contract is the most commonly used contract for projects in the ranges of £500,000 to £10 million and £20 million to £50 million. The JCT forms were updated in 2011 to take into account changes introduced by the Local Democracy, Economic Development and Construction Act 2009. The Joint Contracts Tribunal (JCT) also took the opportunity to make further amendments relating to the Bribery Act 2010.

7 The publisher, Thomas Telford, is owned by the ICE.

fragmentation of the construction industry. Management contracting and construction management stem from the process where main contractors no longer employed large workforces to carry out the works but instead relied upon subcontractors to carry out the physical works on site. These methods are often appropriate for large projects where there is benefit to be gained by commencing work before the design stage is complete.

2.3 Partnering

Partnering is a further more radical collaboration, reflected in PPC2000 and TPC2000 (both amended in 2008). Commentators remain sceptical about PPC2000, particularly during challenging economic times, and have questioned the whole approach of partnering under PPC2000 where all parties enter into a single contract. However, some clients and sectors, in particular the social housing sector, have adopted the PPC2000 suite and have used the contract effectively for many years.

2.4 International

The Fédération Internationale Des Ingénieurs-Conseils (FIDIC) suite of contracts is widely recognised and used internationally.[8] Interestingly, this is not the case in UK. However, the 1957 FIDIC Red Book was based on the Overseas (Civil) Conditions of Contract, a form published in 1956 by the Association of Consulting Engineers and modelled on the Institution of Civil Engineers Form, which was drawn up mainly for the domestic market in the United Kingdom.

3. Building information modelling (BIM) – impact on standard forms and procurement

The government's construction strategy requires that all government projects use a full, collaborative, two-dimensional computer model (Level 2) by 2016, with all project and asset information, documentation and data being electronic. It is intended that the industry will move to fully integrated BIM (BIM Level 3) thereafter.

BIM is defined by the Construction Project Information Committee supported by the RIBA as:

> *digital representation of physical and functional characteristics of a facility creating a shared knowledge resource for information about it forming a reliable basis for decisions during its life cycle, from earliest conception to demolition.*

BIM is effectively a way of approaching the design and documentation of a project, using three-dimensional computer technology which is shared amongst the design and construction teams, incorporating cost, programme, design, physical performance and other information regarding the entire life cycle of the building in the construction information/building model.

The following questions arise: what are the legal and contractual implications of BIM? Do standard forms require amendment to account for the use of BIM? Does the party managing the BIM model acquire additional risk and liability?

---

8 Fédération Internationale des Ingénieurs–Conseils (International Federation of Consulting Engineers) is an international federation of associations of consulting engineers representing the profession in their respective countries. Its secretariat is in Switzerland.

Level 2 BIM provides data and information in a three-dimensional environment, with each member of the design (and possibly construction) team creating and maintaining its own model. These models and databases work together with the use of proprietary technology, and this consolidated model, comprising individual levels prepared by each discipline, is often referred to as a 'federation model in a common data environment'. Level 3 BIM, on the other hand, uses a single project model, accessible to all team members.

As to whether there will be any change in the traditional legal position, the consensus appears to be that the use of BIM at Level 2 does not require wholesale change to the traditional forms of contract or allocation of responsibilities between the parties. However, as BIM moves towards Level 3, changes to building contracts may well be required.

At present, there is no UK standard BIM protocol. However, this will be required at some point in the future. Appendix 20 of the (UK) Government Construction Client Group's "Strategy Paper" (downloadable from www.bimtaskgroup.org) provided a draft illustrative BIM protocol for discussion, but it is thought that this protocol is too brief.

To have any legal recourse, parties are likely to require the BIM protocol to have status in the building contract as a contract document. Notably, the JCT contract amendment introduced in December 2011 in the Public Sector Supplement (Fair Payment, Transparency and Building Information Modelling) requires the BIM protocol to be a contract document.

In summary, Level 2 BIM is unlikely to change the current legal landscape of the construction industry provided that the BIM protocol addresses risk allocation and other elements. However, as the construction industry moves towards Level 3 BIM, contractual relationships and risks are likely to change, resulting in more sophisticated contractual arrangements.

4. Dispute resolution techniques

4.1 The spectrum of dispute resolution methods

Many different labels have been given to the wide range of dispute resolution techniques available in the United Kingdom. In reality there are only three distinct processes and all dispute resolution techniques are built upon these. They are:

- negotiation – the problem-solving efforts of the parties themselves;
- mediation or conciliation – a third-party intervention which does not lead to a binding decision being imposed on the parties; and
- an adjudicative process – where the final outcome is determined by a third party who does impose a binding decision on the parties.

Professor Green of Boston University labelled these as the three pillars of dispute resolution. His chart was adapted by Gould *et al* (1999) and is reproduced at Figure 1.[9]

9 N. Gould, P. Capper, G. Dixon and M. Cohen (1999) *Dispute Resolution in the Construction Industry*, London: Thomas Telford.

Figure 1: The dispute resolution landscape

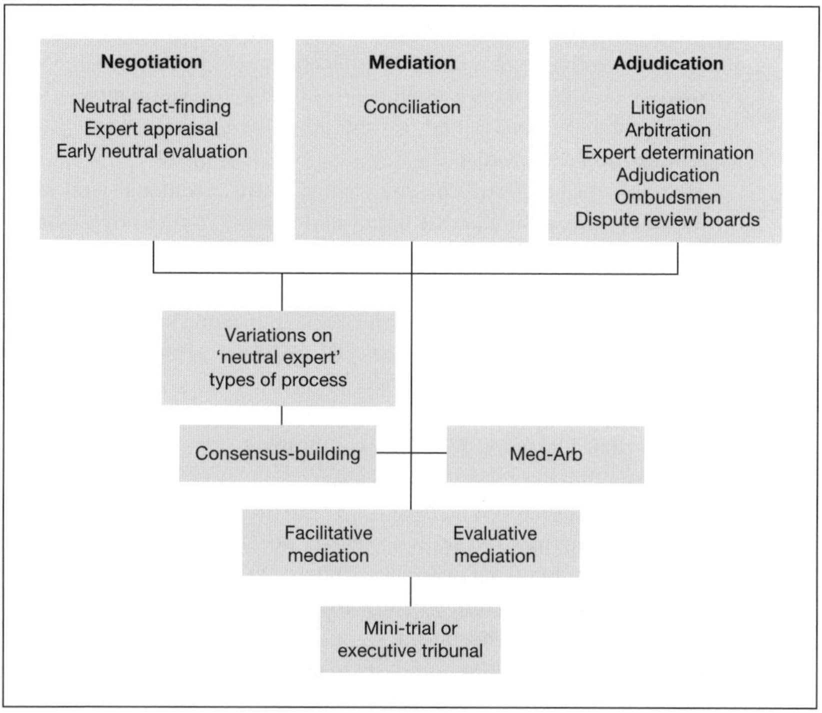

Adapted from a chart by Professor Green of Boston University (1993).

4.2 Overview of dispute resolution techniques

The basic principles of the most frequently encountered dispute resolution techniques are as follows.

(a) *Negotiation*

The parties work out between them how to resolve any issues that have arisen. Power to settle the dispute rests with the parties.

(b) *Mediation and conciliation*

The parties agree on an independent, third-party neutral system to facilitate discussions between them, with the goal of reaching a settlement. The power to settle remains with the parties, but the process is led by a mediator.

(c) *Expert determination*

The parties agree by contract that a third party will make a binding decision on them. The terms are therefore governed by the contract. In most cases the decision of an expert will be final, and it will not be possible to appeal that decision. This means that the decision of an expert finally determines the dispute without further recourse.

(d) ***Adjudication***

Adjudication under Section 108 of the Housing Grants, Construction and Regeneration Act 1996 was introduced in May 1998. The detailed procedure for adjudication is set out in secondary legislation known as the Scheme.[10] The Local Democracy, Economic Development and Construction Act 2009 and the updated Scheme revise some aspects of the adjudication process. Adjudication has been widely used in the construction industry and applies not only to building contracts but also to professional appointments.

If the act applies to a contract, then either party may request the appointment of an adjudicator to be made within seven days of serving a notice of dispute, and the adjudicator has 28 days from issue of the referral within which to issue a decision. That decision will bind the parties and in most cases be readily enforceable in the Technology and Construction Court (TCC). The TCC is the part of the High Court that deals with construction-related litigation.

(e) ***Arbitration***

For arbitration to apply, the contract between the parties must contain a written agreement to arbitrate. Where it applies, the parties might choose to refer to or incorporate an arbitration procedure, such as the Construction Industry Model Arbitration Rules. Alternatively, the arbitration can simply be covered by the applicable legislation, such as the Arbitration Act 1996. Many jurisdictions around the world contain legislation dealing with arbitration, often based upon the United Nations Commission on International Trade Law (UNCITRAL) Model Law.

(f) ***Litigation***

The courts have inherent jurisdiction to hear a dispute in respect of just about anything. In the absence of any other procedure, the parties will have a right to refer their matter to an appropriate court. The procedure is governed by the Civil Procedure Rules, and the nature, complexity and value of the dispute will determine which court will hear a particular dispute.

Courts have the widest jurisdiction and, in addition to determining disputes and declarations, they can also issue charging orders, summon witnesses and involve third parties in the dispute as necessary.

Note that bankruptcy and insolvency proceedings such as administration and the winding-up of companies are not primarily governed by the Civil Procedure Rules but by the Insolvency Act and related regulations. In some circumstances a clear debt may be recovered more economically and easily by serving a statutory demand or a winding-up petition rather than commencing an action in the court.

(g) ***Dispute boards***

Interestingly, dispute boards sit somewhere between avoidance and dispute resolution. Their genesis is in dispute review or recommendation boards (DRBs).

---

10 The Scheme for Construction Contracts (England and Wales) Regulations 1998 (Amendment) (England) Regulations 2011 (SI 2011/2333).

Three dispute board members are appointed at the start of a project. They become familiar with the project by reviewing some of the project documentation and also regularly visiting the site during the course of the works. If and as issues arise, they can be asked for their non-binding recommendation. This may relate to general disagreements or disputes. Often their recommendations are used to resolve disputes between the parties, thus avoiding formal disputes.

Dispute adjudication boards (DABs), on the other hand, while following a very similar pattern, make formal written decisions which bind the parties in respect of any disputes that arise. There is therefore a clear distinction between a DRB and a DAB. Generically they are called dispute boards (DBs).

There is one variation on the theme and that is a 'combined dispute board' that was developed by the International Chamber of Commerce (ICC). The ICC's Combined Dispute Board procedure provides for recommendations or decisions. The parties may request the dispute board to deliver either a recommendation or a binding decision. If the parties cannot agree, then a dispute board can decide whether simply to issue a non-binding recommendation or a written binding decision.

5. Growth of alternative dispute resolution in the United Kingdom

5.1 Trends

Alternative dispute resolution (ADR) has attracted a great deal of attention in the United Kingdom since the mid-1980s. It refers to processes that are alternatives to the traditional binding dispute resolution procedures of litigation and arbitration. It is alternative in the sense that it provides a faster and more economic dispute resolution procedure. Originally ADR was used to describe a consensual alternative approach which helps to maintain business relationships. Broader definitions could include adjudication, negotiation or mediation, or indeed some other form of contractual dispute resolution technique.

5.2 Mediating construction disputes

Mediation has now been used, in the commercial context, for the resolution of disputes in a wide range of industry sectors, both before starting and during formal proceedings. It can of course be used, in theory, at any stage, not just during litigation but also when other forms of dispute resolution, such as arbitration, are contemplated or progressing.

The use of mediation within contracts or as part of a dispute escalation clause has also become more popular, not just in the construction industry but in other commercial sectors as well.[11] A large range of dispute resolution techniques are available for use in the construction industry. Arbitration is still the default dispute resolution procedure, because it was originally included as the only dispute resolution procedure in the most popular standard form of contracts.

Previously, data concerning the effectiveness of mediation in the construction

---

11 See, for example, the dispute escalation clause in *Cable & Wireless Plc v IBM United Kingdom Ltd* [2002] EWHC 2059.

industry, whilst available, was somewhat limited. To address this, an evidence-based survey was developed between King's College London and the Technology and Construction Court (TCC). A summary report of the final results was published on May 7 2009 and can be downloaded for free.[12]

Research undertaken by King's College London, in association with the TCC, shows that mediation is used to resolve about 35% of all disputes that go to court in relation to construction work.[13]

In brief, the findings show the following:

- Mediation now plays an important role in the TCC and is an indispensable tool for settling cases before they go to trial.
- Parties do not generally wait until a hearing is imminent before attempting to settle their dispute, and successful mediations are mainly carried out during the exchange of pleadings or as a result of disclosure.
- Where a settlement was reached prior to judgment, the most successful method used was conventional negotiation, not mediation.
- In the vast majority of cases, mediation is undertaken on the parties' own initiatives.
- Surprisingly, only a low number of typical mainstream construction disputes (such as claims for variations, delays and site conditions) come before the court. The common disputes that reach the TCC are those involving defects, payment issues, design issues and professional negligence.
- For the vast majority of mediations in construction disputes, the mediator is appointed by agreement of the parties, rather than by an appointing body.
- The cost savings attributed to successful mediations are a real incentive for parties to consider mediation.

5.3 The English courts' approach to mediation

The English courts have, since the early 1990s, encouraged mediation. In 1993 the Commercial Court started encouraging ADR by making orders directing the parties to attempt mediation and thereafter to inform the courts of the steps taken to ADR if it failed. Although the scheme was non-mandatory, the aim of the orders was to impose substantial pressure on the parties to mediate and 233 ADR orders were made between 1996 and 2000.[14] In 1996 the Court of Appeal also established a voluntary

---

12 The report can be downloaded from www.fenwickelliott.co.uk/. Nicholas Gould, Partner, Fenwick Elliott LLP and Senior Visiting Lecturer King's College London led the research with coordination and drafting assistance from Claire King, Assistant Solicitor, Fenwick Elliott LLP.

13 See N. Gould, C. King and P. Britton (2010) Mediating Construction Disputes – An Evaluation of Existing Practice. Kings College London, London, p49. The report was a collaborative project involving several contributors, with support throughout from the Society of Construction Law and the Centre of Construction Law & Dispute Resolution, School of Law, at King's College London. It is the first piece of empirical research ever undertaken jointly between the Technology and Construction Court and an academic institution. In the foreword to this final report Lord Justice Jackson notes that: "Empirical data are far more valuable than the anecdotal evidence about litigant behaviour which sometimes informs decisions." The report also includes a preface by Lord Woolf (architect of the UK's present Civil Procedure Rules and a great advocate of mediation). The report can be downloaded at: www.fenwickelliott.co.uk/mediating-construction-disputes-download.

14 See Department for Constitutional Affairs (now Ministry of Justice), "Court-based initiatives for non-family civil disputes: the Commercial Court and the Court of Appeal", by Professor Hazel Genn, Faculty of Laws at University College London, Executive Summary.

ADR scheme and the Central London County Court implemented a voluntary mediation pilot scheme in April 1996.

One of the key aims of Lord Woolf's recommendations in his review of the civil justice system and access to justice reports of 1995 and 1996 was to encourage ADR, especially at an early stage before matters had reached litigation.

The courts are active supporters of ADR, including mediation, and the use of ADR is encouraged at all stages of the litigation process. This approach is reflected in the Civil Procedure Rules, the pre-action protocols and the court guides for particular courts. The guidance and rules that relate to construction disputes can be found in the second revision of the second edition of the TCC Guide, in effect from October 1 2012,[15] and the Pre-Action Protocol for Construction and Engineering Disputes.

Further, courts will generally enforce mediation and impose cost penalties. By way of illustration, in the case of *PGF II SA v OMFS Company and another*[16] the TCC considered submissions that a party should not have Part 36 costs because of its failure to communicate a pleading point and refusal to mediate.

On the refusal-to-mediate point, the judge held that the defendant had unreasonably refused to respond to a suggested mediation. The judge held that, in failing to respond to the suggested mediation, the defendant had refused to mediate and the mediation had a prospect of success. Accordingly, it had been unreasonable for the defendant to refuse to mediate and the conduct was a matter to be taken into account in the exercise of discretion as to costs incurred after the relevant period. Given his views on this point and the pleadings issue, in all the circumstances, he ordered that there was to be no order for costs for that period.

5.4 Multi-tiered dispute resolution processes

The courts will enforce multi-tiered dispute resolution provisions. In *The Channel Tunnel Rail Group Limited v Balfour*,[17] Lord Mustill emphasised that:

> *having made this choice I believe that those who make agreements for the resolution of disputes must show good reasons for departing from them ... that having promised to take their complaints to the experts and go if necessary to the Arbitrators, that is where the Appellants should go.*

The courts will also enforce agreements to mediate where they are part of such a procedure. In *Cable & Wireless plc v IBM United Kingdom Limited*,[18] the court was asked to award a stay of proceedings while the parties undertook the ADR processes provided for within the contract. The ADR provisions were held to have binding effect.

---

15 In brief, the purpose of the TCC Guide is to provide practical guidance on using the TCC and to set out an overall framework for litigation in the TCC. The TCC Guide is designed to ensure effective case management of proceedings. The court can impose sanctions, including orders for costs, if the parties fail to comply with its requirements. The TCC Guide is to be applied in conjunction with the principles of the Civil Procedure Rules, including the overriding objective prescribed in Part 1.1 of the rules. Parties are expected to be familiar with the rules and the overriding objective in Part 1.1. The purpose of the TCC Guide is to explain how the substantive law, rules and practice directions are applied in the TCC. If the TCC Guide does not give specific guidance on a procedural matter, the parties are expected to act reasonably and in accordance with the TCC Guide and the overriding objective (reference is made to section 1.1, TCC Guide).

16 [2012] EWHC 83 (TCC).

17 *The Channel Tunnel Rail Group Limited v Balfour Beatty Construction Limited* [1993] 61BLR1, HL.

18 [2002] EWHC 2059.

Notably, the ADR clause was a sufficiently defined mutual obligation upon the parties to go through the process of initiating mediation, selecting a mediator and at least presenting the mediator with their cases and documents. Since the clause described the means by which such an attempt should be made, the engagement required not merely an attempt in good faith to achieve resolution of the dispute, but also the participation of the parties in the procedure specified. The procedure was of sufficient certainty for a court readily to ascertain whether it should have been compiled with.

However, a note of caution was sounded in the case of *Balfour Beatty Construction Northern Limited v Modus Corovest (Blackpool) Ltd.*[19] In this case the mediation agreement was characterised as nothing more than an 'agreement to agree'. Unlike the mediation agreement in *Cable & Wireless*, it was held to be too uncertain to be enforced by the court. The judge went on to say that he would only stay a claim and counterclaim for mediation if he concluded that:

a) the party making the Claim and or Counterclaim was not entitled to summary Judgment on that Claim and/or Counterclaim, ie, that there was an arguable defence on which the other party had a realistic prospect of success; and

b) the best way of resolving that dispute was a reference to mediation.

6. Expert determination

Expert determination is a creature of contract. The parties agree by contract to refer a dispute to a third party who will then decide that particular issue. The third party might decide a technical or valuation issue, as is common, but, in theory, an expert can determine any dispute which the parties agree to refer. Traditionally, expert determination was used for valuing shares in private companies or certifying profits or losses of companies during sale and purchase. In the construction industry expert determination has been, and is, used for determining value, either of an entire account or sometimes in relation to parts of an account, such as variations.

There are many instances when adjudication is available, and so expert determination has been somewhat eclipsed. However, expert determination can still be used and may be applicable where the Housing Grants, Construction and Regeneration Act 1996 does not apply. Internationally, expert determination is still encountered, often as part of a multi-stage dispute resolution procedure. It is also used in property-related agreements such as development agreements. Finality is a fundamental feature of expert determination and this sets it apart from other forms of dispute resolution. The provisions in the contract for expert determination frequently state that the decision of the expert shall be final and binding on the parties. The courts have taken the view that the decision of an expert will therefore be enforced regardless of any errors.

It is now accepted that when parties agree by contract to refer a dispute to a person as an expert, then the expert's determination is binding on the parties. In *Campbell v Edwards* the Court of Appeal had to consider the expert determination of

19 *Balfour Beatty Construction Limited v Modus Corovest (Blackpool) Limited* [2008] EWHC 3029 (TCC); and *Construction Industry Law Letter*, February 2009, p2661.

a valuer. Lord Denning recognised that the reason for upsetting the decision of valuers no longer existed, and therefore it was now possible to recognise the binding nature of an expert's decision. Lord Denning stated:

> *In former times (when it was thought that the valuer was not liable for negligence) the court used to look for some way of upsetting a valuation which was shown to be erroneous. They used to say that it could be upset, not only for fraud or collusion, but also on the ground of mistake: see for instance what I said in* Dean v. Prince. *But those cases have to be reconsidered now. I did reconsider them in* Arenson v. Arenson *[1973] 2 WLR 553. I stand by what I said there. It is simply the law of contracts. If two persons agree that the price of property should be fixed by a valuer on whom they agree, and he gives a valuation honestly and in good faith, they are bound by it. Even if he makes a mistake they are bound by it.*

Lord Denning was simply giving effect to the contractual arrangement between the parties. The parties had agreed to be bound by the expert's determination (in that case a valuation) and so the parties were obliged to give effect to the decision. It was not for the court to interfere and come to a different valuation. If the valuer had made a mistake or if one party was arguing that the decision was erroneous, then that was irrelevant. Provided that the valuer had done what he had been asked to do, the parties were bound by it, subject to fraud or collusion. In *Campbell v Edwards* Lord Denning said that "fraud or collusion unravels everything". The only exception, therefore, is where a party can show fraud or collusion by the expert.

Campbell was approved by the Court of Appeal in *Jones v Sherwood Computer Services plc*,[20] where an expert was asked to determine a valuation in respect of a sale-and-purchase agreement. One party was not satisfied with the outcome and challenged the reasoning behind the determination. The Court of Appeal stated that the expert had been asked to determine a level of sales, and that is exactly what the expert had done. As the expert had asked the right question, the decision had to be enforced. This approach has been followed and adopted in subsequent cases.

Expert determination can be an economic way of finally resolving valuation disputes. An expert can consider both parties' arguments and then come to a definitive conclusion about the value.

Expert determination could be used more frequently in the construction industry. It may be included within the contracts at the outset (subject to the availability of an adjudication), or it may be that the parties are able to agree to use an expert to resolve the valuation aspects of a dispute that has already arisen.

7. Adjudication

Adjudication is well established and a common occurrence within the construction industry and other common law jurisdictions.[21]

---

20 [1992] 1 WLR 277.

21 Adjudication in England, Wales and Scotland was introduced in May 1998 by the implementation of Part 2 of the Housing Grants, Construction and Regeneration Act 1996. Its use has been reasonably well documented and the number of appointments made by the adjudicator-nominating bodies demonstrates its wide use, as do the regular surveys produced by the Adjudication Reporting Centre, based at Glasgow Caledonian University. Other common law jurisdictions where adjudication has been introduced are Australia (now all of the states from Australia), Singapore and New Zealand.

In 1994 Sir Michael Latham issued his final report reviewing procurement and contractual arrangements in the construction industry.[22] He identified industry inefficiencies, and condemned existing industry practice as adversarial and incapable of delivery for its clients. He also urged reform and recommended that adjudication should be the normal form of dispute resolution.

Adjudication was introduced in England, Wales and Scotland in May 1998 under the Housing Grants, Construction and Regeneration Act 1996 (HGCRA). Section 108 in Part 2 of that act introduced a right to adjudication for any contracts in writing that came within the definitions in Sections 104 and 105. The requirement for construction contracts to be in writing was repealed on October 1 2011 by Part 8 of the Local Democracy, Economic Development and Construction Act 2009. In effect, most of the frequently encountered construction and engineering contracts involving the carrying-out of construction operations, whether by way of new refurbishment, repair or maintenance or otherwise, were covered. Professional appointments also fall within the jurisdiction of an adjudicator.

Adjudication does not apply to a residential occupier carrying out work to a house that he occupies, or intends to occupy, as a residence. Neither does it apply to a series of specific exclusions within the act, including the drilling for or extraction of oil or natural gas, minerals tunnelling or boring, or the assembly, insulation or demolition of plant and machinery or erection or demolition of steelwork for the purposes of providing access to plant or machinery on a site where the primary activity is nuclear power, power generation or water or effluent treatment. Also excluded are sites where the primary activity relates to chemicals, pharmaceuticals, oil, gas, steel, or food and drink. Reference must be made to Sections 104 and 105 in order to deal specifically with these exclusions.

The key provision of the act is Section 108. Assuming that the HGCRA applies to a particular construction contract, then Section 108 provides any party with the right to refer a dispute at any time to adjudication. The noticeable features of Section 108 are as follows:

- There must be a dispute. In other words, a dispute must have crystallised between the parties before it can then be referred to an adjudicator. For example, there could be a dispute about the amount that should be paid in respect of a particular monthly valuation. Any matters that make up that dispute could then be referred to an adjudicator, subject to the scope of the Notice of Adjudication.
- The construction contract must provide that notice can be given at any time in respect of the dispute. In other words, any party can refer the dispute at any time to an adjudicator. This ability to refer the dispute at any time cannot be restricted.
- Once the dispute has been referred, an adjudicator should be appointed and the dispute referred to that adjudicator within seven days of issue of the notice. The emphasis here is for the parties either to agree an adjudicator promptly or for an adjudicator-nominating body to appoint one sufficiently

22 M. Latham (1994), *Constructing the Team*, London: HMSO.

quickly for the referring party to refer the dispute to the adjudicator before the seven-day deadline has expired. There are a number of adjudicator-nominating bodies in the United Kingdom, of which the Royal Institution of Chartered Surveyors is the most widely recognised.

- The decision must be given within 28 days of issue of the referral. The referral must be issued to the responding party and the adjudicator simultaneously on or before the expiry of the seven-day referral period. It is important to note that the referral could be made within just a couple of days after issue of the Notice of Adjudication. In that case, the 28-day period would start from the issue of the referral and so adjudication would proceed quicker than a responding party might anticipate. If the adjudicator has accepted jurisdiction, then the adjudicator is obliged to complete the decision within the 28-day period (or any other properly extended period).
- The referring party can extend the period by up to 14 days, but any further extension must be approved by both parties. There is very little leeway available to the adjudicator, who must reach a decision and communicate it to the parties.
- There is an obligation on the adjudicator to act impartially and fairly. In effect, this means that the adjudicator must give both parties a reasonable opportunity of putting their case and responding to the case before them.
- The adjudicator's decision will be binding. The courts have taken a robust attitude to the enforcement of adjudicators' decisions and, provided that the adjudicator has jurisdiction to make a decision and has not lost it along the way because of some procedural error or breach of natural justice, there is a very high chance that the decision will be enforced.[23]
- Finally, an adjudicator has statutory immunity unless acting in bad faith.

As to current trends in adjudication, statistics published by the Adjudication Reporting Centre are shown in Figure 2.[24]

In summary, in 2007 there was a 5% reduction from the previous year in adjudication referrals, bringing the number of referrals down from 1,506 to 1,432. The previous year, however, saw an increase of 5%. From 2002 to 2008 there was a steady decline in the number of referrals, with 2006–07 being an exception when the number of referrals increased by 5% from the previous year.

It is worth noting that the act only applies to construction operations that are carried out in England, Wales or Scotland.[25] Further, parties cannot contract out of the act by choosing the law of another country.[26]

Statutory-backed adjudication originated in the United Kingdom but has slowly spread to other common law countries. Adjudication has now received backing throughout all the states in Australia, New Zealand, Singapore and most recently

---

23 See the first reported case on enforcement, *Macob Civil Engineering v Morrison Construction* [1999] BLR 93, and the first appeal case of *Bouygues UK Ltd v Dahl-Jensen UK Ltd* [2000] EWCA Civ 507.

24 P. Kennedy, J. L. Milligan, E. McCluskey and L. C. Attanach, Report no. 10, June 2010, Glasgow Caledonian University.

25 See Section 104(7) of the Housing Grants, Construction and Regeneration Act 1996.

26 *Comsite Projects Ltd v Andritz AG* [2003] EWHC 958 (TCC).

Figure 2: Current trends in adjudication

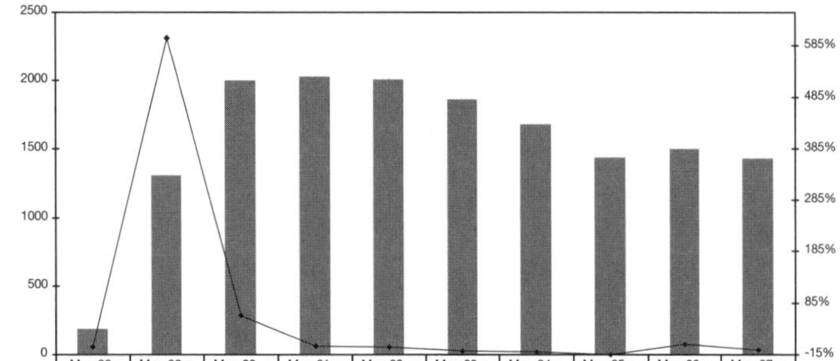

	May 98 – Apr 99	May 99 – Apr 00	May 00 – Apr 01	May 01 – Apr 02	May 02 – Apr 03	May 03 – Apr 04	May 04 – Apr 05	May 05 – Apr 06	May 06 – Apr 07	May 07 – Apr 08
No. of Adjudication referrals	187	1309	1999	2027	2008	1861	1685	1439	1506	1432
% increase/decrease	0%	600%	60%	1%	-1%	-7%	-9%	-15%	5%	-5%

Malaysia. After much debate the Construction Industry Payment and Adjudication Act 2012 of Malaysia received royal assent on June 18 2012.[27] It came into force on June 22 2012, and so Malaysia now has a statutory payment-and-adjudication regime for construction contracts.

8. Dispute boards[28]

The terms 'dispute review board' (DRB) and 'dispute adjudication board' (DAB), collectively dispute boards (DBs), are relatively new ones. They are used to describe a dispute resolution procedure that is normally established at the outset of a project and remains in place throughout the project's duration. The board may comprise one or three members who become acquainted with the contract, the project and the individuals involved with the project in order to provide informal assistance, recommendations about how disputes should be resolved and binding decisions.

The one-person or three-person DBs are remunerated throughout the project, usually by way of a monthly retainer, which is then supplemented with a daily fee for travelling to the site, attending site visits and dealing with issues that arise between the parties by way of reading documents, attending hearings and producing written recommendations or decisions if and as appropriate.

DABs have come into use more recently because of the increased globalisation of adjudication during the course of projects, coupled with the increased use of DRBs, which originally developed in the US domestic major-projects market. DRBs were apparently first used in the United States in 1975 on the Eisenhower Tunnel. The use of DRBs has grown steadily in the United States, but they have also been used internationally. However, DRBs predominantly remain the providence of US domestic construction projects. As adjudication developed, the World Bank and FIDIC opted for a binding dispute resolution process during the course of projects,

27 Rules of Malaysia, Act 746, Construction Industry Payment and Adjudication Act 2012. English translation.

28 See N. Gould (2012), "Enforcing a dispute board's decision: issues and considerations", *ICLR*, p442.

and so the dispute adjudication board evolved from the DRB system. The DRB provides a recommendation that is not binding on the parties.

The Dispute Resolution Board Foundation (DRBF) reported that as a result the recommendations of the Joint Consulting Board were followed, and these included several administrative procedural changes, the settlement of a variety of claims and an improvement in relationships between the parties. The project was also completed without litigation.

According to the DRBF, the records from December 2003 show that there were 340 contracts comprising DRBs that were currently active in 2003.[29] In regard to those projects, 1,261 recommendations were given by the DRBs and, according to the DRBF's records, only 28 matters went beyond the DRB process. In other words, only 2.2% of those disputes that were referred to the DRB progressed to arbitration or litigation. Harmon updated the DRBF database, recording that out of 2,753 disputes referred to the DRB panels, 327 (12%) disputes went on to a further dispute resolution process (mediation, arbitration or litigation).[30]

A more positive way of looking at this is that DRBs seem to work well in dealing with disputes at first instance. More recent statistics have been compiled by the DRBF, and reported by Harmon.[31] DBs have been used on at least 2,150 projects between the DRBF's inception in 1975 and 2010, including, amongst other things, tunnels, highways, rail, light rail, bridges, airports, container ports, buildings, schools, hospitals, sports stadiums, metro systems, pipelines, pumping stations, water treatment works, shopping centres, power plants, nuclear power plants, oil platforms and waste facilities. These projects were not just in the United States but worldwide (and therefore involved DRBs and DABs).

The important distinction then between DRBs and DABs is that the function of a DRB is to make a recommendation which the parties voluntarily accept (or reject), while the function of a DAB is to issue written decisions that bind the parties and must be implemented immediately during the course of the project. The DRB process is said to assist in developing amicable settlement procedures between the parties, such that the parties can accept or reject the DRB's recommendation.

An example of a recent high-profile DB procedure is that adopted for the London Olympics 2012. The Olympic Delivery Authority (ODA) set up an Independent Dispute Avoidance Panel (IDAP) comprising 10 construction professionals under the chairmanship of Dr Martin Barnes. Disputes not resolved by the IDAP were then to be referred to an adjudication panel, comprising 11 adjudicators under the chairmanship of Mr Peter Chapman.[32] As to the success of the dispute resolution

---

29 A. A. Matthews, "The First Dispute Review Board", *DRBF Forum*, 1(1) (1997); K. M. J. Harmon, "A Case Study as to the Effectiveness of Dispute Review Boards on the Central Artery/ Tunnel Project", *J Profl Issues Engineering Education Practice*, 1(1) (2009), 18–31.

30 K. M. J. Harmon, "Using DRBs to Maintain Control of Large Complex Construction Projects", *Dispute Resolution Journal*, 67(1) (Feb–Apr 2012), 70–75.

31 DRBF (2010), "Database of Projects", www.drb.org/manual/Database_2005.xls, 22 April 2010; K. M. J. Harmon, "To be or not to be – that is the question: Is a DRB Right for Your Project?" *Journal of Legal Affairs and Dispute Resolution in Engineering and Construction* (Feb 2011), 10–16.

32 Ellis Baker, "Is it all necessary? Who benefits? Provision for multi-tier dispute resolution in international construction projects", paper presented to a joint meeting of the Society of Construction Law and the Society of Construction Arbitrators, January 2009, paper number 154.

machinery, the ODA has not to date released any information on the IDAP and its successes and/or failures. It remains to be seen whether this information will at some point be made available, in particular given the inherently 'private' nature of the process.

9. Arbitration

Arbitration is a process, subject to statutory controls, whereby formal disputes are determined by a private tribunal chosen by the parties. It is an alternative to litigation and has been used for resolving disputes for some time.

Arbitration in England and Wales has legislative support in the form of the Arbitration Act 1996. The Arbitration (Scotland) Act 2010 applies to Scotland. The act provides a legal framework for arbitration, including recognition of the process, the arbitrator, the procedures, and also the award and enforcement of the award. Arbitrators receive their powers from the provisions of the act, in the absence of any agreement between the parties.

The Departmental Advisory Committee on Arbitration produced two reports: a substantial report on the Arbitration Bill, dated February 1996, and a shorter supplementary report on the Arbitration Act 1996, dated January 1997. The reports are used by the English courts as aids to interpreting the act.

The act was based on five main objectives:

- to ensure that arbitration is fair, cost-effective and rapid;
- to promote party autonomy (ie, to respect the parties' choices);
- to ensure that the courts have supportive powers at appropriate times;
- to ensure that the language used is user-friendly and readily accessible to the parties; and
- to follow the model law (which is used internationally) wherever possible.

Parties can agree to arbitrate once a dispute has arisen. However, it is more common to encounter an agreement to refer future disputes to arbitration. Many of the standard-form contracts contain arbitration provisions. Section 6(1) of the act recognises the distinction between an agreement to refer existing disputes to arbitration and an agreement to submit any future dispute to arbitration.

An arbitrator might be appointed by agreement of the parties. Alternatively, if the parties are unable to agree and have already identified an appointing institution within their arbitration agreement, that institution would then have the power to appoint the arbitral tribunal. For example, the President of the Royal Institution of Chartered Surveyors is frequently included within building contracts as the person to appoint an arbitrator.

Section 33 of the act requires a tribunal to act fairly and impartially between the parties. Each party must be given a reasonable opportunity to put its case and also to deal with the case of its opponent. Further, the tribunal should adopt procedures suitable to the circumstances of a particular case. They should avoid unnecessary delay or expense in order to provide a fair means for resolving the dispute.

Section 29 of the act provides immunity for the arbitrator. The arbitrator is not liable for anything done or omitted in the discharge of the function as an arbitrator, unless the act or omission is in bad faith. The immunity does not apply if an arbitrator resigns, but the court has the power to grant the arbitrator relief from liability if the court considers the circumstances appropriate.

The Construction Industry Model Arbitration Rules (CIMAR) were drafted to comply with the act, and they were adopted by JCT as the rules for an arbitration arising under a JCT contract. The rules set out the available procedures that are to be followed during an arbitration: the appointment of the tribunal, the joining of parties, the powers of the arbitrator, evidence and documents, procedure, hearings, provisional relief, sanctions, awards, remedies and costs. The rules anticipate that the parties might hold a documents-only arbitration, or one with a short hearing, as alternatives to an arbitration with a full hearing.

The arbitrator's award is final and binding on the parties, unless they agree to the contrary. The award by an arbitrator can, with leave of the court, be enforced as if it were a judgment of the court. The standing of an arbitration award is therefore that of a court judgment and so is easily enforced. Moreover, an arbitrator's award is in reality final and conclusive, and the opportunity to challenge an award is extremely limited.

An arbitrator need not make one composite award in respect of a dispute. It is possible to issue interim awards before issuing the final award. Any matters dealt with in an interim award are final. Indeed, substantial issues may well be dealt with during the course of an arbitration, perhaps leaving only the costs to be dealt with in the final award.

If the parties settle their dispute, then the arbitrator can issue, in the same way that a court can issue, a consent award recording the settlement agreement of the parties.

Previously the JCT suite of contracts provided arbitration as the fallback dispute resolution machinery provision, the consequence being that if parties did not specifically amend the contract to state that legal proceedings applied, arbitration would apply. This is no longer the case and in the 2005 suite of forms, arbitration still exists but is no longer the default position. For arbitration to apply, the parties must make an express election.

10. A specialist court

The Technology and Construction Court (TCC) is part of the Queen's Bench Division of the High Court; it was originally known as the Official Referees Court until it was relaunched as the TCC in October 1998. The TCC is a specialist court that deals with technology and construction disputes, and other disputes that involve questions or issues that are technically complex, such as IT disputes, EU procurement disputes and professional negligence claims, as well as enforcement of adjudication decisions and challenges to arbitrator's decisions. TCC cases are heard by specialist judges in both London and regional courts.

Over the past 15 years the court's reputation has steadily grown, and despite the proliferation of both adjudication and arbitration its caseload continues to increase both in the form of traditional litigation and through assisted methods of alternative dispute resolution. Interestingly, the TCC is the only court that operates a judge-led mediation service ('the Court Settlement Process').

Unlike judges in other divisions of the High Court, TCC judges are known for taking a hands-on approach to managing disputes, with each claim allocated to one particular judge who will also if possible be the trial judge. Despite the complex nature of many of the disputes, this approach has led to the majority of cases being dealt with within a 12-month period, and arguably this makes the TCC the fastest commercial court in the world.

Another particular characteristic of the TCC is that in addition to the Civil Procedure Rules, and in particular Part 60 (Technology and Construction Court claims) and its Practice Direction (PD 60), proceedings are governed by the Technology & Construction Court Guide. The guide does not add to or amend the rules; rather, its purpose is to explain how the substantive law, rules and practice directions are applied in the TCC.

10.1 The Costs Management Pilot

The Costs Management Pilot started in the TCC and Mercantile Courts on October 1 2011 and ran until March 31 2013. The pilot was monitored by means of questionnaires and follow-up phone calls in order to evaluate how effective costs management is in terms of controlling costs and keeping clients informed about the overall costs position (not just their own budgeted costs) and what additional workload this imposes on judges and court staff. The pilot aimed to bring to light practical problems and provide the opportunity for improvements before full implementation.[33]

The pilot was governed by Practice Direction 51G (PD 51G). This provides that, for those claims that fall within the pilot, each party will have to file and exchange a costs budget in the form set out in Precedent HB (Form HB) at the same time as filing the case management information sheet.

The costs budget requires reasonable allowances to be made for:

- *intended activities:* for example disclosure, preparation of witness statements, etc;
- *identifiable contingencies:* for example specific applications or resisting applications; and
- *disbursements:* in particular court fees, counsel's fees, any mediator or expert fees.

The court will have regard to any costs budget filed at any case management conference or pre-trial review and will decide whether or not it is appropriate to make a costs management order (CMO). If the court decides to make a CMO, it will, after making any appropriate revisions, record its approval of a party's budget and may order attendance at a subsequent costs management hearing (by telephone, if appropriate) in order to monitor expenditure.

Henry v NGN,[34] handed down on May 16 2012, is the first reported decision on

---

33 See L Neuberger MR (2012) "Proportionate Costs: The Fifteenth Lecture in the Implementation Programme", Law Society, May 29.

34 *Sylvia Henry v News Group Newspapers Ltd* [2012] EWHC 90218 (Costs) (May 16 2012) (www.practicallaw.com/1-519-5935). Ms Henry was a member of Haringey's social work team assigned to the tragic case of Baby P. A settlement in favour of the claimant was reached shortly before trial. Master Hurst accepted that the defendant's tactics had inevitably increased the claimant's costs.

costs management under the Defamation Costs Management Pilot that has been in force since October 1 2009, which is governed by PD 51D. In a ruling on a preliminary issue for detailed assessment, the Senior Costs Judge Master Hurst held that the claimant was not entitled to claim any more costs than in her court-approved budget. The costs at issue were almost £300,000 and Master Hurst gave permission to appeal even before it had been sought.[35]

Master Hurst referred to the mandatory nature of PD 51D and decided that, owing to the claimant's failure to comply with the provisions of PD 51D and inform the defendant and the court of the extra costs, there was no good reason to depart from the approved budget:

> *Whilst, as I have said, I have no doubt that the Claimant could make out a very good case on detailed assessment for the costs being claimed, the fact is the Claimant has largely ignored the provisions of the Practice Direction and I therefore reluctantly come to the conclusion that there is no good reason to depart from the budget.*[36]

Subsequent to the pilot scheme, reform of the arrangements for civil litigation costs became a reality on April 1 2013 through the Legal Aid, Sentencing and Punishment of Offenders Act 2012 (enacted May 2012).

10.2 PFI/PPP

There has been significant investment in both private finance initiatives (PFIs) and private public partnerships (PPPs) since their introduction into the United Kingdom by the Conservative Government in 1992. However, despite the complex nature and often high value of the projects, only two disputes have reached the court in recent times, *Midland Expressway v Carillion Construction Ltd & Ors*[37] and *Emcor Drake & Scull Ltd v Sir Robert McAlpine Ltd.*[38]

Clearly, disputes sometimes happen in PFI/PPP projects. However, given the long-term commercial relationships that typically form the basis of many PFI/PPP projects, it is often in the parties' best interests to try to resolve their differences without resorting to formal legal proceedings before the courts.

A common dispute resolution procedure (DRP) which is often adopted in PFI/PPP contracts is a 'tiered' DRP, which allows the parties to continue to work together whilst disputes are resolved. The first stage often involves without-prejudice negotiations; if these prove unsuccessful then the parties put their case before an expert or adjudicator; and only if this fails will the dispute be decided by the courts or arbitration.

Steps have been taken to standardise the dispute machinery on PFI/PPP contracts, some examples of which are set out below. However, generally speaking, given the bespoke nature of PFI/PPP contracts it arises that parties tend to agree their own mechanisms for determining disputes.

---

35 See also www.legalfutures.co.uk/features/actual-budget-catastrophe, by Andy Ellis, the costs lawyer who acted for the defendant NGN.

36 *Sylvia Henry v News Group Newspapers Ltd* [2012] EWHC 90218 (Costs) (May 16 2012), paragraph 69 of the Approved Judgment.

37 [2005] EWHC 2963 (TCC).

38 [2004] All ER (D) 81.

(a) *The Standardisation of PFI Contracts (SoPC) Version 4 (March 2007)*

Historically, commentators have criticised the amount of time and money that parties have spent negotiating and ultimately drafting the PFI/PPP agreements (including various bespoke DRPs). In the wake of these criticisms the UK government produced the SoPC. The aim of SoPC is to provide guidance on the key issues that arise in PFI projects and in particular to "reduce the time and costs of negotiation by enabling all parties concerned to agree a range of areas that can follow a standard approach with extended negotiations".[39]

Consequently, Chapter 28 of SoPC provides parties with a model dispute resolution process which can be adapted to suit project requirements. The model DRP involves a three-stage process as follows:

- The authority and contractor consult with each other for a fixed time period (possibly involving different levels of internal consultation) in an attempt to come to a mutually satisfactory agreement.
- If consultation fails, the parties may then (except in the case of certain types of dispute) put their case forward for an expert to decide. The expert is appointed from a panel (such as the RICS) whose appointment is regulated by the contract. It may be appropriate in certain circumstances to substitute other forms of ADR for this type of expert determination. Disputes relating to the mechanics of price variations may go to a financial expert agreed between the parties at the time.
- If either party is dissatisfied with the expert's decision, it may refer the matter either to arbitration (itself a form of ADR) or to the courts for a final and binding decision. The method of appointing the arbitrator should be set out in the contract.

(b) *Centre for Effective Dispute Resolution (CEDR)*

In September 2002 CEDR published its model dispute resolution terms for PFI/PPP and long-term contracts which, unlike the SoPC, provide parties with a much more flexible approach to dispute resolution. Despite this flexibility, it is not as widely used as may be expected.

The procedure provides parties with the full range of dispute resolution mechanisms including negotiation, mediation, adjudication, expert determination, arbitration and litigation. It also contains a provision for the appointment of a project neutral. There is an optional provision that prevents disputes of a certain value going further than the adjudication stage.

11. Forbidden processes

By contract, generally speaking, almost any dispute resolution procedure can be devised and the courts will uphold it. The question is whether the subject matter of the dispute offends English law. For example, in the case of *Pearce v Brooks*[40] a

39 Paragraph 1.2.1 of SoPC Version 4 (March 2007).
40 [1866] LR 1 Exch 213.
41 *Everett v Williams* (1725) 9 LQ Rev 196.

contract was held to be illegal where a prostitute had hired a carriage for the purpose of her trade. Further, a contract by two highwaymen to ambush a coach was illegal.[41]

Where parties provide for a dispute to be determined by a third party, for example arbitration, adjudication or an expert, that third party will be bound by certain rules. By way of illustration, an arbitrator could not decide the outcome of a case by simply tossing a coin since he would not be discharging his obligation to weigh up the facts and the law applicable to the dispute in a judicial manner.

It is important to note that once parties have decided on their chosen form of dispute resolution, they cannot subsequently adopt a different method. This is demonstrated by *Channel Tunnel Rail Group Limited v Balfour Beatty*,[42] where the parties were obliged to follow the contractual dispute board procedure rather than submit their dispute to the court. Further, where there is a valid arbitration agreement yet a party attempts to circumvent or avoid arbitration by instead choosing to proceed to court, the courts, under Section 9 of the Arbitration Act 1996, will order that legal proceedings are stayed.

Generally, consumers benefit from a good deal of legislative protection. While discussion of such protection is beyond the scope of this chapter, consumers are, for example, protected against unfair dispute resolution procedures under a variety of legislation.

12. Proposal for reform

Key legislative changes took place in 2012 following the introduction of the Local Democracy, Economic Development and Construction Act 2009, which amended the Housing Grants, Construction and Regeneration Act 1996 – in particular in relation to new payment and adjudication rules.

Other relevant areas of reform are set out below.

12.1 Health and safety

The United Kingdom has the lowest number of non-fatal accidents and the second-lowest number of fatal accidents at work in Europe; despite this, the level of red tape that small and medium-sized organisations face is staggering. In June 2010 the government announced that Lord Young, the Prime Minister's official advisor on health and safety law and practice, would carry out a review of health and safety law in the United Kingdom. In his foreword to the report, Lord Young said he wanted to free businesses from unnecessary bureaucratic health and safety burdens and to put common sense back into health and safety. The key recommendations were:

- the consolidation of current health and safety regulations into a single set of accessible regulations;
- to produce clear, practical guidance focused on small and medium-sized businesses engaged in lower-risk activities;
- the United Kingdom to take the lead in cooperating with other EU member states to ensure that EU health and safety rules for low-risk businesses are not overly prescriptive, are proportionate and do not try to eliminate all risk.

---

42 *The Channel Tunnel Rail Group Limited v Balfour Beatty Construction Limited* [1993] 61BLR1, HL.

In response to Lord Young's findings, the UK government commissioned The Good For Everyone Report which gave details of the findings from a systematic review of health and safety regulations in the United Kingdom. The report noted that, overall, the UK's health and safety regulations are broadly supported, but that not every piece of regulation contributes to a healthier and safer workplace. It proposed simplifying current health and safety regulations in order to assist businesses and to ease their health and safety regulatory burden. It is hoped that by 2014 these changes will have been implemented and that the total number of regulations will have reduced by 50%.

12.2 Late payment of commercial debts

In 2009, a report by the European Commission found that there were €1.9 trillion (£1.6 trillion) worth of late payments in the European economy, €1.1 trillion of which is owed to small and medium-sized enterprises. In light of these findings the European Commission unsurprisingly concluded that late payments are still a problem within the European Union. Therefore, in January 2011 Directive 2011/7/EU of the European Parliament and of the Council on combating late payments in commercial transactions (Late Payments Directive 2011) was adopted and came into force in March 2011. EU member states then had two years to implement it into domestic law, and it was brought into force within the United Kingdom as from March 16 2013.

The revised directive recognises current UK legislation and practice as an exemplar and essentially mirrors existing UK legislation and practice. The main legislative difference is that the revised directive requires public authorities to have a maximum 30-day payment term (with the exception of the healthcare sector). This legislative change effectively mirrors current practice across the UK public sector. The revised directive also establishes a single rate of compensation (compared with the three rates depending on the size of the debt, available in UK legislation). The European Commission believes that, once introduced by all EU member states, the new rules could mean an extra £150 billion being made available to businesses across Europe, helping to relieve cash flow problems.

12.3 Public Finance Initiative

After many years of PFI and PPP in the United Kingdom, there are now concerns over whether it really does deliver value for money. In late 2010 the UK government effectively froze all new PFI projects and is only now in the process of rejuvenating some specific sectors which it feels may produce value for money. It remains to be seen whether PFI will resurface again in the UK construction industry or whether some new funding procedure for long-term concession projects will be developed.

13. Conclusion

The United Kingdom has a well-developed and effective system for determining disputes. This ranges from statutory enactments, such as adjudication and arbitration, to alternative forms of dispute resolution such as mediation. A number of the UK's dispute resolution methods, such as statutory adjudication, have been adopted in other common law jurisdictions.

In addition the United Kingdom has highly specialised and dedicated courts to deal with technical and highly complex construction disputes. These factors make the United Kingdom a favourable place in which to have construction disputes determined.

As to possible changes to improve the position further, some areas of the law, such as statutory limitation periods, may benefit from fixed and clearer time periods – in some countries the limitation period is fixed at 10 years. Such changes would allow the insurance market to respond accordingly and provide greater certainty regarding issues such a latent defects. This would benefit individual homeowners.

About the authors

Ferdinand Adadzi
Partner, AB & David
ferdinand@abdavid.com

Ferdinand Adadzi graduated from the University of Ghana with an LLB (first-class honours) and holds an LLM from the University of Alberta. Mr Adadzi specialises in corporate transaction and project advisory services.

Mr Adadzi currently leads AB & David's procurement, private finance initiative, public-private partnership (PPP) and infrastructure group. He is part of the team preparing the PPP Law for Ghana and is involved in a number of major PPP transactions in the health, water, railways and real estate sectors. Mr Adadzi was part of the team that advised on the negotiation and implementation of Ghana's $547 million Millennium Challenge Compact. He has worked as an international expert on the development of the Procurement and Concessions Regulations and Manual for the Republic of Liberia.

He also lectures on business and company law at Central University College, one of the leading private universities in Ghana.

Oscar Aitken
Partner, Carey y Cía
Oaitken@carey.cl

Oscar Aitken is a partner and leads Carey's engineering and construction, and labour and immigration groups.

He has extensive experience of contracts for all phases of engineering and construction work, including: design and build; engineering, procurement, construction; engineering, procurement and construction management; and build, operate, transfer. His practice spans from the early stages of project development to bidding, negotiation and preparation of contractual documents, claims management and dispute resolution.

Mr Aitken is co-chair of the Dispute Resolution Sub-Committee of the International Construction Projects practice group of the International Bar Association.

He graduated from the Universidad de Chile Law School (distinction maxima) and was admitted to the Bar in 1989. In 1991, he obtained an LLM from the University of Michigan, United States.

Fabio P Alem
Partner, Madeira, Valentim & Alem Advogados
fabio.alem@mvalaw.com.br

Fabio P Alem is a partner in the arbitration and litigation department of Madeira, Valentim & Alem Advogados in São Paulo, Brazil. He holds a law degree and an LLM in comparative contract law. He has specialised in complex and strategic litigation involving construction and corporate law for over 12 years, based in São Paulo and Madrid. He has led teams in major arbitrations and strategic cross-border litigation involving major Brazilian and multinational companies.

Haward Álvarez
Associate, García & Bodán
haward.alvarez@garciabodan.com

Haward Álvarez is an associate attorney in the corporate area with extensive experience of infrastructure issues, having advised Nicaragua's main construction companies. He has a postgraduate degree in mediation and arbitration (dispute resolution), which combines well with his specialisation in public sector contracting. As a result of his specialist degree in public sector contracting, he has counselled construction companies from the start of the bidding process through to execution of the project.

He also spent around one year working at the Commission of Infrastructure of the National Assembly of Nicaragua.

Mr Álvarez leads the team of attorneys that advises the consortium developing the construction of Nicaragua' new Military Hospital, the flagship project of Nicaragua's military medical team, which will be one of the most modern hospitals in Central America.

Maria Alejandra Arboleda González
Associate, Posse Herrera Ruíz
alejandra.arboleda@phrlegal.com

Maria Alejandra Arboleda is an associate at Posse Herrera Ruiz. Her practice focuses on dispute resolution.

Before joining Posse Herrera Ruiz, she worked at a law firm in Paris, where she was involved in the defence of states and investors in investment arbitration before the International Centre for the Settlement of Investment Disputes and international commercial arbitration under the International Chamber of Commerce Rules (Paris).

She has been involved in domestic and international arbitration regarding large infrastructure projects for roads and refineries, among others.

David Arola
Associate attorney, Peckar & Abramson, PC
darola@pecklaw.com

David Arola received his law degree from the Universitat de Barcelona, Spain, in 2005 and then moved to the United States, where he obtained his law degree from Nova Southeastern University in 2006. His practice has a strong focus on international clients that conduct business in the United States and Latin America.

Mr Arola is licensed to practise in the State of Florida and in Spain, and in the US District Courts for the Southern and Middle Districts of Florida. Mr Arola is part of Peckar & Abramson's Latin American practice group.

Cadian T Baker
Paralegal, Peckar & Abramson PC
cbaker@pecklaw.com

Cadian T Baker is a paralegal with Peckar & Abramson, a leading and innovative law firm in construction law. Ms Baker holds both a JD and an MBA. She has served as lead paralegal on various complex litigation matters, and has assisted with arbitrations and mediations. She also works with Peckar's corporate compliance and integrity practice group. In addition to her paralegal duties, Ms Baker works closely with the firm's commercial, civil, and general litigation partners on researching and analysing legislative changes that affect the construction industry.

David Bateson
Partner in charge, King & Wood Mallesons
david.bateson@hk.kwm.com

David Bateson is a partner in the firm's Hong Kong office, where he specialises in dispute resolution, including arbitration, litigation and alternative dispute resolution throughout Asia.

Mr Bateson has been a Hong Kong resident since 1980. He has extensive experience in disputes concerning construction, resources, joint ventures, shareholder agreements, telecommunications, banking and finance, and investor/state.

He is a practising mediator and arbitrator, with extensive experience involving more than 60 arbitrations in Asia, the Middle East and Europe. He has acted as chairman, party-appointed arbitrator or sole arbitrator under the auspices of numerous arbitration institutions.

He is on the arbitral panels of the Hong Kong International Arbitration Centre, the China International Economic and Trade Arbitration Commission, the Singapore International Arbitration Centre (SIAC), the Federation of Indian Chambers of Commerce and Industry Arbitration and Conciliation Tribunal, and the Asia-Pacific Regional Arbitration Group.

Rouven F Bodenheimer
Partner, Lungerich Lenz Schuhmacher Rechtsanwälte
bodenheimer@lls-law.de

Rouven Bodenheimer specialises in conflict resolution and renders advice on corporate law and construction law in particular. Besides civil court proceedings, he has been involved in various arbitration cases governed by different arbitration rules. He also has broad experience in *ad hoc* arbitration proceedings and in the work of dispute adjudication boards.

Professor Bodenheimer studied law in Goettingen, Cambridge, Leuven and Bonn, and completed his legal training in Dusseldorf, Tel Aviv and London. He obtained an additional master's degree in business mediation from Humboldt University in Berlin and Viadrina Frankfurt/Oder. He now lectures on mediation and international arbitration on the joint master's programme of the universities of Humboldt Berlin and Viadrina Frankfurt/Oder, and on mediation at the University of Hannover. He is also a professor of international law at the University of Applied Management in Erding.

Sophie Bourgois
Junior associate, Stibbe
sophie.bourgois@stibbe.com

Sophie Bourgois is part of Stibbe's real estate and construction practice group. She specialises in arbitration and alternative dispute resolution. She has assisted arbitrators in proceedings under the International Chamber of Commerce, Belgian Centre for Arbitration and Mediation, Dubai International Arbitration Centre, and United Nations Commission on International Trade Law rules. She also acts as counsel in sport-related arbitration and commercial litigation.

Ms Bourgois is currently training to become an accredited mediator for civil and commercial disputes.

Jonnathan Bravo
Associate, Navarro Sologuren, Paredes, Gray Attorneys
jbravo@npg.pe

Jonnathan Bravo is a member of the engineering, construction and infrastructure department of Navarro Sologuren, Paredes, Gray Attorneys in Peru. He graduated from the Law School at Pontificia Universidad Católica del Perú, and specialises in construction law, public procurement and dispute resolution methods in construction.

In particular, he advises private constructors and supervisors, as well as public entities. He has also been involved in a number of infrastructure projects in the public sector, and has trained in the design of construction and engineering contracts, construction management contracts and international standard construction contracts, such as the International Federation of Consulting Engineers (FIDIC) models.

He is a member of the Dispute Resolution Board Foundation and the Peruvian Society of Construction Law. He has co-authored articles on public procurement, administrative law and public-private partnership regulation in Peru.

Giuseppe Broccoli
Founding partner, BDA – Studio Legale
broccoli@bdalaw.it

Giuseppe Broccoli is the founding partner of BDA – Studio Legale. He specialises in construction and energy projects.

He advises clients on project development (including tenders), drafting and negotiation of contractual documents, and claims management. Mr Broccoli also has significant experience in national and international arbitrations involving construction-related disputes and has recently acted as counsel in International Chamber of Commerce (ICC) and London Court of International Arbitration international arbitrations.

He has also recently assisted Italian contractors with construction works in the energy industry to be carried out in the Middle East, the Russian Federation and South and Central America.

Jerry Brodsky
Partner, Peckar & Abramson PC
jbrodsky@pecklaw.com

Jerry Brodsky is a partner in Peckar & Abramson's Miami office and is director of the firm's Latin American practice group. Having been born and raised in Peru, Mr Brodsky is trilingual (English, Spanish and Portuguese) and has spent his entire legal career representing members of the construction industry in risk management and the resolution of disputes in the United States, the Caribbean and Latin America. In the past few years he has been involved in the support of firm clients pursuing and undertaking public-private partnership projects in the United States.

Mr Brodsky holds a BSc in industrial engineering from Lehigh University and a law degree, *magna cum laude*, from the University of Miami School of Law.

Cyril Chern
Secretary, Dispute Board Federation
c.chern@chern.net

Cyril Chern, the secretary of the Dispute Board Federation (DBF), is also a barrister at Crown Office Chambers, London, and a chartered architect, chartered arbitrator, accredited mediator and adjudicator. He holds the degrees of BArch in architecture and engineering and JD (Law). He is a fellow of both the Chartered Institute of Arbitrators and the Dispute Board Federation, is on both the International Federation of Consulting Engineers (FIDIC) President's List of Adjudicators and its Assessment Panel, and is a dispute board trainer for FIDIC, the DBF, and the International Chamber of Commerce.

Dr Chern is the author of *Chern on Dispute Boards* (1st and 2nd editions; Wiley-Blackwell), *International Commercial Mediation* and *The Law of Construction Disputes* (Informa). He is also the co-author of *Emden's Construction Law* and its "ADR and Dispute Boards" section (LexisNexis). His newest books, *The Commercial Mediator's Handbook* and *Construction Delay and Damage*, are being published in early 2014.

Danielle J Cole
Partner, Peckar & Abramson PC
dcole@pecklaw.com

Danielle Cole is a partner with Peckar & Abramson, working on its contracts and risk management, international construction and public-private partnership teams. Ms Cole collaborates with clients to facilitate the successful procurement, performance and completion of commercial construction and infrastructure projects, by providing counsel, advocacy, and transactional and project assistance through all project phases, and in complex mediation, litigation and arbitration proceedings.

Ms Cole is recognised for construction in *Chambers USA* and *Georgia Super Lawyers®*, and is AV Preeminent® Peer Review Rated by *Martindale-*

Hubbell®. She is chair of the International Construction Division of the American Bar Association Forum on the Construction Industry, past-chair of the Atlanta Bar Association Construction Law Section, a member of the Contract Documents Forum of the Associated General Contractors of America and the team developing the ConsensusDocs® joint venture and teaming agreements, and a past director of the National Association of Women in Construction, Atlanta Chapter.

Sergio Corrales
Partner, García & Bodán
sergio.corrales@garciabodan.com

Having been the director of the litigation department and chief litigator of García & Bodán, Sergio Corrales has extensive experience in litigation, in particular in relation to real estate and real estate development, construction and related issues. He is the principal consultant and counsels the firm's litigation team on all procedural issues, structuring strategies for cases in which the firm represents clients as both plaintiffs and defendants, assessment of evidence, litigation and dispute resolution, including arbitration proceedings both in law and in equity.

He also counsels the corporate and transactional team on reviewing and negotiating contractual terms aimed at helping the parties to avoid disputes, conflicts and litigation.

Diederik De Block
Associate, Stibbe
Diederik.Deblock@stibbe.com

Diederik De Block specialises in construction law. He has been involved in several important construction projects (including a number of public-private partnership projects), advising either public authorities or private parties, drafting and/or negotiating contracts, and intervening in litigation or arbitration. Previously, Mr De Block also worked as part-time assistant at the University of Ghent. In 2011 he completed a secondment at Herbert Smith, London.

Jonathon DeBoos
Senior associate, Clayton Utz
jdeboos@claytonutz.com

Jonathon DeBoos is a senior associate at Clayton Utz, Melbourne, and holds degrees in science and law. During his time at Clayton Utz, Mr DeBoos has worked on disputes relating to major infrastructure projects, commercial property, power plants, oil and gas projects and foreign investment, and has been involved in litigation in the supreme courts of Victoria and New South Wales and arbitrations under ICC, International Centre for the Settlement of Investment Disputes, Dubai International Arbitration Centre, the Institute of Arbitrators & Mediators Australia and SIAC arbitration rules. Since 2006 Mr DeBoos has served as the deputy secretary general of the Australian Centre for International Commercial Arbitration and on the executive committee of the Australasian Forum for International Arbitration (AFIA).

José Luis Echevarría Petit
Partner, Echevarría Leunda & Echevarría Petit
jlep@echevarríaabogados.com

José Luis Echevarría Petit is a doctor of law and social sciences (University of the Republic), a master of commercial law (University of Montevideo) and a professor of administrative contracts.

He is the partner in charge of Echevarría Leunda & Echevarría Petit, a law firm founded in 1951 which specialises in corporate, commercial, administrative, labour and international commercial law, as well as litigation and arbitration.

He is a member of the National Bar Association, the Administrative Law Institute and the Uruguayan Chamber of Commerce, and is president of the Canada-Uruguay Chamber of Commerce.

He specialises in administrative law and public-private partnerships (PPPs), and has assisted the Canadian government in investigating PPPs in Canada.

He has co-authored several books and publications, and has spoken at conferences both in Uruguay and abroad, on administrative law, procurement and PPPs.

Terencio García
Partner and regional director, García & Bodán
terencio.garcia@garciabodan.com

Terencio García is a leading lawyer in Nicaragua and founder of García & Bodán, the first Nicaraguan law firm to expand within the Central America region. He has extensive experience of infrastructure issues, having served as the attorney and Nicaraguan representative of important local and multinational companies in the infrastructure field.

He also has extensive experience of dispute resolution, having participated in conferences hosted by the International Chamber of Commerce (ICC) on the topic of dispute board resolution.

Mr García has been involved in the structuring and negotiation of construction contracts of great significance in Nicaragua. He has also counselled construction companies from inception through to liquidation, which has given him a more complete picture of how to advise companies in this sector.

Lucy Goldsmith
Associate, Fenwick Elliott LLP
lgoldsmith@fenwickelliott.com

Lucy Goldsmith is an associate at Fenwick Elliott LLP, the United Kingdom's largest specialist construction and engineering solicitors. She specialises in all major forms of dispute resolution, including arbitration, litigation, adjudication, mediation and expert determination. She has been involved in several complex high-value disputes involving civil engineering and energy projects, including highways, bridges, tunnels, power plants, wind farms and biomass plants.

Ms Goldsmith has experience with all major standard forms of contract (eg, FIDIC, Joint Contracts Tribunal, New Engineering Contracts and Institution of Civil Engineers) and dispute resolution procedures including mediation, adjudication, international arbitration and litigation under various rules, including ICC and LCIA. She has dealt with disputes under various systems of law, in addition to English law.

Ms Goldsmith holds an MSc in construction law and arbitration from King's College London. She regularly contributes articles to industry publications (eg, *Building* magazine, *Construction Industry Law Letter*).

Katherine González Arrocha
Director for Latin America, ICC Dispute Resolution Services
International Chamber of Commerce
International Court of Arbitration
katherine.gonzalezarrocha@iccwbo.org

Katherine González Arrocha is a Panamanian lawyer. She specialises in international dispute resolution.

She joined the Secretariat of the ICC International Court of Arbitration in Paris in 1996 and managed arbitration cases in the Ibero-American team, first as assistant counsel and from 1998 as counsel. In 2004 she was appointed secretary of the ICC Commission on Arbitration and senior counsel for ICC Dispute Resolution Services. She is now director for Latin America of the ICC International Court of Arbitration, based in Panama City.

She also works as an independent practitioner and sits as an arbitrator. She has authored several articles and given frequent lectures on international dispute resolution around the world. She holds a law degree from the University of Santa María La Antigua (Panama) and an LLM in arbitration, ADR and litigation from the University of Paris II (Panthéon-Assas).

Nicholas Gould
Partner, Fenwick Elliott LLP
ngould@fenwickelliott.com

Nicholas Gould is a partner and solicitor advocate at Fenwick Elliott LLP, the United Kingdom's largest specialist construction and engineering solicitors. He advises, drafts, negotiates and settles construction documents, and provides strategic contract and dispute avoidance advice. His dispute resolution experience spans negotiation, alternative dispute resolution, adjudication, arbitration and litigation, not just in the United Kingdom but internationally. He acts for contractors, employers and governments in the construction, engineering, infrastructure, transport, energy, oil and gas, and process engineering sectors.

Mr Gould regularly acts as lead mediator in multimillion, multi-party mediations and is an accredited adjudicator, also sitting on international dispute boards. He is chairman of the International Chamber of Commerce International Centre for Expertise, past chairman of the Society of Construction Law and visiting senior lecturer at King's College London. Mr Gould has published widely in the area of construction law and dispute resolution. He is co-author of the report "Mediating Construction Disputes: An Evaluation of Existing Practice" launched in February 2010.

Jaime Gray
Partner/founder, Navarro Sologuren, Paredes, Gray Attorneys
jgray@npg.pe

Jaime Gray is one of the founders and a partner in the engineering, construction and infrastructure department of Navarro Sologuren, Paredes, Gray Attorneys in Peru. He holds degrees in law and business law, and has specialised in construction law, public procurement and dispute resolution methods in construction for more than 20 years in Peru and Panama.

In particular, he has led Navarro Sologuren, Paredes, Gray Attorneys in a number of leading projects in the construction and engineering sectors in Peru, including hydropower plants, highways and transport infrastructure projects.

He is president of the Society of Construction Law in Peru, has been ranked in *Chambers and Partners* in the projects area and has been recommended in the field of construction law by *Who's Who Legal* in 2008 and 2012.

Roberto Hernández-García
Managing partner, COMAD, SC
rhernandez@comad.com.mx

Roberto Hernández-García is a Mexican lawyer who specialises in public and private construction, national and international procurement, and national and international disputes. He is managing partner of leading Mexican law firm COMAD.

Mr Hernández has acted as counsellor in relevant construction and infrastructure projects in Mexico, Europe and Latin America, involving the procurement, negotiation, contracting and dispute stages of projects for the execution of highways, transmission lines, substations, petrochemical plants, chemical plants, industrial plants, metro transportation systems and hospitals, among others.

He has acted as a sole dispute board adjudicator for several contracts in Central America under the International Federation of Consulting Engineers model contracts and the International Chamber of Commerce (ICC) rules, and is a fellow of the Dispute Board Federation and its representative for Latin America.

He has served or is serving as: co-chair of the International Construction Projects Committee of the International Bar Association (2009–11); chair of the Construction Disputes Committee of ICC Mexico; steering committee member of Division 8 of the American Bar Association Construction Forum; and an adviser to CAIC Mexico (Construction Arbitration Centre).

Alfonso Iglesia
Partner, Cuatrecasas, Gonçalves Pereira
alfonso.iglesia@cuatrecasas.com

Alfonso Iglesia is a partner in the litigation and arbitration group of Cuatrecasas, Gonçalves Pereira in Madrid. He specialises in construction and engineering law and civil liability. He has extensive experience as a lead lawyer in national and international arbitration and court proceedings.

During more than 20 years as a lawyer, he has participated in many important civil liability and construction engineering cases in Spain. He has represented Spanish and foreign companies in national and international projects, advising them on all stages from the contract negotiation phase to defence before the courts of justice or in arbitration.

Mr Iglesia is an associate professor of civil law at the University of Comillas, ICADE, of Madrid. He is recommended for dispute resolution, arbitration, construction and product liability by several directories, including *Chambers Global, Chambers Europe, PLC Which Lawyer, Expert Guides, Who's Who Legal, European Legal Experts, Best Lawyers* and *Legal 500.*

Philip Jeyaretnam
Managing partner, Rodyk & Davidson LLP
philip.jeyaretnam@rodyk.com

Philip Jeyaretnam is managing partner of Rodyk & Davidson LLP. He graduated from Cambridge University in 1986 and was a visiting Fulbright fellow at Harvard Law School in 1991. He was admitted to the Singapore Bar in 1988, and was appointed senior counsel in January 2003. Mr Jeyaretnam was president of the Law Society of Singapore from January 2004 to December 2007. He was the founding chairman of the Society of Construction Law, Singapore.

Mr Jeyaretnam is named as a leading individual for dispute resolution in both *Chambers Asia Pacific 2012* and the *Legal 500 Asia Pacific 2012.* He is a member of the Public Service Commission, the constitutional body that oversees the public service in Singapore. Mr Jeyaretnam also chairs the board of Maxwell Chambers, Asia's premier integrated dispute resolution facility.

Sumeet Kachwaha
Partner, Kachwaha & Partners
skachwaha@kaplegal.com

Sumeet Kachwaha is a founding partner of New Delhi-based firm Kachwaha & Partners.

Mr Kachwaha has been involved in more than 30 construction arbitrations, including one as a sole arbitrator. He has also been involved in several power projects, and has advised on the privatisation of railways, roads, airports and other infrastructure projects.

Mr Kachwaha enjoys some of the highest ratings from law directories in the dispute resolution field. He also features in the procurement section of *Who's Who International.* He recently completed a three-year term as chair of the Dispute Resolution and Arbitration Section of the Inter-Pacific Bar Association. Current appointments include co-vice chair of a sub-committee of the International Construction Project Committee of the International Bar Association, vice president of APRAG, and advisory board member of the KLRCA.

William G Kelly
Partner, Goldberg Segalla LLP
Wkelly@goldbergsegalla.com

William G Kelly is a partner in the construction practice group of Goldberg Segalla, with an emphasis on construction, product liability and catastrophic injury litigation. He has litigated multimillion-dollar construction defect cases, including one recent case that involved every floor of a vertical college campus located in Manhattan. He has also represented manufacturers based in mainland China in various litigation matters.

Mr Kelly has lectured for the American Bar Association and the New York State Bar Association, and has been selected to act as a member of the faculty for the Judicial Institute, providing trial guidance for newly elected New York Supreme Court judges. He has also lectured several times in Shanghai and Taipei, addressing international litigation issues.

Mr Kelly holds the highest Martindale rating of AV Preeminent and has been selected for inclusion in *Super Lawyers Corporate Counsel* edition and *Metro New York Super Lawyers*.

Rory Kirrane
Partner and head of construction law and engineering, Mason Hayes & Curran
rkirrane@mhc.ie

Rory Kirrane is partner and head of construction law and engineering at Mason Hayes & Curran. He has extensive experience in contentious and non-contentious construction issues. He advises and represents on all aspects of construction contracts.

Mr Kirrane has acted for a broad range of construction interests in conciliation, adjudication, arbitration and court proceedings in both advancing and defending claims.

Mr Kirrane has particular expertise in complex regulatory energy matters. He leads a team which advises the majority of the leading banks operating in and lending into Ireland on wind energy project finance transactions.

Mr Kirrane previously worked for a leading international construction law practice and has particular knowledge of international construction matters. He is qualified to advise on Irish and English law, and has experience of the FIDIC, JCT and ICE forms of contract.

Benoît Kohl
Of counsel, Stibbe
benoit.kohl@stibbe.com

Benoît Kohl concentrates on real estate law and general construction law. In addition to negotiating contracts, providing legal advice and structuring operations in relation to these matters, he has dealt with various disputes both before the courts and in arbitration. He also often acts as an arbitrator in such matters.

Mr Kohl is a professor at the law faculty of the University of Liège, where he heads the department for law of obligations and contract law. In 2010 he was appointed guest lecturer at the University of Paris II (Panthéon-Assas), where he teaches European construction law. In 2011 he was appointed president of the European Society of Construction Law.

Since September 2012, he has also been the co-president of Cepani40, an association of young arbitration practitioners operating under the auspices of the Belgian Centre for Arbitration and Mediation.

Tuomas Lehtinen
Partner, Castrén & Snellman Attorneys Ltd
tuomas.lehtinen@castren.fi

Tuomas Lehtinen specialises in international construction and projects, dispute resolution and banking. He has several years of experience in dispute proceedings in both arbitration (*ad hoc* and institutional) and civil courts. Dr Lehtinen is frequently appointed as an arbitrator, his expertise covering international trade contracts, project agreements, bank guarantees and trade finance issues such as letters of credit.

Dr Lehtinen is a doctor of laws and a docent in contract law and international trade law at the University of Turku. He wrote his dissertation on "International trade contracts and letters of credit", and has also authored several books and articles on international trade and guarantees. Dr Lehtinen is a frequent lecturer at universities and seminars.

Chambers Europe, Chambers Global, Best Lawyers and *PLC Which Lawyer* rank Dr Lehtinen among Finland's leading legal experts.

Claus H Lenz
Partner, Lungerich Lenz Schuhmacher Rechtsanwälte
lenz@lls-law.de

Claus H Lenz is a founding partner of Cologne-based law firm Lungerich Lenz Schuhmacher, which was set up in 1995. Mr Lenz's main fields of activity relate to work contracts in the construction industry and for complete industrial plants, as well as in the machinery business, both domestically and worldwide. Mr Lenz is also an expert in international commercial arbitration and alternative dispute resolution, and has served on numerous arbitration panels and dispute boards during his career to date, including the German Institution of Arbitration, the ICC, the SIAC, the Stockholm Chamber of Commerce, the Kuala Lumpur Regional Centre for Arbitration and the Cairo Regional Centre for International Commercial Arbitration.

Having worked in Singapore for several years, Mr Lenz is well acquainted and experienced with the legal aspects of all kinds of business activities in Southeast Asia.

Victor Madeira Filho
Partner, Madeira, Valentim & Alem Advogados
victor.madeira@mvalaw.com.br

Victor Madeira Filho is a partner in the construction and infrastructure department of Madeira, Valentim & Alem Advogados in São Paulo, Brazil. He holds a degree in law, and has specialised in construction law for over 12 years while based in São Paulo and Miami. He has also worked as counsel for Companhia Siderurgica Nacional. He has led teams in major transactions involving mining, steel, railway and port projects.

Adrián Martínez Benoit
Deputy director for Latin America, International Chamber of Commerce Dispute Resolution Services
adrian.martinez-ext@iccwbo.org

Adrián Martínez Benoit holds an LLB from the University of Panama and an LLM in international dispute settlement from the University of Geneva and the Graduate Institute of International and Development Studies. Based in Panama City, he currently acts as deputy director for Latin America of the International Chamber of Commerce (ICC) International Court of Arbitration.

Before joining the ICC, he served as in-house counsel for a major energy sector corporation and as a corporate lawyer for a boutique law firm in Panama City. He has also performed academic research in investment arbitration.

David Ofosu-Dorte
Executive chairman, AB & David
david@abdavid.com

David Ofosu-Dorte has considerable experience in construction and engineering contracts. He has worked on several international assignments in West Africa, including Ghana, Nigeria and Liberia. His areas of expertise include finance, infrastructure development, procurement, PPPs and international consulting for governments, regulatory agencies, international organisations and the private sector.

Mr Ofosu-Dorte also led the development of Ghana's National PPP Guidelines, and was engaged by the World Bank to prepare the PPP chapter of Ghana's Local Government Finance Law and the design of a PPP Resource Centre for Ghana.

According to Chambers & Partners Global he has been described by clients as having a "terrifically focused, hands-on approach and brilliant business sense". He is also recognised as one of the world's leading procurement lawyers by *Who's Who Legal*.

Carolina Posada Isaacs
Partner, Posse Herrera Ruiz
Carolina.posada@phrlegal.com

Carolina Posada is a partner at Posse Herrera Ruiz. Her practice focuses on dispute resolution, dealing with local and international arbitration and litigation.

She has an active litigation practice before the civil and administrative courts, and has also acted as an attorney and secretary before several arbitration tribunals.

She has worked for local and international clients in large infrastructure disputes and insurance and reinsurance disputes, as well as disputes involving contractual liability and torts.

Bruce Reynolds
Partner, Borden Ladner Gervais LLP
breynolds@blg.com

Bruce Reynolds is chair of the international construction projects group and a partner in the construction group of the Toronto office of Borden Ladner Gervais. He is the only Canadian lawyer recognised as one of the 10 most highly regarded construction law practitioners internationally, and is noted by *Who's Who Legal* as "'a top practitioner', enjoying an 'impressive' reputation as chair of the firm's international construction projects group".

Mr Reynolds specialises in the litigation, arbitration and mediation of construction claims, construction liens, surety bond claims, construction insurance claims, product liability and architects' and engineers' errors and omissions claims, as well as in the drafting and negotiating of contracts for major industrial and infrastructure projects, including public-private partnerships, and construction, engineering, architectural equipment supply and technology licensing contracts.

Mr Reynolds is a certified specialist in construction law by the Law Society of Upper Canada, and has been inducted into the American College of Construction Lawyers.

Melvin See
Partner, Rodyk & Davidson LLP
melvin.see@rodyk.com

Melvin See is a partner of Rodyk & Davidson LLP. Mr See graduated from the National University of Singapore in 2001. He was admitted to the Singapore bar in 2002 and as a non-practising solicitor of England and Wales in 2004. Mr See's main areas of practice encompass building and construction disputes, corporate and shareholder disputes, insolvency cases and medical malpractice matters. He is also an accredited associate mediator of the Singapore Mediation Centre and the subordinate courts.

Sonja Stark-Traber
Senior associate, Schellenberg Wittmer Ltd
sonja.stark-traber@swlegal.ch

Sonja Stark-Traber is a senior associate in Schellenberg Wittmer Ltd's dispute resolution and construction group in Zurich. Her main areas of practice are national and international commercial arbitration and litigation, with a particular focus on national and international construction disputes and public procurement matters.

Ms Stark-Traber has acted as counsel and co-counsel in a wide array of disputes relating to construction and engineering projects, sales contracts, including post-M&A disputes, distribution agreements, joint ventures and the pharmaceutical and automotive industries.

Ms Stark-Traber graduated from the University of Zurich School of Law in 2001 and was admitted to the Swiss bar in 2005. In 2009, she obtained an LLM in commercial law with distinction from the University of Edinburgh, Scotland. She is a member of several professional associations, including the International, Swiss and Zurich Bar Associations, and she regularly publishes in her fields of practice.

Andrew Stephenson

Partner, Clayton Utz
astephenson@claytonutz.com

Andrew Stephenson heads the Clayton Utz construction group and the international arbitration group in Melbourne, Australia. He recently retired after six years from the Clayton Utz national board. Mr Stephenson has over 30 years' experience in contentious and non-contentious matters relating to all types of major project. He advises clients in relation to contract drafting and negotiation, the allocation of risk, in major projects, the management of those risks, and dispute resolution (negotiation, mediation, litigation, and domestic and international arbitration).

He is a senior fellow of Melbourne University Law School lecturing in construction risk and dispute resolution. He has also lectured at Monash University, Queensland University of Technology and Queensland University, and regularly presents at industry conferences.

He is also the Australian correspondent for the *International Construction Law Review*, published in London.

Ioannis Vassardanis

Managing partner, Alexander Vassardanis & Partners
i.vassardanis@vassardanis.gr

Ioannis Vassardanis has acted as counsel in numerous construction projects in Greece and abroad, and has been appointed as arbitrator in numerous international and domestic arbitrations. He has also acted as counsel in many alternative dispute resolution procedures mainly related to construction issues and as an expert/adjudicator in expertise cases related to construction/technical matters.

Mr Vassardanis is treasurer of the Hellenic Society for Technology and Construction Law, and Council Member of the Greek Arbitration Association. He is also a member of other international construction and arbitration-related organisations and associations.

He has been selected as a notable practitioner in the areas of dispute resolution and construction by many international organisations, including in dispute resolution, by Chambers & Partners (*Chambers Europe 2013*).

Mr Vassardanis has written numerous articles and contributions in many international books and journals, including the chapter on Greece in the *International Handbook on Commercial Arbitration*, Supplement 72, December 2012.

Rony Vermeersch

Partner, Stibbe
rony.vermeersch@stibbe.com

Rony Vermeersch focuses on real estate, construction and liability law. He specialises in construction and engineering contracts, property development, PPP (especially design–build–finance–maintain contracts), joint ventures, industrial projects and product liability. In addition to the negotiation of agreements and the setting-up of structures in these matters, Mr Vermeersch acts as a litigator in both state court and arbitral proceedings.

Mr Vermeersch is chairman of the Belgian Council of the International Project Finance Association, composed of major Belgian industrial players.

He also heads the joint real estate and construction, energy, and environment and permits practices of Stibbe.

Sharon Vogel

Partner, Borden Ladner Gervais LLP
svogel@blg.com

Sharon Vogel is regional leader of the international construction projects group at Borden Ladner Gervais. A partner in the Toronto office, Ms Vogel practises construction and surety law, working primarily on matters involving construction disputes relating to projects including highways, railways, tunnels, pipelines, industrial facilities, commercial buildings and condominiums in various jurisdictions.

Ms Vogel specialises in the negotiation, mediation, arbitration and litigation of construction disputes, including surety bond claims, construction liens, trust claims, delay claims, construction insurance claims and architects' and engineers' errors and omissions claims. She has extensive experience drafting construction contracts on behalf of owners, developers, general subcontractors, subcontractors and suppliers. She has appeared at all levels of court, including the Ontario Superior Court, the Court of Appeal and the Supreme Court of Canada.